THE GUNFLINT LODGE COOKBOOK

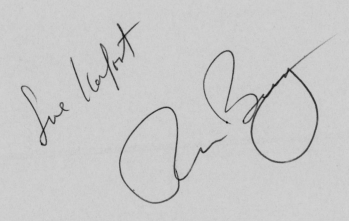

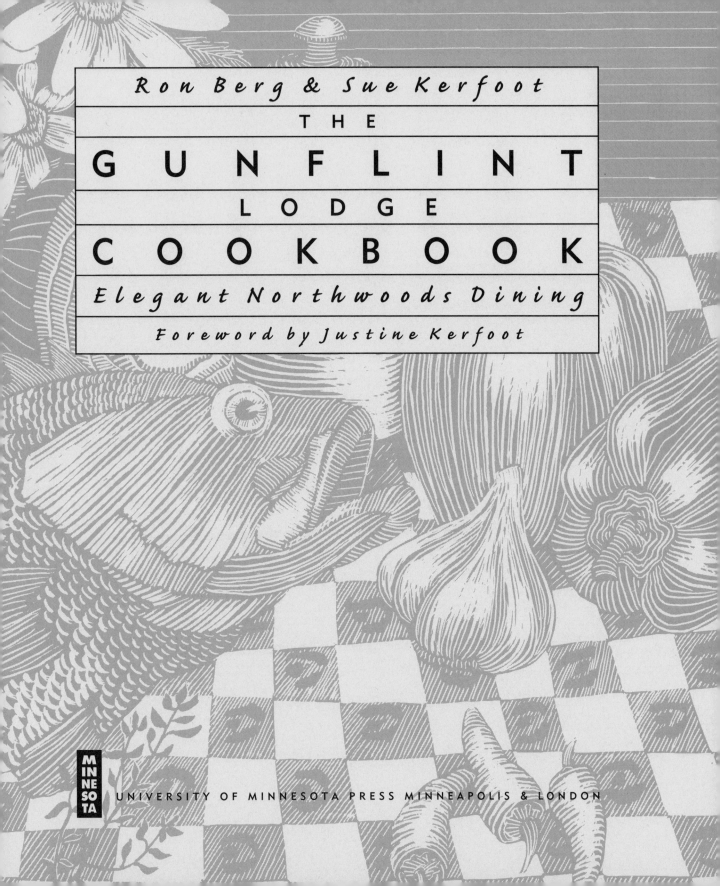

Ron Berg & Sue Kerfoot

THE

GUNFLINT

LODGE

COOKBOOK

Elegant Northwoods Dining

Foreword by Justine Kerfoot

UNIVERSITY OF MINNESOTA PRESS MINNEAPOLIS & LONDON

Published by the University of Minnesota Press
111 Third Avenue South, Suite 290
Minneapolis, MN 55401-2520

Book and cover design: Diane Gleba Hall
Cover art: Iconomics®/Dorothy Reinhardt
Printed in the United States of America on acid-free paper

Library of Congress Cataloging-in-Publication Data

Berg, Ron.
    The Gunflint Lodge cookbook : elegant northwoods dining / Ron Berg and Sue Kerfoot ;
    foreword by Justine Kerfoot.
        p.   cm.
    Includes index.
    ISBN 0-8166-2831-9 (pbk.)
    1. Cookery. I. Gunflint Lodge. II. Kerfoot, Sue. III. Title.
    TX714.B394   1997
    641.5—dc21   97-14009

With love to my Dad,
who was always there for me,
and to my daughter, Sommer,
my biggest fan and best fishing buddy.

R. B.

C O N T E N T S

FOREWORD

Justine Kerfoot

I first came to Gunflint in 1927. At that time the access to the lodge was a narrow dirt road forty-five miles long. The resort consisted of a main lodge and five small log cabins. The cabins were built along the shore and housed our guests, who were all fishermen. The main lodge was divided into a store to accommodate the needs of the Indians and a dining room to provide meals for the fishermen. The kitchen was located behind the dining room. Gas lamps and kerosene lanterns turned night into a hazy day in the lodge and cabins. Heat and cooking were dependent on wood.

The kitchen was the vital factor on which everything depended. It was endowed with a big cast iron stove, six feet by three feet with a four-inch-thick top. The stove must have been acquired from an old logging camp. It took a lot of stoking with wood to get it heated up. The food was placed over the firebox where it would cook steadily. When the food was done, it was shoved to another part of the stove where it remained warm at a constant heat.

Additional goodies in the kitchen were a pitcher pump that connected to an enclosed spring under the lodge and a sink leading to a covered pit. Fresh food was kept in a two-compartment ice box. One half was filled with ice; the other half served to preserve the food.

Two important units served to supplement the kitchen. The root cellar maintained a temperature of about 40°F winter and summer. Here all the canned goods, potatoes, and onions were kept. The second unit was a dry storage building where sacks of flour, sugar, and other dried foods were stacked.

Later, when we acquired more know-how, we built a screen house. The house had to be located where it could get a steady breeze, and it had to be so tight that no fly could find an entrance. In this house the fresh meat was hung with great care so that every side was exposed to the air. The skin on the meat would dry and form a coating that preserved the meat and made it very tender.

But the kitchen itself was the queen of the lodge. She made demands that kept us all hard at work. Take, for instance, the cutting of wood. It sounds innocent enough, but it was a project that required constant physical work from all of us.

All the stoves for the cabins and the kitchen stove used wood. Various woods had their own attributes for this job. Birch was the hottest burning and most desir-

The first dining room at Gunflint was located at the north end of the lodge facing the road, which was considered more interesting to look at than the lake. The furniture in the picture was made by George Bayle in Grand Marais. Justine copied his design when she made furniture for the dining room in the new lodge in 1954. Her furniture was used for forty years before being replaced. Some of it is still used today.

able. This wood, however, contained a lot of sap that left a residue of creosote in stove pipes and became a fire hazard. Jack pine also burned very hot, but it threw sparks. Aspen burned clean but gave a minimum of heat. Balsam was used only as a last resort.

Each fall a year's supply of wood had to be harvested. The trees were cut down with an ax, and the limbs were removed. The trunks were sawed with a crosscut saw into eight-foot lengths. This was all before the era of chain saws. If a person worked alone, the saw was a single five-foot-long wide-toothed handsaw. Two people working together could use an eight-foot saw with an upright handle on each end. They would pull the saw back and forth in rhythm. When the logs

were all cut to length, they would be loaded by hand onto a trunk and hauled to a staging area.

At the staging area a mandrel was mounted permanently on a table. One end of the mandrel had a three-foot-diameter circular saw blade attached; the other end had a counterweight. Normally a belt ran from a gasoline motor to the weighted end of the mandrel to turn the saw blade. We didn't have a motor. I jacked up our Model T Ford and put the belt from the counterweight over the rear tire. By wedging the accelerator down, the car tire turned the saw blade. It was a machine that OSHA would love.

Just to the side of the saw blade was a V-shaped table attached to a swing. The tree lengths would be fed in one end of the table until they stuck out past the end of the saw blade. The table was swung forward past the spinning saw blade to cut the logs into two-foot lengths. The lengths were then thrown onto a pile. When we were done, the pile of wood was literally as high as a house. Because of the danger involved, only my husband, Bill, and I did this job. I fed the saw. Bill received and threw aside the newly cut pieces. As we worked together it became a very rhythmic process of cutting and throwing.

The next step was to split each piece of wood with an ax. The split wood was stacked with the bark side up to shed the rain. Hopefully the wood could dry some before we had to use it. If by chance we ran short of wood, it meant a fresh cut of "green timber," which did not burn with ease and made the cook most unhappy.

One fall when we ran short of wood for the kitchen stove, our cook, Aggie Jackson, said she would help me cut wood. Her terms were to start at daylight and see how much we could produce. I showed up at 6:00 A.M. to be disdainfully greeted by Aggie with, "Fer Christ sake, I thought you were going to sleep all day." I felled and limbed the trees. We sawed and split them for two days. When we were through, there was a sizable pile. I acquired a whole bunch of new muscles and ached all over. Aggie carried on in the kitchen as if she had been on a holiday.

Another endless demand from the kitchen was ice. To keep our ice box full so that it could preserve our fresh foods, we had to have an ice house and a large sawdust pile plus all the necessary equipment for cutting ice. Some of this equipment included large tongs for pulling the cakes of ice from the water, a spud bar for breaking the cakes apart, shovels for keeping the area free of snow, an ax for opening the sawdust pile, ramps for sliding the cakes to ever higher layers, and small tongs for handling the ice in the summer.

The whole process began in the fall. All the sawdust was shoveled out of the ice house and piled like a tall teepee. Cold weather would freeze the outside to form a crust. The crust insulated the inner cone, leaving it warm and dry.

Around December 10, Gunflint Lake froze. As soon as the lake was safe to walk on, an ice field had to be established. The field had to be far enough away from shore so that the saw being lifted up and down would not touch the lake bottom. The top of the field also had to be kept free of any snow from subsequent snowfalls or from blowing wind. If the snow is allowed to accumulate, it freezes into slush ice, which does not hold

Justine hauling firewood with a sled dog.

The original lodge after a heavy fall snowstorm. We know it is fall because the lake is not frozen over. In the spring all the snow melts before the ice goes off the lake.

in the summer as long as clear blue ice. The blue ice is formed by freezing water from below with no snow in it. Also, a cleared ice field freezes much faster than one covered by snow, which acts as insulation from the cold.

The ideal time to harvest ice is when the ice is seventeen to twenty inches thick. The longer one waits, the thicker the ice gets and the heavier the cakes are to handle. Because Gunflint froze late, we frequently were caught putting up ice on the heavy side. The ice would be at the perfect thickness over the holiday season, but we had winter guests to take care of then. By the time our guests were gone, the ice was two feet and going on to three feet thick. Often the temperature was 20° below zero.

Finally the guests were gone. It was time to harvest ice. The first step was to shovel a path from the ice field to the ice house. This cleared path would allow the ice to slide more easily.

Back at the ice field, Bill and I would lay out a grid across the field. A hole large enough to take an ice saw was chopped through the ice in one corner. The ice

saw was a six-foot saw with large teeth and a handle that extended across the top like a T. The ice is sawed in an up-and-down motion, and the cakes were broken apart with a spud. With the large ice tongs, each cake is pulled up out of the water and dragged to the ice house. In the ice house one cake is placed against the next cake in the same order that they came off the field. That way they fit tightly with no space between the cakes. The ice was stacked higher and higher until it reached the top of the ice house. As the ice was stacked, sawdust from the open pile was used to fill an opening five to six inches thick between the ice and the ice house walls. There was also a little sawdust put between the layers. If sawdust was not available, sphagnum moss was used. The moss is found in swamps and is two to three feet thick. It is clean and makes good insulation. But it must be gathered every year because the moss only lasts one year.

Bill would start the sawing process. Across the lake, the Indian neighbors were watching our progress. When the time came for sawing, they all snowshoed over in a long line to help haul. An Indian girl and I took the ice from the field, hauled it to the ice house, layered it and shoveled in the sawdust. It took two to three days to fill the ice house with several tons of ice, which had to last all summer. When the ice was taken from the ice house and headed to the kitchen, all the sawdust had to be washed off. It was this same ice, chipped, that cooled our drinks.

In later years I used my sled dogs hitched to a toboggan to pull the ice to the ice house. They quickly found the job to be boring. One year I had the brilliant idea of using the car to haul ice. A hole was put in the back wall of the ice house. The car was backed up to the outside of this wall. A long rope was tied to the car's bumper and fed through the hole in the ice house and out to the ice field. There I attached the rope to the toboggan. When the toboggan was full of ice, two of us walked back to the ice house. I got in the car and pulled forward until my helper told me to stop. At that point the toboggan should have been just outside the ice house. Due to slow communications, I didn't stop in time. The entire ice house was almost pulled down. We went back to using the sled dogs.

Speaking of ice reminds me of the kitchen's most constant demand—water. Although we had a lake of pure water at our doorstep, we didn't have the pump to get the water to the kitchen for cooking and doing the dishes. The Blankenburgs, the original owners of Gunflint Lodge, had tapped into a spring under the lodge. They dug a pit about three feet in diameter and ten feet deep for the water to run into. The pit was lined with rocks. Immediately above it was the kitchen sink. The water was drawn up into the sink by means of a pitcher pump. As the fishermen became more numerous, this system proved to be inadequate.

We solved the problem by bringing a fifty-five-gallon drum into the kitchen. The drum was placed several feet off the floor at about the height of the stove. It was Bill's job to keep this full. His last job each night was to make several trips up from the lake carrying two pails of water with a shoulder yoke to fill the reservoir. Heaven help us if the cook came into the kitchen next

morning and there was no water. The reservoir would be filled again at midmorning and late afternoon.

For hot water, I fastened pipes together that ran in a circuitous route through the firebox in the stove over to another fifty-five-gallon drum. The water was heated quite effectively. To wash dishes it was dipped out and carried to the sink where the dishes were washed. Before breakfast Bill or I would use a pail to haul hot water to the guest's cabins. Each cabin has its own pitcher and basin for washing.

During the winter months we fed guests in our home. This added another hundred feet to the water trail. The water drum was just inside my kitchen door. Whenever the kitchen door was opened, you had to watch for Toots the calf. She hung out around the kitchen and liked to take a drink from the water drum. Hot water came from large pots that were heated on the wood cook stove. Every Saturday night we would fill a large wash tub with hot water for family baths. As each person got out, a couple of buckets of water would be thrown out the door and replaced with buckets of fresh hot water.

The next demand from the kitchen was food—fresh produce and meat! At that time the wholesale houses from Duluth delivered only as far as Grand Marais. We had to haul everything from town up to the lodge. The exception was Don Brazell, who trucked pop, beer, and candies to the resorts. If we were lucky, he might bring up a box of groceries or our mail. We often suggested to guests that they stop to pick up mail or groceries for us.

My dad, George Spunner, became part of the solution to our food supply problems. He lost all his property in the 1930 financial crash. His spirit was broken and he became our gardener. Fresh vegetables were difficult to acquire, but Dad's garden carried us through. His strawberry bed was superproductive. There was always an abundance of lettuce, carrots, radishes, cabbage, rhubarb, onions, and, of course, a year's supply of potatoes. Tomatoes and sweet corn would never make it. The deer like all the fresh greens, too. After

Grandpa Spunner and Justine in his garden. The garden was located on the site of the present outfitting building.

many experiments, Dad discovered that a row of moth balls placed around the garden would act as a deterrent to deer.

My mother, Mae, decided we should raise chickens for food. The baby chicks came in cartons by mail. Mother kept them behind the kitchen stove so they would remain warm. They grew and finally had to be put outside. I built a chicken house and a wire yard to contain them. The chickens reached the fryer stage and were ready to be harvested for the dining room. When I went to gather them, the chickens were gone. After a diligent hunt, I discovered several weasels had taken over. The chickens had been killed by a nip in the neck.

Next Mother decided that fresh eggs were a necessity, so we went into the egg business. All went well until a skunk discovered this new bounty. One night I lay in wait for the skunk. One shot and it was gone, but the skunk had its revenge. As it was dying the skunk emitted its odiferous gland fluid. Horrible at first, the odor became less noticeable as summer went on. Every rainy spell that summer, the strong odor took on new life and permeated the air.

The most difficult demand of any kitchen is a good cook. A good cook is great, but sometimes I would have settled for even a competent cook. These were the times when a cook was taken ill or quit and the interim fell on my shoulders.

Basically cooks are divided into two categories: meat cooks, who do the basic meals, and pastry cooks, who do pies and cakes. In more recent times this includes breads and cookies, too. For the pastry work some of my neighbors—Marj Estle, Mary Schoenoff, and Kay Warren—came to my rescue. Those were a few of the people I recall.

Petra Boostrom, the owner of Clearwater Lodge, gave me her recipe for bread, which had lots of phrases like, "Till it feels right." I had difficulty attaining that exact moment when the dough felt just right, when it was kneaded perfectly, when it rose the right amount, or when it was baked with a perfect grain. It was also amazing how many old-time guests would step into the kitchen and give me a hand during the crisis. I wonder if it was a case of survival.

Many of the cook crises seemed to occur when I was raising a family. The children managed to add a little more excitement to the situation. I recall when my son Bruce was at the toddling age and able to feed himself with a spoon. I was preparing breakfast with the dining room full. I put Bruce in a high chair with a spoon and a bowl of oatmeal covered with milk. I slid his chair to one side out of the way. Not getting his usual attention he picked up the bowl and turned it upside down over his head.

Dishes were always washed and dried by hand. One day when Butchie (our Indian neighbor who worked for me for many years) was washing dishes, she looked out the window to watch Bruce toddle up the path to the outside "biffy" with a kitten in his arms. He came back out of the "biffy" without the kitten. I was busy cooking when Butchie told me this. I stopped what I was doing to investigate the situation. The kitten had been dropped down the hole and had managed to crawl up to a ledge and was cursing its fate with plaintive meows. What comes first? Cooking or rescuing the kitten from its smelly fate? The kitten had to wait.

During all of these situations the kitchen was the vital point around which everything revolved. It was not only in the lodge but carried over to shore lunches. Here the party went ashore on a smooth rocky ledge

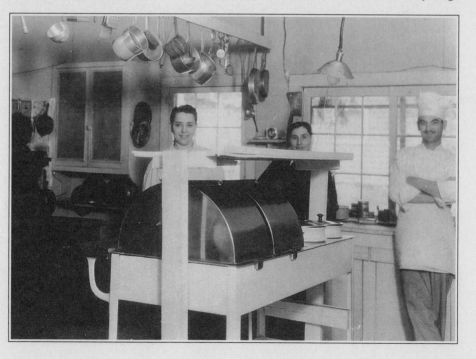

The kitchen in the original lodge. The chef, Frank, is on the right, Lillian ("Butchie") Plummer is in the middle, and a waitress from Europe is on the left.

Butchie Plummer, Aggie Jackson, and Sharon Kerfoot in front of the original lodge about 1950. Aggie learned to cook in the logging camps that her father, George Langtree, ran. She cooked at the lodge off and on until the mid-1970s. Butchie did everything from being Bruce's nanny to guiding to helping in the kitchen to cleaning cabins.

Justine cooking a shore lunch for guests in the early 1930s.

scraped clean from the receding ice floes of years ago. A seagull sailed overhead, took note of possible feed, and then hurried off to notify his friends of his new find.

A circle of rocks indicated a previous fire. Wood was quickly gathered, a fire started, and a pail of water, for coffee, was hung from a green branch over the crackling sticks. The freshly caught fish were filleted by the guide, dipped in cornmeal, and dropped into a hot skillet. Potatoes and vegetables were included in the food provided by the kitchen, which was always with us whether we were in the lodge or out on a scenic remote shore where a light breeze crossed the water and puffy clouds danced across the sky. The seagulls landed where the fish cleaning had taken place and in a few minutes everything was gone.

Bruce and his wife, Sue, have also had their own share of adventures with cooks quitting in the middle of the season. From Bruce's standpoint, the most difficult time occurred during the summer of 1973. Their son Robert was born in September of that year. By the end of June it was apparent that the dinner cook was not going to work out. The only question was whether she would quit or be fired.

Well, she quit on the Sunday morning of the first smorgasbord of the season. Sue was as big as a house. Bruce was insisting he should cook because standing on her feet would be too much. Sue argued harder and won (?) the right to prepare the smorgasbord.

From 7:00 A.M. until 3:00 P.M. she stood and cooked. Of course, the staff helped as much as they could. They were afraid that Robert would be born in the middle of the kitchen. At 3 o'clock, smorgasbord started on time. Sue walked out the back door of the kitchen and went to bed.

The next morning it was obvious that another solution would have to be found. The only other solution was for Bruce to cook. It took ten days to get another cook. Bruce did every dinner during that time. That staff wasn't sure quite how to react. What Bruce lacked in cooking skill, he made up for in speed and cleanliness. Sue was available for technical support: recipes and quantities. Naturally, it was one of the hottest periods of the entire summer. The kitchen must have been fifteen degrees hotter than anyplace else. Bruce was continually called out of the kitchen to make decisions about running the resort. The new cook was greeted with open arms.

Over the nearly seventy years I have been at Gunflint, the kitchen has evolved from a small primitive area to a modern stainless steel wonder. One thing has always remained constant—the need to put out consistently good food. Our cooks have provided every type of fare from logging camp meals to smorgasbords to family-style meals and, now, gourmet meals. In the following pages Ron, our head chef, and Sue will share with you some of the recipes and techniques that they now use. After the book is published, Ron will go back to developing new recipes and techniques. I intend to stay around for another decade or so to see what he comes up with.

PREFACE

Gunflint Lodge started serving meals in 1925 to the first visiting fishermen. The kitchen has been serving ever since. In the old days most guests took all their meals in the main dining room. The capabilities of the cooks varied, but generally good-quality meals came out of the kitchen. At any rate, people were asking for recipes and a cookbook.

In 1991 Ron Berg joined our staff as the head chef. Ron brought with him skills far beyond what any previous cook had. He wanted to be able to serve gourmet meals without being tied to the grind of the same menu day after day. By offering four or five entrées each day and changing them daily, Gunflint adapted its menu format to fit Ron's ideas. The partnership has worked out better than anyone expected.

Along with success came more requests for recipes and a cookbook. Ron and Sue discussed putting together a cookbook every time there was a batch of recipe requests. It became one of those things they were going to do one day.

During the summer of 1994 Lisa Freeman from the University of Minnesota Press came to Gunflint to discuss a possible book with Justine Kerfoot. While Justine, Sue, and Lisa were talking, the subject of a Gunflint Lodge cookbook came up. The university press had been casually discussing the possibility of publishing a cookbook. The timing was right for both parties, and a deal was struck.

Surprisingly, both publisher and authors had independently felt that a seasonal arrangement of recipes might work. From the authors' standpoint, that's how the year runs. Changing a menu daily allows room to adapt easily to seasonal changes in available food and the number of guests. Also the authors were not trying to write a comprehensive cookbook covering all aspects of daily cooking. They just wanted to share some recipes that had worked well at the lodge.

So paging through this book will take you through the seasons. Obviously some recipes could go into any season. But others, such as the game recipes, seem to fit better in the fall and winter than other seasons. The fish cookery chapter gives you all the techniques, tips, and hints to cook fish from your most recent fishing trip or fish from the grocery store. As an experienced fishing guide and chef, Ron has a vast amount of knowledge about fish cooking to share with you. At Gunflint Lodge, the entrées are primarily accompanied by a vegetable and a choice of wild rice pilaf, a potato, or a bread custard. Recipes for many of these are given in one chapter.

Then there are two chapters devoted to desserts and breads. Finally, some recipes are for seasonings, stocks, and sauces that are basic to many recipes.

Each seasonal chapter begins with an essay by Sue describing a part of life at Gunflint Lodge during recent years. Interspersed among the recipes you will find plenty of tips from the kitchen for making your cooking easier. Ron will tell you how to adapt and change recipes easily to vary your daily meals. He has also included more detailed information on aspects of cooking that may be unfamiliar to you. Menu suggestions are often given.

Some recipes, those you might use for special occasions, are long and involved. Ron has broken many of the more complicated recipes into sections. These can be prepared in advance and then assembled on the day they are to be served. Other recipes can be done in just a few minutes when you get home from work. Some of the quick recipes have been identified in the Table of Contents to help you on those days when it's 5 o'clock and you don't know what to serve for dinner. The secret to all the recipes is using top-quality ingredients.

As you try the recipes, be a little adventurous! Ron has created many of his recipes by seeing or reading what another chef does and adapting the recipe or technique or ingredients to what is available at the lodge. With a little practice you can do the same thing. Cooking doesn't have to be drudgery. With courage and practice anyone can learn to be an innovative cook. Don't be discouraged if everything doesn't turn out perfectly the first time. Ron's first attempts often need adjusting, too. So have some fun trying these recipes. Then adapt them to your style and your family's taste.

ACKNOWLEDGMENTS

To get where we are is not a solo trip. Mentors and colleagues are many, and I hope any I have inadvertently left out will forgive me. Although cooking has been my passion since childhood, my tenure in the profession didn't really begin until quite late in life. Steve and Denise Kaminski, owners of the now closed Redwood Inn in Rice, Minnesota, took me on as a part-time cook in 1986. At the time I was teaching junior high English full-time. For the next four school years I spent most of my waking weekend hours behind the line at Redwood. My summers were spent at my cabin at the end of the Gunflint Trail working as a fishing guide—another passion. Steve and Denise encouraged me to help develop a country French menu that was to signify the Redwood Inn.

During those years at the Redwood Inn, I worked with many fine chefs. One in particular stands out, Tim Bromenshenkel. Tim came to the Redwood as a meat-and-potatoes cook who absorbed knowledge faster than anyone I have ever met. Soon we were competing to put our creations on each night's menu. Many of the recipes in this book owe their initial creation to Tim.

Steve was always trying to persuade any chefs he met to come to the restaurant to work with us in the hope that this exposure would improve our techniques and give us inspiration. One such was Bernard LaFon, a retired French chef who, earlier in his career, had traveled with his own brigade of chefs from one French embassy to another in North Africa, preparing important diplomatic dinners. To our advantage, somewhere along the line he married a school teacher from Edina and ended up in Minnesota.

Jay Sparks, then chef at the 510 Restaurant in Minneapolis, was another who spent a day in the kitchen at the Redwood Inn teaching and inspiring us. He must have chuckled when he read a review of the Redwood Inn by Jeremy Iggers in the Minneapolis *Star Tribune*, for some of the entrées Iggers mentioned in his review were variations of recipes Jay had shared with us.

There are also many fine people with whom I have worked and learned along the way: in particular, my capable sous-chef at Gunflint Lodge for several years, Gene Buchholz; the irrepressible Danny Hanson; the exceptionally talented Ban Rith Yung; Steve Meyers, a skillful speed demon behind the line; my friend John Roscoe and his "traveling food show"; and my coworkers on the line over the years whom I depended on so greatly and who never let me down, Jean Oleheiser, Bill Messina, and Curtis Martinson.

Finally, I would like to thank Bruce and Sue Kerfoot for believing in me and giving me the chance to live my dream.

Ron Berg
Seagull Lake

If a resort has served meals for as long as Gunflint Lodge has, there are always requests for favorite recipes. When Ron Berg started cooking for us, the occasional request turned into a steady stream. Ron and I discussed putting together a cookbook to meet these requests.

A casual conversation with Lisa Freeman of the University of Minnesota Press in 1994 started the process that culminated in this book. Lisa and Todd Orjala, also from the University of Minnesota Press, have helped Ron and me go from wannabe authors to published authors. It would have been impossible without their help.

My husband, Bruce, and my mother-in-law, Justine, both offered steady encouragement as I tried to write for the first time since college.

Sue Kerfoot

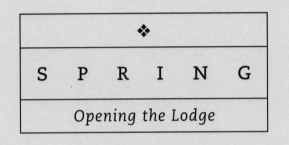

SPRING

Opening the Lodge

SPRING

Opening the Lodge

When Bruce and I were first married, Gunflint Lodge was closed in the winter. The cabins were covered with snow and ignored. The main lodge stood without heat and absorbed the cold until it was colder inside than out. Our schedule was relatively relaxed. Sure, there were chores to do but there was also time to sit down with the newspaper for an hour after lunch or spend a day ice fishing.

With the approach of spring everything changed. Winter's relaxed pace ended about the middle of April. The opening of the resort for the summer season was only a few weeks away.

Opening the lodge was not a matter of opening the door. Every year there were spring projects to be done. We had planned the projects all winter but suddenly their number expanded in leaps and bounds. The time to do all these projects shrank with ever increasing speed.

For me the most difficult part was starting the opening chores in the lodge the first morning. If we were lucky, it was raining and not snowing that first morning. The lake was still covered with gray ice. Everything seemed gray, even the remaining snow. Bruce went down before breakfast to light the stoves—an oil stove and a fireplace in the lounge. The same in the dining room. With no heat all winter, the rooms warmed up very slowly. No matter how well we thought the fall cleaning had been done, every room looked like no one had cleaned it in years.

There was only one thing to do—dig in and start cleaning. Usually we had a couple of girls on the staff to help. Hot water was hauled by the bucketful from our house on the hill. It was still too cold at night to put water in the lodge. Besides, Bruce was working on his projects. As in most marriages, I always felt that his projects had much greater urgency to him than my need for water in the lodge. He seemed to feel the reverse.

The girls and I started in one corner and worked our way around the lounge and dining room. First we moved the lounge furniture into the dining room. Then we washed the ceiling of the lounge. Next it was the walls followed by the fireplace rocks. The lounge floor was washed. A coat of wax was put on. Another coat of wax was put on. Finally, we carried (no dragging) all the furniture from the dining room to the lounge.

Now into the dining room, where we repeated the process. Then on to the office and repeat the process a third time. At last it was time to move into the kitchen.

When the water was hooked up to the main lodge, we started to clean the kitchen. The girls started washing in the kitchen in between working on the cabins. The trick was to time your days. The girls worked in the cabins on nice sunny days as they were outside a lot going between buildings. They worked in the lodge on rainy days because that was all in one building. Not only did more get done that way but everyone stayed happier.

After the water was in the main lodge, Bruce and a helper started to put water into all the cabins. It was either a project that went very quickly and was finished in a few days or one that dragged on forever. One fall we had someone other than Bruce drain the water system in the cabins. The man had never done it before and was not careful to drain everything.

The following spring Bruce paid the price. Every cabin had broken pipes and not just one. There were three, four, and five breaks in each cabin. Bruce ordered replacement parts for two weeks. Every night he came in soaking wet and covered with mud from belly crawling under cabins trying to reach pipes. The worst ones were behind walls; he had to tear out the wall to repair the pipe. A three- or four-day project grew into two weeks.

Before and after putting the water in, Bruce and his helpers worked on spring projects. Every year there were minor repairs to be made in cabins, and major improvements were always scheduled in one or two cabins. Some years Bruce would be trying to finish up a new cabin. We always got cabins done just minutes before the first guests arrived.

Most of the cabins had been cleaned thoroughly the fall before and stayed clean because no one was in them all winter. Spring-cleaning in cabins consisted of making beds, cleaning bathrooms after the water was turned on, and washing windows. Usually I sent the girls out to do the cabins alone. By then I knew which girl should be put in charge and which one needed to be told what to do.

Each day we looked forward to the mail to see how many reservations and deposits came in. In those days, almost all reservations came by mail. Long-distance calls were expensive and only used for emergencies. There was a sense of satisfaction as we marked off each reservation in the books. All deposits were particularly welcome.

As opening day came closer food, candy, pop, beer, dairy products, trading post merchandise, and gasoline were delivered. Salesmen stopped by every day. Neighbors called to see if you had the vital part they needed for one of their repairs or did they have to go to town. Sometimes we had someone in town who could get the part for them.

Bruce and his helpers put the docks back in the water. Somehow they never seemed to go back together quite right. Adjustments and repairs were made. Next the boats were put in the water. Spark plugs were changed on all the motors just before they were put on boats. The gas tanks were filled.

I was trying to keep up with the mail, answer the telephone, and supervise the girls. Bruce and I both went down to the trading post at night to price new gifts. It was always a surprise to see how much stuff we had ordered. Hopefully everything would fit into the store and, more important, sell.

Through it all there was a never-ending parade of food, office supplies, business records, laundry, and cleaning supplies moving down from our house to the lodge. Basically we moved the operation of our business from one location to another every spring. The reverse happened in the fall.

The summer staff arrived on a regular basis during the first weeks of spring. Some were old hands and welcomed back as part of the family. Others were here for the first time. The new ones usually had little experience and had never lived this far from a town. All of them were given chores. There never seemed to be enough time to train everyone. While most stayed for the season, a few decided it wasn't for them and left. Bruce and I decided one or two were not for us and they also left.

Finally opening day arrived. It was the Friday before the walleye season opened. Gunflint bustled with unaccustomed activity. The dinner cook was in the kitchen baking bread and pies and nervous about the first night's dinner. Things still weren't quite organized. The dining room staff didn't know where anything was. Often they had never waited tables before. Out in the front office there was the last bit of dusting to do and the last bag of trash to take out. Just after lunch Bruce and I ran up to put on new Gunflint sweatshirts. Down on the waterfront the dock boy got all the boats and motors set up —cleaned, gassed, and ready to go. The bait man delivered live bait. Every time we looked out the window, another boatload of campers went down the lake, usually in overloaded boats. Hopefully the waves weren't too high and they wouldn't get swamped.

In early afternoon the guests started to check in. By now the cook and waitresses had asked us at least a hundred questions. We were running back and forth checking in guests and answering questions from the kitchen. Nerves were frayed.

All the fishermen wanted to talk with Bruce and the guides. They asked, "Who is my guide going to be? When did the ice finally go out? Do you think it will rain tonight? Can I get a thermos of coffee to take in the boat? Which boat is mine? What time do you serve breakfast in the morning?"

In the space of a few hours we were back in the resort business. All the stress and dirt and hard work of the past few weeks was forgotten. We had guests to take care of now. The reason for all the work was apparent.

Eventually dinner started. It was not perfect but we got through it. The scared waitress approached her first table. The guests didn't bite her. The cook didn't growl at her when she turned in the order. Bruce was in the dining room with a cup of coffee in his hand going from table to table to chat with guests. I was in the kitchen giving directions to the waitresses. Everyone was in a good mood. There was almost a festive air about the lodge. The fishing season opened at midnight!

The end of the day came. The last guest had checked in. The last dinner dish was washed. All the guests had gone back to their cabins to catch a nap before going out for the midnight opener. Bruce and I trudged up to our house. We were dead tired but we were also excited. Spring was here and a new season had started!

Ron's Introduction

Spring comes late to the northwoods. So it is heartening to "Les Hiverants," the locals who spend long winters in the far north, to see and hear the signs of approaching spring after months of winter. I once heard Dorothy Molter, the late, famous "root beer lady" of Knife Lake, characterize the area as "ten months of winter followed by two months of cold weather."

Beginning in early spring, the long silence of winter is gradually broken. From the raucous tempo of the spring peepers to the haunting wail of the first loon, the season builds in intensity. Flights of seagulls appear even before the ice is completely gone. Black bears and their cubs are seen foraging for meager spring rations. Occasionally a doe and her fawn are glimpsed stealing through the sparse spring foliage, melting into the background at the first hint of alarm.

At Gunflint Lodge the kitchen celebrates the arrival of spring with fresh herbs and vegetables of the season to complement the bounty of the lakes and woods. Entrées such as pepper grilled lake trout with spring onion sauce, pan roasted breast of chicken with fresh chive cream sauce, broiled salmon fillet princesse topped with fresh asparagus spears and Parmesan cheese with asparagus sauce, or beer batter fried fillet of walleye appear on the constantly changing menu.

Spring and early summer often provide fast fishing action on Gunflint and other nearby lakes. Gunflint's fishing guides are booked months in advance. The guides provide adventurous forays into the backcountry for guests who are looking for action catching some of the wide variety of fish inhabiting the area lakes: walleyes, lake trout, rainbows, brook trout, splake, northern pike, and smallmouth bass. Trophies abound in these waters. Minnesota's state record walleye was caught up here.

One of the best things about going out with a guide is the shore lunch. What could be better than to be sitting under a great pine looking out over a wilderness lake, feasting on the morning's freshly caught fish your guide has prepared over a campfire?

For the younger guests, "Fishing Fun" provides a guided half-day of fishing. It's not unusual to have a miniature set of fillets from a small perch or smallmouth bass caught by one of the children delivered to the kitchen for the chef to prepare for the young diner's pleasure.

◎ Beer Batter Fried Walleye Fingers

There must be a hundred different ways to make a beer batter and I have tried most of them. This is the one I have found to be the lightest, crispiest, and most grease-free. It also happens to be the simplest—just flour, salt, pepper, paprika, and, of course, beer.

1½ c. all-purpose flour
1 T. salt
1½ tsp. freshly ground black pepper
1½ T. paprika
1 (12-oz.) can of beer, plus more as needed
Flour, as needed for dredging
1½ lb. walleye fillets, cut into finger-size pieces
Tartar sauce or cocktail sauce (pages 103, 104)

In medium bowl, with a whisk combine flour, salt, pepper, and paprika. Whisk in beer until mixture is the consistency of heavy cream. Let stand for 15 minutes. Whisk in more beer to thin out if necessary. It is important that the batter not be too thick.

Heat deep-fat fryer to 360°F. Place 1 cup of flour in a bag or a shallow pan such as a pie tin. Shake or dredge walleye pieces in the flour. Remove the pieces one at a time from the flour; shake off excess flour. Dip flour-coated walleye in the batter and drop gently into the hot fat. Repeat with the remaining walleye, being careful not to crowd the fryer. Remove with a slotted spoon when golden brown and crisp; drain on paper towels. Serve immediately with choice of tartar sauce or cocktail sauce. Makes 6 appetizer servings.

▶ TIP: For an entree or for shore lunch, you can batter fry larger pieces or whole fillets depending on the capacity of your fryer.

Leek and Wild Mushroom Tart with Honey Madeira Sauce

This rich and savory first course is my interpretation of one served by Chef Tim Bromenshenkel at the Radisson Hotel in St. Cloud, Minnesota. It could also be served as an evening entrée for 4 to 6 when combined with a tossed green salad, a loaf of crusty French bread, and a bottle of Pinot Noir.

Tart Crust

¾ c. flour
Pinch of salt
¼ c. chilled shortening
1½–2 T. cold water

In medium bowl, sift flour with salt; cut in shortening until rice-sized. Add water; toss with a fork to moisten. Use hands to form dough into a ball. Cut into two pieces; shape each into a disk. Wrap with film and refrigerate for at least 2 hours before rolling.

Preheat oven to 400°F. On floured surface, roll out dough. Place in 10-inch tart pan with removable bottom or in 9-inch pie pan. Cut a round disk of wax paper an inch or so larger than the pan; line dough with it. Fill shell with pie weights, dry beans, rice, etc., to hold dough in place while baking. Place pan on cookie sheet; bake for approximately 15 minutes. Remove paper and pie weights. Set aside. Reduce oven heat to 375°F.

Cooking with Wine and Spirits

✳ When a recipe calls for a dry white or red wine, which wine should you use? Before today's box wines (which keep well due to their vacuum bag design) I followed Julia Child's advice from one of her cookbooks and used a good-quality dry white vermouth for most recipes that called for a dry white wine. The wine's herbaceous flavors were a plus, but the best reason for using it was that it kept a long time in the refrigerator after being opened. Unfortunately, there was no equivalent red wine that was both well suited for cooking and a good keeper.

All that has changed, of course, with the readily available box wines. For any recipe that calls for a dry red wine, I would recommend one of the box reds, such as a burgundy, Cabernet Sauvignon, or a zinfandel. If the recipe calls for a dry white wine, use a box white, such as a Chablis or sauvignon blanc. I still prefer dry white vermouth for some recipes, especially those involving seafood or turkey, but will use one of the box whites if necessary.

Besides working well for cooking, these box wines are suitable for everyday drinking. While in no way comparable to most bottled wine, they fit a niche. For example, it is not likely that I would open a bottle of red wine to accompany a meat loaf or a burger, but I would certainly have no qualms about having an accompanying glass of one of the box reds, such as a burgundy or a Cabernet Sauvignon.

Should you use the same wine to cook with that you are drinking with the meal? It depends. If the amount of wine amounts to only a splash or so for deglazing a pan, I will frequently use the same wine I have opened for dinner. But if the wine is exceptionally exquisite, I wouldn't want to part with even a splash of it and the splash will come from a box instead.

Spirits such as cognac or brandy, bourbon, scotch whiskey, and apple brandy (the French Calvados or the American equivalent, applejack) add flavor and excitement to many preparations. If a recipe calls for cognac, a good-quality brandy may be readily substituted. In fact, there are so many dishes that benefit from a quick flambé with brandy, I keep a bottle in my cupboard instead of my liquor cabinet.

Tart Filling

3 T. butter

½ tsp. minced garlic (about 1 small clove)

½ c. sliced leeks, white part only

12 oz. wild mushrooms, such as shiitake, crimini, or oyster, tough stems removed, thinly sliced; substitute a combination of wild and domestic or use all domestic

¼ c. dry white wine

Kosher salt and freshly ground black pepper to taste

4 eggs, beaten

1 c. milk

1½ c. heavy cream

½ c. grated Swiss or Gruyère cheese

In 10-inch skillet over medium heat, melt butter. When sizzling, add garlic and leeks. Sauté for 1 minute without browning. Add mushrooms; toss and stir until cooked through and soft. Increase the heat to high; add wine. Reduce until wine is nearly gone. Season to taste with salt and pepper. Set aside.

In medium bowl, whisk eggs, milk, and cream together. Set aside.

To assemble tart, sprinkle Swiss cheese evenly over baked crust. Top with leek and mushroom mixture. Pour egg custard mixture over to within a quarter inch of top of crust.

Bake at 375°F until filling is set, about 30 to 45 minutes. Remove to wire rack; cool for 15 to 20 minutes before serving.

Honey Madeira Sauce

1 c. chicken or beef stock, homemade or low-salt canned

¼ c. Madeira wine

1½ tsp. chopped shallots

1½ tsp. heavy cream

1½ tsp. honey

2–3 tsp. cornstarch mixed with water

1–2 T. butter, cut in small pieces

Kosher salt to taste

While tart is cooling, make sauce. In heavy-bottomed saucepan over high heat, combine stock, Madeira wine, and shallots. Reduce by half. Whisk in cream and honey. Thicken to a saucelike consistency with the cornstarch slurry. Remove from heat; whisk in butter to taste. Season to taste with salt. Strain through a fine sieve. Keep warm.

Cut the warm tart into 8 or 10 pieces. Serve in a pool of sauce. Makes 8–10 appetizer servings.

▶ TIP: For the best flavor and consistency, homemade stock is recommended for the honey Madiera sauce. When canned stocks are greatly reduced, the results are usually less than satisfactory.

Soups

Cream of Spinach Soup

You will love this emerald green soup even if you don't like spinach. The optional anisette enhances the flavor so subtly that no one will guess what it is.

5 T. butter
1 medium onion, chopped
5 T. flour
4½ c. cold chicken stock
10 oz. fresh leaf spinach or 10-oz. box of frozen
    leaf spinach, thawed and squeezed to remove
    most of the moisture
1 c. half-and-half
Salt and white pepper to taste
Nutmeg to taste
1–3 tsp. anisette liqueur (optional)
Freshly grated Parmesan cheese
Croutons

In medium saucepan, cook onion in butter until translucent. Stir in flour. Cook slowly, stirring for 1 minute to cook the flour. Whisk in chicken stock. Bring to a simmer over medium heat, stirring constantly until mixture thickens and comes to a boil. Stir in fresh spinach leaves; remove from heat. Let stand for 10 minutes. In a blender or food processor with steel blade, puree soup mixture in small quantities. Return to saucepan; add half-and-half. Season to taste with salt, pepper, and nutmeg. Add anisette liqueur if desired. Garnish with some freshly grated Parmesan cheese or a few buttery crisp croutons. Serves 6.

Fishing Camp Chowder

This is an old-fashioned fish chowder that you will grow to crave. The soup was legendary at the annual fish camp I hosted for friends for more than twenty years. Some who wandered by the pot of simmering fish heads and bones needed to be cajoled, berated, and downright humiliated into eating their first bowl of the finished product, but they always came back for seconds.

3 T. butter
2–3 c. chopped onions
2–3 c. ½-in. cubed potatoes
1 qt. white wine fish stock (page 149) or ¼ c. wine
    plus 4 (7-oz.) bottles clam juice
½ c. half-and-half
½ c. heavy cream
½ lb. walleye fillets, cut into cubes (use more as
    desired)
Salt and freshly ground black pepper to taste
Tabasco sauce to taste
Butter to taste (optional)
Oyster crackers

In medium stockpot, cook onions in butter until transparent. Add potatoes, white wine fish stock, or clam juice and wine. Reduce heat; simmer until potatoes are tender. Add half-and-half, cream, and walleye. Simmer for 10 minutes or until fish is cooked. Season to taste with salt, pepper, Tabasco sauce, and optional butter. Serve with oyster crackers. Serves 4–6.

▶ TIP: To make a lighter version, omit cooking the onions in butter. Start by combining the onions, potatoes, fish stock, or clam juice and wine. Substitute evaporated skim milk for the half-and-half and the cream. Omit the optional butter.

Fish

Salmon Fillet Princesse

"Princesse" is one of those recipe names that gives a good indication of what might be in it, which in this case is usually asparagus. In the same vein are dishes named "Florentine," which surely contain spinach; "Veronique," which most likely include grapes; and "Provençal," in which tomatoes, garlic, and basil are probably abundant. Fresh asparagus makes this dish an obvious choice for spring. A freshly caught stream trout would substitute wonderfully for the salmon.

Serve with Gunflint wild rice pilaf (page 112) and, perhaps, a salad of mixed greens tossed with red onions and sun-dried cranberries, plus a bottle of chilled chardonnay or fumé blanc for an elegant spring dinner.

12–18 fresh asparagus spears
1½ T. butter
3 T. minced onion
1½ T. flour
1 c. chicken stock, homemade or low-salt canned
½ c. heavy cream
Salt and white pepper to taste
6 (7-oz.) salmon fillets
6–8 T. butter, melted
Salt and freshly ground black pepper to taste
Water or white wine as needed
4–6 oz. freshly grated Parmesan cheese

Trim approximately a half inch off the butt ends of the asparagus and discard. Line up the asparagus spears so the tips are even and cut the spears in half. Set aside the bottom ends while you blanch the tips. In medium skillet three-fourths full of boiling water, cook tips until crisply tender (about 3 to 4 minutes). Taste part of a tip to check for doneness. Cool quickly in ice water; drain on paper towels. Refrigerate until needed.

In heavy-bottomed saucepan over low heat, melt 1½ tablespoons of butter. Add onion; cover. Cook over low heat until onions are transparent. Stir in flour. Cook slowly, stirring, for 2 minutes without browning. Gradually whisk in chicken stock. Continue cooking slowly, whisking constantly, until mixture boils and thickens. Cut bottom ends crosswise into ½-inch pieces and add to thickened stock. Reduce heat to very low; simmer 10 minutes. If mixture gets too thick, thin with a little water or additional chicken stock.

In food processor with steel knife, puree mixture. Strain through a fine sieve into a clean saucepan, pressing down hard on the solids. Whisk in cream; cook over low heat until thickened and smooth. Season to taste with salt and white pepper. Keep warm while fish cooks.

Preheat oven to 450°F. Spray a shallow-sided cookie sheet with nonstick cooking spray. Lay salmon fillets on it with the skin side down. Brush with melted butter. Season to taste with salt and black pepper. Pour a little water or white wine in pan. Bake for 3 to 5 minutes. Place three asparagus spears on top of each serving of fish; top with Parmesan cheese. Return to oven; bake an additional 3 to 4 minutes or until cheese is melted and salmon is done as desired. Place each serving of salmon on a warm plate; spoon the asparagus cream sauce around the fish. Serves 6.

A Guide to Preparing Asparagus

✳ Whether to peel or to snap, that is the question. The tough, woody lower section of a stalk of asparagus needs to be removed before cooking. To do this, one usually grasps the asparagus spear by the tip and the butt end and bends until it snaps in two. The area where it breaks is usually the border between tender and woody.

Snapping is quicker, to be sure, but the peeled stems look nicer, in my opinion, and are more uniform in length. It has always offended my thrifty soul to look upon a pile of snapped stems. So, I usually peel asparagus.

Pepper Grilled Lake Trout with Spring Onion Sauce

Here is a delicious taste of the far north: lake trout with fresh cracked pepper and a creamy sauce made with the green tops of the first spring onions.

1 c. clam juice or fish stock (page 149)
1 c. dry white wine or dry vermouth
1½ c. heavy cream
1 bunch green onion tops, cut into 1-in. lengths
Salt and white pepper to taste
2½ lb. lake trout or salmon fillets
Fresh coarsely ground black pepper, as needed
6–8 T. butter, melted
Kosher salt to taste
Fresh chives or green onion tops

In medium saucepan over medium-high heat, combine clam juice or fish stock with wine or vermouth. Reduce by three-fourths. Add cream; reduce to 1 cup.

Place green onion tops in a blender; pour sauce over onions. Let stand for 5 minutes, then puree. Strain; season to taste with salt and white pepper. Return to saucepan; simmer. Hold over very low heat.

Grind coarse black pepper to taste over lake trout fillets. Press in lightly with the heel of your hand. Brush with melted butter; season to taste with kosher salt. Grill lake trout on a clean oiled grill over hot coals starting with the peppered side down. Remove to heated plates. Top with sauce. Garnish with fresh chopped chives or thinly sliced diagonally cut green onion tops. Serve at once. Serves 6.

▶ TIP: Sauce may be made ahead. Store in preheated thermos for several hours or refrigerate until needed. If refrigerated, heat slowly and serve immediately or the fresh green color will soon be lost.

Fillet of Walleye with Shrimp Sauce and Swiss Cheese Au Gratin

Walleye and shrimp are a wonderful flavor combination. This was the first feature item I ever put on a menu. Since it was a French restaurant, it was listed on the menu as "Sandré aux Crevettes Gratinée."

Shrimp Sauce

5 T. butter
5 T. all-purpose flour
2 c. white wine fish stock or quick fish stock (page 149)
½ c. heavy cream
2 T. chopped shallots
8 oz. frozen or fresh small shrimp (50–60 count) or larger shrimp, cut up
Dry white vermouth or dry white wine
Salt and white pepper to taste

In heavy-bottomed saucepan over low heat, melt butter. Stir in flour; cook slowly for 2 minutes without browning. Remove from heat; whisk in fish stock all at once. Cook over medium heat, whisking constantly until mixture thickens and comes to a boil. Reduce heat to low; slowly whisk in cream. Simmer 3 minutes, whisking occasionally to prevent scorching.

In stainless-steel saucepan over high heat, combine shallots, shrimp, and vermouth or wine. Bring to a boil; reduce by three-fourths. Strain sauce into shrimp mixture. Season to taste with salt and white pepper. At this point, the sauce may be kept warm while preparing the fish or cooled and refrigerated or frozen for later use.

Walleye Fillets

2½ lb. walleye fillets
Melted butter
Salt to taste
Dry white wine as needed
5 oz. grated Swiss cheese
Paprika
Chopped fresh parsley

Preheat oven to 450°F. Place walleye fillets skin side down in a shallow pan. Brush each fillet with melted butter and season lightly with salt. Pour wine around fillets to a depth of ⅛ inch to prevent sticking. Bake for 4 to 5 minutes or until fish is barely done. Remove from oven; drain well. Transfer fillets with a spatula to a lightly buttered shallow-sided casserole large enough to hold all the fillets in a single layer. Spoon shrimp sauce evenly over fillets; sprinkle with Swiss cheese, paprika, and parsley. Return to oven until cheese is melted and sauce is bubbly around the edges. Serves 6.

Two Bottoms

✳ Tom Mooniets, an Ojibway Indian from Fort Hope, Ontario, worked one summer as a guide for Voyageur Canoe Outfitters on Saganaga Lake. On this particular day he was fishing with a party on Northern Lights Lake, nine miles and one portage away. Around 10:00 that morning it began to rain. It turned out to be a memorable rainstorm indeed, for it continued on well into the night and dropped more than four inches. As everybody scrambled for their rain gear, Tom reached into his packsack for his. As the rain poured down, Tom rummaged frantically through the pack. In disgust he threw the packsack to the bottom of the boat. "Damn!" he exclaimed. "Two bottoms!"

Fillet of Walleye Provençal

Guests who drop off fish from a day's catch for their evening meal often leave the manner of preparation up to me. This recipe resulted from a flight of fancy with a guest's fish.

4 (6–8-oz.) walleye fillets
¼ c. butter, melted
Salt and freshly ground black pepper to taste
1 c. dry white wine
¼ c. heavy cream
Salt and white pepper to taste
¼ c. tomato, peeled, seeded, and cut into
   ¼-in. dice
¼ c. fresh basil, chopped
¾ c. freshly grated Parmesan cheese

Preheat oven to 450°F. Place walleye fillets on a 10-by-15-inch buttered cookie sheet. Brush fillets with melted butter. Season lightly with salt and black pepper. Pour wine around fillets. Bake walleye for 4 to 6 minutes or until just barely done. Remove from oven. Pour wine cooking juices into a skillet. With a long spatula, carefully move walleye fillets to a shallow-sided casserole large enough to hold the fillets in a slightly overlapping layer.

Place pan containing the cooking juices over high heat; bring to a boil. Reduce until syrupy; add cream. Reduce over high heat until thickened. Pour any juices that have accumulated around the walleye fillets into the sauce. Season to taste with salt and white pepper. Stir in tomatoes and basil. You may substitute chopped chives, parsley, or another herb for the basil.

Pour the sauce over walleye fillets; sprinkle with Parmesan cheese. Return casserole to oven; bake until cheese is melted and casserole is bubbling around the sides, about 3 to 4 minutes. Serves 4.

◑ Alaskan Bush Scallops

This easy recipe for turning northern pike into morsels that taste remarkably like scallops comes from Justine Kerfoot's daughter Pat. In the tradition of the Kerfoot family, Pat and her husband, Jim, wrested an American plan resort out of the Alaskan bush some years back. The fly-in resort was situated on a lake that held a healthy population of northern pike, from hammer handles to wall mounters. As everyone knows, boredom is the mother of culinary invention, and thus one desperate evening these tasty scallop-like morsels sprang into being.

> Northern pike fillets, skinless
> All-purpose flour
> Vegetable oil
> Salt and freshly ground black pepper
> Tartar or cocktail sauce (pages 103, 104)

Use a sharp knife to cut the Y-bones out of each fillet in a long strip. When you finish, you will have three long pieces. Discard the Y-bone strip. Cut the remaining boneless pieces into 1-inch cubes. When ready to cook, heat a heavy skillet with about ⅛ inch of vegetable oil over medium heat. Season the cubes with salt and freshly ground black pepper. Dredge in flour. Shake off excess flour. Sauté in hot oil until golden brown. Serve with tartar or cocktail sauce.

Opening Day Walleye Fillets with Morel Mushroom Cream Sauce

Spring is a time when two great and seemingly unrelated events coincide: the long-awaited fishing opener finally arrives and the woods abound with morel mushrooms. What better way to celebrate these wondrous events than to pair the springtime bounty of the woods and waters in an unforgettable feast. The perfect accompaniment to this sumptuous dish would, of course, be buttered wild spring asparagus.

> 3 T. butter, melted
> 2 tsp. fresh lemon juice
> 4 (6–8-oz.) walleye fillets
> Salt and pepper to taste
> Paprika
> ½ c. dry white wine
> 12 fresh morel mushrooms
> 1¼ c. heavy cream
> Freshly chopped chives

Preheat oven to 450°F. Combine butter and lemon juice. Place walleye fillets skin side down on a baking sheet. Brush with lemon butter. Season lightly with salt, pepper, and paprika. Pour wine around the fillets. Bake on top rack of oven for 4 to 6 minutes or until fish is just barely done. Remove fillets with a long spatula to a heated serving platter. Cover with foil to keep warm while making the sauce.

Pour remaining juices and butter into a medium skillet. Bring to a simmer over medium heat. Add morels (halved, if large). Cook, tossing and turning until they soften and give up their juices. Increase heat to high. Cook until wine and mushroom juices are reduced to a couple of tablespoons. Add cream. Boil rapidly until reduced to a saucelike consistency, about 4 to 5 minutes. Add any juices that have accumulated around fillets to sauce. Continue cooking for 30 seconds. Remove from heat. Season to taste with salt, pepper, and drops of lemon juice. Spoon sauce over the fillets. Sprinkle with chives. Serves 4.

Chicken

Poached Breast of Chicken Stuffed with Mushroom Duxelles with Spring Leek Pudding and Chardonnay Glaze

The pudding is made with the first leeks of spring, which are especially flavorful and sweet. Accompany this elegant spring entrée with either wild rice pilaf or one of the garlic mashed potatoes.

Mushroom Duxelles Stuffing

1 lb. fresh mushrooms
2 T. butter
4–6 T. finely chopped shallots or leeks
½ c. dry white vermouth or white wine
¼ c. heavy cream
1 c. fresh white bread crumbs
Salt and freshly ground black pepper to taste

In food processor with steel knife or by hand, finely chop the mushrooms. Gather a handful at a time and place in a clean towel. Twist towel around mushrooms; squeeze to remove as much liquid as possible from mushrooms. Repeat with remaining mushrooms.

In skillet over medium-low heat, melt butter. Add squeezed, minced mushrooms. Sauté mushrooms until they begin to separate, about 4 to 5 minutes. Add shallots or leeks; continue cooking until transparent. Add vermouth or wine; reduce three-fourths. Add cream; reduce for 2 minutes. Stir in bread crumbs. Season to taste with salt and pepper. Refrigerate until needed.

Leek Pudding

2¼ c. thinly sliced leeks, white and pale green parts only
1 c. julienne sweet onions such as Vidalia, Walla Walla, or Texas (substitute yellow onions)
3 T. butter
3 eggs, beaten
¾ c. heavy cream
¾ tsp. roasted garlic puree (page 38)
Salt and white pepper to taste
Drops of lemon juice to taste

In medium skillet over medium-low heat, sauté leeks and julienne onions in butter without browning until onions are transparent, about 10 to 12 minutes. Cool. In small bowl, whisk eggs with cream, roasted garlic puree, salt, white pepper, and lemon juice. Combine with leeks and onions. Divide mixture between six 4-ounce ramekins that have been sprayed with nonstick cooking spray. Refrigerate until ready to bake.

Chicken Breasts

6 (6–8-oz.) boneless skinless chicken breasts

Place chicken breasts between sheets of plastic wrap; pound gently to flatten each one to about ¼ inch thick. Spread about one-sixth of duxelles stuffing on the bottom side of one flattened chicken breast. Fold any of the thin jagged edges over the stuffing and roll up beginning with one of the long sides. Repeat for remaining breasts.

Place one of the stuffed breasts along the edge of a 12-by-15-inch square of plastic wrap. Roll tightly in the wrap a couple of times, then fold in the sides and complete rolling. Place wrapped breast on a second sheet of wrap and repeat. Wrap remaining breasts. Recipe may be completed to this point and the stuffed chicken breasts refrigerated until ready to cook.

Preheat oven to 350°F. Bring a saucepan or large high-sided skillet of water to a boil. Gently drop the wrapped chicken breasts in the water. Return water to just a simmer; turn off the heat and cover. The chicken breasts will be done after 20 minutes, at which time they may be removed for serving or they may remain in the water for several minutes more if need be.

While the chicken breasts are poaching, bake the leek puddings at 350°F for 15 to 20 minutes or until set and lightly browned. Let stand 3 minutes before serving.

Chardonnay Glaze

¼ c. chardonnay wine
1½ c. chicken stock, homemade or low-salt
   canned
1 T. cornstarch dissolved in 2 T. chicken stock
Salt and white pepper to taste
1 T. butter
Chopped parsley

Pour wine in small heavy-bottomed saucepan; reduce to 1 tablespoon over high heat. Add chicken stock; boil until reduced to 1 cup. Add cornstarch and chicken stock mixture. Thicken to the consistency of heavy cream. Season to taste with salt and white pepper. Swirl butter into the sauce to finish.

To serve, unmold leek puddings onto six heated plates by cutting around the edge of each ramekin with a small paring knife and inverting onto the center of each place. Cut wrapping off poached stuffed chicken. Slice each serving into four to five diagonal slices. Fan out around the pudding. Spoon the chardonnay glaze over the top. Garnish with a sprinkling of chopped parsley. Serves 6.

Using Herbs

✳ Many of us can remember when canned and frozen vegetables were the norm and produce departments at supermarkets carried little more than iceberg lettuce, carrots, onions, potatoes, garlic, celery, and tomatoes. During the "produce explosion" of the '70s and '80s, supermarkets became showcases for fresh produce from around the world. The buzz word was "fresh," and producers responded to consumer demand.

The first time I tasted mushrooms that were not out of a can was a defining moment for me. The difference in flavor was astounding. I never bought canned mushrooms again.

The discovery of fresh herbs was another such moment. The fresh herbal flavors added a new dimension to much of the food I cooked. I may have rejected canned mushrooms, but I still kept a complement of dried herbs alongside my spices. Today I use both fresh and dried herbs in my cooking.

I use fresh herbs when the recipe would benefit from the fresh flavors of the herbs, otherwise I use the dried. A good rule of thumb is to use fresh herbs in dishes with shorter cooking times or where the fresh flavor of the herb is desired, and dried herbs in dishes that require lengthier cooking.

To substitute dried herbs for fresh, use approximately one-third as much of the dried. For example, if the recipe calls for 1 tablespoon of chopped fresh herb, use 1 teaspoon of the dried. As with any seasoning, more or less may be added to taste.

Here are two good ways to increase the flavor of dried herbs:

1. Rub the herbs between the palms of your hands, crumbling them into the food you are seasoning. This releases the flavor-carrying oils in the herbs.
2. Chop the dried herbs with a tablespoon or so of fresh parsley. This moistens the dried herbs, increasing their flavor.

Rosemary Grilled Chicken with Pommery Mustard Sauce

Marinades add great flavor to grilled meats. Here chicken breasts are marinated with fresh lemon, two kinds of mustard, and rosemary. For a low-fat version, omit the sauce.

1–1½ tsp. fresh lemon juice
1½ T. chopped fresh rosemary (or 2 tsp. dried)
1½ T. Pommery whole grain mustard
1½ T. Dijon mustard
1 tsp. salt
⅜ tsp. black pepper
1 clove garlic, minced
½ c. olive oil
6 (6–7-oz.) boneless skinless chicken breast
    halves
½ c. chicken stock, homemade or low-salt
    canned
2 T. Pommery or whole grain mustard
1 T. cornstarch mixed with 2 T. cold water
¼ c. butter, melted
Salt and freshly ground black pepper to taste

In medium steel bowl, combine first 7 ingredients. Slowly whisk in olive oil. Pour sauce over chicken breasts. Marinate for 2 to 6 hours in refrigerator.

Just before grilling chicken, make mustard sauce. In small heavy saucepan, whisk together chicken stock and mustard. Add cornstarch and water mixture. Simmer over medium heat until thickened to the consistency of heavy cream. Slowly whisk in the melted butter; season to taste with salt and freshly ground black pepper. Keep warm but do not bring to a boil or the sauce will separate.

Remove chicken breasts from marinade. Grill over hot coals until juices run clear when pricked with a fork. Do not overcook. Place grilled chicken breasts on heated plates; spoon warm sauce over each serving. Serve immediately. Serves 6.

Grilled Tenderloin Steak with Horseradish Cream and Fresh Chives

I feature this popular steak on the menu from early spring until I totally exhaust our half-dozen chive plants, sometime around late June or early July.

1 T. butter
6 shallots, minced
1 c. heavy cream
1½ T. prepared horseradish
1½ T. Dijon mustard
4 (6–8-oz.) tenderloin steaks
Salt and freshly ground black pepper or Gunflint
    seasoned salt (page 146)
6 T. chopped fresh chives

In small heavy saucepan, melt butter. Sauté shallots for 1 minute over medium heat. Add cream, horseradish, and mustard; reduce by one-third. Season to taste with salt and pepper. Keep warm.

Season steaks to taste with salt and pepper or Gunflint seasoned salt. Grill over hot coals or sauté in heavy skillet until desired doneness. Serve the steaks in a pool of horseradish cream sauce. Sprinkle chives over steaks. Serves 4.

▶ TIP: To speed up the cooking time as well as to enhance the presentation, cut each tenderloin steak into two smaller steaks. Serve these "tournedos" side by side in a pool of sauce topped with the chives as above.

Meat Temperatures

✳ When roasting or grilling meats to the desired degree of doneness, always allow for carryover cooking. Carryover cooking is the tendency of meats to continue to increase in temperature when removed from the source of heat. Larger pieces of meat will experience a bit more of an increase than smaller pieces such as steaks. I would remove a steak destined to be medium rare from the grill at 110°F for the rare side of medium rare or 120°F for the medium side of medium rare. This allows for about a 10 degree increase from carryover cooking. A roast of pork will always be juicy and cooked sufficiently if removed between 140 and 145°F, allowing for an approximate 10 to 15 degree increase.

I consider most of the published temperature guides to be much too high. On the one hand, they don't allow for sufficient carryover cooking and, on the other, opinions of doneness differ. I believe a rare steak is properly cooked with a cool red or at most, a warm red center. If it is cooked to the often-suggested temperature of 120°F, the internal temperature will likely rise to near 130°F owing to carryover cooking, producing what I would call a medium steak. The only steaks without controversy, it seems, are those cooked medium well or well done. Everyone agrees a medium-well steak should be a light pink inside while a well-done steak has no pink showing at all.

In any event the best thing to do is experiment. Buy a good-quality instant-read thermometer and use it to determine the temperatures you prefer. Experienced grillers use a finger to press the steak to determine done-

◙ Mustard Peppercorn Grilled Sirloin Steak

This recipe is a culmination of several favorite ways to grill steaks: pressing coarse cracked black pepper into the meat along with minced garlic, marinating the steak in a mixture of Dijon mustard and oil, and flavoring the steak with fresh lemon (usually mixed with melted butter for a final brushing just before removing the steak from the grill). The recipe puts most of this together, with excellent results.

2½–3 lb. top sirloin steaks
Freshly ground coarse black pepper to taste
½ c. Dijon mustard
3 T. vegetable oil
1½ tsp. fresh lemon juice or to taste
Salt or Gunflint seasoned salt (page 146) to taste
¼ c. thinly sliced green onion tops, cut diagonally

Coarsely grind pepper onto steaks; press in with the heel of your hand. In small bowl, combine mustard, vegetable oil, and lemon juice while whisking to form an emulsion. Reserve 3 tablespoons for brushing on steaks while grilling. Place steaks on a large cookie sheet. Coat on both sides with remaining mustard mixture. Marinate at room temperature for 1 hour or in the refrigerator for 2 to 4 hours.

Season steaks with salt or Gunflint seasoned salt to taste. Place seasoned side down on an oiled grill over hot coals. Season with additional salt or Gunflint seasoned salt. Turn steaks, brushing with reserved mustard mixture. Grill until desired doneness. Remove to hot plates or a hot serving platter. Sprinkle with the sliced green onions. Serve immediately. Serves 6.

▶ TIP: If you are grilling only one or two individual steaks, use a fork to mix together on a plate 2 tablespoons of mustard with 2 teaspoons of vegetable oil and a squeeze of fresh lemon juice. Pepper the steaks and lay them in the mixture, turning them over until well coated with the mustard. The sirloin steaks may be left whole and sliced for serving after grilling or cut into individual servings before marinating.

ness. This isn't as difficult as it sounds. As meat cooks it becomes firmer. A rare steak feels soft when prodded whereas a well-done steak is quite firm.

I have also known chefs who disdained thermometers, instant-read or otherwise, even when roasting larger cuts of beef. Their trick was to insert a long metal skewer into the thickest part of the roast and leave it there for 30 seconds. Then they would remove the skewer and touch it to their lower lip—if the skewer was cold, the roast wasn't done; if it was warm, it was rare. By the time the skewer had moved from warm to very warm, it was time to remove the roast for medium rare.

Consider the following chart only as a guide to determine how you prefer your meats cooked. Keep in mind that certain meats that are easily contaminated with harmful bacteria, such as ground meats like hamburger, should always be cooked well done. Pork should always be cooked to a serving temperature of at least 150°F to kill any trichinae, which cause trichinosis.

In the kitchen at the lodge I use the lower temperature in each category to determine when meats are cooked to the proper degree, allowing for carryover cooking:

90°F to 110°F	**Rare** (cool to warm red center—inside looks pretty much uncooked)
110°F to 120°F	**Medium rare** (hot red center—inside looks cooked)
120°F to 130°F	**Medium** (dark pink center)
135°F to 145°F	**Medium well** (light pink center)
150°F to 160°F⁺⁺	**Well done** (cooked throughout—no pink showing)

Camp Spaghetti Sauce

If you know why it is called "fishing" and not "catching," then you'll know why a hearty spaghetti dinner might be welcome in a fishing camp. For a meat sauce, add browned Italian sausage, ground beef, venison, bear, or whatever's on hand when you add the tomatoes.

4 cloves garlic, minced
¼ c. olive oil
1½ c. chopped onion
1 c. diced green pepper
1 (6-oz.) can tomato paste
2 (28-oz.) cans whole tomatoes
¾ c. dry red wine
2 tsp. dry oregano
1½ tsp. dry basil
¼ tsp. dry thyme
2 bay leaves
½ tsp. Worcestershire sauce, or to taste
1½ T. sugar, or to taste
1–2 T. chicken base, or to taste
Freshly ground black pepper to taste
1–2 T. whole fennel seed, or to taste (optional)
¾–1 tsp. crushed red pepper, or to taste (optional)
¼ c. chopped parsley (optional)

In large Dutch oven over medium-low heat, sauté garlic in olive oil for 1 minute without browning. Add onion and green pepper; sauté slowly until onion is translucent.

To crush tomatoes quickly, drain juice from one of the cans into the sauce. Put tomatoes into the bowl of a food processor with metal blade. Pulse 5 or 6 times to chop coarsely; add to the sauce. Repeat with the second can of tomatoes. Stir tomatoes into vegetable mixture. Cook, stirring, for a minute or so to warm paste and mix it with the vegetables. Stir in crushed tomatoes, wine, herbs, Worcestershire sauce, sugar, chicken base, and pepper, and the optional fennel and crushed red pepper if you decide to use them. Simmer uncovered for 1½ hours or until the sauce cooks down and thickens. Taste; add additional sugar if needed to adjust the acidity or sweetness to your taste. Near the end of the cooking time, add additional chicken base, if needed, to adjust flavor and seasoning. If using parsley, simmer another 15 minutes. Makes about 2 quarts of sauce.

▶ TIP: Use of a good-quality chicken base gives this sauce flavor and seasoning. If you don't have it, add salt to taste near the end of the cooking time. Adding sugar to a tomato-based sauce helps smooth the acidity of the tomatoes and sweetens the sauce. Home-canned tomatoes, if available, will produce the finest-tasting sauce. Sliced fresh mushrooms may be added to the simmering sauce during the last half hour or so of cooking.

Cooking Pasta Ahead

✳ Pasta may be cooked several hours or even a day or two ahead of time. Cook pasta according to the package directions, making sure the pasta is cooked al dente (still a little firm in the middle). Drain and return to the pan. Run cold tap water over pasta until perfectly cold. Drain and place in a bowl. Toss pasta with olive oil to coat. Store covered in the refrigerator until ready to use.

Pasta can be reheated in several ways, depending on how you plan to use it. If you are topping or combining it with a sauce, simply put the amount of pasta you need into a colander or sieve. Lower into a pan of simmering water for a minute or so until the pasta is hot. Remove, drain, and serve. The cold pasta may also be combined with a sauce by tossing it with sauce in a skillet over medium heat until everything is hot.

To make plain buttered pasta or buttered pasta with garlic, bring the butter or butter and garlic to a sizzle. Add a splash of water. When the water is simmering, add pasta. Toss until heated through. The water prevents the pasta from sticking to the bottom of the pan.

Always serve pasta on heated plates.

Pork

Apple Wood Smoked Loin of Pork with Applejack Brandy Cream

A good accompaniment for this pork roast is horseradish mashed potatoes (page 115).

2½ lb. boneless pork back loin
Gunflint seasoned salt (page 146) or kosher salt to taste
Freshly ground black pepper to taste
2 c. apple wood chips mixed with ½ c. hickory wood chips
2 shallots, coarsely chopped
1 small onion, coarsely chopped
3 red Delicious apples, cored and coarsely chopped
1 c. applejack brandy
2 c. chicken stock, homemade or low-salt canned
½ c. heavy cream
1 T. cornstarch dissolved in 2 T. water
Salt and white pepper to taste
Fresh apple slices and parsley sprigs

Season pork loin with salt and black pepper. A bone-in rack of pork or other pork roast may be substituted for the boneless loin. The length of cooking time varies with the heat of the coals and the ambient temperature. Cover wood chips with cold water to soak while starting the charcoal. Use a covered BBQ kettle cooker or other suitable smoker-cooker following manufacturer's directions for roasting meats. When coals are ready, place pork on rack in cooker. Sprinkle a couple of handfuls of wet wood chips over the hot coals and cover. Cook with light smoke until internal temperature of the pork reaches 150°F. Remove and keep warm.

In medium saucepan, combine shallots, onion, apples, and applejack brandy. Bring to a boil over high heat;

Filling the Smoker

✻ The lodge BBQ smoker is a massive commercially built unit on wheels. During the summer it is fired up every Sunday for our weekly cookout for guests and visitors featuring smoke-roasted chicken and BBQ ribs. It is also used frequently to turn out delicious entrées such as this one. And since one or two pork loins take up so little room, we take the opportunity to fill up the smoker with one, two, or more of the following: mushrooms (for making cream of smoked mushroom soup and smoked mushroom steak butter), tomatoes (for sauces and soups or to oven roast later), sides of brined fresh salmon (for appetizers or pasta dishes), or perhaps chicken breasts (soups, appetizers, and salads). You can do the same at home with any extra room in your cooker.

One of the easiest foods to smoke at home is mushrooms. Simply put the mushrooms in a shallow pan and toss lightly with vegetable oil.

If you have your own smoker, follow the manufacturer's instructions for hot smoking. If you have a covered BBQ grill, light a 10-briquette fire on one end of the grill. Soak hardwood chips (such as hickory or apple) in water for 1 hour. When coals are covered with gray ash, sprinkle hardwood chips over coals. Put mushrooms into a shallow pan and coat lightly with oil. Place mushrooms at the opposite end of the grill. Cover and smoke. Cook until mushrooms are soft and browned from the smoke.

reduce by one-half. Add chicken stock; bring to a boil. Reduce by one-third. Whisk in cream. Strain into a clean saucepan, pushing down hard on onions and apples. Return sauce to medium heat; bring to a simmer. Thicken to a saucelike consistency with cornstarch slurry. Season to taste with salt and white pepper.

To serve, slice pork into ⅛-inch slices. Fan out on bottom half of heated plates. Pour a ribbon of sauce over bottom half of pork slices. Garnish with a fresh apple slice fan and parsley sprigs. Serves 6.

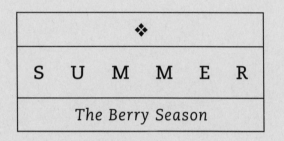

SUMMER

The Berry Season

SUMMER

The Berry Season

One of the summer events many of us living on the Trail look forward to is the berry season. We have an abundance of wild raspberry and blueberry patches surrounding us. Intensely flavored wild strawberries are also found, although the berries are small. A big strawberry measures only one-quarter inch across! And because the plants are right on the ground, picking them is a back-breaking job. Bruce picked strawberries for two hours one summer not too long ago. Much of the picking was on his knees. He got enough berries for three jars of the best strawberry jam I've ever tasted. Most of the time, however, we would rather wait for the blueberries and raspberries to ripen. It is easier and more rewarding to pick them.

By early June we are noting the amounts of sunshine and rain that come as warm weather and sunshine are essential when the bushes are flowering. Warm rains get the berries started; plentiful sunshine ripens them. Additional rain a few weeks before the berries ripen pays dividends in big fat berries. Without enough rain, the berries end up being hard little balls. Without enough sunshine, the berries never truly ripen.

After the middle of July it's time to start checking each of our secret berry patches. Everyone has a secret patch. You usually meet your neighbors there because, as it turns out, this is also their secret patch. We all save a few patches of lesser quality to tell inquiring novices about.

Blueberries grow underneath jack pine on rock outcroppings. Because there is so little soil on top of the bedrock, the blueberries need rain at regular intervals. Raspberries grow best in logged-over areas. I usually find the biggest berries on bushes growing out of rotting piles of tree slashing left over from logging operations. There must be some nutrient in the rotting wood that the berries need.

Berry pickers are divided into several groups. One group finds a promising patch and starts picking. They stay put until the bushes are cleaned. Bruce's mother, Justine, fits this group. The second group is the wanderers. That's where I belong. My group is looking for only the biggest and plumpest berries. We wander from bush to bush only picking the best. It's our contention that because only the biggest berries are picked, the bucket is filled quickly. Those who stay in one spot feel they fill their buckets the quickest because they don't waste time walking around.

There are also subcategories of pickers such as clean or dirty. Clean pickers make every attempt to get only berries. They leave branches and leaves on the bush. I fit in that group. Bruce and his mother belong to the dirty bunch. The two of them are interested in stripping the berries off the bushes as efficiently as possible. They usually fill their pots quite a bit faster than I do. I claim that the leaves and branches in their pots are the only reason they fill up first.

Another subcategory deals with eating while picking. People in my group virtuously don't eat as they pick. We are more concerned with how many berries we can bring home. My children have always belonged to the eater's group. For them it's one for the pot and one for the mouth. Or maybe two or three for the mouth. They trust that Mom will bring home enough berries to finish filling the jars for jam and pies.

Sometimes you meet more than just your human neighbors when berry picking. When our son Robert was about four, he and Justine went blueberry picking. They found a promising patch and sat down to pick. After a few minutes Robert said, "Grandma, I see a horse." Grandma said fine and just continued picking. Robert repeated that he saw a horse and Grandma just kept picking. Finally after he said it the third time, she looked up. About five feet away looking down at them was a big moose. They all stared at each other. After a minute or so the moose ambled off. Grandma and Robert continued picking.

Bruce and I like to go out on a Sunday afternoon to pick raspberries. After a couple of hours, we'll come home with a big pailful. Bruce tops the pail off in the raspberry patch by his mother's house. It's called Sue's Patch but Bruce does all the work tending it. During the season we can easily make a dozen jars of jam each time we go out. It's a good thing because we have a long list of people waiting for their winter supply of jam. When our sons were growing up, they felt like abused children when we ran out of homemade jam.

As good as raspberry jam is, the best way to eat raspberries is for dessert the night they are picked. Just sit down with a big bowl of berries covered with milk or cream. Looking at the price of fresh raspberries in a grocery store makes me realize how luxurious this simple dessert is.

For us, picking blueberries involves an expedition down the Granite River at least once a season to one of our secret patches. After receiving reports from canoers that the berries are at their peak, we'll agree on a date and line up participants. Some members of the party gather pails; others get boats and canoes ready; someone brings snacks; a few just show up. At the appointed time, give or take fifteen minutes, the flotilla leaves the dock. Each boat tows a canoe over to Little Rock Rapids. At the rapids, passengers are transferred from boats to canoes. A couple of minutes later all the canoes have shot the rapids and are paddling on to Little Rock Falls. Once again everybody gets out. The canoes are portaged over to the downstream side of the falls. Finally we all get in for the last half-mile paddle to the berry patch. Upon arrival, everyone scrambles off to their favorite corner of the patch.

When the pails are full, it's time for a snack. On a hot day some will go swimming. Others take their shoes and socks off and just dangle their feet in the water. An occasional canoe party goes by. The loons call and dive on the opposite shore. Time seems to float on by with the river's current.

Eventually someone gets the party organized for the trip home. It's a reverse of the trip down with one big difference. Now we carry a precious cargo of wild blueberries. There is enough for blueberry pies and jam all winter long.

Ron's Introduction

Beginning near the end of June as the fishing slows a bit and the mosquitoes, black flies, and no-see-ums wane in intensity, families on vacation fill up Gunflint Lodge. An influx of canoeists jumping off into the Boundary Waters Canoe Area Wilderness and the Quetico for a week or two of high adventure also filters through the lodge. The dining room fairly buzzes with excitement as folks discuss the day's or week's adventures already experienced or soon to come.

Behind the scenes the kitchen is highlighting the season with soups such as walleye, corn, and wild rice chowder. Entrées feature such choices as herb broiled trout fillets with julienned Roma tomatoes, Parmesan cheese, and lemon beurre blanc; grilled steaks topped with various savory butters; chicken and linguine with wild mushrooms, roasted tomatoes, fresh basil, and Parmesan cheese; and roasted salmon fillets with summer herb beurre blanc and Roma tomato concassé.

Summer in the northwoods is also wild berries for the picking—blueberries, raspberries, and June berries to name a few. Blueberries make their appearance in both entrées and desserts. Pan-fried walleye is served with a blueberry butter sauce while dessert might include blueberry maple bread pudding with a tart lemon whipped cream or a warm blueberry crisp with vanilla ice cream.

It's a great time for outdoor BBQ. Every Sunday Gunflint does just that over its giant outside covered grill featuring BBQ ribs and chicken with all the trimmings of summer—fresh sweet corn, au gratin potatoes, and fresh fruits and vegetables.

Gunflint Lodge Walleye Cakes

Here is a melt-in-your-mouth appetizer with green onions, shrimp, and crab meat, sautéed golden brown and served with sauce Moutarde de Meaux, a creamy coarse-grain mustard sauce.

Walleye Cakes

4 green onions, green part only

1 tsp. butter

3½ oz. jumbo lump crab meat, picked over and shredded, or substitute imitation crab meat (surimi)

8 oz. boneless, skinless walleye fillets, cut into 1-in. cubes

3½ oz. small uncooked shrimp, peeled and deveined

1 whole egg

1 c. heavy cream

1 T. Dijon mustard

1½ tsp. Worcestershire sauce

1½ tsp. Tabasco sauce

¼ tsp. salt, or to taste

⅛ tsp. white pepper, or to taste

Crosscut the green part of green onions ⅛ inch thick. In small skillet over medium heat, combine green onions and butter. Cook until onions are tender. In medium bowl, combine cooked onions and shredded crab; set aside. Put walleye, shrimp, and egg into food processor bowl with metal blade. Process for 1 minute. Scrape down sides of bowl. Process on high speed for 2 minutes.

Scrape bowl again. Slowly add cream while machine is running. Scrape bowl. Process for 10 seconds longer to make sure cream is incorporated. Scrape into large bowl. Add mustard, Worcestershire sauce, Tabasco sauce, salt, and white pepper. Fold in crab and green onion tops. Fry a small portion in a little butter to taste for seasoning.

In large skillet, sauté ½-cup portions at medium-high heat for approximately 2 minutes per side, or until browned on both sides and cooked through. Keep warm until ready to serve. Makes about 6 cakes.

Sauce Moutarde de Meaux

1 c. fish stock (page 149) or clam juice

1 c. heavy cream

1½ tsp. Moutarde de Meaux or other whole grain mustard to taste

Salt and freshly ground black pepper to taste

Combine fish stock and cream; reduce by one-half. Strain through a fine strainer. Thicken with a little cornstarch mixed with milk if necessary to reach a saucelike consistency. Whisk in mustard; season to taste with salt and black pepper. Return sauce to a simmer and serve. Makes about 1 cup.

To serve, thaw walleye cakes if frozen and reheat uncovered on a flat pan at 350°F for about 10 to 12 minutes or until heated through. Place cakes in a pool of sauce. Serve immediately.

▶ TIP: These cakes may be made up to 2 days ahead and refrigerated or they may be frozen for up to 3 months.

Eggs Chimay

The French are big on eggs as an appetizer. Consider the easy and delicious Oeufs Mayonnaise, which is nothing more than a halved hard-boiled egg set on lettuce leaves and covered with a tarragon- and Dijon-flavored home-made mayonnaise. The following recipe is also French. This easy first course is my personal favorite to serve for dinner guests at home.

Mushroom Duxelles

1 lb. fresh mushrooms
2 T. butter
4–6 T. finely chopped shallots or leeks
Salt and freshly ground black pepper

In food processor with steel knife or by hand, finely chop mushrooms. Gather a handful at a time and place in clean towel. Twist towel around mushrooms. Squeeze to remove as much liquid as possible from mushrooms. Repeat with remaining mushrooms.

In skillet over medium-low heat, melt butter. Add squeezed minced mushrooms. Sauté mushrooms until they begin to separate and not stick together, about 4 to 5 minutes. Add shallots or leeks; continue cooking until onions are transparent. Season to taste with salt and black pepper. Set aside.

Eggs Chimay

6 hard-boiled eggs, cooled and peeled

Cut each hard-boiled egg in half lengthwise and carefully remove the yolk. Push yolks through a fine wire mesh sieve into a medium bowl. Add approximately an equal amount of mushroom duxelles to the sieved yolks; mix well. Set aside.

Mornay Sauce

4 T. butter
4 T. flour
2 c. milk
¼ c. cream
Salt and white pepper to taste
¼ c. freshly grated Parmesan cheese or a combination of grated Parmesan and grated Swiss cheese
Additional freshly grated Parmesan cheese for topping

In medium heavy-bottomed saucepan over medium-low heat, melt butter. Stir in flour, cook slowly for 1 minute without browning. Remove from heat; whisk in milk all at once. Raise heat to medium; return saucepan to burner. Whisk constantly until mixture thickens and comes to a boil. Remove from heat; add cream, salt, and white pepper to taste. Stir in cheese; let sit for about 5 minutes while cheese melts. Sauce should be the consistency of a gravy. If too thick, thin with a little milk or additional cream.

Mix about 3 tablespoons of the mornay sauce into the duxelles-egg yolk mixture to make a thick paste. Season to taste with salt and white pepper.

Cut a thin slice off the bottom of each white half so that it will sit upright. Use a small spoon to fill the whites with duxelles stuffing, rounding the stuffing off to the edges of the whites to make them look like whole eggs with half whites and half stuffing. Continue with the remaining whites and stuffing, placing two stuffed halves each in six individual gratin dishes as you go.

Spoon the mornay sauce over the stuffed eggs. Top with additional grated Parmesan cheese. Cover with plastic wrap. Refrigerate until ready to serve. These may be made up to 2 days ahead.

To serve, preheat oven to 375°F. Bake individual gratin dishes for 15 to 20 minutes or until bubbling around the edges. Serves 6.

Soups

Wild Rice and Smoked Chicken Soup

At Gunflint Lodge we smoke boneless skinless chicken breasts over apple wood chips for this soup. Smoked chicken or turkey from the supermarket works just as well.

2 T. butter
1 c. carrots, ¼-in. pieces
1 c. celery, ¼-in. pieces
1 medium onion, ¼-in. pieces
¼ tsp. minced garlic
4½ c. chicken stock, homemade or
    low-salt canned
1 (8-oz.) can whole tomatoes, chopped,
    juice included
2 c. cooked wild rice
1–1½ T. fresh tarragon, chopped
White pepper to taste
Julienned smoked chicken or turkey breast
    as desired

In large stockpot, melt butter. Add carrots, celery, onion, and garlic; cover. Cook over low heat until carrots are tender. Add chicken stock and tomatoes. Simmer uncovered for 20 minutes. Add wild rice, tarragon, and pepper to taste. Bring to a simmer. To serve, place a portion of julienned smoked chicken breast in bottom of bowl and ladle in the hot soup. Makes about 8–10 servings.

Walleye, Corn, and Wild Rice Chowder

Here is an elegant walleye chowder all dressed up with some of Minnesota's choicest products—walleye pike and wild rice from clear northern lakes, red potatoes, sweet corn, and other produce from the rich agricultural heartland.

1½ T. butter
¼ tsp. minced garlic
1 small onion, diced
¼ c. diced carrots
1 rib celery, diced
2 c. fish stock (page 149)
¾ tsp. chopped fresh thyme leaves
1 c. diced unpeeled red potatoes
1 c. cubed walleye
¾ c. whole-kernel corn, cut fresh from the cob or
    use frozen
½ c. cooked wild rice
1 c. heavy cream
Tabasco sauce, to taste
Salt and freshly ground black pepper to taste

In large saucepan, melt butter over low heat. Add garlic, onion, carrots, and celery. Cover pan; cook vegetables until tender. Add fish stock, thyme, and potatoes. Simmer until potatoes are tender. Add walleye, corn, wild rice, and cream; simmer for 10 minutes. Season to taste with Tabasco sauce, salt, and pepper. Makes about 6 servings.

▶ TIP: For a lighter soup, substitute half-and-half or evaporated skim milk for the cream.

Fish

Herb Broiled Trout Fillets with Julienned Roma Tomatoes, Parmesan Cheese, and Lemon Beurre Blanc

These fresh flavors perfectly complement the ambrosial taste of fresh trout.

Beurre Blanc

¾ c. dry white wine
1 T. freshly squeezed lemon juice
2 tsp. minced shallots
2 T. cream
¼ c. unsalted butter, cut into 8 pieces
Salt and white pepper to taste
½ tsp. grated lemon peel

In stainless-steel skillet or saucepan, combine wine, lemon juice, and shallots. Reduce over high heat until only 2 to 3 tablespoons of liquid remain. Add cream; reduce for 30 seconds more. Add butter all at once, whisking constantly until butter is incorporated into the sauce. Immediately remove from heat. Strain into ceramic or stainless-steel bowl. Whisk in salt, white pepper, and lemon peel. Store in small thermos for up to 4 hours.

Trout Fillets

2½ lb. trout fillets: brook, rainbow, splake, or lake trout
3–4 T. butter, melted
Salt and fresh ground coarse black pepper to taste
3 tsp. minced fresh basil
1½ tsp. minced fresh parsley
1½ tsp. minced fresh chives
Dry white wine or dry white wine and water
6 small Roma tomatoes, the sides sliced off and cut into julienne strips
4–6 oz. freshly grated Parmesan cheese

Preheat oven to 450°F. Spray shallow-sided baking sheet with nonstick cooking spray. Lay trout fillets in prepared pan with the skin side down. Brush with melted butter. Season to taste with salt and black pepper. Combine basil, parsley, and chives. Sprinkle evenly over fillets. Pour white wine or wine and water around fillets to keep them from sticking to the pan. Bake for 3 minutes. Remove from oven. Spread julienned tomatoes evenly over fillets; sprinkle with Parmesan cheese. Return to oven for 2 to 4 minutes to finish cooking the fish and melt the cheese. Serve with lemon beurre blanc poured around fish. Serves 6.

▶ TIP: The lemon beurre blanc is easy to prepare; however, a drizzle of melted butter mixed with a little fresh lemon juice to taste makes an easy and delicious substitute.

Roasted Salmon with Summer Herb Beurre Blanc and Roma Tomato Concassé

In this recipe the salmon is roasted on an oiled pan. Roasting makes the skin crispy and gives the salmon a wonderful buttery flavor and aroma.

Beurre Blanc

2 T. chopped fresh basil
1 T. snipped fresh chives
1 T. minced parsley
1 tsp. chopped fresh tarragon (optional)
¾ c. dry white wine
1 T. white-wine or champagne vinegar
2 tsp. minced shallots
2 T. cream
4 oz. unsalted butter, cut into 8 pieces
Salt and white pepper to taste

In small bowl, combine basil, chives, parsley, and tarragon. Refrigerate until needed, bringing to room temperature before using.

In stainless-steel skillet, combine wine, vinegar, and shallots. Reduce to 2 to 3 tablespoons over high heat or until bottom of pan is covered with bubbles. Add cream; cook until thickened. Add butter all at once; whisk constantly until all but a few small pieces of the butter are incorporated into the sauce. Immediately remove from heat; strain into ceramic or stainless-steel bowl. Whisk in salt and white pepper to taste. Store in small thermos for up to 4 hours.

Roma Tomato Concassé

3 c. water
3 Roma tomatoes
1 T. butter
Salt and freshly ground black pepper to taste

In medium saucepan, bring water to a boil. Blanch tomatoes for 20 to 30 seconds. Remove with slotted spoon; place in bowl of cold water. Remove from water, core, and peel. Cut in half crosswise and gently squeeze out seeds. Cut into ¼-inch pieces. In small skillet over medium-low heat, melt butter; add diced tomatoes. Stir gently until hot and steaming. Remove from heat. Season to taste with salt and black pepper. Keep warm.

Salmon Fillets

Vegetable oil or nonstick cooking spray
6 (7-oz.) salmon fillet portions with the skin on if possible
3–4 T. butter, melted
Salt and freshly ground black pepper to taste

Preheat oven to 450°F. Lightly oil a cookie sheet with vegetable oil or nonstick cooking spray. Lay salmon pieces on cookie sheet with skin side down. Brush fish with melted butter; season to taste with salt and black pepper. Bake fish until done as desired. With spatula, remove salmon to heated plates. In small bowl, combine herb mixture and beurre blanc. Spoon 2 to 3 tablespoons of sauce over each serving of salmon. Garnish with a mound of warm Roma tomato concassé. Serves 6.

Salmon with Champagne and Wild Raspberries

Here's a romantic dish for two. Start with a bottle of champagne, a couple of fresh salmon fillets, and a basket of wild raspberries. If wild raspberries are out of the question, use fresh ones from the market. Accompany this with the rest of the champagne, Gunflint wild rice pilaf (page 112), or buttermilk, wild rice, and toasted pecan cakes (page 112) and steamed buttered spinach or other fresh green vegetable.

2 (6–8-oz.) salmon fillets
2 T. butter, melted
Salt and freshly ground black pepper to taste
⅓–½ c. champagne
½ c. fresh raspberries
½ c. heavy cream
Dash of Grand Marnier or other orange liqueur to taste (optional)
Salt and white pepper to taste
¼ c. fresh raspberries for garnish

Preheat oven to 450°F. Lay salmon fillets in pie pan or small baking sheet that is just large enough to hold the fillets without overlapping. Brush salmon with melted butter. Season lightly with salt and black pepper. Pour champagne around salmon to a depth of ¼ inch. Bake until salmon is just barely done.

Remove from oven. Drain juices from the salmon into small saucepan. Cover salmon and keep warm. Add raspberries to the salmon juices; bring to a boil over medium-high heat. Boil 1 minute. Add cream; reduce until thickened. Add any additional juices from the salmon to the sauce. Strain sauce into another saucepan, pressing down on the raspberries. Add optional Grand Marnier to taste. Season to taste with salt and white pepper. Keep warm.

Return salmon to oven for 1 to 2 minutes to reheat. Place salmon fillets on two heated plates. Top each with several tablespoons of the sauce. Sprinkle with a few fresh raspberries. Serve immediately. Makes 2 servings.

Grilled Salmon with Corn and Pepper Compote and Spicy Smoked Chili Corn Sauce

The idea for this dish came from Suzy Croften, a chef in the Chicago area.

Corn and Pepper Compote

2 T. butter
3 T. finely chopped red pepper
3 T. finely chopped green pepper
3 T. finely chopped red onion
¼ c. sweet corn, cut fresh from the cob or frozen whole kernel
Kosher salt to taste

In skillet over medium-low heat, melt butter. Add red pepper, green pepper, red onion, and sweet corn. Cook stirring frequently until onions are transparent and peppers are soft. Season lightly with kosher salt. Makes about ¾ cup. Keep warm.

Spicy Smoked Chili Corn Sauce

2 c. chicken broth, homemade or low-salt canned
2¾ c. sweet corn, cut fresh from the cob or frozen whole kernel
½–⅔ of a whole dried chipotle chili pepper with seeds (remove stem)
1⅓ c. heavy cream
Salt to taste

In heavy-bottomed saucepan, combine chicken broth, sweet corn, and chipotle pepper. Bring to a boil over high heat; reduce by about one-third. Add cream; continue reducing by about one-half. Pour entire contents of saucepan into blender; blend for 2 to 3 minutes. Strain through a fine sieve, pushing down hard on the solids. Season to taste with salt. If too thick, thin with additional chicken broth. Keep warm.

Salmon Fillets

6 (7-oz.) salmon fillets
6–8 T. olive oil
Salt and freshly ground black pepper to taste
Chopped fresh parsley for garnish (optional)

To serve, brush salmon fillets with olive oil and season lightly with salt and pepper. Grill the salmon on a clean oiled grill over hot coals starting with the seasoned side down. When lightly browned, turn and finish grilling until done as preferred. Remove to heated plates. Spoon the corn and pepper compote over each serving. Top with 3 to 4 tablespoons of the spicy corn sauce. Garnish with a sprinkling of chopped parsley. Serves 6.

▶ TIP: The sauce's heat comes from chipotle chilies, which are dried smoked jalapeños. They are quite hot. Since most of the heat is in the seeds, you can add the smaller amount of chipotles and shake out all of the seeds if you are fainthearted. If the sauce still turns out too fiery for your taste, add a little honey or maple syrup to tone it down. I have found this to be a kind of all-purpose sauce. Here at the lodge, it has been served with roasted round of Plains buffalo, venison saddle, chicken breasts, both roasted and grilled pork, and this wonderful grilled salmon.

Pan Seared Scallops with Raspberry Beurre Rouge

This popular dish was passed along by Chef Jay Sparks of D'Amico Cucina in Minneapolis to Tim Bromenshenkel and me some years ago. Chef Sparks used only raspberry vinegar in his reduction; the addition of port wine was Chef Tim's variation. The port adds a nice color and a rich sweetness to the sauce.

Raspberry Beurre Rouge

½ c. raspberry vinegar
¼ c. port wine
½ c. unsalted butter, cut into 8 pieces
Salt and white pepper to taste

In medium skillet over high heat, reduce raspberry vinegar and port wine until syrupy. Whisk in butter until only a few small pieces of butter remain. Remove from heat; whisk until all butter is incorporated. Season to taste with salt and white pepper. Keep warm in a bowl over warm water.

Scallops

14 large sea scallops
¼ c. vegetable oil
2 leaves green kale
Fresh raspberries for garnish

In medium skillet over high heat, heat vegetable oil until hot but not smoking. Dry scallops with paper towels. Season with salt and white pepper. Place scallops in hot oil; sauté until golden brown on both sides. Remove to a warm plate covered with a paper towel to drain.

To serve, pour half of sauce onto each plate. Place a piece of green kale in the center; place a scallop on it. Arrange six additional scallops around the edge of the sauce with a fresh raspberry in between each one. Serve immediately. Serves 2.

▶ TIP: To serve more, the scallops may be sautéed in batches or in two skillets. Be sure not to crowd the scallops or they will steam instead of browning.

◖ Buttermilk Fried Smallmouth Bass Fillets

This is a delicious all-purpose breading strategy for any game fish. The buttermilk provides a subtle tangy flavor to these crisply fried morsels.

Cooking oil, as needed
2 c. buttermilk
⅛ tsp. cayenne pepper
2½ lb. boneless, skinless smallmouth bass fillets
1½ c. all-purpose flour
1½ tsp. kosher salt
1½ tsp. freshly ground black pepper
2 tsp. paprika

Heat oil in deep fryer or high-sided skillet to 375°F. In large bowl, combine buttermilk and cayenne pepper. Soak bass fillets in the buttermilk mixture for 10 minutes. In another large bowl, whisk together flour, salt, pepper, and paprika. One at a time, lift bass fillets out of the buttermilk, letting excess buttermilk drip off. Dredge each fillet in seasoned flour. Shake off excess flour and drop into hot oil. Fry until golden brown and crisp. Drain on paper towels. Serve immediately. Makes 6 servings.

▶ TIP: A tasty variation of this recipe is bass fillets with crispy onion rings. Peel a medium onion and cut into ⅛-inch slices. Separate onion slices into rings and soak in buttermilk with the fish fillets. Dredge onion rings in the seasoned flour and fry along with the fish until crisp and golden brown.

Chicken and Linguine with Wild Mushrooms, Roasted Tomatoes, Fresh Basil, and Parmesan Cheese for One or Two

This is the all-time favorite pasta dish at Gunflint Lodge. I have tried to kill it, but popular demand always puts it back on the menu. Each serving is made to order and on busy nights there are pans of pasta everywhere. One hot August night I'll never forget, I put out 44 of these. I can always count on two to three tables of lodge staff in addition to our regular dinner count when this is on the menu.

2 T. olive oil
4 oz. chicken breast meat cut into
    ¼-in. by 1½-in. strips
½ c. sliced fresh wild mushrooms, such as
    shiitakes (substitute button mushrooms)
1 T. finely chopped shallots, green onions, or
    regular onions

1–2 tsp. minced garlic
2 T. chopped fresh basil
¼ c. chopped roasted tomatoes (page 36)
½ c. cored, seeded, and chopped tomatoes
½ c. chicken stock, homemade or low-salt
    canned
Salt and freshly ground black pepper to taste
1–2 T. butter
4 oz. cooked linguine
¼ c. freshly grated Parmesan cheese

In medium skillet, heat olive oil over high heat. When oil is hot but not smoking, add chicken breast strips and mushrooms. Sauté for 1 minute, stirring frequently. Add shallots, garlic, basil, roasted tomatoes, fresh tomatoes, and chicken stock. Continue cooking over high heat, tossing and stirring occasionally until liquid is reduced by three-fourths. Season to taste with salt and pepper. Add butter and pasta. Toss until everything is combined and thoroughly heated. Turn out onto heated plate. Top with Parmesan cheese. Makes 1 generous or 2 smaller servings.

Roasted Tomatoes

✱ Roasting tomatoes concentrates their flavor. Consider them a fresher-tasting alternative to sun-dried. Roasting is also an excellent way to preserve your own homegrown tomatoes since the roasted ones freeze well. We buy Roma tomatoes in large amounts during the summer when their flavor is at peak and their price is lowest, and roast and freeze them. During the winter season, we thaw and use them as needed in pasta dishes, sauces, and breads.

    Roma tomatoes, cut in half lengthwise
    Olive oil
    Kosher salt and freshly ground black pepper

Preheat oven to 250°F. Brush tomato halves with olive oil. Arrange cut side up on baking sheet. Sprinkle tomatoes lightly with salt and pepper. Bake for 2 to 3 hours or until tomatoes are about half to three-fourths dried (similar to dried apricots). Store in covered container in refrigerator for 4 to 5 days or freeze for up to 6 months.

    The two recipes that follow are Chef Tim Bromenshenkel's of the St. Cloud Radisson.

Roasted Tomato Cream
A full-flavored sauce for pasta and fish. I often use this sauce along with a basil cream sauce to serve with salmon or lake trout.

Grilled Breast of Chicken with Chive, Parmesan Cheese, and Toasted Black Peppercorn Sauce

Toasting gives the pepper's flavor a boost.

1 tsp. coarsely crushed black peppercorns
1 tsp. butter
2 tsp. minced shallots
¼ c. dry white wine
¾ c. heavy cream
2 T. freshly grated Parmesan cheese
3 T. chopped fresh chives
⅛ tsp. nutmeg
Salt to taste
6 (6–8-oz.) boneless skinless chicken breasts
Kosher salt to taste

In skillet over medium heat, toast peppercorns for 3 minutes, stirring constantly. Let cool for a few minutes; add butter. When melted, add shallots. Sauté shallots and peppercorns together for 15 seconds. Add wine; reduce until nearly gone. Stir in cream; reduce until thickened to saucelike consistency. Add Parmesan cheese, chives, and nutmeg and season to taste with salt. Keep warm while grilling chicken.

Season chicken breasts with salt. Grill over hot coals until browned and just cooked through. Serve with a ribbon of sauce over each chicken breast. Serves 6.

½ c. dry white wine
2 T. minced shallots
1¼ c. heavy cream
1 c. roasted tomatoes
Salt and freshly ground black pepper to taste

In medium skillet or saucepan over medium-high heat, combine wine and shallots. Reduce to 2 tablespoons. Add cream; cook until thickened. Place roasted tomatoes and cream mixture in blender. Let stand for 5 minutes; puree until smooth. Drain into clean saucepan. Bring to a simmer. Season to taste with salt and pepper.

Roasted Tomato Pesto

Delicious tossed with pasta or added to a cream sauce.

2 T. chopped fresh basil
1 c. roasted tomatoes
2 cloves garlic, peeled
3 T. freshly grated Parmesan cheese
1 T. pine nuts, walnuts, or almonds
1 tsp. salt, or to taste
1 tsp. freshly ground black pepper, or to taste
¼ c. olive oil

In food processor with steel knife combine all ingredients; process until smooth. Makes about 1½ cups.

Pork

Tenderloin of Pork with Roasted Garlic–Country Mustard Crust, and Bourbon and Green Peppercorn Sauce

The "crust" in the title is not a crust in the crunchy sense, but is rather a savory coating that is rubbed on the meat before roasting and baked on like a dry glaze. The result is juicy, tender meat surrounded by the flavorful crust. The accompanying green peppercorn cream sauce spiked with bourbon adds an earthy pungency.

All this would be nicely accompanied by roasted vegetables (page 109) and celery mashed potatoes (page 115). Choose a sauvignon blanc or fumé blanc to drink with the dinner.

1 T. butter

1 shallot, minced

3 T. bourbon or scotch

1½ T. canned green peppercorns, drained and crushed

1 c. heavy cream

1 tsp. Dijon mustard

Salt to taste

2½ lb. pork tenderloins

¼ c. roasted garlic puree (page 38)

¼ c. coarse grain mustard

1 T. vegetable oil

1 tsp. paprika

½ tsp. kosher salt

Black pepper to taste

In small saucepan over medium-low heat, sauté shallot in butter 1 minute without browning. Add bourbon and green peppercorns. Boil until bourbon is reduced to 1 tablespoon. Add cream; continue reducing until thickened. Stir in mustard. Season to taste with salt. You may add some additional whole green peppercorns if you desire. Keep warm.

In small bowl, combine roasted garlic puree, coarse grain mustard, oil, paprika, salt, and pepper. Place pork tenderloins in a shallow-sided pan. Liberally spread garlic-mustard mixture over tenderloins. Bake at 450°F until pork reaches 150°F, about 10 to 15 minutes. Remove from oven; let stand in warm place for 10 minutes before slicing and serving.

To serve, slice pork tenderloins on the diagonal; fan out on heated plates. Spoon sauce over each portion. Serve remaining sauce on the side. Serves 6.

Roasted Garlic Puree

✱ Cut off top third of as many whole heads of garlic as you want to roast. Discard tops or save for another use. Brush cut surface of the garlic with olive oil. Wrap tightly in aluminum foil. Roast at 350°F for about 1 hour or until garlic is soft. Remove from oven; let cool. To puree, squeeze the garlic cloves from the heads. Place in food processor with metal blade. Puree until smooth. Refrigerate until needed.

Beef

Grilled Tenderloin Steak with Ancho Chili Sauce and Cilantro Cream

The versatile dried ancho chili adds delicious flavor and mild heat to this steak sauce. Cilantro-flavored sour cream tops the steak.

2 ancho chilies, stems removed and seeded
Olive oil
2 whole cloves of garlic, peeled
2 whole shallots, peeled
½ c. tomato juice
½ c. chicken stock, homemade or low-salt canned
2 tsp. lime juice, or to taste
Honey or maple syrup to taste
Kosher salt and pepper to taste
½ c. sour cream
3 T. fresh cilantro leaves
¼ tsp. kosher salt
6 (6–8-oz.) tenderloin or other steaks

Soak chilies in hot water for 30 to 40 minutes. In small skillet over medium-low heat, sauté garlic and shallots in olive oil until lightly browned. Add tomato juice, chicken stock, and drained chilies. Bring to a simmer. Cook slowly for 10 minutes. Pour chili mixture in blender or food processor with metal blade. Puree until smooth, adding lime juice, honey or maple syrup, salt, and pepper to taste. Strain through fine sieve to remove pieces of skin. Keep warm.

In food processor with metal blade, combine sour cream, cilantro leaves, and kosher salt. Keep refrigerated until needed. To serve, season steaks with salt and pepper. Grill over hot coals on oiled grill until desired doneness. Serve in pool of ancho sauce. Top with cilantro cream. Serves 6.

▶ TIP: To enhance presentation of these steaks, put the cilantro cream into a squeeze bottle and squeeze out into a spiral design on top of each steak. The tenderloin steaks may be cut in half into 3–4 ounce tournedos for quicker grilling.

◖ Hickory Grilled Steak

Choose your favorite steaks for this easy summer cook-out. If you prefer, use another wood for flavoring such as mesquite or apple wood.

> 1 clove garlic per steak
> 1 steak per person
> Freshly ground black pepper
> Salt or Gunflint seasoned salt (page 146)
> 1 c. wood chips

Finely chop a clove of garlic for each steak. Sprinkle about half of the garlic over one side of each steak. Set pepper grinder to coarse; grind black pepper to taste over the steak. Use the heel of your hand to press garlic and pepper into the meat. Turn steaks over; repeat procedure on the other side. Let steaks sit at room temperature for 30 to 60 minutes to absorb flavors. Just before grilling, season the steaks to taste with salt or Gunflint seasoned salt.

Soak hickory chips in water for at least 10 minutes. When coals are ready, sprinkle a handful of hickory chips over the coals. Lightly oil the grill. Place steaks on grill. The chips will soon begin to smoke and eventually flame up. This will both flavor and sear the steaks. Grill steaks until done as desired.

Serve the steaks topped with a pat of butter (optional) on heated plates. Keep accompaniments simple—perhaps a baked Yukon Gold potato fluffed up and topped with butter and freshly grated Parmesan plus a simple salad or green vegetable. A bottle of red zinfandel would complete this simple feast.

Grilled Steaks with Savory Steak Butters

Summertime is grilling time! Here are a quartet of steak butters to top your favorite steaks. All of the following butters may be made ahead and refrigerated or frozen until needed. Use a heavy-duty mixer with paddle attachment or a food processor with metal blade to mix these butters. They may also be combined by hand.

Garlic Herb Butter

Besides topping a juicy grilled steak, this versatile butter has a multitude of uses. Use it to sauté fresh mushrooms in, serve it as a savory spread for homemade bread or rolls, or make hot garlic herb bread to serve with pasta.

> 8 oz. butter, softened
> 4 cloves garlic, very finely minced with ¼ tsp. salt
> 3 T. chopped chives
> 1 T. chopped parsley
> 1 tsp. chopped fresh thyme
> Fresh lemon juice to taste (about 2–3 tsp.)
> White pepper to taste

Combine all ingredients and mix well. Roll into logs; wrap in wax paper. You may also pipe into rosettes with a pastry bag and star-shaped tip.

Smoked Mushroom Butter

Bits of smoked mushrooms permeate this steak butter. Additional flavor comes from a reduction of red wine, the juice from the smoked mushrooms, and glacé de viande (page 149), which itself is beef stock reduced to the nth degree.

6 T. minced smoked mushrooms
¼ c. red wine
1 cube glacé de viande (page 149)
2 T. smoked mushroom juice
8 oz. butter, softened
Salt and freshly ground black pepper to taste

Squeeze mushrooms to remove excess juice. Reserve 2 tablespoons juice; set mushrooms aside. In small skillet, combine wine, glacé de viande, and mushroom juice. Reduce by one-half. Let cool before using.

Combine cool wine mixture and butter, salt, and pepper; mix well. Roll into logs; wrap in wax paper. You may also pipe into rosettes with a pastry bag and star-shaped tip.

Roasted Garlic and Chèvre Butter

A nice combination of flavors that go just right with a grilled steak.

8 oz. butter, softened
3–4 T. roasted garlic puree (page 38) to taste
1 oz. goat cheese (chèvre)
Salt and freshly ground black pepper to taste
Chopped parsley (optional)

Combine all ingredients until well mixed. Roll into logs; wrap in wax paper. You may also pipe into rosettes with a pastry bag and star-shaped tip.

Béarnaise Butter

This tangy tarragon-flavored butter is a delicious alternative to béarnaise sauce. Use it to top a grilled steak or any grilled or broiled fish or seafood.

8 oz. butter, softened
1 T. béarnaise reduction (page 152), or to taste
1 T. finely chopped parsley
1–2 T. fresh lemon juice to taste
Salt and freshly ground black pepper to taste

Combine all ingredients until well mixed. Roll into logs; wrap in wax paper. You may also pipe into rosettes with a pastry bag and star-shaped tip.

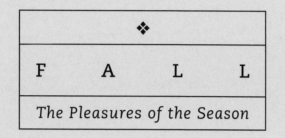

❖

F A L L

The Pleasures of the Season

FALL

The Pleasures of the Season

Fall is my favorite time of the year. I'm sure this comes from the fact that it's the end of the season. Right after Labor Day everyone seems to get a second wind. The end is in sight. When Justine ran the resort, any business after Labor Day was considered a bonus. Even when Bruce and I were married, there wasn't much September business. We thought it was really daring to stay open to the first of October.

Everything has changed now. Several years ago the state of Minnesota started to promote fall color, and this awakened interest in fall vacations. September and October are now as busy as June. People come up for watercolor workshops, for the end of the trout fishing season, for moose calling, for fall color, and for the last hike of the season. Those of us who live here have not quite adjusted to the increase in business. Of course, we have no difficulty spending the extra money. It's just that we still want to do all the things we used to do during the fall.

Trout fishing in fall is high on our list. The end of September is the closing of the lake trout season. As the water cools, the fish gradually come up from deep water. They will spawn during the fall in shallow water. There is often a window of time between when the trout come into shallow water and when the season closes. It's the best time for fast action. On a perfect day, we will sit in the boat on a flat calm lake. The sky is blue. Gold and red leaves are mixed in with green pine trees. Peering over the edge of the boat, we can look throughout the water and see the trout bite on the bait. It's almost more fun to watch the fish bite than to worry about catching them. Of course, freshly caught lake trout for dinner is nothing to turn down.

Hunting season is an important part of fall for many of the people living here. I have never chosen to go deer hunting but partridge hunting is something I've done for years. It's the best excuse I know of to get out in the woods during the fall. There never seems to be enough time for taking a hike in the woods. Hunting, however, is different. Bruce and I will go for an hour or two and just drive around the back roads. We may or may not even see a bird. The success of the hunting is not determined by how many birds we get. Over the entire fall if we get enough birds for one or two partridge meals, it's a successful hunting season.

Bruce and his mother have hunted deer forever.

Again the success of the hunt is not totally determined by the number of deer shot. Several years ago we had a foreign exchange student from France live with us. Bertrand expressed an interest in going deer hunting. Several times before the season opened, Bruce took Bert out to make sure he knew how to safely use a rifle. The hunting laws were explained to him. Bruce and our sons decided on the perfect stand for Bert.

On the morning of the hunt, Bruce and the boys got up before dawn. Bruce made a big "hunter's" breakfast for them. I preferred to sleep in. The four of them took off. By mid-morning Bert returned home just as excited as could be. He had seen a deer! He never got a shot but just seeing the animal was more than he had anticipated. He slowly explained to us that he would never be able to do anything like that in his country. There just weren't enough animals and it was a very expensive sport. Later that afternoon Bert's family in France called. Without even knowing the language, I could hear the excitement in his voice as Bert retold the story. We all shared in Bert's pleasure. It was as if each hunter had just shot a trophy deer himself. Even Bruce's mother, with all her years of seeing deer, was thrilled about Bert's deer.

One of my personal fall pleasures is pinecone picking. It doesn't sound very exciting. We gather pinecones each fall to use in decorating the lodge for Christmas. Of course, all the cones have to be gathered before the snow flies. During October I go out to get a supply. One of my "secret" spots is filled with soaring red and white pines. The ground between them is covered with soft moss. There are more cones beneath any one tree than I could ever use. Just like berry picking, I wander from tree to tree looking for the biggest, newest, and best. It's my own little world where all the stresses of the day evaporate. The silence is broken only by an occasional bird or squirrel. After an hour's picking, I come home refreshed and ready to get back to work.

Several years ago I woke up to a perfect fall day. It was too nice a day to work, so I decided to take the day off. Bruce was gone but Justine agreed to go on a picnic lunch to North Lake. I had some misgivings about my ability to pull the boat up the rapids to North but Mother assured me that she would help. This statement was spoken by an eighty-seven-year-old woman who had had arthroscopic surgery on one knee, a partial replacement on the other knee, and a replacement of the right shoulder, all within the past six months. Needless to say, she was not overly agile. As had happened many times in the past, I would supply the brawn and she would supply the brains.

We packed our lunch and took off. The blue water of the lake was surrounded by a forest of greens and yellows, oranges and reds. The sky was clear. Even the wind on the boat ride down was warm.

After about a twenty-minute ride, the rapids came into view. We landed and I helped Mother out of the boat. On the way down our strategy had been planned. Mother held on to me with her good left arm. I walked her to a rock about a quarter of the way up the rapids. Then I went back and brought the end of the rope on the front of the boat to her. As I pulled the boat up, Mother snaked the rope through her hands. When the boat got to Mother, she held it while I tied the end of the rope to a tree farther up the rapids. Then Mother held on to me and walked to where the end of the rope was tied. We repeated the process three times until the boat was at the top of the rapids. Then we were free to take off and explore North Lake.

On the way back down the rapids, it was Mother's brain and my brawn again. I had never shot these rapids myself in a boat but, of course, Mother had many times. At the top of the rapids, the motor was turned off and tipped up. My place was at the bow of the boat with a paddle in hand. Mother would give directions, "Go left. A little bit more. Keep it straight until we get past the big rock. Now get to the right a bit." Pretty soon the boat was at the bottom of the rapids without ever having touched a rock. We motored home. It had been a perfect fall day.

Ron's Introduction

The passing of Labor Day marks the unofficial start of autumn in the northwoods. Guests include fall fishermen, bug-savvy canoeists, hikers, hunters, and others who have come to relax and enjoy the changing of the season where it begins in Minnesota.

Beginning in late August and early September, touches of sunny yellow appear in the leaves of aspen and birch and hints of auburn subtly shade the maple leaves. Summer is waning. Warm days are followed by crisp nights. One morning a frost covers the leaves of bunchberry and sparkles off the lichens and mosses. By late September the woods are in full color with bright yellows and brilliant splashes of red amidst the constant green of the pines. On the edges of beaver ponds and marshes, stands of tamarack blaze golden in the sun.

It is a glorious time to be outdoors. Mosquitoes and black flies are virtually nonexistent. Leaf-covered trails into the forest beckon us, and the sparkling blue of the lakes with their multicolored shores is tempting.

All this vigorous activity and cool weather sharpens the appetite and the kitchen responds with hearty autumn fare: roasted butternut squash and leek soup, grilled lake trout topped with a slightly spicy ancho chili maple honey glaze, grilled breast of chicken choucroute mornay, pan roasted tenderloin of pork with bacon, mushrooms, and horseradish, and wild game of all kinds.

Pickled Northern Pike

This is good pickled fish! Just be sure to let everything "age" in your refrigerator for at least 5 days before sampling and your patience will be well rewarded. This takes several days to put everything together, plus the aforementioned "aging" period. Oh, and don't worry about the bones in the northern pike; they are so softened by the pickling process you will never notice them. This makes a great appetizer served with crackers.

1 c. white vinegar

¾ c. white sugar

2 bay leaves

3 whole cloves

½ tsp. whole allspice

1 tsp. whole mustard seed

½ tsp. whole black peppercorns

½ c. sweet white wine (a cheap brand)

1 c. pickling salt

2 qt. cold water

1 to 1½ lb. skinless northern pike, walleye, or any freshwater game fish with rib bones removed, cut into 1-in. pieces

1½ to 2 c. additional white vinegar

1 medium onion, thinly sliced

½ lemon, thinly sliced

Day one. In a nonreactive saucepan set over high heat, combine vinegar, sugar, bay leaves, cloves, allspice, mustard seed, and peppercorns. Bring to a boil; reduce heat. Simmer for 5 minutes. Cool. Add wine. Pour pickling syrup into a plastic or glass container; cover tightly. Let sit at room temperature for 4 days.

Mix pickling salt with cold water; stir thoroughly to dissolve salt. Pour over cut-up skinless fish and refrigerate for 48 hours.

Day three. Drain fish; rinse with cold water. Cover fish with vinegar. Refrigerate for 24 hours.

Day four. Drain fish, but do *not* rinse. Discard vinegar. Layer fish, onion, and lemon in one or more glass or plastic containers. Do not pack too tightly. Cover with pickling syrup. Cover tightly; refrigerate for at least 5 days, stirring fish at least once. Store covered with the pickling syrup in refrigerator for up to 6 weeks. Makes approximately 4–5 pints.

▶ TIP: Recipe may be doubled. The spices and sugar may be adjusted to suit your taste. Pimiento pieces may be added for color.

Mushrooms Au Gratin

Serve these creamy mushrooms with crusty bread as an elegant appetizer.

1 c. fresh white bread crumbs
¼ c. shredded Swiss or Gruyère cheese
¼ c. freshly grated Parmesan cheese
1 T. chopped parsley
1 lb. fresh mushrooms, halved or quartered
    if large
4 tsp. clarified butter
3 T. finely chopped shallots, green onions
    (white part only), or onions
1 tsp. minced garlic
Pinch of dried thyme
¼ c. dry sherry
1 c. heavy cream
Salt, pepper, and cayenne pepper to taste
1 T. butter

In medium bowl, combine bread crumbs, cheeses, and parsley. Set aside.

In large skillet over medium heat, sauté mushrooms in clarified butter with shallots, garlic, and thyme until mushrooms are softened and lightly browned. Deglaze with sherry. Bring mixture to a boil. Add cream; reduce until thickened to a saucelike consistency. Season to taste with salt, pepper, and cayenne. Spoon into shallow gratin or casserole dish and top with the crumb-cheese mixture. May be made to this point up to a day ahead, covered, and refrigerated.

To serve, dot the crumbs with butter. Bake in pre-heated 375°F oven until crumbs are lightly browned and gratin is bubbling around the edges. Serves 6–8.

Soups

Roasted Butternut Squash and Leek Soup with Sour Cream, Crisp Bacon, and Scallions

This is a quintessential fall soup, resplendent with the golden color of fall leaves. The hearty flavor of squash is complemented by a dollop of tangy sour cream and crisp smoky bacon bits.

5 lbs. butternut squash
4 T. butter
3 large leeks, cleaned and chopped
1 medium onion, chopped
5 c. chicken stock, homemade or low-salt canned
1 tsp. dried thyme
½ c. heavy cream or half-and-half (optional)
1¼ tsp. salt, or to taste
½ tsp. freshly ground black pepper
½ c. sour cream
4 T. chopped chives or green onion tops
8 slices crisp bacon, crumbled

Preheat oven to 400°F. Cut squash in half lengthwise; scrape out seeds. Place cut side down on a cookie sheet. Pour very hot tap water around squash to a depth of ¼ inch. Bake until tender, approximately 40 minutes, adding additional water as needed. Remove from oven; let cool to room temperature. Remove squash from shells and reserve.

In medium saucepan, cook leeks and onion in butter until tender. Add squash, chicken stock, and thyme. Simmer for 30 minutes. Puree in food processor with metal blade. Add cream if desired. Season to taste with salt and pepper. Garnish each bowl with dollop of sour cream, chives, and bacon before serving. Serves 8.

Roasted Apple and Pumpkin Bisque

My good friend and former Redwood Inn colleague, Chef Tim Bromenshenkel, passed this idea along to me. It has been a hit whenever we have served it.

6 apples, peeled, cored, and halved
Nonstick cooking spray
Cinnamon to taste
2 T. butter
1 small onion, chopped
1 small leek, chopped
4 c. chicken stock, homemade or low-salt canned
½ c. apple juice
1 (16-oz.) can Libby's pumpkin
½ c. heavy cream
1 c. half-and-half
Ground nutmeg to taste
Ground white pepper to taste
2 T. maple syrup, or to taste (optional)
Sour cream

Preheat oven to 400°F. Place apples, cut side down, on oiled cookie sheet. Spray apples liberally with nonstick cooking spray and sprinkle with cinnamon. Bake for 40 to 50 minutes or until tender. Meanwhile, melt butter in a stockpot. Add onion and leek. Cover; cook about 20 to 30 minutes or until tender. Add chicken stock, apple juice, roasted apples, and pumpkin. Bring slowly to a simmer, stirring frequently. Simmer over very low heat for 1 hour. Puree in food processor with metal blade. Return to stockpot. Add cream, half-and-half, nutmeg, pepper, and optional maple syrup. Heat thoroughly. Garnish with a dollop of sour cream before serving. Serves 8.

Minnesota Salmon and Wild Rice Chowder

For a while we were using chinook salmon raised in some of the old iron ore pits in the northern part of Minnesota. The firm has since gone out of business, but the name for this hearty soup remains the same by using Minnesota-grown wild rice.

1 T. butter
1 small red onion, finely chopped
½ leek (white part only), finely chopped
½ tsp. fresh minced garlic
½ c. celery, diced
½ tsp. fresh thyme leaves
1½ T. all-purpose flour
3 (8-oz.) bottles of clam juice
½ c. roasted tomatoes, chopped (page 36)
     (substitute 1 c. canned tomatoes, chopped)
1 c. cooked wild rice
¼ lb. salmon, cut into ¾-in. chunks
1 c. heavy cream
1½ T. chopped fresh basil (substitute 1 tsp. dried)
Salt and pepper to taste

Melt butter in stockpot. Add onion, leek, garlic, celery, and thyme. Cover; cook until vegetables are tender. Stir in flour. Simmer slowly for 3 to 4 minutes. Whisk in clam juice; cook until thickened. Add tomatoes, wild rice, salmon, cream, and basil. Simmer for 5 to 10 minutes or until the salmon is cooked. Add salt and pepper to taste. Serves 6.

Fish

Seafood Stuffed Shrimp

This is an elegant and expensive entrée for a special occasion. For the stuffing, you can use all three of the shellfish mentioned or just one of them, according to taste and availability. Bay shrimp are small uncooked shrimp. At Gunflint Lodge, seafood stuffed shrimp are served with a béarnaise sauce (page 152) sometimes paired with a grilled or sautéed tenderloin steak. If making your own béarnaise seems daunting, serve with a simple lemon butter or butter flavored to taste with fresh lemon juice, minced shallots, and fresh tarragon.

Stuffing

4 oz. frozen crab meat or surimi imitation crab
2 oz. bay shrimp
2 oz. bay scallops
1 c. soft fresh bread crumbs
1½ T. butter, cut into bits
¼ c. water
1 c. finely chopped celery
1½ T. finely chopped onions
2 T. chopped fresh parsley
2–4 T. heavy cream
Salt and white pepper to taste
Fresh lemon juice to taste
1 dash Worcestershire sauce, or to taste
1 dash Tabasco sauce, or to taste

In food processor with steel blade, coarsely chop crab. In small bowl, combine chopped crab and bread crumbs with a fork. Refrigerate until needed.

In food processor with steel blade, coarsely chop shrimp and scallops. In large skillet over medium-high heat, simmer butter, water, celery, and onions. Cook until celery is tender and all the water is evaporated. Add chopped shrimp and scallops to hot celery and onion mixture. Stir over low heat until seafood is cooked. Add to crab-bread crumb mixture along with parsley; mix well. Stir in just enough cream until desired consistency. Season to taste with salt, pepper, lemon juice, Worcestershire sauce, and Tabasco sauce. Refrigerate 1 to 2 hours.

Shrimp

24–30 large shrimp, peeled and deveined
Butter, melted
Paprika
Dry white wine
1½ T. fresh minced garlic
Lemon wedges

Preheat oven to 450°F. Butterfly the shrimp. Lay cut side down. Use about a tablespoon or so of stuffing for each shrimp and shape stuffing into a ball; place on top of shrimp. Curl tail of shrimp over the stuffing; place in baking dish. Continue with remaining shrimp.

Drizzle shrimp and stuffing with melted butter. Sprinkle with paprika. Pour wine around shrimp to keep them from sticking. Stir garlic into the wine. Bake for 7 to 10 minutes or until the shrimp are just done. Arrange on warm plates and garnish with lemon wedges. Serves 6.

▶ TIP: Leftover stuffing may be frozen. The stuffing is wonderful as well in roasted chicken breasts, also served with béarnaise sauce.

Saganaga Lake Trout Dijon

This is a recipe I picked up from one of the cabin folks on Saganaga Lake. Just the thought of this savory preparation makes me want to grab my trouting gear and head out on the water. There are no amounts listed for ingredients because they're not needed. After a time or two you will have this down just the way you like it.

Lake trout or other fish fillets
Dijon mustard
Bread crumbs, dry or fresh
Dry white vermouth
Melted butter
Salt and freshly ground black pepper
Chopped onions
Paprika

Preheat oven to 425°F. Cut trout fillets into serving-sized pieces. Smear fish liberally with mustard. Coat with bread crumbs. Lay with skin side down in buttered baking pan. Drizzle first with vermouth, then with butter. Season to taste with salt and pepper. Smother with onions; sprinkle with paprika. Bake for 10 to 20 minutes or until a fork will just go through the fish.

Smallmouth Bass with Garlic Butter, Chives, and Mushrooms

Fighting warriors of the north! Fun to catch, but hell to clean. These feisty fish are delicious eating. Serve the following with lots of crusty French bread for sopping up the garlic butter.

6–8 T. butter
1–4 cloves garlic, crushed
2½ lb. bass fillets
Salt
Pepper
Paprika
Dry white wine or water
8 oz. fresh mushrooms, quartered
Chopped fresh chives

Preheat oven to 450°F. In small saucepan, melt butter. Add garlic cloves; remove butter from heat. Let butter and garlic steep for 5 to 10 minutes; remove garlic and discard. Brush ovenproof pan with some of the garlic butter; place fillets skin side down. Brush fillets liberally with butter. Season with salt and pepper. Sprinkle with

Sag Lake Folks

✱ The Canadian side of Saganaga Lake at the very end of the Gunflint Trail is still home to several year-round residents. These are hardy folks who make their living running fishing camps, guiding, and trapping. A trip to the nearest town, Grand Marais, involves a six- or seven-mile trip down the lake via boat or snowmobile and a fifty-eight-mile drive. Twice a year, at freeze-up and ice-out, they are isolated for one to two weeks while travel on the lake is impossible. Not one of them would change places with any of the rest of us.

Art Madsen, ninety-one, came to Sag Lake in the thirties by way of freighter canoe through Quetico Park, where he was working as a park ranger. He proved up a piece of property on Red Pine Island, building a house-

boat to live in, just in case his offer to purchase was refused by the crown. The boat still exists, now up on blocks at the water's edge, and has been one of Art's more popular rental units over the years he has run Camp Sagonto.

Just around the corner from Art's is the Chippewa Inn, now run by the third generation of Powells to live and work on Sag. Dick and Sherry Powell live in a hand-hewn log cabin on a rocky point near the main lodge of the fishing camp. Dick's parents, Bill and Dorothy, built the lodge in its present location. He had earlier built the camp at the entrance to the northeast arm, but moved it nearer to customs to be closer to boat and canoe traffic.

Dick's grandfather, Jack Powell, homesteaded on

paprika. Pour a little wine or water around fillets to keep them from sticking to the pan. Bake for 5 to 7 minutes or until fish is barely cooked. While fish is baking, in a small skillet sauté mushrooms in remaining garlic butter until lightly browned. Remove bass to heated serving plates (along with the cooking juices). Spoon on sautéed mushrooms. Sprinkle with chives, if you have them. Serves 6.

◙ Grilled Lake Trout with Ancho Chili Maple Glaze

In this easy recipe, which is a variation on a Bobby Flay preparation, ancho chili powder flavors a sweet mustardy glaze for lake trout or salmon. This is one of our most popular fish dishes.

¼ c. real maple syrup
1 T. Dijon mustard
1 T. ancho chili powder
6–8 T. butter or margarine, melted
Kosher salt to taste
Salt and freshly ground black pepper to taste
2½ lb. lake trout or salmon fillets

In small bowl, whisk together maple syrup, mustard, and ancho chili powder; refrigerate. Bring to room temperature before using. If sauce is too thick, thin with a little warm water. May be prepared several days ahead.

Prepare trout fillets for grilling by brushing with melted butter; season with kosher salt. Grill trout on clean oiled grill or on a grill screen made especially for grilling fish over hot coals. Remove to heated plates. Top with the ancho chili maple honey glaze. Serve at once. Serves 6.

▶ TIP: Ancho chilies are dried poblanos. They are not excessively hot but deliver a pleasant warmth with a fruity and somewhat woodsy flavor. Ancho chili powder is available at some specialty stores and by mail order. It is easy, however, to make your own from dried ancho chilies using an electric coffee or spice grinder. Destem the anchos and shake out the seeds. Break the chili into 1-inch pieces and grind to a powder. Shake the powder through a wire mesh sieve to remove the coarse particles and store in a container in a cool dark place.

nearby Saganagons Lake, now in Quetico Park. In one famous incident his grandfather ferried a cow up to Saganagons all the way from Ely in 1927. The cow was to provide fresh milk for the family, a welcome change from dehydrated. The cow rode on a large raft, which they propelled with two canoes tied alongside powered by outboard motors. At the portages, the cow was harnessed to the raft and pulled it across, while the men portaged the canoes and motors. Unfortunately the cow fared poorly on the wild hay harvested by the Powells and eventually furnished winter meat for the family.

Up on the northeast arm of Saganaga is Betsy Powell's camp, Shady Rest. Betsy's late husband, Frank Powell, was Bill Powell's brother, and Bill's wife, Dorothy, was Betsy's sister. All but Betsy have passed on. For years she guided her guests on Saganagons Lake, portaging in gear and bait and rowing a boat or paddling a canoe while the guests fished.

Irv Benson operates Pine Island camp on the north side of Red Pine Island. Irv, a native of Duluth, Minnesota, came north shortly after World War II, in which he served as a pilot. He met Tempest Powell, Bill and Frank Powell's sister, fell in love, and was married. Tempest, who was born on Saganagons Lake, grew up in the bush and passed on her lifetime of wilderness skills to Irv. Tempest has now crossed her last portage, but Irv still traps and runs his camp.

These men and women represent a dying breed of rugged individuals who will soon be gone forever. With them will go the skills and knowledge of a lifetime.

◉ Garlic Butter Broiled Walleye with Chive and Cheese Sauce

This recipe is a good example of how a flight of fancy can produce a popular addition to the menu. One night a guest dropped off a couple of walleye fillets in the kitchen for me to prepare for his dinner. When asked how he wanted them cooked, his answer, was "Surprise me."

I began by broiling his catch in garlic butter and white wine. Then, after a quick trip to the lodge herb garden to cut a few fresh chives, I reduced the broiling juices, added a splash of cream, and finished the sauce with Parmesan and chives.

Serve this with one of the bread custards (page 117) and a fresh green vegetable, such as asparagus or broccoli. A bottle of chardonnay or sauvignon blanc would complement everything nicely.

2½ lb. walleye fillets
¼ c. butter
2 tsp. minced garlic
Salt and freshly ground black pepper
1 c. dry white wine
3–4 T. heavy cream
Salt to taste
Tabasco sauce to taste
2 T. freshly grated Parmesan cheese
2 T. chopped fresh chives

Preheat oven to 450°F. Place walleye fillets on a 10-by-15-inch cookie sheet. In small saucepan over low heat, melt butter. Stir in garlic. Brush fillets with garlic butter. Season lightly with salt and pepper. Pour wine around fillets. Bake walleye for 4 to 8 minutes or until just barely done. Remove from oven. Carefully pour wine and fish juices from fish into a small skillet.

Remove walleye to a shallow-sided serving casserole large enough to hold the fillets in one layer. Cover the fish with foil and keep warm.

Reduce juices by half; add cream. Reduce until thickened and saucelike. Season to taste with salt and Tabasco sauce. Reduce heat to low; whisk in any juices that have accumulated around the fish. Add Parmesan cheese to sauce. Stir until cheese is melted. Stir in chives. Spoon sauce over fish and serve at once. Serves 6.

Chicken

Grilled Chicken Breasts with Artichoke and Roasted Tomato Ragout

The best part of the artichoke is combined with sweet roasted tomatoes, fresh herbs, and smoky bacon in this versatile vegetable stew. The ragout also nicely complements roasted rack of lamb or grilled lamb chops.

4 strips bacon, cut into ¼-in. dice
4 tsp. minced garlic
2 T. minced shallots
½ c. roasted tomatoes (page 36), julienned
½ c. artichoke hearts, fresh or frozen,
    cut into bite-size wedges
¾ c. chicken stock, homemade or
    low-salt canned
2 T. fresh basil leaves, cut in julienne strips, or 1
    tsp. dried
6 (6–8-oz.) boneless chicken breasts,
    with or without the skin as desired
2 T. olive oil
Salt and freshly ground black pepper or Gunflint
    seasoned salt to taste (page 146)
3 T. unsalted butter
Kosher salt and freshly ground black pepper
    to taste

In medium skillet, sauté bacon over low heat until browned. Pour out all but a film of bacon fat. Add garlic and shallots; sauté for 1 minute without browning. Add roasted tomatoes, artichoke hearts, and chicken stock. Increase heat to high. Cook mixture until liquid is reduced to 3 to 4 tablespoons. Stir in basil. Remove from heat. Set aside.

Brush chicken breasts lightly with olive oil. Season to taste with salt and pepper or Gunflint seasoned salt.

Grill over charcoal or hardwood coals beginning with the skin side down until cooked through. The chicken breasts may also be sautéed. Remove from grill and keep warm while completing the ragout.

Heat ragout to a simmer over medium heat. Remove pan from heat; stir in butter until incorporated. Season to taste with kosher salt and pepper. Serve immediately over grilled chicken breasts. Serves 6.

Roast Chicken with Spinach and Swiss Cheese Stuffing and Portabella Gravy

The stuffing for this chicken is equally delicious with fish, turkey, and pork.

Spinach and Swiss Cheese Stuffing

¾ c. diced celery
1 medium onion, diced
1 clove garlic, minced
¼ c. butter
¼ c. dry white vermouth or white wine
½ tsp. Knorr-Swiss Aromat seasoning to taste
    (optional)
1 tsp. sage to taste
8 c. dried French bread cubes
⅓ lb. fresh spinach, cooked, squeezed, and
    chopped or half of a 10-oz. box frozen spinach,
    thawed, squeezed, and chopped
4 oz. Swiss cheese, shredded
1 c. hot chicken stock, homemade or
    low-salt canned
Salt and freshly ground black pepper to taste

In medium skillet over low heat, sauté celery, onion, and garlic in butter until onion is transparent. Add vermouth to vegetable mixture. Simmer for 5 minutes. In medium bowl, combine vegetable mixture with bread and spinach. Add Knorr-Swiss Aromat, sage, and Swiss cheese; toss together. Add hot chicken stock to moisten the stuffing. Taste; correct seasoning with salt and black pepper.

Roast Chicken

3½ to 4 lb. whole chicken
Gunflint seasoned salt (page 146) or salt and
  pepper

Preheat oven to 325°F. Stuff chicken loosely with stuffing just before roasting; truss. Any remaining stuffing may be baked in a shallow baking dish. Place chicken in a shallow-sided roasting pan (a 10- or 12-inch cast-iron skillet works well, both for roasting and for making the gravy later). Season chicken with Gunflint seasoned salt or salt and pepper. Roast for approximately 35 to 40 minutes per pound or until skin is golden brown and juices from thickest part of thigh run clear when pricked with the point of a knife. Reduce roasting time about 10 minutes per pound if roasted unstuffed.

Remove chicken to a warm platter. Cover loosely with foil. Let rest for about 20 minutes while you make the gravy.

Portabella Gravy

3 T. fat from roasting pan
4 oz. portabella mushrooms, cut into ½-in. dice
3 T. flour
1½ c. chicken stock, homemade or
  low-salt canned
2 T. dry white vermouth or white wine
Salt and freshly ground black pepper to taste

Pour fat and drippings into a measuring cup. Reserve 3 tablespoons of fat. Discard remaining fat. Add any liquid drippings to chicken stock. Add reserved fat to roasting pan. Place over medium heat. Add portabella mushrooms. You may substitute any wild or domestic mushrooms or a combination for the portabellas. Sauté until lightly browned. Reduce heat to low. Stir in flour. Cook stirring for about 30 seconds. Whisk in chicken stock and vermouth. Increase heat to medium high. Whisk constantly until gravy thickens and comes to a boil. Reduce heat to low; simmer for a couple of minutes. Season gravy to taste with salt and pepper. Whisk in any juices that have accumulated around the chicken. Serves 4.

Grilled Breast of Chicken Choucroute Mornay

This dish with its surprising combination of flavors was inspired by a recipe in Larousse Gastronomique, *a massive compendium of French cookery. A grilled breast of chicken is served on a bed of sauerkraut braised with aromatic vegetables in white wine and chicken stock. It is then gratinéed with a creamy Swiss cheese sauce (Mornay). This is a perfect repast for a cold fall evening!*

Sauerkraut

1 lb. sauerkraut, washed in cold water and
  disentangled
3 T. finely diced leek, white part only (optional)
½ small onion, stuck with one clove
3 T. finely diced carrot
½ rib celery, whole
Bouquet garni—combine 1 tsp. juniper berries,
  6 whole peppercorns, and 1 small clove of
  peeled garlic, and tie in a cheesecloth bag
¼ c. dry white wine
⅓ c. chicken broth
Salt to taste
2 T. butter, melted

Preheat oven to 300°F. In buttered casserole, pile half of sauerkraut. Lay diced vegetables, celery rib, and bouquet garni on top. Cover with remaining kraut. Pour on wine and chicken broth. Season lightly with salt. Drizzle melted butter over the kraut. Cover; bake for 2 to 2½ hours, or until liquid is almost gone. Cover and keep warm or refrigerate until needed.

Mornay Sauce

4 T. butter
4 T. flour
¼ tsp. dry mustard, or to taste
2 c. chicken stock
½ c. heavy cream

Salt and ground white pepper to taste
¼ c. grated Swiss cheese or a combination of
  Swiss and Parmesan cheeses

In medium saucepan over low heat, melt butter. Whisk in flour and dry mustard. Cook slowly for 30 seconds without browning. Remove from heat; whisk in chicken stock all at once. Return to medium heat. Continue cooking, whisking constantly until stock comes to a boil and thickens. Reduce heat to low; simmer for 2 minutes. Whisk in cream. Season to taste with salt and white pepper. Whisk in cheese; heat slowly until cheese is melted. Cover and keep warm or refrigerate until needed.

Breast of Chicken

6 (6-oz.) boneless skinless chicken breasts
Salt and freshly ground black pepper to taste
Additional grated Swiss or combination of Swiss
  and Parmesan cheeses for topping

Season chicken breasts lightly with salt and pepper. Grill over hot coals on charcoal or gas grill until just cooked through. The chicken breasts may be broiled or sautéed instead of grilled. Remove and keep warm or refrigerate until needed.

Preheat oven to 400°F. Cover bottom of 9-by-13-inch casserole or individual gratin dishes with sauerkraut mixture. Place grilled chicken breasts on top of sauerkraut, overlapping slightly if necessary. Cover breasts with Mornay sauce; top with additional grated cheese. Place in oven 5 to 10 minutes until sauce is bubbling around the edges and cheese is melted. Serves 6.

▶ TIP: All the elements of this recipe may be made up to 2 days ahead and refrigerated either separately to be put together later or already assembled and oven-ready. To serve, preheat oven to 350°F and bake for 30 to 40 minutes for the larger casserole (20 to 25 for the individual gratin dishes) or until casserole or gratins are bubbling around the edges and cheese is melted.

Pork

◉ Pork Chop Massimo

This is the recipe of Massimo, the Swiss banker son-in-law of my good friends David and Pat Undlin. He loves the Gunflint country because it reminds him of his family's mountain retreat in the Alps (without the mountains, of course). He prepared this delicious pork chop wrapped with a strip of hickory smoked bacon, then sautéed with white wine, fresh rosemary, and sweet cream for me on one of his visits. It has become a favorite on the lodge menu.

6 (8-oz.) pork chops, each wrapped with a slice of bacon across the meaty portion of the chop and secured with a toothpick
Salt and freshly ground black pepper to taste
Olive oil
¼ c. dry white wine
Sprig of fresh rosemary
1 c. heavy cream
Salt and freshly ground black pepper to taste

Preheat oven to 400°F. Season the bacon-wrapped pork chops with salt and pepper. In small skillet, sauté pork chops in olive oil until nicely browned on both sides. Remove chops to another pan. Bake until they reach an internal temperature of 150°F. Remove from oven. Keep warm.

Pour excess oil from skillet. Deglaze with wine and rosemary sprig; reduce by three-fourths. Add cream; reduce until thickened, about 5 to 8 minutes. Remove rosemary sprig; season to taste with salt and pepper. Serve pork chops with sauce. Garnish with a fresh rosemary sprig. Serves 6.

Pan Roasted Tenderloin of Pork with Bacon, Mushrooms, and Horseradish

The smoky flavor of bacon mingles nicely with the pungency of horseradish in this creamy mushroom sauce for pork. This entrée has graced our fall menus for several years, attesting to its ongoing popularity. Try this with the ancho maple glazed carrots (page 110) and your favorite mashed potatoes on the side.

3 slices bacon, cut into julienne strips
2 T. shallots
8 oz. fresh mushrooms, quartered
1½ c. chicken stock, homemade or low-salt canned
Vegetable oil to coat bottom of skillet
2½ lb. whole pork tenderloins
Salt and pepper or Gunflint seasoned salt (page 146) to taste
3 T. brandy
2½ T. butter
2½ T. flour
½ c. heavy cream
Prepared horseradish to taste
Salt and freshly ground black pepper to taste

Preheat oven to 400°F. In heavy skillet, fry bacon until crisp. Remove with a slotted spoon. Drain on paper towels. Set aside.

To remaining fat in pan add shallots and mushrooms. Sauté over medium-low heat until mushrooms are soft and lightly browned. Add chicken stock. Cook over medium-high heat until reduced by one-third.

Meanwhile, in large skillet over medium-high heat, add thin film of vegetable oil. Season pork tenderloins. Brown tenderloins in hot oil, frying in batches if necessary. When browned, remove to a small shallow-sided cookie sheet just large enough to hold the tenderloins set about 1 to 2 inches apart to allow for heat circulation. Pour out any excess oil. Carefully pour in brandy to deglaze the pan. Scrape to dissolve any of the crusty brown bits on the bottom of the pan. Pour brandy into reducing chicken stock.

Bake pork tenderloins to desired doneness or an internal temperature of 150°F. Remove from oven. Let stand in a warm place for 10 minutes.

Strain mushroom mixture into a small skillet; set aside mushrooms and shallots. In heavy saucepan over low heat, melt butter and stir in flour. Cook, stirring, for 1 to 2 minutes without browning. Remove from heat. Whisk in mushroom liquid. Whisk constantly over medium-low heat until mixture boils and thickens. Add cream; whisk until smooth. Strain into mushrooms and shallots; mix well. Add horseradish, salt, and pepper to taste. Keep warm.

To serve, slice pork tenderloins diagonally into slices; fan out on plates. Spoon mushroom horseradish sauce over each serving and sprinkle with the crisp bacon. Serves 6.

◨ Grilled Venison Saddle with Jack Daniels and Green Peppercorn Sauce

Similar to the bourbon and green peppercorn sauce served with the pork tenderloin on page 38, the green peppercorn sauce that accompanies this grilled venison steak has a pedigree—Jack Daniels Tennessee whiskey. Although technically not a bourbon (it's not made in Bourbon County, Kentucky), Jack Daniels adds a charcoal-filtered smoothness to this sauce. For a side dish, choose either the buttermilk, wild rice, and toasted pecan cakes (page 112) or the wild rice pudding (page 113).

6 (6–8-oz.) venison steaks

Salt and pepper or Gunflint seasoned salt
    (page 146) to taste

1 T. butter

2 T. vegetable oil

¼ c. Jack Daniels Tennessee whiskey

2 tsp. water-packed green peppercorns,
    drained and crushed

1 c. heavy cream

1 tsp. cornstarch and 2 tsp. water combined

½–¾ tsp. Dijon mustard to taste

¼–½ tsp. salt, or to taste

1 tsp. additional whole green peppercorns

Season venison steaks with salt and pepper or Gunflint seasoned salt. In large skillet over medium-high heat, sauté in butter and oil until desired doneness. Remove from heat; keep warm while making the sauce.

Pour out excess fat in skillet. Return to heat; deglaze by adding Jack Daniels and green peppercorns. Flambé, gently shaking pan until flames die. Add cream; bring to boil. Simmer for 2 minutes. Add cornstarch mixture; cook until thickened. Whisk in mustard and salt to taste. Add whole green peppercorns. Makes about 1 cup. Spoon sauce over steaks; serve immediately. Serves 6.

Venison—From Field to Freezer

✳ Hunters know that proper handling and butchering are essential for good-eating venison. For best results, the meat should be boned out and all fat removed. Since almost all venison fat is on the exterior of the meat (venison has little or no fat marbling), this is easily accomplished. Be forewarned that venison fat sets records for achieving rancidity in the freezer.

To freeze, wrap the meat first in plastic wrap and then in freezer wrap. Venison properly butchered, wrapped, and frozen in this way lasts for well over a year with no loss of flavor.

◑ Campfire Grilled Big Game Steaks

Grilling venison, moose, elk, and other big game chops and steaks over charcoal or, better yet, over the coals of a campfire best suits these wild viands. Keeping it simple, this basic recipe uses only salt and freshly ground black pepper plus real butter flavored with a little fresh lemon juice. Butter adds a rich flavor that margarine lacks. This method is also outstanding with beef steaks.

6 (6–8-oz.) big game steaks
Freshly ground coarse black pepper
6 T. butter, melted
1½ tsp. fresh lemon juice
Kosher salt to taste

Grind coarse black pepper to taste over sides of each steak; press into meat with heel of your hand. Let sit at room temperature for 30 to 60 minutes before grilling. In small bowl, combine butter and lemon juice.

Grill steaks over hot charcoal or wood coals, turning only once. After turning, brush each steak generously with the lemon butter. Season to taste with kosher salt. The salt will draw some of the steak juices to the surface to mingle with the lemon butter and black pepper, forming a delicious glaze. For the juiciest steaks, do not grill beyond medium rare, certainly no more than medium. Serves 6.

Grilled Venison Steak with Juniper Berry Cream

¼ oz. juniper berries
2 T. gin
1 T. finely chopped shallots
½ c. demi-glacé (page 149; substitute good-quality homemade chicken or beef stock lightly thickened with cornstarch)
1 c. heavy cream
Salt and freshly ground black pepper to taste
1½ tsp. butter (optional)
4 (6-oz.) venison steaks
Melted butter
Gunflint seasoned salt (page 146)

Crush juniper berries. Place in bottom of medium skillet over medium-high heat. Add gin and shallots; flambé. Add demi-glacé and cream; reduce until thickened. Season to taste with salt and pepper. Whisk in optional butter. Keep warm.

Brush venison steaks with melted butter. Season with Gunflint seasoned salt. Grill to desired doneness. Place on warmed plates. Top with sauce. Serve immediately. Serves 4.

Roast Grouse with Horseradish Cream Sauce

Rough grouse are often plentiful in the northwoods. They are delicious—and dumb, especially in the deep woods where hunting pressure is light. Prepare them as you would pheasant, or chicken for that matter. The white breast meat is generous and one grouse is sufficient to serve two. To complete this northwoods feast, serve grouse either topped with the sauce on a bed of wild rice or sided by half an acorn squash baked with butter and brown sugar. Irv Benson, trapper, resort operator, and year-round resident and character on the Canadian side of Saganaga Lake, even claims to feed four hungry men with just one grouse. His secret? He bones out the breast, cuts the meat into strips, and deep fries it in a beer batter.

1 grouse—whole, skinned
Salt and freshly ground black pepper to taste
2 T. oil
1 T. butter
2 T. minced shallots, green onion, or onions
2 T. brandy
1 slice of bacon, cut in half
½ c. chicken stock, homemade or
    low-salt canned
2 oz. fresh small button or quartered mushrooms
    (optional)
¼ c. heavy cream
1 T. prepared horseradish, or to taste
Salt and freshly ground black pepper to taste

Preheat oven to 350°F. Truss grouse so that legs are close against body. Dry bird with paper towels; season with salt and pepper. In small heavy skillet over medium-high heat, brown grouse in oil and butter. Remove grouse. Pour off all but a film of remaining fat. Add shallots; sauté 1 minute or until lightly browned. Return grouse to skillet. Pour brandy over bird; ignite. Shake skillet gently until flames subside.

Lay bacon strips over grouse breast. Add chicken broth and optional mushrooms. Bake uncovered, basting occasionally with broth for 25 to 40 minutes or until juices run clear. Overcooking will result in a dry tough bird. When done, remove grouse to heated serving dish. Cover lightly with foil. Keep warm while preparing sauce.

Pour juices into small saucepan; reduce by one-fourth. Stir in cream and horseradish; reduce over medium-high heat until thickened. Season with salt and pepper.

To serve, cut grouse in half with poultry or kitchen shears. Place half a grouse on each plate; spoon on sauce. Serves 2.

▶ TIP: If you are not a fan of horseradish, a few quick changes will produce roast grouse with sherry mushroom sauce. Simply add the optional mushrooms and omit the horseradish. After adding the cream and reducing, stir in a tablespoon or so of dry sherry to taste. Simmer for a minute or two before serving. It's a tossup as to which one I like better.

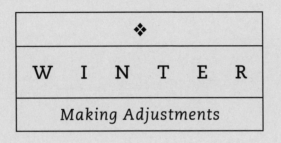

❖

W I N T E R

Making Adjustments

WINTER

Making Adjustments

Spending the winter in the northwoods has always required a bigger adjustment for those of us coming from the city than any other season. Before marrying Bruce, I lived in a Chicago suburb. My employer was a large bank in downtown Chicago. My morning trip to work was via a commuter train filled with hundreds of other commuters. I dressed appropriately to the job—business suits, heels, and nylons. Little allowance was made for weather when deciding what to wear to work. After work, all the attractions and entertainment of a major city were available. As a young college graduate, I took advantage of as many of them as my time and money would allow. It was a time of great fun and few responsibilities. But in the background was this guy in the northwoods who called every week and I wrote to every day.

Like many before me, the lure of the north proved irresistible. Bruce and I were married one October day. After a short honeymoon we arrived back at Gunflint in mid-November. What a change! There were so many new things to see and do and learn—even now it overwhelms me.

The first step was learning how to dress appropriately for the weather. Twenty-five years ago, most city people had yet to discover L. L. Bean. Very few city dwellers wore any type of hiking boot. Bruce told me, "Don't buy any boots in the city. Even if you knew what to get, you couldn't find them in Chicago." So my birthday present was my first pair of Bean boots. I've never been without a pair since. They were quickly followed by a pair of Sorel boots (rubber bottoms, leather tops, and a ½-inch felt liner throughout) for real winter weather. Another important purchase was a pair of choppers—wool mittens covered with a leather shell. It was patiently explained to me that gloves won't keep your hands as warm as mittens in really cold weather. Slowly every item of my winter apparel was changed to something more functional. The concept of layering clothes was taught to me. Eventually the great day arrived when I was trusted to dress myself before going outside.

Another big step was learning to cook. Quite frankly, Bruce was a much better and more experienced cook than I was. That winter he suffered through my learning process. It could not have been too bad because he gained twenty pounds in four months.

But the northwoods added another challenge to learning to cook—planning. The nearest grocery store was forty-five miles away! If you didn't have it or couldn't borrow it from a neighbor, there was no going to the corner store. Of course, I always seemed to lack that one essential ingredient to make the recipe. Gradually I learned to plan a week's worth of dinners, list the necessary ingredients, and get most of them during a weekly trip to town.

We also kept a large supply of canned goods on hand during the winter. Just like Justine used to do, in the fall we would stock up on cases of commonly used foods. As the children came and I served more meals to guests during the winter, Bruce built me a huge larder in the basement of our home. My weekly trips to town centered on fresh produce, dairy products, and bread.

An additional challenge to my self-taught cooking lessons was moose meat. That fall Bruce had filled our freezer with a moose he had shot. It was to be our winter's meat. Bruce had lived off wild game all his life. No big deal, he said. I had never eaten it and could hardly cook beef. With suggestions from Bruce and lots of failures, eventually I achieved meals where you could easily chew the meat. The only plus in the entire process was that Justine has never been known for her cooking skills. As a result I never heard, "Why don't you get my mother's recipe?" from Bruce.

The lack of neighbors was another new experience for me. If you live forty-five miles from the nearest town of any size, the result is that you have very few neighbors. The lodge was closed all winter. Bruce, Justine, and I were the only ones who lived here during this time. There was no year-round staff. For fifteen miles in every direction, we had a total of fourteen neighbors. In Chicago, I could hear the girl next door practicing her flute in her bedroom!

Over the years, more and more people have moved permanently to the area. The lodge business has grown, necessitating a permanent staff. There are now four resorts open all year on Gunflint Lake. Several couples have chosen to retire to their cabins in the woods. More than forty people live on Gunflint year-round. Pretty soon we'll be an urban area.

When you live in the city, the mailman brings your mail to your door six days a week. I soon learned in the late sixties that when you lived on the Gunflint Trail the mail came three days a week from October to May. It was a mixed blessing. On one hand, there was no correspondence to be answered on the off-days. The downside was that there were no daily newspapers either. Slowly the post office added daily delivery for three more months and then finally for the last three months. Today we also have all the other quasi mail services of UPS, Federal Express, faxes, and E-mail.

Our feelings of isolation were intensified by a total lack of television and radio reception. All U.S. radio and TV transmissions were blocked by a 300-foot ridge located a half-mile behind the lodge. For the first five years of our marriage we didn't own a TV. We finally found a radio good enough to get one station out of Thunder Bay, Ontario. When the news magazines came, Bruce and I would read them from cover to cover just to feel a part of what was happening in the rest of the country.

There was only one night that first winter that I particularly felt isolated. Bruce was gone to a sports show. His mother was off on vacation somewhere. I was home alone with only our dog, Itzy, for companionship. My city fears of being alone at night were coming to the surface. Itzy was really restless. She kept getting up to look out the window. The fur would stand up on her neck. I let her out. Then she wanted in. Five minutes later it was out again. The outside flood light was on. I couldn't see anything except deep shadows. Finally I stepped outside to see if I could hear anything. There was a pack of wolves very close to the house. Their howling sounded like it was right next to me. A chill went down my spine. I stepped back into the house and called Itzy in. For the next few minutes I sat inside and tried to convince myself that it was silly to be afraid.

What could the wolves do to me? I was inside; they were outside. The phone rang. I jumped. It was Bruce calling from the sports show. Needless to say, he found the entire incident extremely amusing. Nothing like a little irritation with your spouse to drive away fear!

Perhaps my biggest adjustment was one that many a small business owner has had to make—living with your job twenty-four hours a day, seven days a week. The jobs I had held in the past were located some distance from my home. When the workday was completed, you left. Your home was an entirely different world. The two worlds never met. Running your own very small business and living on the business property is entirely different.

The first thing I noticed was that we always had work to do. The projects were just in the next room or out the door. It was kind of like being in college when you always knew you could be studying a little bit more. Every day when we got up there was a list of projects to be worked on. Some of them surrounded us. One year we painted new signs in the living room for the hiking trails. It was more comfortable than in the crowded workshop. You also worked faster just to get the project done and out of the living room.

Another change was our topics of discussion over meals. If you and your spouse work at different jobs, dinnertime discussions about work might merely consist of "It was a good day." Bruce and I always found different things to discuss about Gunflint Lodge. It varied from current projects to the next season's advertising to the next ten years' building projects. This is not to say that we didn't do our share of gossiping about the neighbors, but Gunflint Lodge always seemed to creep into our conversations.

The biggest difference when you live at your business is the telephone. It always rings, day and night, seven days a week. No one ever wanted to miss that one caller who wanted to make a reservation. If they didn't get an answer, they might call someone else. When we were first married in the late sixties, there wasn't any staff during the winter to help answer the phone. There weren't even answering machines then. Now a staff person answers the phone from 7:00 A.M. to 10:00 P.M. all winter long. In-between those times, we answer the phone.

Winter at Gunflint will always be a uniquely challenging time for those of us who live here. I think I have adjusted but there is always a winter to test my adjustment. As I am writing this in April 1996, the winter of 1995–96 might just have been a testing winter. In January we had temperatures of –50°F. That's not windchill. There was a two-week period where the temperatures warmed to –25°F during the day. The snowfall was over 150 inches and no melting.

Bruce and I got away for three weeks in Florida during late February and early March. We came home to snowbanks taller than me. By the end of March the roads were still covered with snow. Nature added another four inches on March 30.

Today is April 8. I can't see out the window of my computer room because of a snowbank. You can drive a truck anywhere on the lake. Most of the dirt roads still have snow on them. The calendar says spring is here but the view from my window is a different story. I keep telling myself that I really like winter in the northwoods.

Ron's Introduction

Winter comes early to the north country and stays late. It is not unusual for snow to fall in October that will stick around until sometime in late April or even early May. For Gunflint Lodge it is our second season and it's nearly as busy as our summer season. Beginning around Thanksgiving and continuing until the end of March, cross-country skiers, snowshoers, dog-sledders, ice fishermen, snowmobilers, and winter campers head north to where the snow is always white and plentiful.

The season begins with a grand buffet on Thanksgiving Day featuring turkey and wild game with all the trimmings. In December guests pitch in to help decorate the lodge for the holiday season. Two large trees are harvested and set up in the lodge to be trimmed and hung with lights. The smell of pine is in the air as balsam wreaths are assembled. It is a magic time. Fires crackle in the fireplaces as guests hang decorations in cozy comfort, while just outside the windows, snow falls in heavy profusion, covering the backs of white-tail deer at the feeders.

Guests and visitors dine by candlelight as a birch and maple fire in the hearth sends out extra warmth. Starters from the kitchen might include the lodge's signature appetizer, a delicate walleye, wild rice, and pistachio nut sausage with sauce beurre blanc. Also on the menu are soul-warming soups such as cream of smoked mushroom and leek or creamy roasted onion topped with croutons and Parmesan cheese. Entrées are hearty and elegant: roast breast of chicken pistache with blackberry sauce, honey-dijon roasted pork loin with cider cream sauce, or walleye and shrimp pot pie with sourdough biscuit crust.

Appetizers

Walleye, Wild Rice, and Pistachio Nut Sausage with Sauce Beurre Blanc

This is our signature appetizer. Although the idea of fish sausage may sound strange, everyone who tries this loves it. This recipe makes enough sausage to serve a small party.

Beurre Blanc

¾ c. dry white wine
1 T. champagne vinegar
2 tsp. minced shallots
2 T. cream
4 oz. unsalted butter, cut into 8 pieces
Salt and white pepper to taste
½ tsp. grated lemon peel

In medium steel skillet or saucepan, combine wine, champagne vinegar, and shallots. Reduce over high heat until only 2 to 3 tablespoons of liquid remain. Add cream; reduce 30 seconds longer. Add butter all at once, whisking constantly until butter is incorporated into the sauce. Immediately remove from heat. Strain into ceramic or stainless-steel bowl. Whisk in salt, white pepper, and lemon peel. Store in small thermos for up to 4 hours.

Walleye Sausage

4 (6–8-oz.) walleye fillets, skinned and cut into
    1-in. chunks
12 oz. small shrimp
4 oz. bay scallops
6 egg whites
2 T. cognac or brandy
⅜ tsp. cayenne
4–6 tsp. fresh lemon juice (1 small lemon)
1½ tsp. walleye sausage seasoning
    (recipe follows)
1 to 1½ c. heavy cream, as needed
12 oz. coarsely chopped imitation crab
2 c. coarsely chopped shrimp
2–3 c. cooked wild rice
4 oz. pistachio nuts, shelled and chopped
½ c. chopped fresh parsley
Salt to taste
Fresh white bread crumbs, as needed for
    proper consistency
Sausage casings

In food processor with metal blade, puree walleye, shrimp, and scallops. Add egg whites, cognac or brandy, cayenne, lemon juice, and walleye seasoning mix. Process for 30 seconds. With machine running, slowly pour in enough cream to produce a mixture that will hold its shape in a spoon. Pour into large bowl. Refrigerate for at least 15 minutes.

In same processor bowl, add crab and shrimp. Pulse to chop coarsely. Fold seafood into chilled sausage mixture. Add wild rice, pistachios, and parsley. If mixture

Taste Tests

✳ When I first developed this recipe and was anxious to get some feedback, I passed out samples to several friends to try along with several sauce ideas. One person, a fellow guide, ignored my suggestions for preparing and saucing the sausage. Viewing it as some sort of aquatic bratwurst, he had stuck it in a pan of water, boiled it up, then put it on a hot dog bun and slathered it liberally with mustard, ketchup, and sweet pickle relish. "Pretty weird stuff," he told me later.

is too soft, add fresh white bread crumbs as needed for proper consistency; mix well. In small skillet, sauté small amount to taste for seasoning. Add salt to taste if needed. Refrigerate for 1 hour.

Stuff sausage mixture into prepared sausage casings; tie into 4-inch links. (If you do not have or prefer not to use casing, you may make small patties of sausage. The patties can be browned and cooked immediately. Then freeze individually on a cookie sheet. The next day wrap patties tightly in plastic wrap and put in plastic bag. To serve patties, thaw and heat to temperature in a 400°F. oven.)

Place sausage links in simmering water; cook gently until internal temperature reaches 165°F. Place sausages in ice water until cold. Wrap individually in plastic wrap. Store in refrigerator for up to 2 days or freeze in bags. Thaw before using. Makes about 20–24 4-inch sausages.

To serve links, sauté sausages in large skillet until nicely browned and heated thoroughly. Slice diagonally; fan out on a pool of beurre blanc (page 153).

Walleye Sausage Seasoning

2 T. ground white pepper
2¼ tsp. ground nutmeg
1 T. ground coriander
¾ tsp. ground cloves
1½ tsp. onion powder
5 T. kosher salt

Combine all ingredients well.

Venison BBQ Cocktail Meatballs

Use any ground big game for this party appetizer. Keep hot in a crockpot or a chafer with fondue forks or tooth-picks nearby. The recipe for the BBQ sauce is one I got from my old friend, Boots Johnson, many years ago and who, I should add, gave due credit to his mom for its creation. Make the BBQ sauce a day ahead to allow for maximum flavor development.

Boots's BBQ Sauce

2 c. catsup

2 c. water

¾ tsp. celery seed

¾ tsp. chili powder

¼ tsp. dried oregano

⅛ tsp. thyme

¼ tsp. red pepper flakes (more to taste)

½ tsp. salt

4 tsp. cider vinegar

¼ c. chopped celery

2 T. chopped celery leaves

½ medium onion, coarsely chopped

1 medium clove garlic, halved

¼ tsp. or more BBQ spice mix (any brand)

Make BBQ sauce a day ahead. In large heavy-bottomed saucepan set over medium-low heat, combine all ingredients; bring to a simmer. Reduce heat to low; simmer slowly for 1½ to 2 hours until reduced and thickened somewhat. Refrigerate overnight. Return sauce to a simmer. Strain before using. Makes about 2½ cups. The sauce may be made ahead and stored in the refrigerator for several months.

Meatballs

2 lb. ground big game, such as venison, elk, moose, about 80 percent lean (substitute ground beef)

2 eggs, slightly beaten

1 c. crushed crackers

1½ tsp. chili powder

½ tsp. garlic powder

2 tsp. Worcestershire sauce

Kosher salt and freshly ground black pepper to taste

Preheat oven to 375°F. In large bowl, combine venison, eggs, crackers, and seasonings; mix well. In small skillet, fry a small piece. Taste for seasoning. Adjust seasonings as needed. Roll into 1-inch balls; place close together on cookie sheets. Bake 10 to 15 minutes until done. May be made ahead to this point and refrigerated or frozen. To serve, thaw if frozen. Reheat in the sauce. Makes about 60–70 cocktail meatballs

Cream of Smoked Mushroom and Leek Soup

Chefs pick up ideas from many places—cookbooks, food publications, and other chefs, to name a few. I developed this soup after working a winemakers' dinner for Bob and Kathy Bennet, chef-owners of Bennet's Bar and Grill in Duluth, Minnesota. Bob had prepared an ethereal creamy smoked wild mushroom soup for this event. This is my interpretation using fresh cultivated mushrooms. A variation of this recipe combining smoked wild mushrooms and fresh mushrooms won first place at the first annual North Shore "Souper Bowl."

1 lb. fresh mushrooms, lightly smoked over apple
    or hickory in stovetop or other smoker
6 T. butter
1 medium onion, chopped
½ leek, sliced
½ tsp. minced garlic
6 T. flour
6 c. chicken stock, homemade or low-salt canned
½ c. half-and-half
½ c. heavy cream
Salt and freshly ground black pepper to taste
Fried julienned leeks (optional garnish)

Fill stovetop smoker with whole mushrooms and smoke. Set aside about a fourth of the mushrooms for slicing; add later to soup. In food processor with steel blade, finely chop remaining mushrooms. Save any juices from the mushrooms.

In stockpot, melt butter; add onion, leek, and garlic. Cover; cook until onion is tender. Stir in flour; cook without browning for 2 minutes. Stir in stock and chopped mushrooms and juices from the mushrooms. Simmer for 20 minutes. Strain. Add half-and-half, cream, and reserved sliced mushrooms. Simmer; season to taste with salt and pepper. Serve garnished with the fried leeks, if desired. Serves 6–8.

▶ TIP: To make optional garnish, finely julienne the white and pale yellow part of 2 leeks. Toss with cornstarch. Deep fry until golden brown. Drain on paper towels. Season to taste with salt.

Creamy Roasted Onion Soup

Not to be confused with French onion soup, this creamy, earthy-tasting soup is flecked with specks of brown from the roasted onions.

2 large onions
Olive oil
4 T. butter
¼ tsp. minced fresh garlic
4 T. flour
4 c. stock, equal parts chicken and beef stock or all one
½ c. heavy cream
Salt to taste
Freshly ground black pepper to taste
Fresh grated Parmesan cheese

Preheat oven to 350°F. Peel and halve onions. Brush small shallow casserole pan with olive oil. Place onions cut side down in pan. Brush tops of onions with olive oil; cover pan with foil. Roast for 45 minutes until nearly tender. Uncover; continue roasting until flecked with brown and cooked through. Puree in batches in food processor with metal blade. Measure out 1 cup of onion puree and set aside. Reserve remaining puree.

In large heavy-bottomed saucepan set over medium-low heat, melt butter. Add garlic; simmer for 30 seconds without browning. Whisk in flour; cook slowly for 1 minute. Remove flour and butter mixture from heat. Whisk in stock all at once. Return pan to medium heat. Cook, whisking constantly, until stock thickens and comes to a boil. Reduce heat; whisk in roasted onion puree. Simmer for 10 minutes. Stir in cream. Season to taste with salt and pepper. Additional onion puree may be added as desired. Top with Parmesan cheese and croutons before serving. Serves 6.

Neeps and Tatties Soup

The following soup was inspired by some Scottish staff who worked here a few summers ago. In Scotland, neeps (rutabagas) and tatties (potatoes) are often served as a side dish. Here they are combined into a savory creamy soup.

1½ lb. rutabagas
3 oz. bacon, cut into ¼-in. dice
1 medium onion, finely chopped
1 small leek, white part only, chopped
1 lb. potatoes
4 c. chicken stock, homemade or low-salt canned
½ c. heavy cream
Salt and freshly ground pepper to taste
Pinch of ground nutmeg to taste
Crisp bacon
Croutons

Peel and cube rutabagas. In medium saucepan filled with boiling water, blanch rutabagas for 3 minutes. Drain and set aside. In large Dutch oven, fry bacon until browned and nearly crisp. Add onion and leek; sauté over low heat until translucent but not browned. While vegetables are cooking, peel and cube potatoes. Add chicken stock, rutabagas, and potatoes; bring to a boil. Reduce heat. Cook at a steady simmer until rutabagas and potatoes are very tender. In food processor with metal blade, puree potato mixture in batches. Return to saucepan. Place over low heat. Add cream; heat until hot. Season to taste with salt, pepper, and nutmeg. Garnish with crisp bacon and croutons. Serves 6.

▶ TIP: If soup is too thick, add additional chicken stock or milk to thin. If soup is not thick enough, add instant potatoes as needed.

Fish

◉ Garlic Parmesan Baked Walleye Fillets

Here is a quick and easy way to prepare walleye fillets for the oven. The fillets may be prepared in a refrigerator-to-oven casserole ahead of time and popped in the oven just before serving.

1 lb. walleye fillets
2 T. butter, melted
2 tsp. fresh lemon juice
Minced fresh garlic to taste
Salt and pepper
Freshly grated Parmesan cheese
Heavy cream (optional)

Preheat oven to 450°F. Lay walleye fillets in shallow casserole. In small bowl, combine butter and lemon juice. Brush over fillets. Sprinkle with fresh garlic. Season lightly with salt and pepper. Bake for 3 to 4 minutes or until about three-fourths done. Remove from oven; sprinkle with Parmesan cheese. Return to oven. Bake until cheese is melted, about 1 to 2 minutes longer. Serve immediately. Serves 4.

For a richer sauce, pour the pan juices from broiled fish into small saucepan. While keeping the fish covered in a warm place, make a sauce by reducing the pan juices by three-fourths. Finish by adding a splash of cream and reducing until saucelike. Spoon sauce over fish before serving.

Behold the Night

✳ A poem once began, "Behold the wonders of the night sky!" Surely the poet must have had the night sky of the northern wilderness in mind when he penned those words, for the wonders are many indeed. From the colored ribbons of cold fire of the aurora borealis to the surreal shine of a full moon on the frozen landscape, the sights are truly wondrous and numerous.

Consider the cathedral of stars from a rocky outcropping deep in the Boundary Waters far from city lights and pollution. Have you ever seen so many? Once while canoeing on a wilderness lake on a moonless night with a friend and her sister, the sister was awestruck by the sheer numbers of stars she could see. "Do we have this many stars back in Omaha?" she asked her sister. Her sister laughed softly and answered, "Only when we can see them."

The aurora borealis or northern lights are an enduring symbol of the far north. They enter our consciousness and remain forever linked to that moment. One fourth of July some years ago, they lit the sky in a magnificent light show that seemed so appropriate for the date. Another night while camped on Hudson Lake in the Boundary Waters, my companions and I witnessed an incredible display of two natural phenomena: a brilliant display of northern lights and a partial eclipse of

Walleye and Shrimp Pot Pie with Sourdough Biscuit Crust

Here's a hearty pot pie for a cozy supper in front of the fire on a cold winter's eve. Chunks of walleye nestle with shrimp, pearl onions, carrots, and mushrooms in an herbal white wine cream sauce under flaky sourdough biscuit crust.

3 T. butter
1 c. diced carrots
1 c. quartered fresh mushrooms
1 c. pearl onions (or 2 large onions,
    cut into ½-in. dice)
¾ tsp. finely chopped fresh thyme
2 T. chopped fresh basil
4 T. butter
4 T. flour
2 c. white wine fish stock (page 149) or clam juice
½ c. heavy cream
Salt and white pepper to taste
1½ to 2 T. sherry wine
1½ c. large shrimp pieces

2 c. walleye, cubed
Freshly baked sourdough biscuits (page 127)

In large Dutch oven over low heat, melt 3 T. butter. Add carrots, mushrooms, and pearl onions. Cover pan; cook until vegetables are tender. Add thyme and basil; remove from heat.

In medium heavy-bottomed saucepan over low heat, melt 4 T. butter; whisk in flour. Cook stirring for a minute without browning. Remove pan from heat; add fish stock all at once. Increase heat to medium; whisk constantly until mixture thickens and boils. Reduce heat to low; whisk in cream. Season to taste with salt and pepper. Add sherry wine to taste. Strain sauce into vegetables. Add shrimp and fish. Simmer over low heat until fish is cooked.

Spoon into individual-sized casserole dishes or into a 2-quart casserole. Top with hot sourdough biscuits. Serve immediately. Serves 6.

▶ TIP: Any freshly baked biscuit may be substituted for the sourdough biscuits.

---

the moon! And on a winter night while snowshoeing across Seagull Lake, I saw the bands of colored light rise and fall across the sky with remarkable energy, the rushing streamers of pale red, yellow, and ghostly green flaring far overhead, then receding before bursting forth again. Although my feet grew numb with cold, I stood transfixed, savoring the sight.

Journey across the ice on a clear January night when the moon is full. It is so cold each breath stings your nose and catches in your throat. Beneath your feet the snow makes that curious squeaky crunching sound it makes when the temperature is well below zero, a cornstarch squeak. The noise of your walking seems out of place and you stop. All you can hear is the sound of your own breathing. What a contrast with summer's raucous cacophony of sounds!

The Indians had a name for each full moon. January's moon, which presided over this spare rocky land frozen tight with ice and snow, was known to the Cree as the Moon of Great Cold. You are amazed at how light it is. You can clearly see the hills around the lake, although they are miles away. Not like dusk exactly, nor like early dawn, this moonlight is infinitely more surreal. It casts long shadows from the pines covering the shore creating a bluish-tinted tableau of black bars across the deep snow beneath. It is a magic time to be out.

Betsy Powell's Fish Cakes

Betsy Powell, a long-time resident of the Canadian side of Saganaga Lake, passed this recipe along to me. In the far north this seems to be a preferred method of preparing the bony northern pike, known in the bush as jackfish.

2 c. ground or pureed raw fish
Freshly ground black pepper to taste
1 c. canned evaporated milk
Dash of nutmeg
4 eggs, beaten
½ c. dehydrated potato flakes
1½ T. salt, or to taste

In medium bowl, combine all ingredients except salt. Beat to a very stiff batter. Add salt to taste. Drop onto a greased griddle or skillet with a spoon. Fry over medium heat until browned on one side; turn to finish cooking. Serves 4.

▶ TIP: To test for seasoning, add 1 teaspoon of the salt. Fry up a small cake and eat it. Adjust the seasoning as needed.

Fishing with Irv

✳ Irv Benson, year-round resident on the Canadian side of Saganaga Lake at the very end of the Gunflint Trail, is well known for his practical jokes. One winter Irv agreed to take local fisherman Tumsey Johnson on his rounds of his trap line so that Tumsey could fish for trout on one of the lakes along the way.

Irv dropped Tumsey and his gear off and continued on to check his traps. When he returned later that day, Tumsey was nowhere to be seen. Tracks indicated he had walked off into the woods, perhaps to warm up or answer nature's call. Not one to pass up such an opportunity, Irv quickly pulled out a rabbit he had caught in one of his traps, hooked it on Tumsey's line, and stuffed the whole thing back down the hole in the ice.

Moments later as Tumsey walked out of the woods, Irv yelled, "Better hurry! Your bobber just went down!"

Running to the hole, Tumsey set the hook and began hauling in the line. As his "catch" cleared the hole, he found himself staring in total disbelief at a dripping wet rabbit dangling at the end of his fishing line.

He looked at Irv, who shook his head solemnly and said, "I dunno, Tumsey, but I think you're fishin' too shallow."

Baked Whole Trout with Eagle's Nest Camp Stuffing

If the prospect of a nobly stuffed warrior of the deep appeals to you, the following recipe will be of interest. Some years ago I spent a week camping on Eagle's Nest Island on Seagull Lake in the Boundary Waters Canoe Area in early June. I fished hard for walleyes but only managed to catch a small lake trout. The following stuffing was cobbled together out of ingredients on hand. The stuffed trout, wrapped in foil and baked over the coals of my campfire, was, as I remember, one of the finest meals I have ever eaten in any camp. This recipe makes enough stuffing for a 3- to 4-pound fish. Recipe may be halved.

Eagle's Nest Camp Stuffing

12 T. butter (1½ stick), divided

2 small cloves garlic, minced

2½ c. fresh bread cubes or coarse crumbs

¼ c. chopped onion

¼ c. chopped celery

2 fresh tomatoes, peeled, seeded, and diced

2 T. chopped fresh basil, or ½ tsp. dried

4–6 T. dry white wine or vermouth

2 T. chopped fresh parsley

Chicken broth or chicken base and water, as needed

Salt and freshly ground black pepper to taste

In 10-inch skillet set over medium heat, melt 6 tablespoons of the butter. Add garlic, sauté for 1 minute without browning. Add bread cubes or crumbs. Toss and stir until lightly browned. Remove to a bowl. Set aside.

Reduce heat to medium low. In same skillet, melt remaining butter. Add onion and celery. Sauté until celery is tender crisp. Add tomatoes and basil; cook slowly for 1 minute. Pour in wine; cook for a minute longer. Combine vegetable and wine mixture with sautéed bread and garlic. Toss together gently with parsley. Add chicken broth as needed to moisten stuffing. Season to taste with salt and pepper. Cool before using.

The Trout

1 (3–4-lb.) whole lake trout, salmon, or other whole fish, eviscerated and gilled

6 T. melted butter combined with 2–3 T. fresh lemon juice to taste

Kosher salt and freshly ground black pepper to taste

Preheat oven to 450°F. The head may be left on or not, depending on aesthetics and/or pan size. Brush prepared fish inside and out with lemon butter. Season with salt and pepper. Loosely fill cavity with stuffing. Use skewers and string to enclose stuffing. Extra stuffing may be baked in casserole. Place on cookie sheet or shallow casserole dish.

Use a ruler to measure fish at the thickest part of the back. For every inch of thickness, you will roast this fish for 10 minutes. That means if the fish were 1½ inches thick, you would roast it for 15 minutes. Since it is stuffed, which slows down the roasting time a bit, add an additional 5 minutes to the total roasting time. After removing from the oven, let the fish rest in a warm place covered with foil for an additional 10 minutes.

If you like, the fish may be moved with a couple of long spatulas to a warm serving platter and garnished with lemon and parsley.

To serve, remove skin from the top of the fish. Slice servings from along the backbone and ribs. Remove backbone and ribs in one piece. Serve remaining fish. Serves 6.

◙ Cajun Shrimp and Linguine

When I cooked at the Redwood Inn (now closed) at the Château Devenois Winery in Rice, Minnesota, a similar version of this pasta dish was one of the restaurant's most popular dishes. The original recipe was developed by owner Steve Kaminski utilizing his secret Sharja seasoning he discovered while working as a private pilot for one of Saudi Arabia's princes. I have substituted Cajun seasoning (a close match) for the Sharja (still Steve's secret) and added tomatoes and green onions. For the best flavor, make this as hot as your taste buds will allow.

2 tsp. butter

1 oz. julienned yellow onions

3-4 oz. bay shrimp (40–50 count per pound)

1½ tsp. Cajun seasoning (page 146)

Water, as needed

2 T. diagonally sliced green onion tops

⅓ c. tomato concassé (diced fresh tomatoes)

4 oz. linguine, cooked al dente

Salt to taste

1 T. chopped fresh parsley (optional)

In medium skillet over medium heat, melt butter. Add onions, shrimp, Cajun seasoning to taste, and enough water to cover the bottom of the pan to a depth of ⅛ inch. Sauté, tossing and stirring until shrimp turns pink and translucent. Add green onion tops and tomatoes; sauté for 30 seconds, stirring frequently. Push shrimp and vegetables to one side of the pan. Add pasta; season with salt to taste. Toss pasta in remaining liquid until hot, adding a little extra water if necessary to prevent the pasta from sticking to the bottom of the pan. Turn pasta and shrimp out onto a warm plate. Sprinkle with optional parsley. Serve immediately. Makes 2 appetizer servings or 1 entrée serving.

▶ TIP: This amount of Cajun seasoning is for medium spicy. Add more or less to adjust spiciness. Use our recipe for Cajun seasoning or substitute any Cajun fish or seafood seasoning.

Crispy Beer Batter Fried Walleye with Mango Sweet and Sour Sauce

With its wonderful combination of flavors and textures, this golden-fried walleye with an Asian-style sweet and sour sauce has become our most popular walleye entrée.

Sweet and Sour Sauce

1 c. sugar

2 tsp. minced garlic

1½ c. rice wine vinegar

2 tsp. chili paste with garlic

2 T. Asian fish sauce

Cornstarch slurry as needed

½ mango cut into ¼-in. dice (other fruits such as fresh peaches, raspberries, wild blueberries, or strawberries or a combination of fruits may be substituted)

Garnish

½ red pepper, finely diced (or a combination of colored sweet peppers)

4 green onions, green part only, finely sliced on the diagonal

Beer Batter

10 oz. all-purpose flour

3 T. paprika

2 T. kosher salt

1 T. ground black pepper

2–3 12-oz. cans beer

All-purpose flour (to dredge walleye in before battering)

6 (8–10-oz.) boneless, skinless walleye fillets, whole or cut into finger-sized strips

Make sweet and sour sauce. Combine sugar, garlic, rice wine vinegar, chili paste, and fish sauce in a heavy bottomed saucepan over medium heat. Bring to a boil and simmer for 4 to 5 minutes until reduced and flavor reaches desired intensity. Thicken with cornstarch slurry. Refrigerate until needed. Serve warm. Makes about 2 cups of sauce.

Prepare garnishes and refrigerate until needed.

Make beer batter. Whisk the flour, paprika, salt, and pepper together until well combined. Whisk in beer to make a thin batter, not much thicker than buttermilk or very heavy cream.

To serve: Dredge walleye in flour and shake off excess. Dip into beer batter and deep fry until golden brown and crisp. Remove and drain.

Cover the bottom of 6 heated plates with 1½ to 2 oz. of the sauce mixed with 1 to 2 tablespoons of the chopped mango. Sprinkle the red peppers and green onion tops over sauce. Place walleye on top and serve. Serves 6.

▶ TIP: Leftover sweet and sour sauce keeps almost indefinitely in the refrigerator in a covered container.

Roast Breast of Chicken with Mushroom and Wild Rice Stuffing

This stuffing works equally well with fish, either with or without the wild rice. The stuffing is rich and creamy and in no way resembles a traditional bread stuffing. The mushroom flavor is intense and the wild rice adds a pleasant nutty crunch to the stuffing.

Mushroom and Wild Rice Stuffing

2½ T. butter
¼ tsp. minced garlic
½ c. finely chopped onions
½ c. finely chopped celery
1 lb. fresh mushrooms, finely chopped
½ c. heavy cream
½ c. fresh white bread crumbs, as needed for consistency
Salt and freshly ground black pepper to taste
2 c. cooked wild rice (about ½–¾ c. uncooked)

In large skillet over medium-low heat, melt butter. Add garlic, onions, and celery. Cook until onions are tender. Add mushrooms. Cook over heat to medium high, stirring occasionally, until most of the liquid has cooked away. Add cream; bring to a boil. Reduce for 2 to 3 minutes. Reduce heat to medium low. Stir in enough bread crumbs to give the stuffing a firm consistency. Season to taste with salt and pepper. Stir in cooked wild rice. Refrigerate until cold before using. Makes about 4–5 cups of stuffing.

Roast Breast of Chicken

6 boneless chicken breasts
Salt and freshly ground black pepper to taste

Prepare chicken breasts for stuffing by placing one breast skin side down on cutting board. With a small sharp knife, start at center of the breast. Hold the knife at a 45-degree angle and cut a pocket by slicing the meat toward the outside edge. Turn the breast and do the same thing to the other half. Don't worry if the pocket doesn't look very neat at this point. Repeat with the remaining breasts.

Stuff the prepared chicken breasts with the cold stuffing. Mold the stuffing into an oblong shape. Press and mold the stuffing into the pocket. Use your hands to mold the chicken breast around the stuffing. Don't worry if the stuffing isn't totally enclosed by the chicken. Repeat with the remaining chicken breasts. Any leftover stuffing may be frozen for several months.

Cut six 6-by-8-inch pieces of aluminum foil. Spray one of them with nonstick cooking spray. Place one of the stuffed chicken breasts in the center of the foil. Fold the sides over two to three times to form a foil boat with ½-inch sides that fit snugly around the stuffed breast. Repeat with remaining stuffed breasts. Refrigerate until ready to bake.

Preheat oven to 375°F. Place prepared chicken breasts on small cookie sheet. Season tops of breasts with salt and pepper to taste. Bake for 20 to 30 minutes until tops of breasts are golden brown and chicken is cooked through. Let rest for 5 minutes, then remove roasted breasts from the foil and serve. Serves 6.

Grilled Turkey Tenderloin with Red Chili Cream Sauce

Turkey tenderloins are great for grilling. Grilled whole, they can be sliced and served with a savory sauce such as this somewhat spicy red chili cream sauce.

2½ lb. turkey tenderloins

4 T. olive oil

Gunflint seasoned salt (page 146) or salt and
    freshly ground black pepper to taste

2 T. butter

2 T. flour

1½ c. chicken stock, homemade or
    low-fat canned

1 T. chopped shallots

1½ tsp. minced garlic (about 2 cloves)

2 T. or to taste finely chopped jalapeño peppers,
    stemmed and seeded, or half of a 4½-oz. can
    chopped green chilies

¾ c. dry white wine

½ c. heavy cream

¼ tsp. dried oregano

Chili powder to taste

Ground cumin to taste

Salt and freshly ground black pepper to taste

Brush turkey tenderloins with olive oil. Season lightly with Gunflint seasoning or salt and pepper. On lightly oiled grill set over hot coals, grill turkey until internal temperature reaches 165°F. Remove to a warm platter; cover loosely with foil. Keep warm while making sauce.

In heavy-bottomed saucepan over low heat, melt butter. Whisk in flour. Cook without browning for 30 seconds. Remove pan from heat. Whisk in chicken stock all at once. Return to medium heat. Whisking constantly, cook until stock thickens and comes to a boil. Remove thickened stock from heat. Set aside.

In medium saucepan, combine shallots, garlic, jalapeño peppers (or canned green chilies) and wine. Cook over high heat until reduced by three-fourths. With a fine mesh sieve, strain thickened chicken stock into wine mixture. Cook sauce at a bare simmer over very low heat for 15 minutes to develop flavors. Whisk in cream, remaining seasonings, and any juices that have accumulated around the tenderloins. Bring sauce to a simmer.

To serve, slice turkey tenderloins on the bias. Fan out the slices. Ladle some of the red chili cream sauce over the top. Serve remaining sauce on the side. Serves 6.

▶ TIP: Adjust the heat by increasing or decreasing the amount of jalapeño chilies, or use the canned green chilies, which have a nice chili flavor without much heat. Commercial chili powders, a blend of ground chilies, garlic, cumin, and oregano, vary greatly in flavor and heat. A pure chili powder such as ground New Mexico red chilies (molido), ground anchos, ground pasillas, or a combination may be used to replace all or part of a commercial chili powder.

Roast Breast of Chicken Pistache with Blackberry Sauce

Chef Tim Bromenshenkel and I developed this recipe while we worked together at the old Redwood Inn in Rice, Minnesota. It has long been one of my favorites. A breast of chicken is stuffed with chicken and pistachio nut mousseline and topped with crisp pistachio bread crumbs, then roasted, sliced, and fanned out on a pool of blackberry sauce. The result is a tour de force of flavor and elegance.

Chicken and Pistachio Mousseline

18 oz. boneless skinless chicken breasts
1 egg white
1 T. cognac or brandy
½ tsp. salt, or to taste
⅛ tsp. cayenne pepper, or to taste
½–¾ c. heavy cream
¼ c. chopped fresh basil
1½ T. chopped fresh parsley
2 oz. pistachio nuts, chopped
1½ c. fresh white bread crumbs

In food processor with metal blade, puree chicken breasts. Scrape down the bowl. Add egg white, cognac, salt, and cayenne pepper. Turn on machine and slowly add cream, stopping to scrape down the bowl once or twice. Scrape into a bowl. Stir in basil, parsley, and pistachio nuts. Stir in white bread crumbs. Fry up a sample and taste for seasoning. Refrigerate until used.

Pistachio Bread Crumbs

2 c. dry white bread crumbs
1 oz. pistachio nuts, very finely chopped
½ tsp. finely chopped fresh rosemary
1 T. finely chopped fresh parsley
Salt and freshly ground pepper to taste

Combine dry bread crumbs with pistachio nuts, rosemary, parsley, salt, and pepper. Set aside.

Blackberry Sauce

1 (16½-oz.) can blackberries in heavy syrup
¾ c. tawny port wine
1 T. raspberry vinegar
6 oz. unsalted butter, cut into 12 pieces
Freshly squeezed lemon juice to taste
Kosher salt and white pepper to taste

Drain blackberries. Reserve juice and berries separately. Measure out half of juice for sauce. Discard remainder. Measure out half of berries for sauce. Reserve remaining berries for garnish. In medium skillet, combine reserved juice with half of reserved berries, wine, and raspberry vinegar. Reduce over high heat until syrupy. Whisk in butter one piece at a time. Continue whisking until only a few small pieces of butter remain unincorporated. Strain sauce into a bowl, whisking through blackberries in the sieve to squeeze out their juices. A hand-held blender may be used to slightly thicken and fluff up the sauce after straining. Add lemon juice, salt, and white pepper to taste. Makes about 2 cups.

Chicken Breasts

6 boneless skinless chicken breasts
Mayonnaise, as needed

Place a chicken breast between two pieces of plastic wrap. Pound to flatten to about ¼ inch thick. Repeat with remaining breasts.

Place about 3 to 4 tablespoons of mousseline along the lower third of the long side of one chicken breast. Roll chicken breast around the stuffing, folding in the sides to enclose the stuffing. Shape with your hands as best you can into an elongated oval. Don't worry about the appearance of the breasts at this point. After the breasts are breaded, they will look fine. Place the stuffed chicken breast on a small sheet pan covered with plastic film. Stuff remaining breasts. Place pan with stuffed breasts in the freezer until firm, about 1 hour.

Remove breasts from freezer. Brush each breast with mayonnaise and dredge in the pistachio bread crumbs.

At this point the breaded chicken breasts may be double-wrapped individually in plastic wrap and returned to the freezer for up to 1 month.

To serve, place breaded stuffed breasts on a small shallow-sided sheet pan. Drizzle with melted butter. Pour about ¼ inch of water around chicken breasts to prevent sticking. Bake at 375°F until crumbs are nicely browned and chicken is firm to the touch, about 20 minutes. Let rest for 5 minutes. Slice and fan out on a mirror of the sauce. Garnish with some of the reserved berries. At the lodge we paint the sauce with heavy cream or with sour cream thinned with a little half-and-half or milk dispensed from a plastic squeeze bottle. Simply squeeze some lines across the sauce and make a design by running the point of a knife through the lines. Serves 6.

▶ TIP: A 1-pound loaf of white bread with the crusts removed yields about 4 cups of fresh white bread crumbs. Leftover mousseline may be frozen up to 1 month.

Pork

Honey Dijon Roasted Pork Loin with Cider Cream Sauce

A distinctively flavored roast pork with a triple dose of apple flavors in the sauce: fresh apples, apple cider (or juice), and apple brandy (such as Calvados or applejack). If you don't have any apple brandy it may be left out with no harm to the sauce. This roast has enough flavor to stand on its own if you decide not to make the sauce. Try the honey-Dijon coating with grilled or broiled salmon.

1 (2½- to 3-lb.) boneless pork loin roast
3 T. Dijon mustard
1½ T. honey
Gunflint seasoned salt (page 146)
Freshly ground coarse black pepper
1 T. chopped carrot
2 T. chopped celery
2 T. chopped onion
1 Granny Smith apple, cored and chopped
½ medium onion, minced
3 Granny Smith apples, cored and chopped
2 T. apple brandy
½ c. chicken stock
1 c. apple cider or juice
3 T. butter
3 T. flour
¼ c. heavy cream
Salt and pepper to taste

Preheat oven to 450°F. In small bowl, combine mustard and honey. Spread heavily over all sides of pork loin. Season with Gunflint seasoned salt. Grind coarse black pepper over roast. In bottom of a roasting pan, spread carrot, celery, onion, and 1 chopped apple. Place pork in pan. Place in oven; immediately reduce heat to 325°F. Roast 1 to 1½ hours or until an instant-read thermometer registers 140°F in the thickest part of the roast. Remove to a carving board. Cover with foil; let set for 30 minutes. Reserve roasting pan to complete sauce.

While roast is cooking, puree 3 apples in a food processor with metal blade. In medium saucepan, combine onion, pureed apples, chicken stock, and apple cider. Bring to a boil over high heat. Reduce heat to low; simmer for 30 minutes. Strain though a fine strainer, pressing down hard on pulp to extract juices. Set aside.

In small saucepan over low heat, melt butter; whisk in flour. Whisk for 1 minute to cook roux; remove from heat. Set aside.

While roast is setting, pour off excess fat from pork roasting pan; place pan over medium-high heat. Add apple brandy and apple and chicken stock liquid to roasting pan. Deglaze the pan, scraping up the crusty brown bits from the pan. Strain into a clean large saucepan. Set stockpot over medium heat; whisk in roux to thicken. Slowly whisk in cream. Season to taste with salt and pepper. Whisk in any juices that have accumulated around pork roast. Heat thoroughly. Strain the sauce into a warm gravy boat or serving bowl.

Slice the pork; fan out the slices on warmed plates. Spoon a couple of tablespoons of cider cream sauce over each serving. Pass the remaining sauce. Serves 6.

Game

◙ Venison and Wild Mushroom Stroganoff à La Minute for Two

This is a quickly made romantic stroganoff for two. Serve over wild rice sided by crusty bread, a salad of mixed greens or a buttered green vegetable such as broccoli, and a nice bottle of Pinot Noir.

1 small clove garlic, minced
2 T. finely chopped onions
3–4 oz. wild or cultivated mushrooms
2 T. butter
6–8 oz. tender venison, cut into narrow strips
2 T. dry sherry or white wine
¼ c. strong beef or game stock
1 tsp. Dijon mustard
½ c. sour cream mixed with 1 tsp. flour
½ tsp. Worcestershire sauce
Salt and freshly ground black pepper to taste
1 c. hot cooked wild rice
Fresh or dried dill weed for garnish (optional)

In large skillet over medium-high heat, sauté garlic, onions, and mushrooms in butter until lightly browned. Add strips of meat. Sauté, tossing and stirring, until meat loses its redness on the outside. Add sherry or wine; bring to a boil. Cook for 30 seconds. Add stock; boil an additional 30 seconds. Remove from heat. Stir in mustard, sour cream mixture, and Worcestershire sauce. Over medium-low heat, slowly reheat contents of skillet until just hot. Season to taste with salt and pepper. Divide hot wild rice between two warm plates; spoon stroganoff over rice. Sprinkle each serving with dill weed. Serves 2.

◗ TIP: This recipe may also be made with leftover rare or medium-rare steak or roast. The only requirement is that the meat come from a tender cut as the cooking time is very short. Venison tenderloin would make this a feast extraordinaire with cuts from the loin a close second followed by cuts of tender round.

Pan Roasted Duck Breast with Sun-Dried Cranberry Sauce

This is also wonderful with venison steaks. Glacé de viande, a concentrated stock essence, is available commercially in some gourmet shops and by mail order. Directions for making your own are in the Gunflint Pantry chapter (page 149).

2 T. dried cranberries (craisins)
¼ c. port wine
2 (6–8-oz.) boneless duck breast
Salt and freshly ground black pepper to taste
1½ T. glacé de viande (page 149)
2 T. red currant jelly or jellied cranberries
Salt and freshly ground black pepper to taste
1 T. butter

In small bowl, soak dried cranberries in wine for 1 hour. Slash fat of each duck breast diagonally without cutting into the meat. Season each breast with salt and pepper to taste. In large skillet, sauté duck breasts skin side down over medium-low heat until skin is crisp and brown and most of the fat has cooked away. Turn duck breasts over; continue cooking until internal temperature reaches 110°F for rare-medium-rare. This doesn't take very long as most of the cooking is done on the skin side. Remove duck breasts to a warm plate. Cover; keep warm while making the sauce.

Pour remaining fat out of skillet; deglaze pan with wine and dried cranberry mixture. Stir in glacé de viande and red currant jelly. Reduce until syrupy. Season to taste with salt and pepper. Swirl in the butter to finish. Keep warm.

Slice each duck breast; fan out on heated serving plates. Spoon sauce over duck. Serves 2.

A Letter from Justine's Husband, Bill

✳ From a letter by Bill Kerfoot published July 9, 1981, in the *Cook County News-Herald*.

The standard American Plan at the lodges, three meals and lodging was $3.75 per day per person. Gateway Lodge on Hungry Jack Lake catered to the wealthier folks and charged $4.50 per day per person.

Guides received $5.00 per day and some go to $7.00 per day on overnight canoe trips.

Fishing, of course, was excellent. Most trolling was done by paddling our Old Town canvas canoes or rowing boat. The swanky fishermen used a quarter horse motor for trolling and a three horse motor for high speed on the lakes.

Hunting was excellent. Lots of deer. A typical family of five would get two deer licenses, one for Dad and one for Mom. They then would go out and get six deer. One for each member of the family and one for the house. That carried them for winter meat.

When Floyd Olson was the Farmer Labor Governor of Minnesota in the early 40's, his actions during his tenure of office were such that the entire Gunflint Trail permanent population turned staunchly Republican and have stayed that way to this day. On election days they

Beef

Gunflint Lodge Chili

When the mercury hides in the bulb of the thermometer and the winter winds howl across Gunflint Lake, shaking clouds of snow from the spruce and pines along the shore, it's time for the skier, snowshoer, and sledder alike to head to the cozy environs of the lodge and enjoy a hot bowl of homemade chili in front of the fireplace. Use any ground or cubed meat you prefer, or leave it out for a vegetarian version.

1 lb. ground beef
1 c. diced celery
1 c. diced onions
½ c. diced green peppers
4 cloves garlic, minced
2 (28-oz.) cans whole tomatoes, crushed
1 (14-oz.) can tomato puree
½ c. hot tap water
2 T. Worcestershire sauce
1 T. salt
2 T. sugar
5–6 T. chili powder, or to taste
½ tsp. dried oregano
½ tsp. ground cumin
3–4 (15-oz.) cans of kidney beans, drained

In large skillet, brown ground beef with celery, onions, green peppers, and garlic. Drain fat. Transfer beef and vegetable mixture to large heavy-bottomed saucepan or Dutch oven. Add tomatoes and tomato puree. In small bowl, combine hot tap water, Worcestershire sauce, salt, and sugar; stir to dissolve salt and sugar. Add water mixture to beef and tomatoes. Stir in chili powder, oregano, and cumin. Bring to a simmer; cook slowly, stirring occasionally, for about 1 to 1½ hours. Add additional seasonings as needed to taste. Stir in kidney beans; reheat to a simmer and serve. Makes about 3 quarts.

would have to drive miles to vote, but they did and still do today.

Every guest cabin in those days had an airtight stove and a Coleman lamp. Also an outside biffy. Several of the lodge operators finally got little Delco light plants and after a fairly short time a few of them got diesels for lights and power. The whole trail was tickled pink when a power line finally came up.

Most of the men in the area did some trapping. Results were pretty good. If they happened to obtain more than the limit of some hides or possibly several that were illegal to trap, these extras were saved. Several of our Canadian neighbors would be contacted before they went up in early winter to the Lakehead (now called Thunder Bay) to sell their furs. They would take our outlaw fur and extra hides we couldn't declare and they would sell them for us up there and bring us the money for them.

Those early days on the Trail were marvelous in many ways. A lot of hard work but progress was made and the development of the area is a dream we hoped would come true.

(signed) Fond Memories,
Bill Kerfoot

◖ Sautéing and Deglazing

Basic Steak and Chop Sauté (with various sauces)

> 4 steaks or chops
> Salt and coarsely cracked black pepper
> 2 T. butter
> 1 T. oil

Dry surface of steaks or chops with paper towels. Season to taste with salt and pepper. Heat butter and oil in large nonreactive skillet over medium-high heat. The butter and oil mixture will foam as the moisture cooks out of the butter. Just as the foam subsides, indicating that the fat is hot enough, put in the meat. Sauté until nicely browned on one side. Turn meat and continue cooking until done as desired. Meats needing a longer cooking time, such as thick steaks and pork chops, should be sautéed over lower heat. Keep steaks or chops warm while making one of the following sauces or one of your own variations. Each of these recipes makes enough for four steaks.

Red Wine Sauce

This is the sauce to use when frying up a fine steak such as a tenderloin or a ribeye or a choice cut of venison from the loin. If you decide to make the sauce using the red wine you are serving with dinner, the sauce may be named after the wine, such as Cabernet sauce or Pinot Noir sauce.

2 T. minced shallots (substitute green onions, white part only)
½ c. dry red wine
1 T. glacé de viande (page 149; optional)
1 T. butter, unsalted preferred (optional)
Salt and freshly ground black pepper to taste

In skillet, sauté meat. Remove from heat. In separate pan, keep meat warm while making sauce. Pour out all but a thin film of fat after sautéing meat. Add shallots; sauté for 30 seconds. Add wine and optional glacé de viande; reduce over high heat until thickened. The sauce will be lightly syrupy if you are using only wine. Remove pan from heat; swirl in butter. Season to taste with salt and pepper. To serve, spoon a little of the sauce over each steak.

▶ TIP: Glacé de viande, if available, not only adds an incredibly rich flavor to the sauce, it does so without adding additional fat. Lacking glacé de viande, ½ cup of reduced homemade game or beef stock may be added along with the wine and reduced together. Thicken with cornstarch if necessary, to achieve the desired consistency.

White Wine and Shallot Sauce

Here is a sauce for steak that uses white wine instead of red.

¼ c. chopped shallots
½ c. dry white wine or dry vermouth
2 T. unsalted butter (optional)
Salt and freshly ground black pepper to taste

After sautéing the steaks, pour out all but a thin film of fat. Add shallots; stir over medium-high heat for 1 minute. Add wine; reduce until syrupy. Remove from heat; swirl in optional butter. Season to taste with salt and pepper.

▶ TIP: You can make a nice shallot sauce by leaving out the wine and doubling the shallots. After removing the steaks and pouring out excess fat, add shallots along with a tablespoon of butter to sauté pan. The moisture in the shallots will deglaze the pan. When shallots are soft and nicely browned, season to taste with salt and pepper and spoon over steaks.

Dijon Mustard Sauce

2 T. minced shallots
¼ c. brandy
1 c. heavy cream
1 T. Dijon mustard
Salt and freshly ground black pepper to taste

After sautéing the steaks, pour off all but a thin film of fat. Add shallots. Cook for 30 seconds. Add brandy to the pan; reduce by half. Add cream; over high heat reduce for 3 to 4 minutes or until thickened. Remove from heat; whisk in Dijon mustard to taste. Season sauce with salt and pepper. Spoon over hot steaks; serve immediately.

▶ TIP: This sauce can be easily transformed into a green peppercorn sauce to serve with either steak or duck breasts. Just add a tablespoon of crushed green peppercorns to the sauté pan along with the shallots. Finish the sauce with a teaspoon of whole green peppercorns. To serve this sauce with chicken breasts or pork chops, substitute dry white wine or dry vermouth for the brandy.

Madeira Cream Sauce

Serve with steak or chicken. A tablespoon of glacé de viande added with the cream gives a rich flavor to this sauce.

⅓ c. Madeira wine
1 c. cream
Drops of lemon juice
Salt and freshly ground black pepper to taste

After sautéing steaks or chicken, pour out remaining fat; add the Madeira to deglaze pan. Cook over high heat until reduced to 1 tablespoon. Scrape up brown bits off pan during cooking. Add cream; reduce over high heat until a saucelike consistency, about 4 or 5 minutes. Add lemon juice, salt, and pepper to taste. Stir any juices that have accumulated around chops into the sauce. Spoon some of the sauce over each serving.

▶ TIP: Omit the cream and substitute 1 cup of good reduced homemade beef or veal stock. Reduce the stock by one-third. Then thicken to a saucelike consistency with a cornstarch slurry. Season to taste with salt and ground pepper. To vary the sauce, substitute Marsala wine for Madeira. Serve with chicken breasts.

Steak Au Poivre

Au poivre is French for "with pepper." Freshly ground or coarse cracked black pepper is a must for this recipe. Store-bought ground black pepper oxidizes soon after grinding and loses its wonderful pepper flavor and aroma, leaving only the sensation of hotness.

4 (6–8-oz.) steaks
3–4 T. fresh coarse cracked or coarsely ground
    black pepper
Salt to taste
2 T. butter
1 T. oil
2 T. brandy
½ c. red wine
1 T. glacé de viande (page 149)

Sprinkle pepper over the steaks on both sides, pressing it into meat with the heel of your hand. Let sit at room temperature for one-half hour. Season steaks with salt. In skillet over medium-high heat, sauté steaks in butter and oil until done as desired. Remove steaks to a warm plate; keep warm. Pour out remaining fat from skillet; add brandy and red wine. Reduce until syrupy. Add glacé de viande; simmer until reduced to a saucelike consistency. Season to taste with salt. Serve sauce over warm steaks immediately. Serves 4.

The Pepper Grinder

✱ Could the pepper grinder be the most useful item in your kitchen? There is simply no comparison between freshly ground and preground pepper. Whole peppercorns, as with other whole spices, keep their pungent flavor locked inside until released by grinding or cracking. Shortly after being ground, pepper oxidizes and loses flavor. Only the heat remains.

Peppercorns grow on vines in such exotic places as India, Sri Lanka, Indonesia, Madagascar, and Brazil. The berry of the pepper vine provides us with three familiar forms of pepper.

Green peppercorns are picked before they are fully mature and are sold in dehydrated or freeze-dried form or packed in brine. They have a fresh pepper flavor.

Black peppercorns are also picked before they are fully ripe, then dried. When freshly ground, they provide a pungent aroma and flavor.

White peppercorns are allowed to become fully ripe, then they are soaked to remove the black outer husk. White pepper tastes different from black. It has a milder, somewhat fermented, flavor and is used in white sauces or other preparations where those unsightly black specks just won't do. During the days of coal- and wood-fired locomotives, white pepper was used routinely in the galley cars so passengers wouldn't complain of soot in their food.

Pepper Roasted Prime Rib of Beef with Brandy Tarragon Jus

Garlic or horseradish mashed potatoes would make a wonderful accompaniment for this roast along with a green salad, crusty bread, and a bottle or two of your favorite red wine. Any fairly tender beef roast such as top round, sirloin tip, or rump roast may be substituted for the rib roast.

1 3–4-lb. bone-in beef rib roast

½ c. crushed black peppercorns

½ tsp. ground cardamom

1 tsp. garlic powder

⅓ c. olive oil

½ c. soy sauce

½ c. brandy

3 T. balsamic vinegar

8 garlic cloves, peeled and crushed

2 T. dried tarragon leaves, crumbled

Reserved juices from roast

Water or beef stock, homemade or low-salt canned, as needed

Reserved marinade, degreased and strained, as needed

1 T. cornstarch mixed with 2 T. water

Place beef roast in large pan. Rub with peppercorns, cardamom, and garlic powder. In medium bowl, combine olive oil, soy sauce, brandy, balsamic vinegar, garlic, and tarragon. Pour over beef; cover. Marinate refrigerated overnight. Reserve marinade. Refrigerate for au jus.

Preheat oven to 450°F. Remove roast from marinade. Wrap in aluminum foil, taking care to avoid tearing the foil on the bottom so that the juices will be retained during roasting. Place wrapped roast in roasting pan; put into preheated oven. Immediately reduce heat to 325°F. Roast approximately 12 minutes per pound to an internal temperature of 110°F for medium rare. Remove roast from oven. Open foil; remove roast to a warm place to rest for at least 30 minutes before serving. Reserve drippings in bottom of foil.

Strain reserved drippings into a measuring cup; degrease. To the degreased drippings add water to measure 1 cup. Pour into small saucepan; bring to a simmer. Thicken very lightly with cornstarch mixture. Taste; correct seasoning if necessary with a spoonful or so of the reserved marinade.

To serve, carve roast into half-inch slices, serving every other cut with the bone. Removing bones before carving will make slicing easier. Serve on heated plates with a spoonful or two of the jus over the meat. Serve remaining jus on the side. Serves 6–8.

❖

FISH

COOKERY

A Compendium of How to
Care for, Prepare, and Enjoy
the Fish You Catch

FISH COOKERY

A Compendium of How to Care for, Prepare, and Enjoy the Fish You Catch

As a fishing guide for seventeen summers at the end of the Gunflint Trail, I amassed a wealth of information about the lakes I fished, the best ways to keep fish fresh tasting, and interesting and unique ways to prepare the catch.

From the beginning I knew there would always be other guides who could catch more and bigger fish, but I figured few of them could match me in preparing shore lunches. Over time gourmet shore lunches prepared over a campfire became my specialty.

I started my clients out with such appetizers as home-smoked lake trout on crackers with horseradish scallion sauce to snack on while I cleaned the fish and got the fire going. The fish we had caught were breaded with pecans or cashews or beer battered. These were served with various side dishes: pommes dauphine (deep-fried potato puffs made with cream puff paste and mashed potatoes), wild rice pilaf, corn on the cob, steamed broccoli, or whatever fresh vegetables I could find. I heated homemade breads and rolls in a reflector oven and served them with my homemade wild berry jams. Sometimes I would bake cornbread in the reflector oven. On one occasion I even baked a cake for a client's birthday in a reflector oven.

What follows is a collection of information I have learned over the years, both as a fishing guide and as a chef, on some of the best ways to take care of what

you catch, some basic cooking methods for preparing it, and a collection of sauces especially for fish.

From Summer Catch to Winter Cache

Proper care of the fish you catch begins as soon as the fish is removed from the hook. Unlike many red meats that benefit from a lengthy aging period, fish flesh garners no such benefits. The truth is, as soon as the fish dies, it begins to deteriorate. It becomes essential, then, to keep freshly caught fish as close to 32°F as possible until we eat or freeze them.

In my opinion, the worst way to take care of freshly caught fish is to put them on a stringer and drag them around in the water beside the boat all day. As the fisherman moves from spot to spot, the fish are hauled in and out of the boat. Soon the entire day's catch is floating belly up in the water. During the years I guided, I would often see fishermen at the cleaning table filleting such fish. The gills were barely pink. The once-firm flesh was now white and soft. Who would want to eat such fish?

Ideally we could ensure the best-tasting fish by keeping them alive until we were ready to eat them. But the popular live wells designed to do just that don't work much better than a stringer, especially when the surface water is warm. Far better to kill the fish quickly with a blow to the head and put it into a cooler packed with ice, preferably crushed or small cubes.

Another method used by commercial fishermen is to place the just caught fish in a mixture of salt, ice, and water. Use proportions of one part salt to two parts each of ice and water. This so-called super cooling method will keep the fish fresh and firm and in tip-top eating condition for up to 3 days, something for the backcountry fisherman to consider.

Freezing Fish for Easy Eating

Here are three unique methods for freezing your summer catch. Be sure to check your state laws before transporting fish. For best eating, use frozen fish within three months.

Cookie sheet method. Wrap each fillet tightly in plastic film. Lay them flat on a cookie sheet. Place in freezer. When frozen, wrap each fillet with aluminum foil. Place the fillets in plastic freezer bags. Squeeze out as much air as possible and twist the top of the bag until it is twisted tight and forms a loop. Secure the loop with a wire twist tie. Place this bag inside another freezer bag and repeat this process with the second bag. This makes a fairly effective airtight seal.

Water glazing method. Freeze the fillets on a cookie sheet. When frozen, dip each fillet several times in ice water or spray several times with cold water on both sides, freezing between each application, until fillets are well glazed with ice. No need to wrap, just place glazed fillets in freezer bags and twist and seal as above.

Ready-to-cook method. Prebreaded fish are great to have on hand. No thawing is necessary before using. Simply remove what you need and deep fry until golden brown. Serve the fingers of fish like the shrimp they resemble with lemon wedges and tartar or cocktail sauce if you like. These are wonderful served with cocktails or as an appetizer. The breading also forms a formidable barrier against freezer burn. (See also beer battered fried walleye fingers, page 7.)

Bread whole fish fillets (not over ½ inch thick for proper deep frying) or chunks or finger-sized strips using a three-step breading (seasoned flour/egg wash/bread or cracker crumbs). Lay individually on a cookie sheet. Cover with plastic film or foil. Place in freezer. When frozen, remove to freezer bags. Squeeze out as much air as possible. Twist and seal in double plastic bags as described above. Do not thaw fish before using. To use, remove amount needed and deep-fry at 360°F.

Walleye and lake trout are the two most sought after species on northern lakes, with smallmouth bass, stream trout, and northern pike not far behind.

Walleye—Minnesota's (and the Gunflint Trail's) Favorite

Walleye, the most sought after fish of Minnesota anglers, is also a popular item on Minnesota menus. The walleye's boneless and delicately flavored white meat takes readily to numerous preparations from the everyday to the gourmet.

But ask any Minnesotan his or her favorite way to enjoy walleye and chances are you'll hear deep-fried or pan-sautéed. Perhaps the ultimate version of this is the lunch prepared over an open fire on the shore of one of Minnesota's sparkling birch- and pine-forested lakes. Nothing can top the freshly caught and crisply fried fillets traditionally served up with fried potatoes and onions and pork and beans out of a campfire-blackened billy.

But don't stop there. Back in camp (or back home in your kitchen), try starting the day with pan-fried walleye fillets and eggs, perhaps scrambled with some cooked wild rice if you have any and maybe some Monterey Jack cheese. How about a walleye club sandwich for lunch? Pan-fry or deep-fry the walleye and layer the crisp fillet with lettuce, tomato, fried bacon, and red onion. Then add tartar sauce or a lemon-basil or Dijon mustard-flavored mayonnaise. If walleye isn't starring on the dinner menu, consider giving it a supporting role as an appetizer. Serve beer batter fried walleye fingers with lemon wedges and a choice of dipping sauces such as homemade tartar and cocktail sauces.

But frying only scratches the surface of the walleye's versatility. Walleyes may be stuffed (wild rice is a favorite), pureed into an airy mousseline, or made into an elegant sausage and artfully sauced. Let your imagination be your master.

Lake Trout

Lake trout are synonymous with the far north. The waters they inhabit have to be clean, cold, clear—and deep. The opening of fishing on the Gunflint often provides fast lake trout action for the angler. The late break-up of the lakes in the far north keeps the surface water cold enough to hold the trout shallow for the first few weeks of the fishing season in mid-May. This makes them easier to find and catch, providing a welcome and delicious alternative to the often difficult-to-catch postspawn walleye.

According to old-timers of the Gunflint, there are really two types of lake trout caught in these waters: the orange-fleshed trout that are native to the backcountry and the white-fleshed trout that have been stocked, probably from Lake Superior stock. However, since the color (and the flavor) of the flesh varies considerably from lake to lake, the trout's diet must certainly be a contributing factor.

Lake trout do not take kindly to being frozen. The somewhat fatty flesh turns rancid quickly. According to the Minnesota Department of Natural Resources, in a study done some years ago, bleeding the fish as soon as it is caught increases freezer life significantly. Cutting off the tail of the fish is the quickest and best way to do this. Yes, this makes a mess of your cooler and you may well prefer instead to eat the trout either fresh or within a month of freezing for the best flavor. The skin may be left on lake trout fillets since, like other trout and salmon, they are virtually scaleless.

Smallmouth Bass

Smallmouth bass have a well-deserved reputation as feisty fighters. They deserve to have a reputation as a fine eating fish as well. The meat is a little sweeter than a walleye's, but most people can't tell the difference, even when they taste them side by side. Clean and prepare them as you would walleye. Be sure to rinse them well to remove all blood.

Stream Trout

Rainbow trout, brook trout, and splake are in various stocked and managed lakes and streams along the Gunflint Trail. They provide excellent eating and may be fried or baked whole, stuffed or unstuffed, or filleted and broiled or sautéed.

Northern Pike

These predators of the deep, known in Canada as jackfish, can grow to twenty to thirty pounds or more. When you are fishing for walleyes and a sudden bite relieves you of your terminal tackle, it was likely a northern's razor-sharp teeth biting through your line. For this reason, people fishing for northern use wire leaders.

Northerns have a reputation for being bony, and because of this, larger northern pike are preferred to small ones, as it is easier to remove the offending Y-bones that grow in a line near the center of each fillet. Filleting northern pike without the Y-bones seems to be an art. I have known many would-be filleters end up with what appears to be a handful of pinkish white burger while attempting such a feat. Those who have mastered the craft are few.

Larger northern pike, like larger lake trout, are favorites for stuffing and baking. Use the eagle's nest camp stuffing (page 77), mushroom and wild rice stuffing (page 80), spinach and swiss cheese stuffing (page 55), or your favorite.

Cooking Fish: A Primer

Deep Frying

During my seventeen summers as a fishing guide, I cooked hundreds of shore lunches over campfires. I discovered that by continuing to feed dry wood to my fire and thus keeping a good flame going, I would have the right amount of heat to produce the correct temperature for frying. To check when that point had been reached, I tossed in a potato or dipped the tail end of a breaded fillet into the grease. If the potato or the fillet sizzled and bubbled vigorously, the grease was ready.

At home in the kitchen it's a different story. If you have a deep fryer appliance, you're all set. Just set it at a temperature of 360°F. Not having such a modern convenience, I use a cast-iron chicken fryer with 4-inch sides filled about half full of vegetable oil. To assess the correct frying temperature, I use a clip-on thermometer. Laying the fish carefully in the hot grease with the skin side down helps to minimize curling.

With all the greasy mess and smells that come with deep frying, you might just want to consider building a fire in the backyard and doing the frying outside.

If you're catchin' 'em big and the fillets are more than ½ inch thick, you will have a difficult time getting the fish done in the center by the time the outside is the right shade of golden brown. For these larger fillets, I suggest either cutting them into finger-sized pieces or dividing them into three or four pieces and then slicing them in half horizontally.

Pan Sautéing

My first choice for this job is a cast-iron skillet, although any heavy frying pan will do nicely. Pour about ⅛ inch of vegetable oil, shortening, or bacon grease into the pan and heat over medium heat until a drop of water dropped into the grease spits and sizzles. Bread the fish fillets using any of the breadings (save the batters for deep frying) or, if you're in a hurry, simply season the fillet with salt and pepper and dredge in plain flour. Shake off the excess and lay the fillets in the hot grease. Use a long-tined fork, tongs, or spatula to turn the fish when golden brown. Continue frying until just cooked through.

Baking

A useful rule of thumb for baking fish in any form—whole, steaked, or filleted—is to bake the fish in a preheated 450°F oven for 10 minutes for each inch of thickness of the fish measured at the thickest point.

Broiling

Years ago I "broiled" fish under the broiler of my oven. Then I found out that what a restaurant refers to as "broiled" is actually baked in a very hot oven. I would challenge anyone to tell the difference between the two "broiled" fish.

Here's how to do it. Preheat your oven to 450°F. Place the fish skin side down on shallow-sided pan such as small sheet pan. In the kitchen at Gunflint, we use a pie tin for single orders. Brush the top of each fillet with lemon butter (2 tablespoons melted butter mixed with 2 teaspoons of fresh lemon juice to taste) and season lightly with salt, freshly ground black pepper, and paprika. Pour a little dry white wine, water, or a combination of wine and water around the fillets to keep them from sticking to the pan and "broil" in the oven until barely done. (Remember the 10 minutes per inch rule.) The fish will finish cooking from the residual heat after they are removed from the oven. If you cook the fish until they flake, you have overcooked them.

That's the basic recipe. Do you want to get a little creative? Add one or a combination of any of the following to taste to the melted butter before brushing the fish: fresh lemon juice, Dijon or whole grain mustard, a fresh herb or combination of fresh herbs, or minced garlic, to name just a few possibilities.

Poaching

While I don't recommend poaching for walleye (I find the resulting texture unappealing), this cooking method works very well with lake trout, whitefish, and many other fish.

Here's the easiest way to poach fillets up to ¾ inch thick. Bring a large skillet or saucepan filled with about 1½ to 2 inches of water or equal parts water and white wine to a boil. Place serving-sized pieces of fish in the boiling water, cover the pan, and turn off the heat. Let sit for 5 minutes. Remove from water and serve with lemon butter or other sauce of your choice.

Grilling

Some fish, such as walleye, are difficult to grill owing to their delicate nature, but with a grill screen made especially for fish, it is possible and delicious. Other fish, such as salmon and lake trout, are a natural for the grill.

You can marinate the fish before grilling (bottled Italian dressing isn't bad) or grill them plain. Place the grill screen over hot coals and let it get hot. Brush the fish lightly with olive oil or vegetable oil and season to taste with salt and pepper. Lay on the grill. When about half-cooked, turn carefully with a flat spatula, brush with butter or lemon butter, and finish grilling.

Traditional Guide's Shore Lunch Breading

This is more or less the traditional breading packed by guides everywhere in the North.

    1 c. flour
    1 tsp. salt
    ½ tsp. black pepper
    2 tsp. paprika
    ⅓ c. corn meal, cracker meal, or potato granules

Put all ingredients in a bag. Shake well to combine. Shake fish in bag to coat before pan frying or deep frying.

▶ TIP: With the exception of the beer batters and the one-step breadings (like the traditional guide's shore lunch breading), you can bread the fish well in advance. Just bread fish fillets or pieces, such as finger-sized pieces, several hours in advance and refrigerate until you are ready to fry them. Or you may bread and freeze them for several months. Your fish will be ready to fry at a moment's notice and as a bonus, the breading acts as an effective barrier against freezer burn.

Crispy Breading

This is a recipe for a classic three-step breading, commonly called an "Anglais" or English breading.

Make a seasoned flour by omitting the corn meal or cracker meal in the traditional guide's shore lunch breading. Coat fish fillets with it. Shake fillets to remove excess flour. Dip into beaten eggs mixed with one of the following: beer, water, white wine, milk, or evaporated milk (about ¼ cup liquid per egg). Then roll in finely crushed cracker crumbs or in dry bread crumbs. Refrigerate until ready to fry.

Guide's Beer Batter

Double the traditional guide's shore lunch breading, omitting corn meal or cracker meal. Divide it in half. Place one-half in a plastic or paper bag and add fish fillets to it. Shake to coat fillets. Put other half into a bowl or pot and beat in enough beer (about 1¼ cup to each cup of flour mixture) until the consistency of heavy cream. Shake the flour-coated fillets to remove excess and dip into the batter and deep-fry in hot (360°F) fat.

Quick Beer Batter

Whisk beer into 1 or 2 cups of pancake mix or Bisquick until the consistency of heavy cream. Add salt and black pepper to taste (you probably won't need any if you're using pancake mix). Whisk in about 1–2 teaspoons of paprika. Dip fillets into flour (or additional pancake mix or Bisquick), shake off excess, and dip into the batter and fry in 360°F fat until golden brown.

The Shore Lunch:
Some Additions and Dividends

✻ Shore lunches are a tradition all over the north country, and what could be better? Shore lunches are pristine northern lakes, the smell of wood smoke and pine, and the best, absolutely the best fish you've ever eaten. On the menu are golden-fried fish, freshly caught that very morning, served up with crisp bacon, fried potatoes and onions, and pork and beans, all washed down with campfire-brewed coffee and topped off with a little something for dessert. And it's all prepared with a humble flair by an itinerant shore chef, perhaps your fishing guide or your Uncle Joe or even yourself. If you pack carefully and pay attention to the heat of your fire, preparing a shore lunch is a snap. Here are a few suggestions for turning your shore lunch into a real shore feast.

Some Additions

Bacon. Few things have more of an affinity with the outdoors than bacon. The sweet smoky aroma of bacon frying over an open fire mingling with the smell of wood smoke is something you're not likely to forget. Gordy Poehls, master guide of Saganaga Lake, showed me this method of frying bacon one bone-numbing, cold, rainy day in early June some years back when we were guiding a party of fishermen together.

Take an entire pound of sliced bacon and carefully add it, unseparated, to the hot grease in your skillet before you add the potatoes. Use a long-handled fork to "shake" the bacon into individual slices as it fries. Remove to paper towels to drain when brown and crisp. The bacon cooks quickly without burning, and all the bacon fat is rendered out to flavor the potatoes and the fish when it's their turn in the pan.

Serve the crisp bacon as an appetizer or put aside to crumble over the potatoes before serving (or save a few slices for yourself to make the guide's deluxe shore lunch walleye sandwich—see Some Dividends, below).

Onion rings. When time permits, onion rings are a delicious and easy addition to a shore lunch. Use the same breading or batter you are using for the fish and deep-fry the breaded rings until golden crisp and brown. Serve as an appetizer or as an accompaniment to the fish.

Fried mushrooms. Here's a real treat that will impress anyone who eats one of your shore lunches. Bread a pound or so of fresh mushrooms using your fish breading. You might have to rinse the mushrooms with water to get the dry breading to stick. Deep-fry until golden brown and serve as an appetizer.

Some Dividends

The guide's deluxe shore lunch walleye sandwich. Place a hot, crisp-fried walleye fillet on a slab of bread, buttered or not as you prefer. Place a couple of thin slices of raw onion over the top and finish with a crisp bacon slice or two if you have them. Spoon on some tartar sauce or lay on a spoonful or two of what many believe to be the tartar sauce of the northwoods, pork and beans, and finish up with another slice of bread.

Kenora fried potatoes. This is the way a guide who worked out of the Kenora area in Canada prepared shore lunch potatoes for his clients. You'll need to pack an extra skillet to fry the fish if you decide to use this recipe.

Dice or slice cold boiled potatoes and fry them in about $1/8$ inch of your choice of shortening. Toss and turn until the potatoes begin to turn brown and crisp and are almost done. Now add as many diced onions and chopped green peppers as you like. Fry until the potatoes are nicely browned and the onions and peppers are tender. Season the whole thing with salt and pepper to taste. Lay slices of American or cheddar cheese over the top of the potatoes. Prop up the pan in front of the fire until the cheese is melted and the fish are ready to serve.

This is a time to relax against a sturdy old jack pine at the edge of a sparkling blue wilderness lake while the wind rustles through the trees.

Cashew Breading

Nut crunchy! Substitute almonds, pecans, macadamia nuts, or whatever nuts you like for the cashews.

4 oz. soda crackers (about ¾ c. pulverized)
    or use cracker meal
1¼ c. salted cashews
1 T. paprika
¾ tsp. salt, or to taste
⅛ tsp. ground red pepper (cayenne)
¾ tsp. white pepper, or to taste
All-purpose flour
2 eggs
Pinch of salt
½ c. liquid

In food processor with metal blade, combine all ingredients. Process until nuts are finely pulverized. Correct seasoning. Makes about 2 cups of breading.

To bread, shake fish fillets in a bag containing plain all-purpose flour. Shake off excess flour. Dip fillets into a mixture of eggs, salt, and liquid. The liquid may be water, beer, white wine, milk, cream, or evaporated milk. Then dredge or shake the fillets in the cashew breading. Place breaded fillets on a pan or plate and refrigerate until you are ready to fry them.

Herbed Breading

To change the flavor simply change the herb. In place of the marjoram, add dill weed, basil, thyme, oregano (with a little grated Parmesan cheese perhaps?), or a combination.

1 c. flour
1 c. bread crumbs
1 tsp. salt
2 tsp. paprika
½ tsp. crumbled whole dried marjoram
2 tsp. fresh chopped parsley or 1 tsp. dried
½ tsp. freshly ground black pepper
2 eggs
6 T. of your choice of whole milk, cream, half-
    and-half, or evaporated milk

In a shallow-sided pan such as a pie tin, combine all dry ingredients. In separate bowl, mix together eggs and milk. Roll fillets in breading; shake off excess. Dip into egg mixture. Let excess drip off; roll in breading again. Refrigerate until ready to fry.

Fish Sauces

Basic Tartar Sauce

This excellent tartar sauce was a staple in my shore lunch box when I worked as a fishing guide. Now it is a staple in the dining room.

1 c. mayonnaise
3–4 T. finely chopped dill pickle
1 T. minced onion
1 T. chopped capers (optional)
1 T. chopped fresh parsley
½ tsp. dried tarragon or dried dill weed
1 tsp. sugar
¼ tsp. salt, or to taste
1 tsp. prepared mustard
½ tsp. fresh lemon juice, or to taste
Freshly ground black pepper to taste
1½ T. finely chopped pimiento-stuffed
    green olives (optional)
1 hard-boiled egg, chopped (optional)

In medium bowl, combine all ingredients; mix well. Refrigerate 1 hour before serving to blend the flavors. Store in refrigerator. Makes about 1½ cups.

Jalapeño Tartar Sauce

This is a spicy variation of the preceding tartar sauce.

1 c. mayonnaise
1½ T. minced red onion
2 T. jalapeños, seeded and finely chopped
½ T. sugar
1 T. prepared mustard
½ tsp. fresh lemon juice
¼ c. finely chopped dill pickle
1 T. chopped fresh parsley
2 T. freshly ground black pepper
¼ tsp. salt

In medium bowl, combine all ingredients; mix well. Refrigerate 1 hour before serving to blend the flavors. Store in refrigerator. Makes about 1½ cups.

▶ TIP: For a hotter tartar sauce, chop the jalapeño with some or all of the seeds included.

Horseradish Tartar Sauce

This deliciously piquant sauce bridges the gap between cocktail sauce and tartar sauce.

1 c. mayonnaise
1 T. horseradish
1½ T. finely minced red onion
6 T. finely chopped dill pickle
1 tsp. Dijon mustard
1 tsp. fresh lemon juice
1¼ tsp. sugar
¼ tsp. salt
A pinch of pepper
1 T. ketchup
1 dash hot sauce
1 T. chopped fresh parsley

In medium bowl, combine all ingredients; mix well. Refrigerate 1 hour before serving to blend the flavors. Store in refrigerator. Makes about 1½ cups.

Cocktail Sauce

This is excellent with deep-fried fish and seafood. Serve as a sauce choice with the beer battered fried walleye fingers (page 7), along with one of the tartar sauces.

½ c. chili sauce
¼ tsp. salt
⅓ c. catsup
¼ tsp. Worcestershire sauce
2 T. prepared horseradish
1 dash hot pepper (Tabasco) sauce (optional)

Combine all ingredients and refrigerate until needed. Makes about 1 cup.

Cucumber Sauce

This mellow sauce is just right with broiled or baked fish.

1 medium cucumber, peeled, seeded, and diced
1 tsp. salt
1 T. minced onion
2 tsp. Dijon mustard
½ c. real mayonnaise
Salt and fresh ground black pepper to taste

Toss diced cucumber with salt. Refrigerate for 15 minutes. Drain well; blot dry with paper towels. Combine with remaining ingredients. Taste to adjust salt and pepper. Refrigerate until ready to use. Makes about ¾ cup.

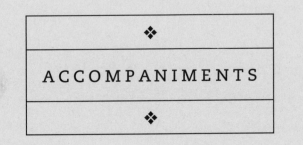

ACCOMPANIMENTS

ACCOMPANIMENTS

Not only do the entrées change every day on the menu at Gunflint Lodge, so do most of the accompaniments. Our most popular side dish is the Gunflint wild rice pilaf (page 112) and, as such, it is on the menu nearly every evening. Wild rice also stars in the buttermilk, wild rice, and toasted pecan cakes (page 112), a natural accompaniment to game dishes, and in the wild rice pudding (page 113), a nice side dish for roasted meats and poultry.

Mashed potatoes are nearly everybody's favorite way to have America's most popular starch. At Gunflint Lodge we have fun with mashed potatoes. We prepare them with garlic and sour cream (page 114), roasted garlic and chèvre (page 114), horseradish (page 115), celery (page 115), and with rutabagas (page 117).

A bread custard is a unique and delicious accompaniment. Think of a bread custard as a savory bread pudding. Made primarily with bread, eggs, half-and-half, and cream, bread custards lend themselves to endless variations. In this chapter you will find recipes for a sun-dried cherry and fresh basil bread custard, a roasted blueberry and wild rice model, and a fall favorite incorporating sun-dried cranberries and fresh thyme.

Fresh vegetables of each season are prepared in countless ways and served every evening—from grilled, roasted, and steamed to sautéed, pureed, and glazed.

Side dishes, like good wine, delight the palate and contribute an exciting overture to the main entrée.

Vegetables

◧ Grilled Summer Vegetables

There are lots of ways to grill vegetables. This is the Gunflint version. Marinating the vegetable in a balsamic vinaigrette before grilling adds flavor.

1½ T. balsamic vinegar
6 T. olive oil
Salt and freshly ground black pepper to taste
1–2 tsp. minced garlic, if desired
2–3 tsp. finely chopped fresh herbs, such as
    rosemary or thyme, if desired
3 medium zucchini, ends trimmed and
    halved lengthwise
3 medium yellow squash, ends trimmed and
    halved lengthwise
1 red onion, peeled and cut into ¼-in. thick slices
8 oz. fresh whole mushrooms

In small bowl, whisk balsamic vinegar and olive oil to form an emulsion. Season with salt and pepper. Stir in garlic and herbs, if desired. Toss vegetables with vinaigrette. Marinate for 1 to 3 hours before grilling.

Drain vegetables in a colander set over a bowl; reserve marinade. Grill vegetables over hot coals until tender crisp. Remove zucchini and yellow squash as it finishes cooking and slice crosswise.

Combine the zucchini and yellow squash with the grilled mushrooms and onions. Toss with reserved vinaigrette. Correct seasoning with additional salt and pepper as needed. Serves 6.

▶ TIP: A grill screen such as is used to grill fish works well to keep the onions and the mushrooms from falling through the grate into the fire.

Provençal Vegetables

These stewed vegetables are a close relative of ratatouille, a French vegetable mélange that invariably includes eggplant. This dish highlights the flavors of fresh summer garden vegetables.

1½ T. olive oil
2–3 tsp. minced garlic
1 small onion, chopped
1 small green pepper, chopped
1 small red pepper, chopped
3 small zucchini, halved and cut into ¼-in. slices
2 tomatoes, seeded and chopped
3 T. dry white wine
1 tsp. Herbes de Provence or Italian herb blend
Salt and freshly ground black pepper to taste

In large saucepan, combine olive oil, vegetables, and wine. Sprinkle with herbs, salt, and pepper to taste. Simmer over medium heat, stirring occasionally, until peppers are tender crisp. Correct seasoning and serve. Serves 6.

Roasted Vegetables ·

On a blustery winter's eve these savory homey vegetables really hit the spot. They are a delicious accompaniment to roasted meats and poultry.

6 carrots, peeled and cut into approximate
    ½-by-2-in. pieces
1 medium rutabaga, peeled and cut into
    ¾-in. cubes
2 medium red onions, cut into ¾-in. squares
1 head garlic, separated into cloves and peeled
3 T. chopped fresh rosemary, or 1 T. dried
2 T. chopped fresh thyme, or 2 tsp. dried
¼ c. olive oil
1 T. balsamic vinegar
1 lb. fresh whole mushrooms
Kosher salt and freshly ground black pepper
    to taste

Preheat oven to 375°F. In large bowl, combine all vegetables and herbs except mushrooms. In small bowl, whisk together olive oil and balsamic vinegar. Pour over vegetables; toss to combine. Spread vegetables in large shallow roasting pan. Roast, stirring occasionally, for about 1 hour. Stir in mushrooms. Continue roasting, stirring once or twice, until tender and lightly browned, about 20 to 30 minutes more. Season to taste with salt and pepper. Serves 6.

◖ Roasted Asparagus

Roasting brings out a new flavor dimension for this favorite spring vegetable.

1 lb. asparagus, stems peeled or snapped
Vegetable oil as needed
Salt and freshly ground black pepper to taste

Preheat oven to 450°F. Place asparagus spears in flat casserole or pan long enough to hold the asparagus; toss with enough oil to coat the spears. Spread the asparagus out in a single layer on a cookie sheet. Sprinkle with salt and pepper to taste. Bake for 12 to 15 minutes, turning once until tender crisp.

Ancho Maple Glazed Carrots

A delicious side dish with a little bit of heat from the ancho chilies and the smooth, satisfying sweetness of real maple syrup.

Ancho Chili Puree

3 dried ancho chilies
Very hot water to cover

Place ancho chilies in medium bowl. Cover chilies with near boiling water. Use lid or small plate to keep chilies submerged. Let chilies rehydrate for 20 minutes. Remove from water. Remove stems and seeds. Puree in a blender (a blender works better than a food processor for this). Add some of the soaking water if not too bitter; otherwise use plain water as needed to achieve a thick puree. Leftover puree may be stored in the refrigerator for several days or frozen for up to 6 months. Makes about ½ cup puree.

Carrots

1¼ lb. whole baby carrots, baby-cut carrots,
   or cut to your favorite size
3 T. butter
¼ c. real maple syrup
Ancho chili puree (recipe follows) to taste
Kosher salt and fresh ground black pepper
   to taste.

Ancho Chilies

✳ At Gunflint Lodge ancho chilies, which are dried poblano chilies, are used in a number of dishes. While not excessively hot, their heat ranges from very mild to medium and the fruity flavors meld well with a variety of preparations. Anchos are one of the sweetest of dried chilies, with flavors of raisins and dried plums accented with undertones of tobacco and coffee. Anchos may be purchased whole dried or in powdered form.

Ancho chilies appear in several recipes in this book. In addition to this carrot recipe, you will find them used in grilled tenderloin steak with ancho chili sauce and cilantro cream (page 39), grilled lake trout with ancho chili maple honey glaze (page 53), and homemade vanilla ice cream with ancho maple caramel sauce (page 141).

In medium saucepan with salted boiling water, cook carrots to taste. Drain. The carrots may be cooked up to a day ahead and refrigerated until needed.

In 10-inch skillet set over medium heat, melt butter until sizzling. Add cooked carrots; stir and toss until heated through and coated with the butter. Whisk together maple syrup and ancho puree to taste; add to carrots. Continue stirring and tossing until coated with glaze and hot throughout. Season to taste with salt and pepper. Serve immediately. Serves 6.

Zucchini Gratin with Sour Cream, Cheddar, and Chive Sauce

Zucchini is a prolific producer, as any home gardener will tell you. In some parts of Minnesota, the story goes, folks lock their cars in late summer to prevent generous friends and neighbors from filling up their back seats with extra zucchini from their gardens. This is a favorite zucchini recipe.

2 lb. medium zucchini, scrubbed and
    sliced diagonally
1 T. butter
½ c. sour cream
1 tsp. all-purpose flour
½ c. grated cheddar cheese
½ tsp. paprika
¼ c. chopped fresh chives
Kosher salt and freshly ground black pepper
    to taste
Milk, if necessary, to thin sauce
¼ c. butter, melted
1 c. crushed crackers (I prefer the premium
    rectangular-shaped crackers, in which case
    24 of them will equal a cup)

Preheat oven to 350°F. In medium saucepan with boiling salted water, blanch zucchini until tender crisp, about 2 to 3 minutes. Remove and drain on paper towels.

In medium heavy-bottomed saucepan over medium-low heat, melt butter. In separate bowl, whisk together sour cream and flour, then whisk into melted butter. Add cheddar cheese; stir until melted. Although the flour will help to keep the sour cream from curdling, for best results, do not bring to a boil.

When cheese is melted, remove from heat. Stir in paprika and chives. Season to taste with salt and pepper. If too thick, thin with a little milk.

Arrange zucchini in a neat overlapping layer in the bottom of a shallow-sided 1½-quart gratin or casserole dish. Spoon sauce over top of zucchini. In small bowl, mix butter and crushed crackers with a fork. Sprinkle buttered cracker mixture over zucchini and sauce. May be made up to a day ahead to this point. Cover and refrigerate until ready to bake.

Bake for about 20 minutes or until bubbling and hot around the edges. Serves 6.

10/30/10 took to Millers very tasty

Buttermilk, Wild Rice, and Toasted Pecan Cakes

Serve these savory little cakes with game, grilled meats, and poultry.

½ c. sifted all-purpose flour
½ tsp. baking soda
½ tsp. baking powder
½ tsp. salt
¼ tsp. freshly ground pepper
1 egg
½ c. buttermilk
1 T. whipping cream
1½ T. chopped shallots
1½ c. cooked wild rice
¼ c. chopped pecans, toasted

In medium bowl, combine flour, soda, baking powder, salt, and pepper. In small bowl, whisk together egg, buttermilk, and whipping cream. Add to dry ingredients; stir until well blended. Add shallots, wild rice, and pecans; mix well. Fry as for pancakes. Makes about 12 2-inch cakes. These may also be frozen at this point and reheated to serve later.

▶ TIP: For variety you can add a ¼ cup or so of roasted corn or dried berries, such as blueberries, cherries, or cranberries.

Gunflint Wild Rice Pilaf

This popular side dish is on the menu almost every day at the lodge.

1 c. wild rice, cooked according to package directions in chicken stock, homemade or low-salt canned
4 T. butter
¼ tsp. minced garlic, if desired
1 medium onion, finely chopped
1 small green pepper, finely chopped
½ red pepper, finely chopped
4 oz. fresh mushrooms, sliced
2 T. chopped parsley
Salt and freshly ground black pepper to taste

In large skillet, melt butter over medium heat. Add garlic, onion, green pepper, red pepper, and mushrooms. Sauté until vegetables are soft. Toss vegetables with cooked wild rice and parsley. Season to taste with salt and pepper. Serves 6–8 as a side dish.

Wild Rice Pudding

This recipe was developed for our first winemaker dinner series. It was a hit and has remained on our menu ever since. The recipe is a variation on an old-fashioned corn pudding.

3 c. cooked wild rice
3 T. finely chopped red pepper
3 T. finely chopped green pepper
¼ c. finely chopped onion
¾ c. shredded Monterey Jack cheese
¾ c. dry white bread crumbs
½ tsp. dry mustard
2 eggs, beaten
1⅓ c. half-and-half
Salt and freshly ground black pepper to taste
½ c. additional dry white bread crumbs
2 T. butter, melted

Preheat oven to 350°F. In medium bowl, combine wild rice, red pepper, green pepper, onion, cheese, bread crumbs, and mustard. In small bowl, whisk eggs and half-and-half. Add to dry ingredients; toss together to mix. Season to taste with salt and pepper. Pour into greased 2-quart casserole. Cover with additional bread crumbs; drizzle with butter. Bake for 40 to 50 minutes or until set. Makes 6–8 servings.

Minnesota Wild Rice

✳ Minnesota ranks as one of the top producers of this native grain. Years ago the price of wild rice fluctuated wildly depending on the harvest. With the development of a wild rice plant that would not shed its grain when ripe, a new industry was born—the growing of wild rice in paddies. While like the commercial tomato, this was not a great gastronomic leap forward, the price has remained fairly stable since its introduction. Lake and river wild rice is available. It costs a bit more, but I prefer it to the paddy rice. Minnesota-grown wild rice must state on the package whether it is paddy grown or not.

▶ TIP: When sweet corn is in high season, substitute it for the wild rice. Follow the recipe using corn cut off the cob from either just-shucked or leftover cooked sweet corn in place of the wild rice. Substitute shredded cheddar cheese for the Monterey Jack.

Potatoes

◙ Garlic and Sour Cream Mashed Potatoes

My general rule of thumb for these potatoes is to add one whole peeled clove of garlic per potato. Add more or fewer garlic cloves to adjust the intensity of the garlic to your preference.

2½ lb. red potatoes, peeled and halved
6–8 large cloves of garlic, peeled and halved
4 qt. cold water seasoned with 1 T. salt
2–4 T. soft butter, if desired
Sour cream as needed; use full-fat, light, or
   nonfat as desired
Salt and freshly ground black pepper to taste

In large saucepan, combine potatoes and garlic in salted water. Bring to a boil over high heat; cook until potatoes are tender. Drain; return to saucepan. Shake the pan with the potatoes over medium-high heat to evaporate remaining moisture. In large bowl, mash potatoes adding butter and sour cream as desired. Season to taste with salt and pepper. Serves 6.

▸ TIP: These garlicky mashed potatoes can be made as light as you like. In fact, if you leave the butter out and use nonfat sour cream, they will be fat-free.

◙ Roasted Garlic and Chèvre Mashed Potatoes

Our first choice for the goat cheese to put in these tangy, garlicky mashed potatoes is an excellent Minnesota chèvre made by Mary Doerr at her Dancing Winds Farm in Kenyon, Minnesota. Substitute another domestic such as a Wisconsin chèvre or an imported French goat cheese.

2½ lb. red or Yukon Gold potatoes,
   peeled and halved
4 qt. cold water seasoned with 1 T. salt
¼ c. roasted garlic puree, more to taste (page 38)
2–3 oz. goat cheese (chèvre), or to taste
¼ c. butter
½ c. warm milk, half-and-half, or cream;
   more if needed
Salt and freshly ground black pepper to taste

In large saucepan, add potatoes to salted water. Bring to a boil over high heat. Cook until potatoes are tender. Drain; return to saucepan. Shake the pan with the potatoes over medium-high heat to evaporate remaining moisture. In large bowl, mash potatoes. Add roasted garlic puree, goat cheese, butter, milk, half-and-half, or cream; mash to desired consistency. Season to taste with salt and pepper. Serves 6.

Horseradish Mashed Potatoes

These potatoes are an excellent accompaniment to beef and game roasts or steaks and salmon.

2½ lb. red or Yukon Gold potatoes, peeled and halved
6–8 cloves garlic, peeled and halved
4 qt. water seasoned with 1 T. salt
1 c. cream
1 shallot, minced
4–8 T. prepared horseradish to taste
2 T. butter, if desired
Salt and freshly ground black pepper to taste
Chopped fresh chives or parsley for garnish

In large saucepan, combine potatoes and garlic in salted water. Bring to a boil over high heat. Cook until potatoes are tender. While potatoes are cooking, combine cream with shallot and horseradish to taste. Bring to a boil; simmer slowly for 3 to 4 minutes. Drain potatoes; return to saucepan. Shake the pan with the potatoes over medium-high heat to evaporate remaining moisture. In large bowl, mash potatoes. Add hot cream mixture and butter. Season with salt and pepper to taste. Serve immediately garnished with chives or parsley. Serves 6.

Celery Mashed Potatoes

These potatoes are a marvelous accompaniment to roasted meats, game, and poultry.

4–5 ribs celery, trimmed
1 small onion, minced
2 T. butter
¼ c. heavy cream
Chicken base or salt to taste
Freshly ground black pepper to taste
2 lb. red potatoes, cut into 2-in. chunks, peeled or unpeeled as desired
Buttermilk or milk as needed

Cut each rib of celery lengthwise into ¼-inch strips. Gather celery strips together and slice thinly crosswise. In skillet over low heat, combine celery and onions with the butter; cover. Cook vegetables until very tender. Add cream, chicken base or salt, and pepper to taste. Simmer mixture very slowly, uncovered, for 15 to 30 minutes. Puree in the food processor with metal blade.

While celery and cream mixture is simmering, in a stockpot cook potatoes in lightly salted water until very tender. Drain potatoes; return them to the stockpot over medium heat. Shake pan to evaporate any excess moisture on the potatoes.

Combine celery puree with potatoes. Mash using a hand-held masher or the paddle attachment of a heavy-duty mixer. Add buttermilk or milk as needed for consistency. Taste and correct seasoning with additional salt and pepper if necessary. Serves 6.

Smoked Gouda Au Gratin Potatoes

These potatoes are excellent served with grilled meats. It is also a good recipe to use with leftover boiled potatoes.

3 T. butter
¼ tsp. minced garlic
¼ c. minced green onions
3 T. flour
½ tsp. dry mustard
⅛ tsp. cayenne pepper
1¼ c. milk
¼ c. cream or half-and-half
Salt and white pepper to taste
2½ c. cubed cooked potatoes
6 oz. grated smoked Gouda

In medium heavy-bottomed saucepan, melt butter over medium-low heat. Add garlic and green onions; cook until onions are soft. Stir in flour, dry mustard, and cayenne. Cook, stirring for 1 minute without browning. Remove from heat. Whisk in milk and cream all at once. Cook over medium heat, whisking constantly until thickened and sauce comes to a boil. Remove from heat. Season to taste with salt and pepper.

Toss potatoes with two-thirds of the Gouda. Add sauce. Transfer to an 8-by-8-inch pan. Sprinkle with remaining Gouda. May be made ahead to this point. Refrigerate until needed.

Preheat oven to 350°F. Bake about 15 to 20 minutes until bubbly around the edges and hot throughout. Serves 6–8.

Swiss Au Gratin Potatoes

These fine potatoes are a distant relative of the French pommes dauphinoise. They are easy to prepare ahead of time and are a nice side dish to serve with roasts and grilled meats.

6 medium-sized potatoes, peeled, cut into
    ½-in. dice
1 small onion, finely diced
2 c. (about 8 oz.) shredded Swiss cheese, mixed
    with ½ c. (about 2 oz.) grated Parmesan cheese
5 T. butter
1 small clove garlic, minced
5 T. flour
½ tsp. dry mustard
1½ c. milk
½ c. cream
Kosher salt and ground white pepper to taste
Butter
Paprika

In large saucepan, cook potatoes in boiling salted water until tender. Drain and cool. Combine cooled potatoes, onion, and half of cheese mixture. Set aside.

In medium heavy-bottomed saucepan set over low heat, melt butter; add garlic. Cook garlic without browning for 1 minute. Stir in flour and dry mustard; cook slowly for another minute. Remove from heat; combine milk and cream and add all at once to flour mixture. Return pan to medium heat. Whisk constantly until sauce comes to a boil and thickens. Remove from heat; season to taste with salt and pepper.

Combine sauce with potato mixture. Pour into 1½-quart gratin or casserole. Sprinkle with remaining cheese mixture. Dot with butter; sprinkle with paprika. May be made up to a day ahead to this point. Refrigerate until ready to bake.

To serve, preheat oven to 350°F. Bake for 25 to 30 minutes or until bubbly around the edges. Serves 6–8.

Rutamousse

Mashed potatoes and rutabagas. People who swear they hate rutabagas have been known to go back for seconds of this.

1 lb. rutabagas, peeled and cut into ½-in. dice

1 qt. water seasoned with ¾ tsp. salt

1½ lb. red or Yukon Gold potatoes, peeled and halved

6 cloves garlic, peeled and halved

2½ qt. of water seasoned with 2 tsp. salt

3 oz. cream cheese (may use low-fat or fat-free)

½ c. sour cream, or as needed (may use low-fat or fat-free)

Kosher salt and freshly ground black pepper to taste

In saucepan set over high heat, combine rutabagas and salted water. Bring to a boil; cook until very tender. Drain; return to pan. Set pan over high heat. Shake pan back and forth to evaporate any remaining moisture. Be careful not to scorch rutabagas.

In another saucepan, combine potatoes, garlic, and salted water; set over high heat. Bring to a boil; cook until very tender. Drain; return to pan. Shake over high heat to evaporate any excess water. Again, avoid scorching.

In large mixing bowl, combine rutabagas, potatoes, garlic, cream cheese, and sour cream. Mash with a mixer or potato masher, adding salt and pepper to taste. Scrape into a serving dish. Serve hot.

May be made up to a day ahead and refrigerated in a bake-and-serve dish. To serve, bake at 350°F for 20 to 30 minutes or until heated through. Serves 6.

▶ TIP: For smoother consistency, puree rutabagas in food processor fitted with steel knife before combining and mashing with the potatoes and remaining ingredients.

Bread-Based Side Dishes

◕ Dried Wisconsin Cranberry and Sage Bread Custard

This recipe lends itself to all sorts of variations. This and the three variations that follow are my favorites.

4 c. Italian or French bread, cut into ¾-in. cubes

1 small onion, chopped

1 rib celery, chopped

4 eggs, beaten

½ c. half-and-half

¾ c. heavy cream

2 tsp. rubbed sage

½ c. dried cranberries

Salt and fresh ground black pepper to taste

Preheat oven to 350°F. In medium bowl, combine bread cubes with the onion and celery. In small bowl, beat eggs with half-and-half and cream. Whisk in sage and cranberries. Season to taste with salt and pepper. Spray 8-inch square glass pan with nonstick cooking spray. Spoon bread mixture into prepared pan. Bake for 30 minutes until puffed and set. Serve hot. Serves 4–6.

Variations: Roasted Blueberry and Wild Rice Bread Custard

1. Combine ¾ c. cooked wild rice with the bread, celery, and onion.
2. Fold in ¼–½ c. roasted blueberries (page 118) in place of the dried cranberries.

3. Substitute ¼ c. sun-dried cherries for the blueberries and 1 T. fresh chopped basil for the rubbed sage.

Roasted Blueberries

✳ Roasting concentrates the flavor of the blueberries. Spray small cookie sheet with nonstick cooking spray. Spread 1 cup of frozen or fresh blueberries in prepared pan. Spray tops of the berries with nonstick cooking spray. Roast at 250°F for 1½ to 2 hours (or more if needed) until berries are about half-dried. Makes about ½ cup.

Duck Marsh Herb Stuffing

The duck marsh in the title suggests the wild rice in this stuffing. This was my traditional Thanksgiving stuffing for many years. It has become the stuffing I serve with our grand Thanksgiving buffet. The stuffing is also delicious in a baked chicken breast.

5 c. dried cubed bread
1 c. cooked wild rice (about ⅓ c. uncooked)
6 T. butter, melted
2 cloves garlic, minced
¾ c. diced celery
1 c. finely chopped green onions, including tops
4 oz. fresh mushrooms, sliced (optional)
¼ c. dry white vermouth or dry white wine
¼ tsp. dried thyme
1 T. dried tarragon
¾ tsp. rubbed sage or poultry seasoning
1 T. honey or pure maple syrup
Hot turkey or chicken stock
2 T. chopped parsley (optional)
Salt and freshly ground black pepper to taste

In large bowl, combine bread cubes and cooked wild rice; set aside. In large skillet over medium heat, melt butter. Add garlic; sauté for 30 seconds without browning. Add celery, green onions, and mushrooms; cook slowly 6 to 8 minutes or until onions are translucent and celery is tender crisp. Add vermouth or wine; simmer for 2 minutes. Stir in herbs and honey or maple syrup; cook for 1 minute. In large bowl, combine vegetable herb mixture with bread and wild rice. Add parsley; toss lightly to combine. Adding hot stock to moisten as desired. Season to taste with salt and pepper. Cool before stuffing bird. Makes 4–6 servings.

BREADS

BREADS

Answers to a few simple questions can make bread-baking much easier to understand. The following are a few of the most common questions I have been asked.

— What is the best flour to use for bread-baking? Higher gluten flours such as those labeled "bread flour" work best.

— How do retail bakeries make some rye breads black? Caramel color, made from caramelized sugar. It is available from specialty bakery shops and some mail order catalogs such as The King Arthur® Flour Baker's Catalogue (800-827-6836).

— How do you determine when bread dough has doubled? Punch a finger into the dough about ½ inch. If the dent remains, the dough has doubled.

— How can you tell when bread has finished baking? Because ovens can vary significantly in temperature, relying on the amount of time given to complete baking or on how brown the bread is can be deceiving. The time-honored way to test for doneness is to tap on the bottom of the loaf. It sounds hollow when it is done. A more accurate way to gauge doneness is with an instant-read thermometer. Bread will have an internal temperature of 190 to 205°F when done. Instant-read thermometers are also available from The King Arthur® Flour Baker's Catalogue and are indispensable in the kitchen for everything from telling when a roast or steak is properly cooked to the correct temperature of the water to mix with yeast.

Wheat and Rye
Sesame Nut Bread

This is a bread recipe I developed some years back. In spite of the hearty ingredients, this recipe produces a light loaf. I thought enough of the recipe to enter it once in a bread recipe contest. Only after mailing in my entry did I notice that I had neglected to include yeast in the ingredient list. Needless to say I didn't win.

2 T. honey
½ c. warm water (110–115°F)
1 T. yeast
¼ c. shortening
1½ c. water
1 c. bread flour
1½ c. whole wheat flour
⅔ c. medium rye flour
1 T. salt
⅓ c. cracked wheat
3 T. toasted wheat germ
3 T. packed brown sugar
⅓ c. sesame seeds
⅓ c. sunflower nuts
2–2½ c. additional bread flour
½ c. broken walnuts
½ c. cooked wild rice (optional)

In large bowl, combine honey and ½ cup warm water. Dissolve yeast in honey-water mixture. Let stand for 10 minutes.

In large saucepan, combine shortening and 1½ cups water. Heat water until shortening melts. Let cool until warm (about 110–115°F) and add to yeast mixture.

With a wooden spoon, add 1 cup bread flour, the whole wheat flour, and rye flour. Beat vigorously until well blended, about 30 strokes. Stir in salt, cracked wheat, wheat germ, brown sugar, sesame seeds, and sunflower nuts. Beat vigorously until well combined, about 25 strokes. Add enough additional bread flour, ½ cup at a time, to make a soft dough.

Turn dough out onto a floured surface. Lightly flour surface of the dough; let rest 5 minutes to allow the water to be absorbed by the dough. Use only as much flour as necessary to prevent the dough from sticking to the surface and knead the dough for 8 to 10 minutes until smooth and elastic.

Let rest for 5 minutes. Flatten dough into a circle and sprinkle the surface with walnut pieces. Fold sides of the dough over the walnuts; knead until walnuts are evenly distributed throughout the dough.

Place in greased bowl, turning to grease top. Cover with plastic wrap and towel. Let rise in a warm place until double, about 1½ to 2 hours. Punch down; turn out onto a lightly floured surface.

Divide into two parts, shape into balls; cover with bowl. Let rise for 15 minutes. Shape into 2 loaves; place each loaf in a greased 9-by-5-inch loaf pan. (May also be shaped into 2 round hearth loaves and placed on a greased cookie sheet that has been sprinkled with corn meal.) Cover with a towel; let rise until doubled. Bake at 375°F for 35 to 40 minutes. If tops of loaves brown too fast, cover loosely with aluminum foil. Remove from pans. Cool completely on wire racks.

Sauerkraut Rye Bread

Developed in 1990, this sauerkraut rye bread has excellent flavor. Shape into buns to use for steamed or grilled bratwurst, kielbasa, or franks…or imagine hot pastrami or corned beef piled high between slices of this hearty rye. It's wonderful toasted, too.

1 c. warm water
2 T. sugar
1 T. dry yeast
2 T. molasses
½ T. salt
1 tsp. vegetable oil
1 c. medium rye flour
1 8-oz. can sauerkraut, drained, squeezed dry, and chopped fine
1½ to 2 c. bread flour as needed

In small bowl, combine warm water (110–115°F) and sugar. Sprinkle yeast over water-sugar mixture. Stir to dissolve. Add molasses, salt, oil, rye flour, sauerkraut, and ½ cup bread flour. Beat 2 minutes at medium speed with a mixer. Gradually stir in enough remaining flour to make a soft dough (will be sticky). Turn out onto lightly floured board; knead for 8 to 10 minutes until smooth and elastic.

Place in greased bowl, turning to grease top; let rise until doubled. Turn dough out onto a lightly floured surface, cover and let rise 15 minutes before shaping into rolls, round hearth loaves, or French-type loaves (can also be put into a loaf pan to make 1 loaf). Place rolls, round, or French-type loaves on greased cookie sheets sprinkled with corn meal. Cover and let rise until doubled. Bake at 375°F for 25 to 40 minutes depending on the shape. Cool on wire racks.

Wild Rice and Honey Bread

This bread is one of our most requested by our guests. The honey makes this a sweeter bread than most, and the wild rice makes it Minnesotan.

⅔ c. warm water (110–115°F)
1 T. sugar
2 T. yeast
⅔ c. honey
½ c. cracked wheat
½ c. medium rye flour or wild rice flour
½ c. oatmeal
1½ c. bread flour
¼ c. vegetable oil
2 tsp. salt
1 c. cooked wild rice
1¼ c. additional warm water
1½ c. additional medium rye flour
2 c. additional bread flour, approximately

In large bowl, combine ⅔ cup warm water and sugar. Dissolve yeast in mixture. Add honey, cracked wheat, rye flour, oatmeal, bread flour, oil, and salt. Beat with mixer for 3 minutes. Stir in wild rice and 1¼ cup warm water. Add rye flour and as much of the additional bread flour as necessary to make a soft dough.

Turn out onto a floured surface and knead for 8 to 10 minutes. Place in greased bowl; cover; let rise until doubled in size. Turn out onto a lightly floured surface. Divide into three portions. Cover with plastic wrap; let rise for 15 minutes. Shape into loaves. Place in greased loaf pans. Let rise until center is 2 inches above the pan (50 to 60 minutes). Bake at 375°F for 30 minutes or until bread tests done. Cool on wire racks.

Crusty Country Bread

This is similar to a French bread recipe but seems easier to make with a greater success rate. I don't know why.

⅓ c. warm water
1 T. dry yeast
4 c. bread flour
2½ tsp. salt
1¼ c. warm water

In large bowl, combine ⅓ cup warm water (110–115°F) and yeast until bubbly, about 5 to 7 minutes. Add flour, salt, and remaining water to the mixing bowl; mix well. Turn out onto a lightly floured surface. Knead 8 to 10 minutes. Do not knead in too much flour or the bread will turn out heavy.

Place in greased bowl; let rise for 3 hours until nearly triple in size. Punch down and let rise until doubled, about 1 to 1⅓ hours. Remove to a floured surface; cut into pieces for French loaves, rolls, etc. Cover with plastic wrap. Let rest for 15 minutes. Shape as desired. Place on greased cookie sheets that have been sprinkled with white or yellow corn meal. Let rise until doubled or more, 1 to 2 hours.

Bake at 425–450°F (depending on the size of the loaves or rolls). Spray loaves or rolls with a mist sprayer of water before putting them in the oven and every minute for the first 6 minutes of bake time. Bake until bread tests done. This will vary with the size of the loaves or rolls. Cool on wire racks.

Painter Family Rolls

I usually shape this dough into round rolls, dip the tops in butter, smear in on the baking sheet, and turn right side up and flatten the roll with the palm of my hand. That's the way I learned to do it from Raymie Painter who learned it from Ma Painter, so many years ago.

½ c. sugar
¾ tsp. salt
3 T. shortening
2 c. water
1½ T. dry yeast
2 eggs, beaten
5–6 c. bread flour

In large bowl, combine sugar, salt, and shortening. Add 1 cup hot water. Let sit until shortening is nearly melted. Add 1 cup water to cool mixture to 110–115°F. Sprinkle yeast over the liquid and let proof until bubbly.

Add eggs and 3 cups flour to the liquid. Beat well. Stir in remaining flour, 1 cup at a time, until soft dough forms. Do not add too much flour or rolls will not be light and fluffy.

Turn out onto a floured surface and knead for 5 to 8 minutes. Place in greased bowl; let rise until more than doubled. Punch down and let rise until doubled. Turn out onto a lightly floured surface; cut into portions. Cover and let rest for 15 minutes before shaping.

Shape and let rise until double. Bake at 400°F for 10 to 15 minutes. Cool on wire racks. Makes approximately 30 rolls.

Black Onion Rye Bread

I collected the recipe for this delicious, moist, oniony black rye in a trade with a professional baker.

1¼ c. medium rye flour
1 T. salt
1 T. shortening
3 c. high gluten or bread flour
¼ c. caramel color (molasses may be substituted, but the bread will not be as dark)
⅓ c. chopped dry onions
1 T. dry yeast
2 c. warm water (110–115°F)
Additional high gluten or bread flour as needed

In large bowl, combine first 7 ingredients in a large bowl. Stir in warm water. Add additional flour to make a soft dough. Turn out onto a floured surface; knead until smooth and elastic, about 5 to 10 minutes. Place dough in greased bowl, turning to grease the top. Cover and let rise until doubled, about 1 to 1½ hours. Punch down and turn out onto a floured surface. Cover; let rest for about 15 minutes. Cut dough in half; shape each half into a French-type loaf. Place shaped loaves on a greased cookie sheet. Cover; let rise until doubled.

Preheat oven to 375°F. Bake loaves on center shelf for 20 to 25 minutes or until loaves test done. Cool on wire racks. Makes 2 loaves.

Sourdough Starter

It's easy to start your own sourdough pot. Dried sourdough starters may be purchased at supermarkets or specialty stores, and by mail order. Some of these dried sourdoughs purport to be from starters begun over a century ago. By following this recipe, you can easily make your own.

1 c. warm water (110–115°F)
1 T. sugar
1½ tsp. dry yeast
1 c. flour

In medium bowl, combine water and sugar; stir until sugar is dissolved. Sprinkle dry yeast over water mixture; stir to dissolve yeast. Stir in flour to make a smooth paste. Cover loosely with a towel. Set in warm place (around 85°F) to sour. Stir a few times each day. After 3 to 4 days (longer if it is cooler), it should be ready to use or to store. Store in loosely covered (to allow the gases to escape) glass or plastic container in the refrigerator. Be sure to label it well. More than once a well-meaning baby-sitter or house guest has thrown away "a vile-smelling jar of something that was rotting in your fridge."

Occasionally sourdough can go bad. If it turns pink or orange and smells dreadfully foul, throw it out as there is no salvation for it. To guard against losing mine, I share it with my friends. On at least two occasions, I asked them to share a cup of their starter with me to replace mine that had gone bad.

Before using your starter, measure out 1 cup of starter in a ceramic or plastic bowl. Stir in 1 cup of warm water (110–115°F). Add 1½ cups of flour (bread flour is best for sourdough breads because of its higher gluten content); beat well. Cover loosely. Place in a warm place to ferment. Sourdough works best around 85°F. At that temperature it will be ready to use in about 12 to 24 hours. Since my kitchen at home isn't that warm, I usually start my sourdough at least 2 days before I plan to use it. The sourdough is ready to use when it has "settled down" and thinned out somewhat. Before using your sourdough, always, without fail, return 1 cup of starter to your starter pot, leaving about 1½ cups of sourdough for your recipe.

You can make sourdough ahead and keep in the refrigerator until needed. For example, you can start your sourdough early in the week, put your 1 cup of starter back, and store the resulting 1½ cups of sourdough for pancakes on Sunday in another container. Just bring the sourdough to room temperature before continuing with the recipe.

Sourdough Pancakes or Belgian Waffles

If I were to pick my favorite thing made from sourdough, it would have to be the ethereally light and crisp pancakes and waffles. One woman I know has fallen so much in love with sourdough waffles that she has bought two Belgian waffle irons and keeps close to a half-gallon of starter on hand to cook up stacks of waffles for her frequent house guests and family members who demand them nearly every Sunday morning.

For a breakfast extraordinaire, drop fresh or frozen wild blueberries or wild raspberries on top of the batter right after ladling onto the griddle or into the waffle iron, cook as usual, then top the results with real maple syrup.

The Sourdough Pot

✳ Sourdough has been around a long time. We know it was in use some 5,000 years ago in Egypt during the time of the pharaohs. It was a staple of early trappers and settlers as the American frontier moved west. The fresh yeast of the time didn't keep well, and a pot of easily replenished sourdough was a valuable possession.

In recent times, sourdough was closely associated with the Alaskan gold rush of 1898. Veteran miners acquired the name "sourdoughs" because nearly every one of them kept a pot of the stuff going to keep himself well supplied with breads, pancakes, and biscuits. They disdained baking powder, which they believed caused gastric distress when eaten on a regular basis.

Evidently, if the following story is to be believed, the use of baking powder may well affect the libido as well. It seems a "soiled dove" named Maud had wandered into an Alaskan mining camp hoping to mine a little gold herself by plying her trade. But business was so slow she had no choice but to move on. As the boat she had boarded was pulling away from shore, the miffed madam bid adieu to the camp's pitiful inhabitants. "Good-bye!" she sang out. "Good-bye, you bakin' powder eatin' sons-of-bitches!"

Sourdough has always been a part of the mystique of the far north. When we hear the name, we can almost hear the wind blowing high in the spruce trees amid the calls of loons echoing from bay to bay on a rocky-shored northern lake. Our mind imagines a trapper or miner nurturing his pot of sourdough in some warm nook in his rough-hewn log cabin and producing tantalizing baked goods from his wood cookstove. Sourdough will do that to you.

Sourdough starters will last indefinitely if properly fed and cared for, barring an errant spoor that will occasionally invade and destroy even the most meticulously kept starters. I have heard of starters that were well over a hundred years old, still going strong, being passed down from generation to generation. In those terms, mine, which has been going since 1973, is young indeed.

The recipe may be doubled, but be sure to use a very large vessel to start the sourdough lest it overflow. Be forewarned that spilled sourdough is not an easy thing to wipe up. And dried sourdough is even worse to remove, so be sure to rinse the bowls, pots, and utensils before the sourdough dries.

1½ c. sourdough
1 egg, beaten
¼ c. dry milk
¼ c. butter, melted
2 T. sugar
¾ tsp. salt
1 tsp. baking soda

Heat griddle or waffle iron. In large bowl, beat together sourdough, egg, dry milk, and butter. In small bowl, combine sugar, salt, and soda. When griddle is hot, sprinkle sugar mixture over the sourdough mixture. Fold together. Have your ladle at hand. Slowly at first and building in intensity, the batter will start climbing the sides of the bowl. As it approaches the top, ladle out your first pancake (3- to 4- inch size are best) or waffle (the Belgian type holds more butter and syrup!). This first one is a test for the cook. To appreciate what you have just accomplished, eat it plain or topped only with perhaps some butter. See if you don't agree that these pancakes and waffles are truly one of life's great pleasures. Serves 3–4.

▶ TIP: Like all sourdough goods, these freeze wonderfully. To use, just remove frozen pancakes or waffles from the freezer and put in the toaster to reheat.

Sourdough Biscuits

Biscuits were a staple of frontier life. In the old west they were often referred to as "pinch offs." The outfit cook would mix up a batch of biscuit dough and then "pinch off" chunks of dough, snuggling them into a warm cast-iron Dutch oven to bake in the coals of the morning fire. When not in use, the sourdough pot was stowed in the chuck wagon in a secure spot. Legend has it that on cold nights, the Cookie would put the pot under his blankets and sleep with it to keep it warm. A cook's reputation was often determined by the heft and loft of his biscuits.

2 c. flour (bread flour or all-purpose)
1 tsp. salt
½ tsp. baking soda
½ c. butter or shortening
1½ c. sourdough starter
½ c. buttermilk
Melted butter or bacon grease

In large bowl, combine flour, salt, and soda. Cut in butter or shortening with a pastry blender until mixture resembles corn meal. In medium bowl, stir together sourdough starter and buttermilk. Add to dry ingredients. Mix with a fork until a dough is formed. Turn out onto a floured surface. Knead 5 or 6 times. Roll out to ½ inch thickness. Cut with a biscuit cutter; place on a lightly greased cookie sheet. For soft-sided biscuits, place them with the sides touching. For crusty biscuits, place them about an inch apart. Brush with melted butter or bacon grease. Set in a warm place (85°F) for 30 minutes to rise. Preheat oven to 425°F. Bake for about 15 minutes until browned and done. Serve hot.

Trapper's Sourdough Bannock

What biscuits were to the west, bannock was to the north. Bannock was one of the three B's of old-time basic back-country provisions—bacon, bannock, and beans. It is nothing more than a large pan-fried biscuit. Here's how a trapper might make his.

1 c. flour
½ tsp. salt
1 T. sugar
¼ tsp. baking soda
1½ c. sourdough starter

In medium bowl, combine dry ingredients. In large bowl, measure out sourdough starter. Sprinkle dry mixture over sourdough. Mix together only enough to moisten dry ingredients. Turn out onto a well-floured surface; knead gently about 10 to 15 times to make a soft but still sticky dough.

Pat biscuit dough into a flat cake about ½ to ¾ inch thick on a floured surface. With your fingers, work a hole in the center of the dough much like a giant doughnut. This helps the bannock to cook more evenly and will make more of the marvelous crust. Warm a cast-iron skillet or other heavy-bottomed frying pan over the campfire or cookstove. Don't get it too hot! Grease the bottom and sides of the pan with some bacon grease or whatever oil or shortening is on hand. Place the bannock in the pan, patting it gently into place. Grease the top of the bannock and set the skillet in a warm place. Let rise for 1 hour.

Place the skillet over low coals and cook until bottom of the bannock is nicely browned. Be careful! There is a fine line between browned and burned. Now flip the bannock over and finish cooking. You can also prop the pan up in front of a low fire and bake until the top is brown and the bannock is done. Break off a steaming hunk and slather it with butter and some homemade wild berry jam if you have it. Always remember, roughing it is for those who just don't know any better.

Sourdough Bread or Rolls

*Although sourdough alone will cause bread to rise suffi-
ciently, the addition of yeast will accomplish this much
quicker. If you have a very warm kitchen (85°F) and lots
of time, the yeast may be omitted.*

 1½ c. sourdough starter
 2 tsp. dry yeast
 ¼ c. warm water (110–115°F)
 2 T. sugar
 1½ tsp. salt
 3 T. dry milk
 2 T. vegetable oil, melted butter or bacon grease
 1–2 c. bread flour
 3 T. butter, melted

In large bowl, measure out sourdough starter. In small
bowl, dissolve yeast in warm water. Stir yeast mixture
into sourdough. Mix in sugar, salt, dry milk, and vegetable oil. Slowly add flour to make a soft dough. Turn
out onto a floured surface; knead until smooth and
elastic, adding more flour if necessary. Shape dough
into a free-form loaf or form into rolls. Place on a well-
greased cookie sheet. Brush with melted butter; let rise
in a warm place until doubled in size. Bake the loaf at
375°F for about 35 to 45 minutes or the rolls at 425°F
until browned and done. Makes 1 loaf or about 12 rolls.

▶ TIP: It's easy to make this sourdough bread or rolls
on your next camping or canoe trip. Before you go you
will need to prepare the sourdough for traveling and
prepack the dry ingredients for the bread.

First, put a cup of sourdough into a large bowl and
work in enough flour to make a soft dough, similar to
a biscuit dough. Using floured hands, form the dough
into a ball. Bury the sourdough ball in your flour sack
and pack as usual.

Next, from the recipe above, combine the yeast,
sugar, salt, dry milk, and one cup of the flour. Place
these ingredients in a container with a tight lid or in a
sealable plastic bag. You will also need about two cups
of additional flour.

At camp reconstitute the sourdough by placing the
sourdough ball in a large nonreactive container such
as plastic or stainless steel. Add enough warm water
to reach the consistency of sourdough. If the amount
in the bowl looks sufficient for your recipe, cover it
loosely and let it work. If additional sourdough is needed,
mix in equal amounts of flour and warm water. A plastic
container with a lid works well if you have to transport
the working sourdough. A good idea is to mix the sourdough the night before and use it the next afternooon
or evening.

When the sourdough is ready, remove a cup of it,
mix in flour as before and return it to the flour sack.
From the remaining sourdough, remove 1½ cups and
place in a large bowl or cookpail. Stir in 4 cups of warm
water, 2 T. vegetable oil, and the prepacked yeast and
flour mixture. Add enough additional flour to make a
soft dough. Follow the kneading, shaping, and baking
directions in the recipe.

Flaky Sourdough Honey Whole Wheat Biscuits

Light and flaky with honey and whole wheat goodness and sourdough tang, these biscuits would have been considered politically correct in some Alaskan mining towns because, in addition to sourdough, this recipe uses yeast and baking powder.

1½ c. sourdough starter
1 T. honey
3 T. warm water (110–115°F)
1½ tsp. dry yeast
1½ tsp. salt
1½ tsp. baking powder
1 c. stone-ground whole wheat flour
½–1 c. all-purpose flour
6 T. shortening
1½ T. toasted wheat germ (optional)
6 T. butter, melted

In large mixing bowl, measure sourdough starter. In small bowl, combine honey and warm water. Stir in yeast. Add to sourdough starter; stir to combine. In another large bowl, combine salt, baking powder, whole wheat flour, and ½ cup all-purpose flour. Cut shortening into dry ingredients until it resembles coarse corn meal. Add dry ingredients to sourdough mixture, stirring well with a fork. Turn onto a well-floured surface; knead gently 6 to 8 times. Roll dough to about ½ inch thickness. Cut with a biscuit cutter. Dip tops in melted butter. Place in greased cake pan with the sides touching. Set in a warm place away from drafts. Let rise for about an hour. Bake at 400°F for 20 to 25 minutes or until golden brown. Makes about 18 biscuits.

Sourdough Wild Blueberry Lemon Bread

Tangy lemon and precious wild blueberries combined in a marvelous loaf!

½ c. shortening
1 c. sugar
2 eggs
1 c. sourdough starter
½ c. milk
1⅓ c. all-purpose flour
¾ tsp. baking soda
½ tsp. salt
1 c. wild blueberries, fresh or frozen
Grated peel of one lemon
¼ c. sugar
Juice of one lemon (about 2–3 T.)

Preheat oven to 350°F. In large bowl, cream shortening, sugar, and eggs. Stir in sourdough and milk. In medium bowl, mix flour, soda, salt, blueberries, and lemon peel. Add to sourdough mixture, stirring only long enough to combine dry ingredients with sourdough mixture. Pour into greased loaf pan. Bake for 1 hour or until the loaf tests done. The bread is done when a toothpick or wooden skewer comes out clean. Combine ¼ cup sugar and lemon juice. Pour over loaf when it comes from the oven. Cool in the pan for 5 minutes before turning out onto a cooling rack. Cool before slicing. Makes 1 loaf.

DESSERTS

DESSERTS

Northwoods activities produce a heavy craving for sweets and the quick energy and psychological lift they provide. Gunflint Lodge is happy to do its part in satisfying such urges with several sources of sweet temptations. For starters, complimentary homemade cookies are available, along with coffee, tea, and hot chocolate, for guests and visitors alike. Freshly baked desserts are a hallmark of dining at Gunflint Lodge.

Homemade and homestyle are the key words for desserts at Gunflint Lodge. For most of the year, a professional baker is employed to make desserts as well as to bake breads and breakfast pastries. An additional task is to produce an endless stream of cookies destined for the bottomless cookie jar at the front desk.

In place of an overflowing dessert cart, nightly dessert offerings consist of one or two different desserts. In the homestyle tradition are numerous varieties of bread puddings, from rhubarb, blueberry-maple, and lemon to a rich chocolate version served with a custard sauce, raspberry puree, and toasted hazelnuts. Cobblers and crisps are also popular, as are freshly baked pies and cakes.

◑ Maker's Mark
Chocolate Bread Pudding

A splash of my favorite bourbon, Maker's Mark, one of Kentucky's finest, and a hint of cinnamon give this rich chocolate pudding considerable élan. In the dining room we serve this warm topped with chopped, toasted hazelnuts in a pool of vanilla custard sauce (crème anglaise) swirled with raspberry coulis (frozen unsweetened raspberries thawed and pureed with sugar and Triple Sec to taste and then strained to remove the seeds).

½ c. heavy cream
¾ c. half-and-half
3 oz. semisweet chocolate chips
4 c. French bread cubes
½ c. sugar
¼ tsp. cinnamon
1 tsp. vanilla
1 T. Maker's Mark or other bourbon
1 large egg

Preheat oven to 350°F. Mix the cream and half-and-half together in a large saucepan. Heat until near boiling. Pour over the chocolate chips in a bowl and stir until all the chocolate is melted. Combine chocolate mixture with bread cubes.

Whisk together sugar, cinnamon, vanilla, bourbon, and egg. Add to chocolate and bread mixture and combine well. Pour into a two-quart baking dish and refrigerate for 15 to 30 minutes before baking. Bake, uncovered, until set and a toothpick comes out clean, about 30 to 40 minutes. Serve warm. Serves 4.

Hot Apple Pie and
Cinnamon Ice Cream Profiterole
with Grand Marnier Custard and
Toasted Hazelnuts

This recipe kind of evolved one night. There were some Grand Marnier custard and toasted hazelnuts left over from a previous dessert, and there were some Granny Smith apples in the cooler that needed to be used. This is the dessert that resulted, and it was such a big hit in the dining room it has been on our menus since.

Everything may be made a day or two ahead except, perhaps, the cream puffs, which are best used shortly after baking. However, even they can be made ahead and frozen to be later thawed and recrisped in a moderate oven for several minutes.

6 cream puffs (recipe follows)
1 recipe warm apple pie filling (recipe follows)
1 quart cinnamon or vanilla ice cream
1 recipe Grand Marnier Custard (recipe follows)
Toasted hazelnuts (recipe follows)

Cut the cream puffs in half. Place a scoop of ice cream inside each puff. Spoon the hot apple pie filling over the ice cream and replace the tops of the cream puffs. Spoon a few tablespoons of the custard sauce over each puff and sprinkle with the toasted hazelnuts.

Pâté au Choux (Cream Puff Paste)

1 c. water
4 T. butter cut into 4 pieces
1 c. flour
¼ tsp. salt
1½ tsp. sugar mixed with a pinch of nutmeg
3–4 eggs

Preheat oven to 475°F. Combine the water and butter and bring to a boil. Mix the flour with the salt and sugar mixture and add all at once to boiling water and butter. Stir with spoon until mixture comes together and cleans sides and bottom of pan. Scrape into a bowl and let cool for five minutes. Add the eggs one at a time and beat until each egg is incorporated before adding the next. At first the mixture will separate as each egg is added, but as you continue to beat, it will all combine into a paste again. When enough eggs have been added, the choux paste should slowly run off the spoon when raised. Add the fourth egg if necessary.

Drop 2-inch round mounds of pâté au choux onto a greased baking sheet. Bake in 475°F oven for 10 minutes. Reduce heat to 375°F and bake until brown and crisp. Poke holes in sides to let moisture out. Cool on racks. Makes about 24 large puffs.

Apple Pie Filling

5 c. apples, preferably Granny Smith,
    peeled, cored, and sliced
¾ c. sugar
1½ T. flour
½ tsp. ground cinnamon
¼ tsp. ground nutmeg
Pinch salt
1–2 T. water, as needed for proper consistency

Combine sugar, flour, cinnamon, nutmeg, and salt. Mix the sugar mixture with the apples in a heavy saucepan. Add a tablespoon of water and heat over medium-low heat until mixture comes to a boil and thickens, stirring occasionally. Let cool and refrigerate until needed. Makes about 2½ cups filling. Serve warm.

Grand Marnier Custard
(also excellent with fresh fruit, chocolate mousse, apple tarts and pies)

2 egg yolks
6 T. sugar
2 T. plus 1 tsp. water
1 T. Grand Marnier liqueur
¾ c. heavy cream, whipped until stiff

Beat the yolks slightly. Combine the sugar and the water in a heavy-bottomed saucepan over medium-high heat. Bring to a boil and cook to the soft ball stage —234–240°F. Pour the hot sugar syrup mixture over the egg yolks and beat continuously until cool. Add the Grand Marnier and let stand until cold. Fold in the whipped cream. Refrigerate until needed. Makes about 1 cup.

Toasted Hazelnuts

Toast hazelnuts in a 350°F oven for 10 to 15 minutes until the white parts are light brown. While hot place in a towel and rub to remove as much of the brown skin as possible. Let cool and chop.

Blueberry Maple Bread Pudding with Lemon Whipped Cream

This northwoods bread pudding may be served warm or cold. Blueberries and maple syrup are a natural together. When my staff and I were developing this recipe, there was considerable discussion as to whether the cream would curdle instead of whipping when the fresh lemon juice was added. Happily this did not occur.

½ c. whipping cream
¼ tsp. grated lemon peel
2 T. powdered sugar
1½ T. fresh lemon juice, or to taste
¼ c. heavy cream
¾ c. half-and-half
¼ c. pure maple syrup
½ tsp. vanilla
2 large eggs
4 c. French bread cubes
1 c. blueberries, fresh or frozen

In medium bowl at medium speed, beat whipping cream. As cream begins to thicken, add grated lemon peel and powdered sugar. Drizzle in the lemon juice and whip until stiff. Refrigerate.

In medium bowl, whisk together cream, half-and-half, maple syrup, vanilla, and eggs. In large bowl, pour cream mixture over bread cubes; mix well. Fold in blueberries. Pour into 2-quart baking dish. Refrigerate 15 to 30 minutes. Preheat oven to 350°F. Bake, uncovered, until set, about 30 to 40 minutes. Serve warm with lemon whipped cream. Serves 4–6.

Heartland Apple Pie

Although apple trees in the far north are as scarce as hair on a walleye's belly, apples from Minnesota's heartland find their way into the lodge larder every fall. Especially esteemed for making this pie are Minnesota-grown Haralson, but any good pie apple will suffice.

2½ c. sifted all-purpose flour
1 tsp. salt
1 c. chilled shortening
⅓ c. ice water
5 c. peeled, cored, and sliced apples
¾ c. sugar
1½ T. flour
½ tsp. ground cinnamon
¼ tsp. ground nutmeg
2 T. butter
2 T. cold milk
1–2 T. sugar

In medium bowl, cut sifted flour and salt with shortening until shortening is the size of a grain of rice. Add ice water. Combine with a fork until flour is moistened. Gather into a ball; cut ball in half. Place each half on a piece of plastic wrap; flatten into a disk about 3 inches in diameter. Refrigerate for 2 hours.

Remove crusts from refrigerator; let warm up for 15 minutes. Flour one pie crust disk; place on a floured surface. Roll out and place in the bottom of a 9-inch pie pan. Pile sliced apples in crust. In small bowl, combine sugar, flour, cinnamon, and nutmeg; sprinkle evenly over apples. Dot with butter. Roll out top crust; place over apples. Flute edges of crust and cut decorative slits. Brush with cold milk. Sprinkle with sugar.

Bake at 450°F for 10 minutes. Reduce heat to 350°F; bake for an additional 40 minutes or until crust is golden brown and filling is bubbling through slits. Place foil over the top if crust is browning too fast. Makes 1 9-inch pie.

▶ TIP: To measure sifted flour, scoop about 3 cups of flour into a sifter and sift onto a piece of wax paper. Spoon the sifted flour into a measuring cup to overflowing and level the top.

Lemon and Wild Blueberry Cheese Pie

The idea of using an entire quart of hard-earned, hand-picked wild blueberries to make just one pie has always seemed ludicrous to me, so I came up with this blueberry-sensible pie. To make this dessert for a crowd, double everything and use a 9-by-13-inch pan.

1 c. all-purpose flour
2 T. powdered sugar
½ c. butter or margarine
3 T. cornstarch
1 c. plus 1 T. sugar
Dash salt
1½ c. hot water
3 T. fresh lemon juice
Rind of one lemon
3 egg yolks, beaten
2 T. butter (optional)
¼ c. wild blueberries, fresh or frozen
3 T. sugar
½ tsp. fresh lemon juice
8 oz. cream cheese
Cream as needed
3 T. sugar
1 T. fresh lemon juice
½ c. whipping cream
2 T. powdered sugar, or to taste
¼ tsp. vanilla extract

In medium mixing bowl, sift flour and powdered sugar together. With pastry blender, cut in butter until mixture resembles corn meal. Chill 30 minutes. Turn into 9-inch tart pan or pie pan; press firmly onto bottom and sides. Bake at 425°F for 10 to 12 minutes. Cool on cake rack.

In medium saucepan, combine cornstarch, sugar, and salt. Whisk in hot water, lemon juice, lemon rind, and egg yolks. Cook over medium heat, stirring, until thickened. Remove from heat; stir in optional butter. Cool while making blueberry cream cheese layer.

In small bowl, crush blueberries with a fork. Scrape crushed blueberries into small saucepan. Add sugar and lemon juice. Bring to boil over medium heat; cook for 1 minute, stirring constantly. Remove from heat and cool.

In medium bowl, beat cream cheese with a mixer, adding just enough cream to make a light fluffy consistency. Add sugar and lemon juice to taste. Stir in cooled blueberry mixture. Spread in bottom of tart crust. Top with cooled lemon filling.

In medium bowl, whip cream with powdered sugar and vanilla until stiff. Spread over lemon filling. Sprinkle with a few fresh or thawed frozen wild blueberries. Hold in refrigerator until served. Makes 1 9-inch pie.

Swedish Kringle

Lemon and almond are the two main flavors in this pastry and they work wonderfully well together. A luscious lemon filling is nestled between a flaky pie crust on the bottom and an almond-scented cream puff top that is glazed with an almond-flavored frosting. Although this dessert can be made ahead and refrigerated, it is best eaten soon after assembling.

Choux Paste

1 c. water
½ c. butter
1 c. flour
3–4 eggs
1 teaspoon almond extract

In medium saucepan over high heat, combine water and butter; bring to a boil. Add all flour; stir until incorporated. The dough will come together in a smooth clump that leaves the sides of the pan. Remove from heat; let cool for 5 minutes. Add eggs one at a time, beating until smooth after each addition. Beat in almond extract. Let cool.

Butter Pastry

½ c. butter
1½ c. flour
Pinch of salt
4–6 T. cold water

Preheat oven to 400°F. In medium bowl, cut butter into flour and salt until mixture resembles coarse corn meal. Stir in cold water until mixture is moist enough to be shaped into a ball with your hands.

Cut butter pastry in half; press or roll out to form two 10–12-inch circles on a large flat cookie sheet.

Pile and spread choux paste on each pie crust. Bake at 400°F for 10 minutes. Reduce heat to 350°F. Continue baking for 40 to 45 minutes. Remove from oven when browned and puffed. Immediately cut around the edge of puffed top. Carefully remove top to a rack to cool.

Lemon Filling

¾ c. sugar
2 T. cornstarch
6–7 T. fresh lemon juice to taste (2–3 lemons)
1½ c. hot water
2 egg yolks, slightly beaten

While crust is baking, prepare lemon filling. In medium saucepan, combine sugar and cornstarch. Stir in lemon juice, hot water, and egg yolks. Over medium heat cook, stirring constantly, until thickened. Cook for 1 minute longer, stirring constantly. Remove from heat. Let filling cool for 15 minutes, stirring occasionally. Spread half of filling over each bottom crust. Replace the tops.

Glaze

1 c. powdered sugar
2 T. melted butter or 2 T. light cream
½ tsp. almond extract

In medium bowl, combine powdered sugar, melted butter (or cream), and almond extract; stir until smooth. Frost tops of the kringle immediately with the glaze. Makes 2 10–12-inch round kringles (about 12–16 servings).

Gunflint Blueberry Pie

In the summer after picking wild blueberries, we freeze them in 5-cup portions to be used throughout the winter for pies.

¼ c. cornstarch
¼ c. cold water
5 c. fresh or frozen blueberries
1 c. sugar
½ tsp. salt
¾ c. hot water
1 T. lemon juice
1 uncooked double pie crust
Milk as needed

Preheat oven to 425°F. In small bowl, combine cornstarch and water. In medium saucepan, combine ½ cup blueberries, sugar, salt, hot water, and cornstarch mixture; simmer, stirring constantly and crushing blueberries with spoon until thickened. Add lemon juice. Remove from heat.

In medium bowl, put remaining blueberries. Pour hot sauce over blueberries; combine. In a 9-inch pie pan, place lower half of pie crust. Pour in blueberry mixture. Top with pie crust. Brush with milk. Bake at 425°F for 30 minutes. Reduce heat to 325°F. Bake an additional 10 to 20 minutes or until nicely browned.

Gunflint Cookies

All summer long we send these cookies out with canoers. When the trips are over, everyone wants the recipe. So here it is. It's a huge recipe but the cookies go fast.

1½ c. margarine
4 c. brown sugar
4 eggs
¾ c. milk
4 tsp. vanilla
6 c. flour
2 tsp. baking soda
1 tsp. salt
10 c. granola
5 c. carob chips (substitute chocolate chips)
5 c. raisins
5 c. peanuts

Preheat oven to 350°F. In large bowl, cream margarine and brown sugar until light and fluffy. Blend in eggs, milk, and vanilla. Add flour, baking soda, and salt. Stir in granola, carob chips, raisins, and peanuts. Using an ice cream scoop, drop portions on a greased cookie sheet. Bake for 8 to 10 minutes. Baking time may vary according to the size of cookies. Allow to cool on cookie sheet before removing. Makes approximately 4 dozen cookies.

Rhubarb Bread Pudding with Strawberry Whipped Cream

Bread puddings are popular at Gunflint Lodge. Not only are they homey and satisfying, they lend themselves to seemingly endless variations. The following bread pudding is a perfect springtime dessert, for it combines two of the garden's early producers—strawberries and rhubarb. Enjoy this on a soft spring evening on the patio or porch while the peepers and crickets play in the background.

Bread Pudding

3 c. cut-up rhubarb
½ c. sugar
3 T. Triple Sec or other orange liqueur,
    or 1 to 2 T. water
2 eggs, beaten
¼ c. cream
⅔ c. half-and-half
½ tsp. vanilla
4 c. cubed French or Italian-style bread

In heavy-bottomed saucepan set over medium heat, combine rhubarb, sugar, and Triple Sec. Bring to a boil. Reduce heat; simmer until rhubarb is very soft. Taste and add additional sugar to taste. Chill before using.

In large bowl, beat eggs, cream, half-and-half, and vanilla. Add bread cubes and chilled rhubarb sauce; fold together until thoroughly mixed. Pour into 8-inch pan or other similar-sized baking dish. Refrigerate for about 30 minutes before baking.

Preheat oven to 350°F. Bake bread pudding uncovered until set and a toothpick comes out clean, about 30 to 40 minutes.

Strawberry Whipped Cream

½ pt. fresh ripe strawberries, hulled and halved
4–6 T. sugar
¾ c. whipping cream
Drops of lemon juice

Put strawberries and sugar in bowl of food processor fitted with a steel knife. Pulse to finely chop strawberries. Set aside to macerate while whipping cream. In chilled bowl with chilled beaters, whip cream to soft peaks. Add strawberries and whip until stiff.

Serve bread pudding warm and generously topped with strawberry whipped cream. Serves 4–6.

Homemade Vanilla Ice Cream with Ancho Maple Caramel Sauce

This dessert created a sensation at one of our fall wine-maker dinners. Most folks (including a majority of the kitchen staff) were shocked when they heard that chili peppers were an ingredient in the dessert. They were even more shocked to discover that it tasted delicious. The flavor of the anchos blends perfectly with the maple and adds just a touch of heat to the sauce, creating a nice contrast to the rich creamy ice cream.

Homemade Vanilla Ice Cream

2 c. whole milk (do not use skim or 2%)
¾ c. sugar
4 egg yolks, lightly beaten
1 c. whipping cream
1 T. vanilla

In heavy-bottomed saucepan set over medium heat, bring milk to a near boil. In top of a double boiler, put sugar and egg yolks and whisk to combine. Slowly whisk in hot milk. Place top of double boiler in bottom pan containing hot water; set over medium heat. With a wooden spoon, stir and cook mixture until it thickens and coats the spoon. Immediately strain into a large bowl. Stir in cream and vanilla. Chill. Freeze in ice cream maker according to manufacturer's instructions. Makes about 1 quart.

Ancho Chili Puree

3 dried ancho chilies
Very hot water to cover

In medium saucepan, bring water to a near boil. Place ancho chilies in a bowl; pour enough hot water over to just cover chilies. Use lid or small plate to keep chilies submerged. Let chilies rehydrate for 20 minutes. Remove chilies from water. Remove stems and seeds. Puree in a blender (a blender works better than a food processor for this). Add some of the soaking water, if not too bitter; otherwise use plain water as needed to achieve a thick puree. Leftover puree may be stored in the refrigerator for several days or frozen for up to 6 months. Makes about ½ cup puree depending on size of the chilies.

Ancho Maple Caramel Sauce

2 c. heavy cream
¾ c. sugar
½ c. pure maple syrup
¼ tsp. maple flavoring
Ancho chili puree to taste

In heavy-bottomed medium saucepan, combine cream, sugar, and syrup. Stir over medium heat until sugar dissolves. Increase heat; bring to a boil. Reduce heat to medium low; simmer sauce until caramel-colored and reduced to 1¾ cups, whisking occasionally, about 35 minutes. Mix in maple flavoring. Add ancho chili puree to taste. Serve warm over homemade ice cream.

◖ Opal's Rhubarb Custard Pie

The late Opal Enzenauer, with her husband, Don, ran Voyageur Canoe Outfitters on the Seagull River for many years. She wrote this recipe out for me on the back of one of their price lists. I'm not sure when I got this recipe, but it must date back to the late 1970s. The cost of renting a canoe per day ($7) is about half of what it is today. And fishing guides, who today charge around $120 per day, were offered a mere $35 per day, up an entire $10 from the season before!

Anyway, this recipe from Opal is sure to become one of your favorites. I have added apple and peach variations that I have developed over the years. And, best of all, the crust is a snap to make!

Crust

2 c. sifted all-purpose flour
2 tsp. sugar
1¼ tsp. salt
⅔ c. vegetable oil
3 T. milk

Preheat oven to 450°F. In a sifter, combine flour, sugar, and salt and sift into an 8-inch or 9-inch pie tin. In small bowl, beat together oil and milk with a fork. Pour over flour mixture. Combine with the fork until all flour mixture is moistened. Remove about one-third for the top of the pie.

With your fingers, press remaining crust mixture as evenly as you can over the bottom and sides of the pie tin. Flute the edges with your fingers if desired. Set aside while making filling.

Rhubarb Custard

1½ c. sugar
3 T. flour
½ tsp. ground nutmeg
1 T. butter, cut into bits
2 eggs
3 c. chopped rhubarb

In medium bowl, mix together sugar, flour, nutmeg, and butter. Add eggs; beat until smooth. Stir in rhubarb. Scrape into prepared pie crust. Crumble reserved crust mixture over top of the filling.

Bake pie on middle shelf of 450°F oven for 10 minutes. Reduce heat to 350°F; bake until filling thickens and bubbles around the edges, about 30 more minutes.

Here are a couple of variations you can try with this pie.

Apple Custard Variation

⅔–¾ c. sugar, depending on sweetness of apples
4 T. flour
½ tsp. ground nutmeg
¼ tsp. ground cinnamon
1½ T. butter, cut into bits
2 eggs
3 c. peeled, cored, and sliced apples

Follow directions for rhubarb custard pie, substituting the above ingredients and amounts.

Peach Custard Variation

Follow directions for rhubarb custard pie, reducing sugar to ⅔ c. and substituting 3 c. of fresh peaches, peeled, pitted, and sliced.

THE
GUNFLINT
PANTRY

THE GUNFLINT PANTRY

My grandmother's pantry always fascinated me. It was a small room off the kitchen, a bit larger than a good-sized closet. The walls were lined with shelves and bins. On the shelves were rows of store-bought canned goods intermingled with jars holding my grandmother's homemade jams and pickles—a colorful melange of summery red strawberry preserves, whole tomatoes, translucent watermelon pickles, and the muted green of tiny whole cucumbers immersed in the brine with great sprigs of her garden dill and slivers of pale garlic. Beneath the heavily laden shelves were bins holding flour, sugar, cereals, and the like. As a boy it seemed to me that the promise of great eating lay within this room.

In the Gunflint Pantry you will find additional recipes and procedures for adding great flavor to your cooking. Here you will learn how to make your own Cajun seasoning and our all-purpose Gunflint Seasoned Salt. Detailed directions will guide you through the making of your own flavorful meat, poultry, and fish stocks, and will tell you how to reduce and concentrate them to add rich flavor to your sauces. Best of all these stock concentrates are virtually fat-free.

Here, also, you will learn how to make classic hollandaise and beurre blanc sauces, plus hints on how to fix them when they fail to hold together. No need to feel guilty about using either of these rich and delicious buttery sauces. Just a tablespoon or two adds sublime flavor to the foods you serve them with. At home I think of hollandaise and beurre blanc as "special occasion" sauces used primarily when entertaining. And after all, isn't an occasional splurge chicken soup for the soul?

Seasonings

Cajun Seasoning

2 T. dried basil

2 T. garlic powder

2 T. gumbo filé

2 T. dry mustard

2 T. onion powder

2 T. dried oregano

½ c. paprika

¼ c. ground black pepper

2 T. cayenne pepper

2 T. ground white pepper

1 c. kosher salt

2 T. dried thyme

In medium bowl, combine all ingredients and mix well. Makes about 3 cups.

Gunflint Seasoned Salt

Use this all-purpose seasoning as we do at the lodge to add tantalizing flavor to cuts of beef, pork, poultry, and game.

1 tsp. Cajun seasoning

1½ tsp. celery salt

2½ tsp. granulated garlic

1½ tsp. onion powder

1½ tsp. lemon pepper

½ c. kosher salt

In small bowl, combine all ingredients thoroughly. Makes about three-fourths of a cup.

The Stock Pot

The secret to many fabulous sauces and great soups is fine stock. In many professional kitchens, because of economy and labor costs, traditional stocks have been completely or partially replaced by commercial bases, those pastes or powders that contain much salt and the essence of the stock it emulates.

Stock is created by simmering bones, water, aromatic vegetables, and seasonings together. If the bones are browned first, the stock will be brown. If they are not, it is referred to as white stock. Browning the bones first also gives the stock a richer, more robust flavor. No salt is added since the resulting stock is often reduced to intensify flavors when used in various sauces.

The type of stock determines the length of time the stock simmers. Beef and game stocks require long, slow cooking to extract all the flavor from the bones and scraps. They should be simmered from 24 to 48 hours. Chicken and other poultry stocks require less time to develop full flavor, about 4 to 5 hours. Fish stocks require as little as 30 minutes.

Once the stocks have finished cooking, they need to be strained and degreased. The stock is first strained through a fairly large sieve to remove the bones and vegetables, then through a very fine sieve to remove the impurities. Degreasing is easiest if the stock is refrigerated until the fat congeals on the surface. Then it can be easily removed.

Once the stock is at this point, it may be used as is or reduced by boiling to reach the flavor and consistency desired. If the stock is reduced by half, or until dark and syrupy, it becomes "demi-glacé" or half-glaze. Demi-glacé is the basis of many sauces. The stock may be still further reduced to a very concentrated essence called "glacé de viande" or meat glaze. Glacé de viande is too concentrated to use as a sauce. Instead, it is used to add a rich flavor to other sauces.

The finest demi-glacé and glacé de viande are made with brown veal stock. Veal bones are quite expensive. Many chefs use a combination of veal and beef bones, and in a pinch a combination of beef and poultry bones will produce a flavorful and gelatinous stock.

Not many kitchens today rely exclusively on the stockpot for soups and sauces. At Gunflint Lodge brown chicken stock is made weekly and a brown veal and beef bone stock is made as needed for making demi-glacé and glacé de viande.

Stocks, either at full strength or reduced, keep for extended periods in the freezer. For the serious home cook, the making of a stockpot full of stock once or twice a year for the purpose of making glacé de viande or demi-glacé is sufficient for sauce-making needs.

Brown Stock

The following stock can be made with veal bones, beef and veal bones, beef and poultry bones, or all poultry bones. The resulting stocks from any of the combinations may be reduced to make either demi-glacé or glacé de viande. Game bones and trim may be used alone or in combination with veal, beef, or poultry bones. In fact, lacking veal bones, I always combine beef or game bones with poultry bones (use about 20 percent poultry to 80 percent beef or game bones) to add more gelatin to the stock. To make this stock, you will need at least a 20-quart stockpot (available through mail order and at restaurant supply houses). If using all poultry bones, cut total simmering time to 4 to 6 hours. To make a white stock, omit the oven browning of the bones and the vegetables.

> 10 lb. veal, beef, game, or poultry bones, or a combination
> 2–3 large onions, cut into large chunks (about 1½ lb.)
> 2–3 carrots, cut into 1-in. pieces (about ¾ lb.)
> 6 ribs celery, cut into 1-in. pieces (about 1–1¼ lb.)
> 1 whole head of garlic, cut in half cross-wise
> 1 bunch fresh parsley
> 5 bay leaves
> 2 T. dried thyme
> 1 T. whole black peppercorns
> 1 (10¼-oz.) can of tomato puree or crushed canned or fresh tomatoes to equal

Preheat oven to 450°F. In large roasting pan, place bones in a single layer. Roast until well browned (about 1 to 1½ hours), stirring every 30 minutes. Remove bones to stockpot. Cover bones with cold water to within 3 inches of top of pot. Bring to a boil on stove. Reduce heat to a simmer. Cook for 1 hour, skimming any fat or other impurities that come to the surface.

Meanwhile, add onions and carrots to the roasting pan; continue roasting, stirring occasionally, until browned and caramelized. Remove with slotted spoon; add to simmering stock. Although the recipe calls for using whole vegetables, vegetable trim such as carrot peels and root ends of celery may be accumulated. They work just as well and are more economical.

Pour off all fat from roasting pan. Deglaze with water, scraping up all the crusty brown bits to dissolve them. Add this to stockpot along with remaining ingredients. Cook at the barest simmer for 10 to 12 hours. The stock should not boil or it will be cloudy. The top of the stock should shimmer with an occasional bubble breaking the surface. The French refer to this as "smiling."

The simmering may be interrupted and resumed as long as the stock is cooled down quickly and refrigerated. This is impractical for the home cook who lacks the resources to quickly cool a large stockpot, not to mention a large enough place to refrigerate it. Best to cook it slowly overnight and finish in the morning.

Strain the stock through a colander to remove the bones and vegetables. Skim off as much fat as possible. Strain though a fine sieve lined with several layers of cheesecloth. Refrigerate the stock until completely cold.

Remove the remaining fat from the surface of the chilled stock. Measure the stock and, if necessary, reduce in a large pan set over high heat to 5 quarts. The stock is now ready to use or freeze.

Demi-Glacé

If you have used all veal bones for your stock, just reduce the stock by half to make demi-glacé. Skim off any impurities, which will appear on the surface as a lighter-colored scum. When reduced, the remaining stock is slightly syrupy and quite gelatinous. Let cool. It will be very firm. To freeze, scoop it out in 1-cup chunks; wrap chunks in plastic wrap. Stocks made with bones other than veal, or those made with combinations of bones, might have to be reduced by more than half to achieve similar results.

Glacé de Viande

Glacé de viande or meat glaze may be made with the above stock or can be made from the second cooking of the bones and vegetables. To use the bones and vegetables, return them to the stockpot; refill with cold water. Simmer as before for 10 to 12 hours and skim and strain as before.

To make the glacé, reduce the skimmed strained stock until quite thick. Again skim as needed to remove any impurities. When the stock has reduced sufficiently, the surface will be covered with large bubbles. The glaze will be dark brown in color and very sticky. Transfer the glaze to smaller and smaller pans as it reduces to avoid scorching.

With rubber spatula, scrape glaze into small cake pan or shallow casserole. Refrigerate until set, then cut into cubes. The cubes will keep for quite some time in the refrigerator if stored uncovered to keep them from molding. They may also be frozen and stored almost indefinitely.

In a similar fashion, "glacé de volaille" (chicken glaze) or "glacé de poisson" (fish glaze) may be made from those respective stocks.

White Wine Fish Stock

This recipe makes enough stock for chowder or for poaching fish. Doubling it makes a stock suitable for a rich sauce. Reserve the heads and bones from the fish you catch, discarding the skin and gills, to use for making this stock.

1–2 lb. (about 4–8 c.) fish heads and bones
½ c. finely chopped onion
⅔ c. dry white vermouth or dry white wine
3½ to 4 c. cold water to cover
2 tsp. fresh lemon juice
½ tsp. dried thyme
6 whole black peppercorns
2 parsley stems

In large saucepan, combine fish heads and bones, onion, and vermouth or wine. Boil over high heat until wine is reduced by half. Add enough cold water to cover bones by ½ inch. Add remaining ingredients; simmer uncovered for 30 minutes. Strain through a very fine sieve or through washed cheesecloth. Refrigerate or freeze until ready to use. Makes about 3–4 cups.

Quick Fish Stock

Here is a quick fish stock that is quite good. Use it in any recipe that calls for fish stock.

1½ c. bottled clam juice
1 c. water
⅔ c. dry white vermouth or dry white wine
½ c. finely chopped onions
3 whole black peppercorns
¼ tsp. dried thyme, crumbled

In medium saucepan, combine all ingredients. Bring to a boil. Reduce heat; simmer for 30 minutes. Strain the stock. Refrigerate or freeze until ready to use. Makes about 3 cups.

Sauces

Proper Consistency of Sauces

Throughout this cookbook such instructions as "reduce to the consistency of heavy cream" and "reduce to a saucelike consistency" are frequently used. The consistency of heavy cream varies according to the amount of butterfat. The heavy cream that you buy in the grocery store is considerably thinner than the approximately 40 percent butterfat cream we use in the lodge kitchen. And what seems a proper "saucelike consistency" to one person may be too thin or too thick for others. So what does constitute the proper consistency of a sauce?

Generally speaking, most sauces, including gravies, should be thick enough to coat a spoon, which means they will be thick enough to coat the food lightly. Overthickening is rarely a problem with reduction sauces. Use water or a light stock to thin out an overthickened sauce.

Guidelines to Making Hollandaise and Béarnaise Sauces

Make sure all of your equipment is perfectly clean. The eggs and the temperature of a finished hollandaise are ideal for bacterial growth. For the same reason, use the sauce shortly after completing. Both hollandaise and béarnaise sauces may be held for a short period either in a bowl set over warm water or in a warm thermos bottle.

Although experienced chefs are able to heat the yolks over direct heat, the hot water method is safer, although slower. As your confidence increases, you will be able to use a hotter heat source and make the sauce more quickly.

A round-bottomed stainless-steel bowl is best for beating the yolks evenly. Also, stainless steel is non-reactive and will not discolor or give your sauce an off-flavor.

Make sure the butter is not too hot or you may scramble the yolks. Also it is of utmost importance that the butter be added very s-l-o-w-l-y at first. Finally, remember that, unless the eggs have been overcooked, a broken hollandaise is usually fixable.

Hollandaise Sauce

Hollandaise sauce is an emulsion sauce made with egg yolks, butter, lemon juice, and seasonings. It is best known as the sauce for Eggs Benedict.

2 egg yolks
2 tsp. cold water
⅛ tsp. cayenne pepper
2 sticks of butter, melted
2–3 tsp. fresh lemon juice to taste
Kosher salt to taste

In small, very clean stainless-steel bowl, combine egg yolks, water, and cayenne pepper. Beat well with a whisk. Set bowl containing yolks over barely simmering water. Whisk constantly for 5 to 10 minutes, watching yolks carefully. The yolks are ready when they've gotten hot and thickened a little. The yolks will be frothy and will have nearly doubled in volume. If the yolks get too hot, they will scramble. If this happens, you must start over as there is no way to fix this.

Remove bowl from the heat. Whisk in butter, drop by drop at first until nearly half of it has been incorporated. Butter may then be added in a thin stream until all has been added. Be careful to add only butterfat and not the milky liquid below. Whisk in lemon juice. If too thick, use some of the liquid from the melted butter, which is quite salty, to thin the hollandaise. Taste and season to taste with salt. Makes about ¾ cup.

Fixing a Broken Hollandaise

✳ Some years ago I took an evening cooking class at the local vo-tech school. The chef-instructor was demonstrating, with the help of a student, how to make a hollandaise sauce. The student was drizzling in the melted butter, added it a little too fast at the start, and the sauce broke (separated). The chef-instructor poured the broken sauce into the garbage and thus missed the opportunity to demonstrate how to fix it.

Knowing how to fix a sauce that has separated gives us added confidence. I have heard of many ways to repair a failed hollandaise. This is the method that works for me.

Pour the broken hollandaise into a glass measuring cup or a small bowl. Wash and dry the stainless-steel bowl and place a teaspoon of Dijon mustard in the bottom. Using a spoon or small ladle, whisk in the broken sauce drop by drop until an emulsion is reestablished; then very, very slowly add the remaining broken sauce. If all this fails, throw the sauce out, chalk it up to experience, and begin again from the beginning.

Béarnaise Sauce

Among the many variations of hollandaise, the most popular is béarnaise sauce, in which the lemon juice is replaced with a tangy shallot-and-tarragon-flavored reduction of white wine and vinegar.

1 recipe hollandaise sauce, lemon juice omitted
1–3 tsp. béarnaise reduction to taste
1 tsp. chopped fresh parsley
Pinch of freshly ground black pepper

In medium bowl, combine all ingredients; whisk together. Makes about ¾ cup.

Béarnaise Reduction

✱ Here is a restaurant trick for making béarnaise. A make-ahead reduction is prepared and added to a hollandaise sauce made without the lemon juice. The reduction takes the place of the lemon juice. The following béarnaise reduction will keep indefinitely in your refrigerator.

6 large shallots, finely chopped
1 T. dried tarragon
3 oz. dry white wine
3 oz. white wine vinegar
1 pinch dry thyme
1½ bay leaves
Pinch of freshly ground black pepper

In nonreactive saucepan over high heat, combine all ingredients. Reduce until only a tablespoon or two of liquid remains. Cool. Remove bay leaves. Store in tightly covered glass container in the refrigerator.

Beurre Blanc

Beurre blanc is sometimes referred to as a hollandaise without egg yolks. Like hollandaise, beurre blanc is an emulsion made with butter (unsalted is preferred since it contains less water than salted). Instead of egg yolks an acidic reduction is used to bind the emulsion together, usually a combination of white wine or vermouth and vinegar, such as champagne or white wine. White wine or vermouth alone may be used to make a beurre blanc if they are acidic enough.

Don't believe what most cookbooks and cooking publications tell you about making a beurre blanc. Contrary to what they say, it is not a difficult sauce to make; it can be made several hours ahead and held until you are ready to use it; and it can be resurrected if broken.

There are three steps to making a beurre blanc:
1. Making the acid reduction
2. Whisking in the butter
3. Adding the final seasoning or flavoring

I usually add a fourth step, which came about when a colleague shared his secret with me for making the light and airy beurre blancs for which he was well known. All he did was to pour the finished sauce into a blender and give it a couple of short bursts to fluff it up. I now use a hand-held blender to accomplish the same thing.

Beurre blancs can be held for several hours in a preheated thermos bottle. This means that you can make the sauce long before dinner and not have to think about it until you are ready to serve.

What if it breaks? A broken or separated beurre blanc is one that is no longer emulsified. Usually this is caused by trying to keep the sauce too hot. Most sources will tell you it can't be fixed. It can. Here's what to do. Place 2 tablespoons of heavy cream in a bowl. Put the broken beurre blanc in a skillet or saucepan and bring to a boil. Remove from heat and drizzle the hot beurre blanc slowly, drop by drop, into the cream while whisking constantly. After about half of the broken sauce has been whisked in and has been reemulsified, you can add the remaining sauce in a thin stream while continuing to whisk. Pour the beurre blanc into a clean preheated thermos to store or use immediately.

Basic Beurre Blanc

¼ c. dry white wine
¼ c. white wine or champagne vinegar
1 T. finely chopped shallots
1 c. (2 sticks) unsalted butter, cut into 16 pieces
Salt and white pepper to taste

In an 8- to 10-inch nonaluminum skillet, combine white wine, vinegar, and shallots. Over high heat bring to a boil; reduce until approximately 3 tablespoons remain, about 5 minutes. Add butter all at once; whisk briskly so that the butter melts evenly. When all the butter except two or three small pieces has been incorporated into the sauce, quickly pour the contents of the pan through a fine sieve into a bowl. Whisk until smooth. Season to taste with salt and pepper. At this point a hand-held blender or a regular blender may be used to fluff up and thicken the beurre blanc. Use immediately or store in a preheated thermos bottle. Makes about 2 cups.

INDEX

Cucumber sauce, 104
Custard
    bread, 107, 117–118
    Grand Marnier, 135
    pie, 142
    See also Pudding

Deglazing sauce, 88–91
Demi-glacé, 147, 149
Desserts, 133–142.
    See also specific desserts
Duck
    breasts, pan roasted, 86
    stuffing, herb, 118

Eggs
    as appetizer, 29
    Chimay, 29
    hard-boiled, 29
    oeufs mayonnaise, 29

Fish and seafood, 11–14, 31–35,
    51–54, 74–79, 95–99
    baking, 98
    breadings and batters, 7, 100–102
    broiling, 99
    cakes, 76
    chowder, 10
    deep frying, 98
    fish cakes, 76
    freezing, 96
    grilling, 99
    pan sautéing, 98
    poaching, 99
    preparing and cooking, 95–99
    sauces, 31–32, 103–104
    sautéing, 98
    seafood stuffing, 51
    shore lunches, 101
    stock, 75, 149
    See also specific fish or seafood

Florentine, 11
Freezing
    fish, 96
    mousseline, 83
    pancakes, 127
    seafood stuffing, 51
    stock, 147
    venison, 60
    waffles, 127

Game, 60–62, 85–86
    and brown stock, 147–148
    chops and steaks, campfire
        grilled, 61
    See also specific game
Garlic
    butter, 40–41, 52–54
    potatoes, mashed, 114
    roasted, 38, 114
    walleye, 74
Garnishes
    leeks, 72
    pimiento, for color, 48
    for walleye, 79
Glacé de viande, 41, 86, 89, 91, 147, 149
Glaze
    almond, 138
    ancho chili maple, 53, 110
    carrots, 110
    chardonnay, over leek pudding,
        15–16
    for chicken, 15–16
    for fish, 53
    frosting for pastries, 138
    mustard, over pork, 38, 84
Gravy
    lumps, preventing, 56
    portabella, 55–56
    See also Sauce
Grilling. *See also* Smoker cooking;
    specific foods

Grouse, roast/roasted, 62
Gunflint Lodge, xiii–xxi
    berrying in spring, 25–27
    fall season, 45–47
    fishing, 5–6
    opening in spring, 3–6
    pantry, 145
    winter season, 65–68
Gunflint seasoned salt, 18, 19, 40, 59,
    146

Hazelnuts, toasted, 134–135
Herbs
    breading, 102
    increasing flavor of, 16
    in stuffing, 118
    using, 16
    See also Seasonings;
        specific herbs
Hollandaise sauce, 150, 151
    fixing, 151
Honey sauce, Madeira, 8–9
Horseradish
    potatoes, mashed, 115
    sauces, 18, 59, 62, 104

Ice cream
    cinnamon, 134–135
    vanilla, 141

Juniper berries, cream sauce, 61

Kerfoot, Justine, xiii–xxi, *xv*, *xviii*,
    xx, xxiii
Kerfoot, Sharon, *xx*
Kringle, 138

Lake trout. *See* Trout, lake
Leeks
    as garnish, 72
    pudding, 15–16

Ron Berg taught English for twenty-three years at Albany Junior High School in Albany, Minnesota. A leave of absence he took in 1990 became permanent when he began working at Gunflint Lodge.

Shortly after purchasing a cabin on Seagull Lake in 1973 Ron began working for Voyageur Canoe Outfitters as a fishing guide. He worked for seventeen summers guiding on Saganaga Lake at the end of the Gunflint Trail, a job he gave up (along with his teaching position) to take the job of executive chef at the Gunflint Lodge.

Ron has worked part-time in the food service business since his college days in St. Cloud. His first paid job as a cook was at his fraternity house.

While teaching in Albany, Ron opened and ran a restaurant in a college bar; spent two summers cooking at Grand View Lodge on Gull Lake near Brainerd, Minnesota; co-managed the food service at Powder Ridge, a local ski area; and finally ended up at the Redwood Inn in Rice, Minnesota, in 1986. This was the place where everything came together and where he spent a magical four years.

Sue Kerfoot worked in a large bank in downtown Chicago for about a year after college. She and Bruce Kerfoot were married in 1968 and she moved to the northwoods. Prior to marrying Bruce Sue knew little about cooking and nothing about running a restaurant. The past twenty-eight years have been a practical seminar in restaurant management. First she had to learn to cook for two people. The next step was learning to order food for the lodge kitchen. Over the years Sue learned every cooking position in the kitchen: baker, breakfast/lunch cook, cook's helper, and dinner cook. Most of the time she did these jobs only when the lodge was short-handed, but one summer she was the dinner cook for the entire summer. It was horrible. Cooking is a task that Sue does well but has no desire for innovation or experimentation. That summer the lodge had a seven-day rotation menu that was followed all summer. The food was good but Ron would have been bored to death.

Sue's strength lies in having the food Ron needs to cook with. She supervises and reminds the staff to do the things that get forgotten: organizing the coolers, cleaning the freezers, using leftovers, and watching the food waste.

Justine Kerfoot has written a weekly column for the *Cook County News-Herald* since 1956. Her *Woman of the Boundary Waters: Canoeing, Guiding, Mushing, and Surviving* also was published by the University of Minnesota Press (1994).

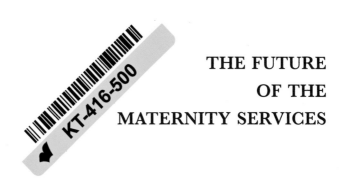
THE FUTURE
OF THE
MATERNITY SERVICES

The future of the
MATERNITY
SERVICES

Edited by
Geoffrey Chamberlain and Naren Patel

RCOG Press

iv

First published 1994
© Royal College of Obstetricians and Gynaecologists 1994

ISBN 0 902331 67 1 (hardback)
ISBN 0 902331 68 X (paperback)

Published by the **RCOG Press** at the
Royal College of Obstetricians and Gynaecologists
27 Sussex Place
Regent's Park
London NW1 4RG

Registered Charity No: 213280

Cover design by Geoffrey Wadsley
Printed by Latimer Trend and Company Limited, Estover Close, Plymouth PL6 7PL

Contents

SECTION II: PROVISION OF SERVICES: WHAT AND HOW?

Preface

Twice a year the RCOG holds a Study Group to consider in depth topics of current interest to the specialty. The publication in August 1993 of the report of the Expert Maternity Group triggered a decision by the College to plan a special study group on maternity services. This two day meeting provided a forum for women who use the service to debate their views with members of the main professional groups, and for all parties to consider the implications of the recommendations in *Changing Childbirth*.

Just as with the Expert Maternity Group, the Study Group identified that high quality care needs to be woman-centred, as well as of a high technical quality. In particular improvements in communication, choice of care and continuity of carer were confirmed, and this is reflected in the detailed recommendations. Both the users and professionals were clear that a good maternity service requires close collaboration between members of all professional groups and agreed that for each woman there should be an appropriate lead professional, acceptable to her.

The work of the Study Group should help to achieve further improvements which will be welcomed by women and health professionals. I am grateful to the conveners and to Miss Sally Barber, Postgraduate Education Secretary of the RCOG, for the effective arrangements for the meeting and to Mrs Sandra Wegerif, Publications Editor at the College, whose efficiency has made early publication possible.

Julia Cumberlege

Back row (left to right): Dr L.F.P. Smith, Professor W. Dunlop, Mr J.A.D. Spencer, Professor A.A. Calder, Professor P.J. Steer, Dr M.J.V. Bull, Mr B.J. Capstick, Dr G.L. Young, Dr M.H. Hall, Dr S. Lawson, Ms A.J. Macfarlane, Ms C. Henderson, Dr W.J. Modle, Professor J.M. Connor, Professor C.H. Rodeck, Dr W. McN. Styles, Dr N.B. Patel, Dr W.J.D. McKinlay, Dr L.I. Zander.

Front row (left to right): Mr S.A. Walkinshaw, Dr S.K. Cole, Mr P.M. Coats, Mrs J. Sleep, Professor L.A. Page, Dr A.P. Rubin, Professor G.V.P. Chamberlain, Baroness Julia Cumberlege, Ms D. Kroll, Ms M.C. McGinley, Ms M.S. Newburn, Dame Margaret Brain, Ms G.L. Halksworth, Mrs J. Allison, Dr M. Reid, Ms S.M. Downe.

x

Participants

Mrs Julia Allison
Director of Midwifery Education, Norfolk College of Nursing and Midwifery, Faculty of Midwifery, Marathon Centre, Norfolk and Norwich Hospital, Brunswick Road, Norwich, UK

Miss Mary M. Anderson
Consultant Obstetrician and Gynaecologist, Lewisham Hospital, High Street, Lewisham, London SE13 6LH, UK

Dame Margaret Brain
Former President, Royal College of Midwives

Dr Michael J. V. Bull
General Practitioner and Hospital Practitioner in Obstetrics (retired), 7 Lewis Close, Risinghurst, Headington, Oxford OX3 8JD, UK

Professor Andrew A. Calder
Centre for Reproductive Biology, University of Edinburgh, 37 Chalmers Street, Edinburgh EH3 9EW, UK

Mr Brian J. Capstick
Partner, Capstick Solicitors, General Accident Building, 77/83 Upper Richmond Road, London SW15 2TT, UK

Professor Geoffrey V. P. Chamberlain
President, Royal College of Obstetricians and Gynaecologists, 27 Sussex Place, Regent's Park, London NW1 4RG, UK

Mr Percy M. Coats
Consultant Obstetrician and Gynaecologist, Royal Surrey County Hospital, Egerton Road, Guildford, Surrey GU2 5XX, UK

Dr Susan K. Cole
Consultant in Public Health Medicine, Scottish Health Services Agency, Information and Statistics Division, Trinity Park House, South Trinity Road, Edinburgh EH5 3SQ, UK

Professor J. Michael Connor
Head of Department of Medical Genetics, Duncan Guthrie Institute, Yorkhill, Glasgow G3 8SJ, UK

Baroness Cumberlege
Parliamentary Under Secretary of State for Health (Lords), Department of Health, Richmond House, 79 Whitehall, London SW1A 2NS, UK

Ms Susan M. Downe
Research Midwife, Derby City General Hospital, Uttoxeter Road, Derby DE22 3NE, UK

Professor William Dunlop
Honorary Secretary, Royal College of Obstetricians and Gynaecologists, Department of Obstetrics and Gynaecology, Royal Victoria Infirmary, 4th Floor, Leazes Wing, Queen Victoria Road, Newcastle upon Tyne, Tyne and Wear NE1 4LP, UK

Dr Martine Eskes
Obstetrician and Gynaecologist, Stichting Ziekenhuis 'De Heel', PO Box 210, 1500 EE Zaandam, The Netherlands

Miss Gillian L. Halksworth
Integrated Midwife, Taff Ely Community/East Glamorgan Hospital, Church Village, Near Pontypridd, Mid Glamorgan CF38 1AB, UK

Dr Marion H. Hall
Consultant Obstetrician and Gynaecologist, Aberdeen Maternity Hospital, Cornhill Road, Aberdeen AB9 2ZA, UK

Ms Christine Henderson
Director of Research and Development and Lecturer in Midwifery Studies, Birmingham and Solihull College of Nursing and Midwifery, Thorne House, 113/115 Anderton Park Road, Moseley, Birmingham B13 9DQ, UK

Mrs Rosemary Jenkins
Director of Professional Affairs, Royal College of Midwives, 15 Mansfield Street, London W1M 0BE, UK

Ms Debra Kroll
Senior Midwife, Obstetric Hospital, University College Hospital, Huntley Street, London WC1E 6AU, UK

Mrs Helen Lewison
Chairman, National Childbirth Trust, Alexandra House, Oldham Terrace, London W3 6UH, UK

Professor Richard J. Lilford
Professor of Obstetrics and Gynaecology, Chairman, Institute of Epidemiology and Health Services Research, Department of Clinical Medicine, 34 Hyde Terrace, Leeds LS2 9LN, UK

Professor B. Garth McClure
President, British Association of Perinatal Medicine and Professor of Neonatal Medicine, Queen's University, Belfast, BT12 6BJ, Northern Ireland

Ms Alison J. Macfarlane
Medical Statistician, National Perinatal Epidemiology Unit, Radcliffe Infirmary, Oxford OX2 6HE, UK

Ms Mary C. McGinley
Head of Midwifery Services/Site Manager, The Glasgow Royal Maternity Hospital, Rottenrow, Glasgow G4 0NA, UK

Dr W. J. David McKinlay
Associate Adviser, North West Thames Region, and Joint Hospital Visit Convener, Royal College of General Practitioners and General Practitioner, Claremont House, 53 Pendle Road, Clitheroe, Lancashire BB7 1JQ, UK

Ms Mary S. Newburn
Head of Policy Research, National Childbirth Trust, Alexandra House, Oldham Terrace, London W3 6NH, UK

Professor Lesley A. Page
Head of Midwifery and Women's Health Studies, Thames Valley University, Queen Charlotte's College of Health and Science, Queen Charlotte's and Chelsea Hospital, London W6 0XG, UK

Dr Naren B. Patel
Vice President, Royal College of Obstetricians and Gynaecologists, Consultant Obstetrician and Gynaecologist, Ninewells Hospital Medical School, Dundee DD1 9SY, UK

Dr Margaret Reid
Senior Lecturer, Department of Public Health, University of Glasgow, 2 Lilybank Gardens, Glasgow G12 8RZ, UK

Professor Charles H. Rodeck
Head of Department of Obstetrics and Gynaecology, University College Hospital, 86–96 Chenies Mews, London WC1E 6HX, UK

Dr Anthony P. Rubin
Consultant Anaesthetist, Department of Anaesthetics, Charing Cross Hospital, Fulham Palace Road, London W6 8RF, UK

Mrs Jennifer Sleep
Director of Nursing and Midwifery Research, Berkshire College of Nursing and Midwifery, Royal Berkshire Hospital, London Road, Reading, Berkshire RG1 5AN, UK

Dr Lindsay F. P. Smith
The General Practice Unit, Department of Epidemiology and Public Health Medicine, Canynge Hall, Whiteladies Road, Bristol BS8 2PR, UK

Mr John A. D. Spencer
Senior Clinical Lecturer and Consultant, Department of Obstetrics and Gynaecology, University College Hospital, 86–96 Chenies Mews, London WC1E 6HX, UK

Professor Philip J. Steer
Head of Academic Department of Obstetrics and Gynaecology, Charing Cross and Westminster Medical School, Chelsea and Westminster Hospital, 369 Fulham Road, London SW10 9NH, UK

Dr William McN. Styles
Chairman of Council, Royal College of General Practitioners and Regional Adviser in General Practice, North West Thames Region, The Grove Health Centre, 95 Goldhawk Road, London W12 8EJ, UK

Dr Deborah Turnbull
Project Manager, Midwifery Development Unit, Glasgow Royal Maternity Hospital, Rottenrow, Glasgow G4 0NA, UK

Mr Stephen A. Walkinshaw
Consultant in Maternal-Fetal Medicine, Liverpool Maternity Hospital, Oxford Street, Liverpool L7 8BW, UK

Dr Gavin L. Young
General Practitioner and Chairman, The Association for Community-Based Maternity Care, The Surgery, Temple Sowerby, Penrith, Cumbria CA10 1RZ, UK

Dr Luke I. Zander
Senior Lecturer, Department of General Practice, United Medical and Dental Schools of Guy's and St Thomas's Hospitals, 80 Kennington Road, London SE11 6SP, UK

Observers

Dr Sheila Lawson
The Scottish Office, Home and Health Department, St Andrew's House, Edinburgh EH1 3DE, UK

Dr W. John Modle
Department of Health, Room 501, Wellington House, 133–155 Waterloo Road, London SE1 8UG, UK

Miss Kathryn Partington
Midwifery Officer, Department of Health, Room G31, Wellington House, 133–155 Waterloo Road, London SE1 8UG, UK

Additional contributors

Dr Dirk van Alten
Consultant Obstetrician and Gynaecologist, Academisch Medisch Centrum, Amsterdam, The Netherlands

Dr Alastair G. Donald
President, Royal College of General Practitioners, 14 Princes Gate, Hyde Park, London SW7 1PU, UK

Dr Michael J. A. Maresh
Department of Obstetrics and Gynaecology, St Mary's Hospital, Whitworth Park, Manchester M13 0JH, UK

Dr Gillian M. McIlwaine
Consultant in Public Health Medicine, Glasgow Royal Maternity Hospital, Rottenrow, Glasgow G4 0NA, UK

Miss Suzanne Tyler
Policy Co-ordinator, Royal College of Midwives, 15 Mansfield Street, London W1M 0BE, UK

Introduction

This century has seen a massive improvement in the safety of childbirth for both mother and baby. This has been brought about by the work of doctors and midwives and also owes much to the improved health of women who have better nutrition and education. However, in pursuing the interests of safety, we must all remember those who are centre stage for pregnancy and childbirth, the mother and her baby. For mother it is one of life's great experiences, for the baby it is the beginning of independent life. In consequence, pregnancy and labour are processes to be guided with a sensitive hand; it is hoped that most doctors and midwives in the Western world do this, but sadly this is not always so.

The publication of the Department of Health's Report on *Changing Childbirth* showed us that there were many good practices going on in the United Kingdom, but their use is by no means universal. Hence, whilst professionals felt that they were giving a good and full service everywhere, this was not so. We hope that the very publication of the report and the public discussion that followed will lead to improved practice in those units that are not already undertaking the aspects highlighted in the Departmental report.

As a part of the promulgation of these ideas, the Royal College of Obstetricians and Gynaecologists, in conjunction with the Royal College of Midwives and the Royal College of General Practitioners, held a two-day Study Group. To this were invited many who have been working in the field of maternity services for a long time. Midwives, GPs, obstetricians, health educators, neonatologists, anaesthetists and representatives of the women themselves – some thirty users spent two days in discussion about how best to take forward ideas into the future maternity service. The papers given and the edited version of the discussions are presented in this volume for a wider public to read. This debate needs to be fuelled and kept going until we have a service in which women having babies are satisfied that they are recognised for the place they should hold in childbirth and their professionals are satisfied that the best service is being given to the fetus and newborn.

Geoffrey Chamberlain
President
Royal College of Obstetricians and Gynaecologists

SECTION I
CHOICE AND RISK

Chapter 1

What are consumer views of maternity care?

Margaret Reid

Introduction

> Even when midwives are trained, apparatus available and transport arranged there
> is a further difficulty to overcome – the attitude of the midwives themselves. The
> giving of anaesthesia in itself involves a certain amount of trouble which some
> midwives seem unwilling to take unless a mother is very insistent in her demands
> for relief (p. 82, RCOG, Population Investigation 1948).

> We are convinced that the most fundamental change that needs to occur is one of
> attitudes on the part of some of the care-givers (p. 12, Department of Health 1993).

The twin themes to this chapter are apparently contradictory. The first is that
despite considerable improvement over the past decades in the clinical obstetric
care that women receive during their pregnancy and childbirth, other aspects of
care, the organisational features and social relations within the service have not
shown such progress. The first quotation at the top derives from one of the earliest
systematic consumer studies in the field of maternity care (published in 1948) in
which women were interviewed about their experiences of the services. It will be
argued that over the years women have continued to make certain requests which
remain largely unfulfilled. Today, even more so than yesterday, many consumers
wish control over the experience; this is often expressed in the research studies
and in this chapter through requests for choice and (better) communication, two
topics which will be discussed in more detail below. Improved continuity of care,
the third issue to be raised, is again a recurrent theme of consumer studies in
maternity care. Good continuity is also seen as very important as it provides a
woman with the opportunity to establish a relationship with a small group of
health professionals. That in turn gives her a stronger feeling of recognition as an
individual and a basis for asserting herself and her wishes.

The consumer literature is often seen as quite critical of the services, and yet it
would be false to conclude without commenting on recent events which hopefully
signal real change; policy documents have at last indicated that the thinking about
the structure and the social relations with the maternity services is showing greater

congruence with consumer wishes. This second theme, that change is occurring, will be briefly taken up later in the chapter before a discussion of research methods.

Consumer wishes

Choice

Women have never all wanted the same kind of childbirth experience. This is evident from responses reported within a wide range of studies. At any point in time a woman might wish to experience a range of options during her childbirth; this range is affected by the age of the woman, her parity, her social class, her ethnicity and of course trends and fashions which shape maternity care as they do other aspects of life. In a study of Scottish maternity service consumers conducted through 15 focus groups Bostock concluded, 'Women want health professionals to acknowledge them as individuals with specific and different needs' (Bostock 1993, p. 14), thinking very much in line with the Cumberlege Report published later that year (Department of Health 1993).

Given that expectations of the experience of childbirth may be varied, providing choice is one organisational way of attempting to match consumer wishes with what is on offer. But consumers report that they are not always given choice or are presented with choice too late to become involved in the decision-making. Furthermore, it is apparent from a wide range of studies that lack of choice may result in less consumer satisfaction. Some examples of key topics will illustrate the case.

In 1979 Oakley reported from her study of 55 London women that 61 per cent of women were offered no choice of hospital by the general practitioner whom they first consulted about their pregnancy. A more recent study of 788 consumers' views from Lothian Region Scotland indicated improvement; 65 per cent of women were offered a choice of hospital and 'type of birth' (e.g. domino delivery) but with significant variations between areas and hospitals; in one area 86 per cent of consumers were offered a choice, and they were also twice as likely to be offered a home birth (Scottish Health Feedback 1993). As revealing, 72 per cent of middle class women from the total sample but only 62 per cent of working class women were offered a choice.

The extent to which women may wish midwife care only, or antenatal care based at their general practitioner is not fully known and three large randomised controlled trials are currently being undertaken to answer such questions. However, a number of studies have indicated women's preference for the more personal ambience and convenience of community-based clinics (Thomas *et al.* 1989). Choice of where to give birth is not always possible and women in rural areas continue to encounter greater problems.

The need for choice is apparent throughout pregnancy. From studies evaluating the policy of giving women their obstetric records to carry, it became apparent that more women were satisfied with their care when they held their notes than those who did not (Elbourne *et al.* 1987). In a study of 1023 women who were surveyed about their attitudes to HIV testing it was found that 94 per cent had no objection to being tested although 55 per cent wished to be asked first (Thomas *et al.* 1989). However, although the choice about whether to undergo screening tests does exist in reality few women do refuse. It still remains the case that some women do not understand the purpose of such tests (Macintyre 1982).

Even hospitalisation can be offered as a choice; Twaddle found that the majority of women requiring additional antenatal care preferred day-care to in-patient admission whereas 57 per cent said that they would be prepared to attend 5 days a week as out-patients (Twaddle in press). Once admitted for the delivery the majority of women preferred small wards to the larger eight-bedded ones (Reid 1991; Glazener *et al.* 1993); however, Reid's study (1991) showed that more women from the higher social classes preferred a single room as did others in certain circumstances (e.g. illness, after a difficult birth).

Choice over management of labour and delivery is not always feasible in the case of difficult deliveries and emergencies. But most births do not fall into those categories and choice becomes more possible – and desirable. In a Glasgow study of 80 first-time mothers McIntosh (1989) found that many of the women from working-class backgrounds reported postive attitudes towards technology and intervention which they found reassuring; other studies (e.g. Oakley 1979) have argued that middle-class women interested in having a positive birth experience hoped to have as little intervention as possible. The Scottish Health Feedback (1993) study found that middle-class/older women (defined as owner occupiers, living with their partner, non-manual occupation) were more likely to feel their preferences during labour and delivery were taken into account than were younger, often single women with partners in manual occupations. Attitudes also varied about the role of the father in the labour suite, some women reporting pressure for a father to be present when the implication was that this was not necessarily what the couple wanted (Barbour 1990).

Postnatally women have been shown to have varying preferences for the length of their stay although there are indications that women judge the stay by the quality of care rather than by the actual number of days (Reid and Garcia 1989).

One final comment about choice: in the past it has been argued that women tend to choose the service with which they are familiar (Porter and Macintyre 1984). Indeed in real life as in some of the above studies women have simply been asked how satisfied they were with the present situation. One way of helping to integrate choice into the system is through the introduction of birth plans although there is as yet little research on their success (or otherwise). Focus group discussion revealed to Bostock the whole spectrum of comments about birth plans, some women reporting them an important part of the birth experience while others felt they were a token gesture: 'There should be someone to help you fill it in. You just get handed it. They ask you what do you want – this or that – pethidine or morphine. Folk dinna ken what these things are' (Bostock 1993, p. 25). As the respondent suggests, choice without information is pointless. Informed choice also depends on good communication, the next issue to be discussed.

Communication

A repeated complaint has been about the lack of information given to women about their baby, reflecting a lack of dialogue between the staff and themselves. Graham and McKee (1979) found in their 1979 study of York first-time mothers that whereas 90 per cent of their sample thought that antenatal care was important 80 per cent had not learned anything from the check-ups and 34 per cent felt that they did not have the opportunity to ask questions. Cartwright (1979), in one of the few national surveys of childbirth, offers a slightly different slant; working class pregnant women wanted to be informed about their pregnancy and labour as much as did middle-class women but were less successful in eliciting information from the staff. However, although one response is to be the 'confident patient', a frequent finding from consumer studies is that women may feel in a double-bind situation; those who ask for advice, who start up the dialogue, may be seen to be difficult whereas the 'passive patients' do not get as much information as some would like.

Attendance at antenatal classes is not always high but it may be important; studies assessing the usefulness of information gained by attending antenatal classes have shown that women who attend do feel better prepared for labour and delivery (Brewin and Bradley 1982; Newton 1991). Information given out at the classes and during antenatal care has been shown to be vague, with a tendency to offer reassurance rather than a proper explanation. Women have shown greater resilience than is often anticipated and studies testify to many women's desire to be more thoroughly informed about potential problems. Shapiro et al. (1983) found that 84 per cent of the women interviewed wanted to know about fetal deformities while only 21 per cent of doctors identified the women's desire for such information. Information was more likely to be given when non-routine tests were being performed (Macintyre 1982).

There are startling examples of lack of communication. Marteau et al. (1988) found that from a sample of 69 women questioned postpartum about tests they had undergone in their recent pregnancy 38 per cent did not know or knew incorrectly whether they had their blood checked for alphafetoprotein; 23 per cent did not know or knew incorrectly whether they had undergone amniocentesis. In a more recent study, Marteau et al. tape-recorded antenatal consultations where screening was discussed and concluded that the routine MS-AFP screening tests for spina bifida and Down's syndrome was usually mentioned but that 'little information was provided about the test, the conditions it screens for and the meaning of either a positive or a negative result' (Marteau et al. 1992, p. 137). In fact a wealth of studies comment on the poor procedures on information and result-giving in this area (Fearn et al. 1982).

There are a number of studies which focus on women's dissatisfaction arising from inadequate explanations of procedural interventions during labour (Kirkham 1983; Windsor-Richards and Gillies 1988). Better feedback on the overall birth experience was something Bostock (1993) found women in her Scottish study requested with the suggestion that the dialogue between professional and expectant mother should be extended to a 'de-briefing session' during the early postnatal period.

Table 1.1   Continuity of hospital care and overall evaluation of care

Same doctor seen at:	Antenatal care rated 'very good'
Every hospital visit	69%
Some hospital visits	49%
No hospital visits	38%

Source: Scottish Health Feedback (1993).

Attitudes of the staff, so crucial to all communication, are often little studied with regard to 'routine' situations. Health professionals reflect more generally held attitudes towards women from different social classes, and towards women of different ethnic groups. Racism is a difficult topic to study, although a few reports have explicitly commented on the racist attitudes of a few staff which inhibited good communication with ethnic minority women (Phoenix 1990).

Continuity of care

The system of antenatal care, the long waiting times, the uncomfortable premises and the hurried consultation remain markers of a system which has not changed despite continued criticisms over the decades (see O'Brien and Smith 1981; Reid and Garcia 1989). Lack of continuity of care, or more accurately, continuity of carer, is another significant part of this unwieldy system resulting in less satisfaction, decreasing the likelihood of individual care and good communication. Overall, the majority of women report that they would prefer continuity of care, that is, to see the same caregiver (or one of a small group) over the duration of their pregnancy. Reid and McIlwaine (1980) found that 85 per cent of women favoured seeing the same doctor for their antenatal care; others have reported an almost equally high percentage of women (77 per cent) attaching importance to continuity of midwifery care ante- and postnatally, and 80 per cent felt that knowing the delivering midwife was important (Melia *et al.* 1991). In the 1987 version of the Lothian study 86 per cent of women wanted to see the same doctor or midwives but in the second run of the study in 1992 only 57 per cent responded as such (Scottish Health Feedback 1993). Of those who saw the same doctor at every hospital visit, however, a significant number were more likely to rate their antenatal care as 'very good' – 69 per cent compared with 49 per cent who saw the same doctor on some hospital visits, and 38 per cent who never saw the same doctor at hospital visits (Table 1.1).

This study well illustrates the important link between a woman's expectations and the care she receives while also underlining the earlier point that women do have different views. Table 1.2 from the same study indicates that within the group of women who 'sometimes or never saw the same doctor', three quarters who did not mind seeing different doctors rated their overall care

Table 1.2   Overall evaluation of care of those who 'sometimes or never saw the same doctor'

	Antenatal care rated 'very good'
Wanted to see same doctor	21%
Did not mind seeing different doctor	79%

Adapted from Scottish Health Feedback (1993).

'very good' whereas only a fifth of those who had wanted to see the same doctors rated their care likewise.

One feature intrinsic to continuity of care is continuity of advice and women have frequently reported that conflicting advice is confusing at any time during maternity care although it is during the postnatal period that complaints are most often recorded. Hillan (1992) noted in her study of women undergoing Caesarean sections that there was considerable dissatisfaction with the postnatal care, specifically with the lack of support and conflicting advice from midwives on the postnatal wards. Research on breastfeeding, too, has shown that women are given conflicting information about breastfeeding (how to feed, how often, etc.), and incidentally, not enough support (Garforth and Garcia 1989; Glazener et al. 1993). In Murphy-Black's (1989) study the number of women breastfeeding was reduced from over 50 per cent to 13.3 per cent by the time the babies were three months old. Comments by the women on the decreasing interest reflected both a lack of understanding of lactation and inaccurate information from the midwives, and later, the health visitors (Murphy-Black 1989). Murphy-Black and others have commented on the number of different health professionals that women see in the early days postpartum.

The lack of support that women sometimes feel they receive during childbirth is also linked to lack of continuity of care. Building support and trust in professional staff is easier when there is a face to recognise, as emerged from Bostock's study of Scottish women (Bostock 1993). Kirke (1980) noted that if care providers are to be more supportive to women they would have to give greater consideration to the psychological and social aspects of care.

Signs of change

The second theme of the chapter is that although we may remain aware of a number of repeated consumer complaints a case can also be made that only within the last few years have high level policy documents reflected far more closely the kinds of service and the kinds of attitudes as those described in many consumer studies. Although the status of these documents is not always clear-cut the Winterton Report (House of Commons Health Committee 1992), the Cumberlege Report (Department of Health 1993) and Provision of Maternity Services in Scotland (Scottish Office 1993) all represent a significant shift in orientation of service to one more women-centred with an emphasis on the concepts described above, choice, communication and continuity.

Even so, it is important to be careful not to over-generalise and to continue to ask, whose voice are we hearing? Thus when planning studies there is a need to avoid the tendency (and a temptation) to exclude 'difficult categories', as has so often been the case in the past. Our information about preferences and dislikes of pregnant women are influenced heavily by the attitudes of primiparous, low risk women, and the experiences of the silent minorities remain under-researched; what are the views of women with multiple births, women with problem pregnancies, ethnic minority women, teenagers, older mothers, travelling women, homeless, refugee and disabled women? These groups have a variety of needs; many already show higher than average rates for maternal and neonatal problems and warrant more time and attention than currently given to them.

Studies tend to be carried out using small samples and to be local rather than national studies; consumer responses are therefore influenced by the good (or bad) practices of the research hospitals. Many of the studies have used questionnaires as the main form of data collection. On this topic Jacoby and Cartwright (1990) sound a note of caution: assessing consumer opinion can be more difficult than it first appears, for it is possible to slant questionnaires to give positive answers. When presented with very general statements about satisfaction women tend to respond positively and yet if asked for more detail, will report ways in which the service could be improved. To gauge more accurately what aspects of the services consumers are genuinely satisfied with it is better to focus on specifics.

Other research methods used may include interviewing women, a good but often quite costly approach, while there is an increasing use of 'focus groups' as a quick (and cheaper) method of obtaining consumer views. This method does not rely on a random sample and may appeal rather more to those who have strong views about certain issues. Given the methodological pitfalls which can easily be encountered, particular importance should be attached to sampling techniques, to randomised controlled trials (where appropriate) and to observational studies as well as the more routine methods and styles of research. Perhaps the message is that regardless of the research methods employed and of the potential difficulties of assessing consumer needs, what consumers want from the services has shone through clearly for many years. Consumer requests are not always complicated, their complaints often straightforward. It is surely time to incorporate the consumer wishes more strongly into the services of the future.

References

Barbour, R. (1990) 'Fathers: the emergence of a new consumer group' in J. Garcia, R. Kilpatrick and M. Richards (Eds) *The Politics of Maternity Care*, pp. 202–16. Oxford: Oxford University Press

Bostock, Y. (1993) *Pregnancy, Childbirth and Coping with Motherhood: What Women Want from the Maternity Services*. Edinburgh: CRAG Secretariat, The Scottish Office, St Andrew's House

Brewin, C. and Bradley, C. (1982) Perceived control and the experience of childbirth. *Br J Clin Psychol* **21**, 263–9

Cartwright, A. (1979) *The Dignity of Labour*. London: Tavistock

Department of Health (1993) *Changing Childbirth*: Parts 1 and 2. London: HMSO

Elbourne, D., Richardson, M., Chalmers, I. *et al.* (1987) The Newbury maternity care study: a randomized controlled trial to assess a policy of women holding their own obstetric records. *Br J Obstet Gynaecol* **94**, 612–19

Fearn, J., Hibbard, B.M. and Robinson, J.O. (1982) Screening for neural-tube defects and maternal anxiety. *Br J Obstet Gynaecol* **89**, 218–21

Garforth, S. and Garcia, J. (1989) Breastfeeding policies in practice – 'No wonder they get confused'. *Midwifery* **5**, 75–83

Glazener, C.M.A, Abdalla, M., Russell, I. *et al.* (1993) Postnatal care: a survey of patients' experiences. *Br J Midwifery* **1**, 67–74

Graham, H. and McKee, L. (1979) *The First Months of Motherhood*. Report of a Health Education Council project concerned with women's experiences of pregnancy, childbirth and first months of life. York: University of York (unpublished)

Hillan, E.M. (1992) Short term morbidity associated with Caesarean delivery. *Birth,* **19**, 190–4

House of Commons Health Committee (1992) Second Report, *Maternity Services* Vols 1 and 2. London: HMSO

Jacoby, A. and Cartwright, A. (1990) 'Finding out about the views and experiences of maternity-services users' in J. Garcia, R. Kilpatrick and M. Richards (Eds) *The Politics of Maternity Care*, pp. 202–16. Oxford: Oxford University Press

Kirke, P.N. (1980) Mothers' views of care in labour. *Br J Obstet Gynaecol* **87**, 1034–8

Kirkham, M. (1983) 'Labouring in the dark: limitations on the giving of information to enable patients to orientate themselves to the likely events and timescale of labour' in J. Wilson-Barnett (Ed) *Nursing Research – Ten Studies in Patient Care*, pp. 81–99. Chichester: John Wiley

Macintyre, S. (1982) Communication between pregnant women and their medical and midwifery attendants. *Midwives' Chronicle*, November, pp. 387-94

Macintyre, S. (1984) 'Consumer reactions to present-day antenatal services' in L. Zander and G. Chamberlain (Eds) *Pregnancy Care for the 1980s*, pp. 9-17. London: Royal Society of Medicine Macmillan Press

Marteau, T.M., Johnston, M., Plenicar, M. *et al.* (1988) Development of a self-administered questionnaire to measure women's knowledge of prenatal screening and diagnostic tests. *J Psychosom Res* **32**, 403–8

Marteau, T.M., Slack, J., Kidd, J. *et al.* (1992) Presenting a routine screening test in antenatal care; practice observed. *Public Health,* **106**, 131–41

McIntosh, J. (1989) 'Models of childbirth and social class; a study of 80 primigravidae' in S. Robinson and A. Thomson (Eds) *Midwives, Research and Childbirth*, Vol. 1, pp. 189–214. London: Chapman and Hall

Melia, R.J., Morgan, M., Wolfe, C.D. *et al.* (1991) Consumer views of maternity services: implications for change and quality assurance. *J Public Health Med* **13**, 120–6

Murphy-Black, T. (1989) Midwives' role in postnatal care. *Nurs Times,* **85**, 54–5

Newton, C. (1991) Patients' knowledge of aspects of labour. *Nurs Times* **87**, 50

Oakley, A. (1979) *Becoming a Mother*. London: Martin Robertson

O'Brien, M. and Smith, C. (1981) Women's views and experiences of antenatal care. *Practitioner* **225**, 123–5

Phoenix, A. (1990) 'Black women and the maternity services', in J. Garcia, R. Kilpatrick and M. Richards (Eds) *The Politics of Maternity Care*, pp. 274–99. Oxford: Oxford University Press

Porter, M. and Macintyre, S. (1984) What is, must be best: a research note on conservative or deferential responses to antenatal care provision. *Soc Sci Med* **19**, 1197–2000

Reid, M.E. (1991) Maternity Patients Views of Single and Shared Accommodation. Report prepared for Greater Glasgow Health Board. Glasgow (unpublished)

Reid, M.E. and McIlwaine, G.M. (1980) Consumer opinion of a hospital antenatal clinic. *Soc Sci Med,* **14A**, 363–8

Reid, M.E. and Garcia, J. (1989) 'Women's views of care during pregnancy and childbirth' in I. Chalmers, M. Enkin, and M.J.N.C. Keirse (Eds) *Effective Care in Pregnancy and Childbirth*, Vol. 1, pp. 131-42. Oxford: Oxford University Press

Royal College of Obstetricians and Gynaecologists and the Population Investigation Committee (1948) *Maternity in Great Britain: a Survey of Social and Economic Aspects of Pregnancy and Childbirth*. Oxford: Oxford University Press

Scottish Health Feedback (1993) *Lothian Maternity Survey 1992*. Report to Lothian Health Council, Edinburgh

Scottish Office (1993) *Provision of Maternity Services in Scotland; a Policy Document*. Edinburgh: HMSO

Shapiro, M.C., Najman, J.M., Chang, A. *et al.* (1983) Information control and the exercise of power in the obstetric encounter. *Soc Sci Med* **17**, 139–46

Thomas, J., Bowen-Simpkins, P., Stewart, G. *et al.* (1989) Survey of attitudes to testing for HIV infection in antenatal clinics in West Glamorgan, *Br J Obstet Gynaecol* **96**, 1405–9

Twaddle, S. (1994) Women's views of daycare for hypertension in pregnancy. *Nurs Times* (in press)

Windsor-Richards, K. and Gillies, P.A. (1988) Racial grouping and women's experience of giving birth in hospital. *Midwifery*, **4**, 171–6

Chapter 2

Views of consumers: what are they and how may they be obtained?

Mary S. Newburn

I have two qualifications for talking about what women want from the maternity services. I work for the National Childbirth Trust (NCT), the largest birth and parenting organisation in the UK with some 56 000 members, 380 local branches and representatives sitting on 96 Maternity Services Liaison Committees. I am also a mother myself. My youngest child was born in 1993 so all the issues to do with pregnancy, birth, breastfeeding, broken nights, bad days and beaming baby smiles are very real and immediate for me.

Having a baby changes a woman's life dramatically. Her body, her time, her thoughts, her freedom, her opportunity to work, her sex life, her future, are all affected. If the father is closely involved, having a baby transforms his life, too. In having, or attempting to have, a baby we experience some of the most profound changes in our lives and some of the most extreme feelings.

The author of *The Mother Zone* describes it like this:

> Motherhood is an unexplored frontier of thought and emotion that we've tried to tame with rules, myths and knowledge. But the geography remains unmapped (Jackson 1992).

Having a baby, she says, has 'so much otherness, so much third-person expertise brought to bear on it' (Jackson 1992).

As a society, we concentrate mainly on how professionals view becoming a mother, rather than asking women themselves what they experience. However, both the Health Select Committee (Health Committee 1992a) and the Expert Maternity Group (Department of Health 1993) made a point of adopting a perspective of first-person expertise. They began by asking what are women's needs and preferences?

Views of consumers: what are they?

In brief, under the present system, it seems to the NCT that women who are healthy and expecting to have healthy babies are often not getting the kind of care they need, and neither are women and babies for whom pregnancy and birth

12

are more complicated or risky. Furthermore, the best use is not being made of obstetric or midwifery skills. We explained our thinking in detail in our evidence to the Health Select Committee (Health Committee 1992a) and in response to the specific questions put by the Expert Maternity Group (Department of Health 1993).

Some of the major complaints from women over many years have been that they were made to feel unimportant. They have seen a succession of different faces and received conflicting advice. Health professionals have not had time to talk and explain, and the midwife providing 'hands-on' care has not felt she had the authority to discuss and agree decisions. Women have also complained about the system of care being authoritarian, with doctors, in particular, assuming they knew what was best and not providing the information women wanted so they could attempt to participate in decision-making. In recent years, conflict has often been most explicit over the issue of home birth. Other contested areas of care include method of delivery for breech babies, birth after a Caesarean section, appropriate forms of monitoring and the progress of labour.

For some time, domino deliveries seemed to provide what many women wanted. In theory a domino delivery meant care from a known midwife in the local community, including assessment and support at home at the beginning of labour, with the birth itself in hospital. However, in practice, there have been problems with both quality and quantity. Where community midwives have been working in large teams or have not been able to work sufficiently flexibly, women have not had a known midwife with them in labour and available to take them home afterwards. Furthermore, the number of domino deliveries available has always been kept very low – never higher than 4.5 per cent (Macfarlane and Mugford 1984) – and many women have been excluded from eligibility, usually including all those having first babies. Flint (1993) describes domino deliveries as having been 'nothing more or less than a confidence trick'.

Changing childbirth

In our evidence to the Health Select Committee and the Expert Maternity Group, we discussed how we would like to see the health professionals working and explained in detail the kinds of qualities women are looking for in the care they are offered.

The Health Select Committee said:

... on our several visits to varied areas we made a point of having informal discussions with women, and found that they echoed the themes and points put by the organisations (Health Committee 1992b, para 37).

They concluded that women should be the focus of maternity care, summing up succinctly that what women want from the service is choice, continuity of care and carer, and control. They went on to make recommendations about how this might be achieved.

When *Changing Childbirth* was published, very much the same understanding was expressed. In her introduction to the Report (Department of Health 1993), Baroness Cumberlege said:

> Considerable evidence examined by the (Expert Maternity) Group points to a set of universal standards that all women want from their maternity care. They want a service that is flexible and responsive to their individual needs, which acknowledges the role of their partners and which communicates effectively. They want improved information that allows them to make informed choices. Above all, women and their partners are seeking a service that is respectful, personalised and kind, which gives them control and makes them feel comfortable in the sense of being at ease in the environment of childbirth and having confidence in their care.

It is most important that the significance of these two reports is appreciated. They show the direction in which women would like the maternity services to change. The challenge for purchasers and providers is to find ways of planning and delivering a woman-centred service.

Continuity of carer

Before the Health Committee enquiry was announced the policy group at the NCT had decided that our priority for change was to see an end to women seeing a succession of strangers who knew nothing about them. Women want to be able to get to know someone with whom they can develop a relationship of confidence and trust. As the Winterton Report said, there is a strong feeling that midwives are particularly well placed to fulfil this need.

The pregnancy, birth and early postnatal days all make demands which women feel they can cope with better if they have someone familiar to turn to who understands their maternity history and what is important for them.

Evidence from the St George's Hospital Know Your Midwife (KYM) Scheme shows numerous ways in which the KYM women had significantly different experiences from those in the randomly selected control group. For example, they were more likely to be able to discuss anxieties in the antenatal clinic, more likely to feel very much in control during labour, and more likely (six weeks postnatally) to feel very well prepared for looking after a baby. They were less likely to have had analgesia or an epidural for pain relief in labour but just as likely as the control group to feel very satisfied with their pain relief (Flint and Poulengeris 1987).

The midwife's role means she provides care for women postnatally, as well as antenatally and during labour. In addition to being with women throughout the process – perhaps because of this – midwives seem quite good at 'tuning in' to women's needs.

In the 1991 Maternity Services Survey of members who had recently had a baby, respondents (n = 2043) were asked about how well health-care professionals had met various of their needs. We asked:

Whether professionals had provided the information women wanted.

How good professionals were at listening and explaining.

To what extent they showed respect and kindness.

Whether professionals seemed to understand what was important for the individual woman.

Though we did not coin the phrase at the time, these four factors looked at in combination could be seen as indicators of woman-centred care. Women consistently rated the midwife who had cared for them at the birth higher than their GP, health visitor or consultant obstetrician, if they saw one (National Childbirth Trust 1991).

In letters, we have heard from women with fertility problems and other medical conditions who have had continuity of medical care. Those who have been able to get to know a specialist doctor have clearly valued the relationship highly. Women who have known a supportive GP report similar views.

The way a woman is made to feel about herself, her birth experience and her mothering can have a profound influence on the baby, the couple and on the family.

Lead professional

Changing Childbirth says women should be able to choose who will be their lead professional, the lead professional being:

the professional who will give a substantial part of the care personally and who is responsible for ensuring that the woman has access to care from other professionals as appropriate.

If a woman was able to get to know a lead professional with whom she agreed the pattern of her care, that person would be able to get to know and value her.

The NCT welcomes the model described by *Changing Childbirth* in which every woman should know one midwife (the named midwife) who ensures continuity of her midwifery care, and that in many instances, the named midwife can be the lead professional. We would also fully endorse the idea that:

In other circumstances, normally when the pregnancy is more complicated, the obstetrician will be the lead professional. (Also that some women, with uncomplicated pregnancies, may prefer to have an obstetrician or GP take this role.)

Women are individuals and they and their families will have diverse needs and preferences. The provision of care should be flexible with all professionals working together constructively. For example, midwives should be able to refer women in their care to a consultant for a specialist medical opinion, and care, if it is considered necessary.

Midwife caseloads

The NCT is very pleased to see initiatives in which midwives are able to work in group practices and have an individual caseload of women for whom they provide care as the lead professional. The small number of midwives working independently in the private sector, are used to this pattern of working but it is still unusual within the NHS.

An audit of birth registers to examine the work of independent midwives in 1980–1991 suggests that this kind of care can be very successful in clinical, as well as social and emotional, terms (Weig 1993). The audit covered 43 independent midwives and the care of 1285 women, of whom 49 per cent were nulliparous and 63 per cent were aged 30 years or over. A total of 89 per cent had a spontaneous vaginal birth, 6 per cent were delivered by Caesarean section and 5 per cent had an instrumental birth. Three quarters of the women gave birth at home. The perinatal mortality rate was 7.7 per 1000 for the whole audit population. There were 221 unplanned transfers to hospital during labour. All these women were accompanied to hospital by their familiar midwives who continued to provide clinical care or support.

The South East Thames Regional Health Authority has recently awarded funds for the development and evaluation of three midwifery group practices, including a group practice of independent midwives. The independent midwives are hoping to secure an NHS contract for providing services in their District. [Since the time of writing, the practice has secured a six-month NHS contract.]

Sadly, it appears that in Scotland self-employed midwives are being prevented from working as lead professionals as some GPs, on the advice of the Medical Defence Union, have been refusing to sign prescriptions for medications or to sanction tests such as laboratory tests, ultrasound or X-ray examinations (Scottish Home and Health Department 1993).

Midwife caseload systems are now being developed within the NHS. The Centre for Midwifery Practice in West London began a new service in November 1993, aiming to provide women with one to one continuity of midwifery care. Midwives work in partnerships, closely linked with four other midwives for support and back-up. The midwife partnerships are affiliated with individual GPs. The project is open to women receiving either midwife-led or consultant-led care. The project is being evaluated and will provide further information about what women and their families find helpful and supportive and what, if any, measurable differences in clinical outcomes can be achieved (Centre for Midwifery Practice 1994).

It is to be hoped that this and other schemes based on midwife caseloads will manage in practice to provide continuity of care for women. Sadly, few of the initiatives to set up midwives working in teams have been successful in this respect (Wraight *et al.* 1993). Notable exceptions include the Scunthorpe and the Taff Ely/Rhondda teams in which the number in the teams are small and the teams are woman-centred rather than ward-centred (Flint 1993).

Perhaps one of the most important potential health gains to be achieved from continuity of midwifery care is an increase in breastfeeding. Jean Keats, speaking at the Royal College of Midwives Professional Day Conference, 24 July 1992, reported that of the mothers in the Taff/Ely Rhondda scheme who started breastfeeding, 91 per cent continued up to and beyond the eighth week. In Scunthorpe, 80.8 per cent of mothers who were cared for by the Winterton Team breastfed compared with 30 per cent of other women having babies in the local maternity unit (Flint 1993).

Views of consumers: how can they be obtained?

There are many ways of researching the views and experiences of consumers. Many of the satisfaction surveys which are undertaken are fairly simple to administer and analyse but limited in their scope and potentially misleading. People's perception of services and their willingness to question or complain are influenced by their expectations and experience of alternatives. Some of the most interesting evidence seems likely to come in the future from studies designed to evaluate the effects of new patterns of providing care.

The effects of doing things differently should be evaluated. Before setting up new patterns of care it is important to take account of existing research, so as not to repeat other people's mistakes. It helps to have identified clear and measurable objectives and it may well be advantageous to get specialist advice on research design.

Finally, I was on Planet Motherhood when *Changing Childbirth* was launched. My baby, Owen, was a few days old and the rest of the universe hardly existed. Coming back to it now with a bit more distance from being a new mother, I realise what an exciting message it bears. It voices the views and needs of users comprehensively and with vision. Within that broad framework, we now need to see innovative projects in every district.

References

Centre for Midwifery Practice (1994) *Newsletter* 5, January

Department of Health (1993) *Changing Childbirth*, Report of the Expert Maternity Group, London: HMSO

Flint, C. (1993) *Midwifery Teams and Caseloads*, Oxford: Butterworth-Heinemann

Flint, C. and Poulengeris, P. (1987) *The Know Your Midwife Report*, 49 Peckerman's Wood, London SE6 6RZ

Health Committee (1992a) *Maternity Services*, House of Commons Paper (HC(1990–91) 430–II), London: HMSO

Health Committee (1992b) *Maternity Services*, House of Commons Paper 29–I, 1991–2, London: HMSO

Jackson, M. (1992) *The Mother Zone: Love, Sex and Laundry in the Modern Family*, Toronto: Macfarlane Walter and Ross

Macfarlane, A. and Mugford, M. (1984) *Birth Counts. Statistics of Pregnancy and Childbirth* (Tables), National Perinatal Epidemiology Unit, Vol. I. London: HMSO

National Childbirth Trust (1991) Maternity Services Survey, (unpublished)

Scottish Home and Health Department (1993) *Provision of Maternity Services in Scotland*, Edinburgh: HMSO

Weig, M. (1993) *Audit of Independent Midwifery 1980-91*, Royal College of Midwives (taken from the abstract by Mavis Kirkham)

Wraight, A., Ball, J. and Seccombe, I. (1993) *Mapping Team Midwifery*. IMS Report Series 242. Brighton: Institute of Manpower Studies

Chapter 3

Review and assessment of models of care using research, information and data: the role of routinely collected data

Alison J. Macfarlane

To review and assess models of maternity care, a variety of complementary approaches are needed. The use of randomised controlled trials to assess the effectiveness of care is now widely accepted. The evidence from systematic reviews of individual trials is used increasingly by people providing care. Use of this research has also highlighted gaps in the available evidence. There are, of course, types of question for which randomised trials are not appropriate and different techniques, including case control and cohort studies, surveys and qualitative techniques are needed to answer them.

Before models of care or specific interventions can be assessed, or the impact of research about their benefits and risks can be monitored, it is important to have baseline information about the extent to which they are or could be used and the choices available. This means that data are needed to describe the services provided, the people who use them and the population from which they come. This chapter focuses therefore on the availability, content and quality of data from routine systems. There is not space here to document sources in detail, but this has been done elsewhere (Macfarlane and Mugford 1984; Barron and Macfarlane 1990; Central Statistical Office 1990; Macfarlane 1990, 1994; Campbell 1991, 1992).

People who work in the services and devote considerable effort to recording information on paper records or in computers and, increasingly, in auditing specific aspects of care are often surprised when the corresponding information is not available more widely or at national level. The National Perinatal Epidemiology Unit in Oxford receives many enquiries for data of this sort. For example, three recent telephone queries were: 'What is the national epidural rate?'; 'What is the average age of a first-time mother in London?'; 'Is there a national figure for the proportion of women admitted to hospital during pregnancy?' For different reasons which will be discussed later, none of these questions could be answered using routine data for England. The first two enquiries came from journalists and the third from the secretary of a Community Health Council. The journalists were more surprised than the Community Health Council secretary about the lack of national data.

Does this matter? It could be argued that local data are sufficient for people's needs. The tenth 'indicator of success' set out in *Changing Childbirth* (Department of Health 1993a) is that: 'All women should have access to information about the services available in their locality.' Similarly, clinical audit has a local focus. Local data can be very misleading and difficult to interpret if they are viewed in isolation. National data and data about the extent of variation between populations or provider units is needed to set them in context. In addition, national data are needed to monitor public expenditure and the way it is distributed and used.

It is also important to recognise at the outset that data are not collected for the United Kingdom as a whole. Each of the four countries of the UK has separate systems for collecting data locally and aggregating them at a national level. In general, Scotland has systems which are more fully developed and contain higher quality data than those of the other three countries. In England, NHS information was reviewed in the mid 1980s by the Steering Group on NHS Information, usually referred to as the Körner Committee (Steering Group on Health Services Information 1985). Wales and Northern Ireland have based some of their new data collection systems on the recommendations of the Körner Committee and have used some of the minimum data sets defined.

English health authorities were asked to implement the Körner Committee's recommendations, without any additional resources, in 1987 and 1988. In fact, many aspects had not been fully implemented by the time the introduction of the NHS internal market in April 1991 brought further changes in data collection. Further disruption is being caused by the restructuring and subsequent abolition of the English regional health authorities which have had a major role in coordinating data collection and collating information. It is a matter for some concern that the way this will be dealt with in the future was not discussed in the document setting out plans for changes at regional level (Department of Health 1993b).

There are also three separate civil registration systems. Birth and death registration in England and Wales is co-ordinated by the Office of Population Censuses and Surveys (OPCS) which also analyses and publishes the data derived from registration. Scotland and Northern Ireland each have their own General Register Offices.

What do the data collected routinely through these and other systems tell us about who provides what care, where, for whom at what cost and with what outcome?

Who provides care?

In general, the introduction of the NHS internal market and the decentralisation of personnel management to NHS trusts has made staffing data more inconsistent. Nevertheless, fairly detailed data are collected about medical staffing in the hospital and community services, making it possible to monitor the numbers of obstetricians and paediatricians, even though neonatologists are not identified separately.

Figure 3.1.   Whole time equivalent numbers of midwives, England and Wales, 1953–87

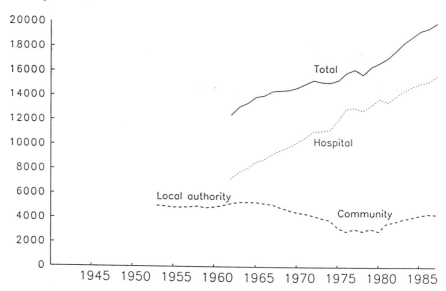

Source: Data from Ministry of Health, DHSS and Welsh Office publications

Data about midwives are less detailed. Figure 3.1 is an attempt to chart long-term trends (Campbell and Macfarlane 1994). It shows 'whole-time equivalent' numbers of midwives, but makes no attempt to adjust for changes over time in the contract hours of full-time midwives or the hours they actually worked. It was impossible to update it any further as the Welsh Office is no longer able to provide separate figures for the numbers of midwives in Wales. This is because they are now grouped together with nurses. Although separate figures are still published for hospital and community midwives in England it is unclear whether they reflect the increasing extent to which midwives work in both hospitals and the community. If we want to monitor the extent to which change is taking place, perhaps a different but more detailed subdivision is needed to reflect the different ways in which midwives are now practising.

The fact that general practitioners are independent practitioners means that data about their activities are more sparse than for directly employed staff. The only routine data about their involvement in maternity care comes from statistics about payments for antenatal and delivery care. This can be very misleading as general practitioners who receive payments vary widely in the extent and type of care they actually provide. Even these inadequate data have become problematic at a national level. It appears to be impossible to obtain reliable data for the years

Figure 3.2.   Numbers of claims by GPs for fees for maternity care, England and Wales, 1963–88

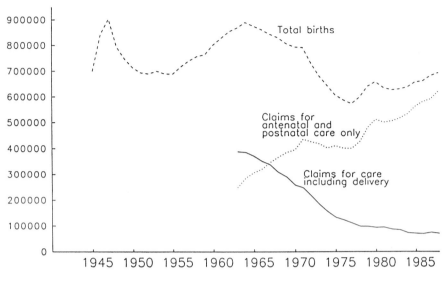

Source: DHSS, FP24 claims by GPs

since 1988 needed to update the graph in Figure 3.2, which is also from the second edition of *Where to be born?* (Campbell and Macfarlane 1994). Data provided by the Department of Health for the years 1989 onwards appear to have been compiled on a different basis and were described as 'not reliable' and 'not necessarily complete'. The numbers of claims by GPs for giving antenatal and postnatal care now appear to exceed the numbers of babies born!

What care is provided?

Trends and variations in interventions in pregnancy and labour, such as Caesarean, induction and epidural rates are of widespread interest to users and providers of services and to the local and national press. Although most units extract this information from notes and produce statistics for perinatal meetings and for reports of hospital or community units, it often does not get passed on to regional or national systems. This can happen if computer systems used in maternity units are not designed to communicate with hospital systems, or if neither is capable of providing records in a form which can be transferred to district or regional computer systems.

A recent article (Macfarlane and Chamberlain 1993) on trends in Caesarean section rates pointed out that Scotland is the only country of the United Kingdom to have a consistent series of data for the last 15 years or so. Its rates are compared

Figure 3.3.   Caesarean rates for hospital births in selected countries

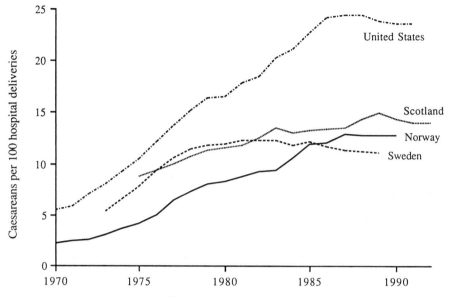

Source: International collaborating effort on perinatal and infant mortality

with those of Sweden, Norway and the United States (Figure 3.3). The other three countries of the United Kingdom had recently changed their data collection systems, thus giving rise to discontinuities in the series of data. Although Wales and Northern Ireland are getting over the initial problems they experienced with their new systems, the incompleteness and poor quality of the data for England collected through the Maternity Hospital Episode System (HES) are a continuing cause for concern.

There has been some improvement in this system since it started in September 1988. Nevertheless, by the financial year 1991–92, data from the Körner minimum data set were collected for only 450 420 or 69 per cent of the 649 014 maternities which occurred in England. (Department of Health 1993c). This does not mean, of course, that the data were not available at local level. One region, North West Thames, which collects and publishes very complete data about deliveries in its hospitals, contributed no data to Maternity HES in 1991–92. In addition, even where records exist in Maternity HES, some individual data items are missing (Middle and Macfarlane 1994).

This explains why the most recent year for which there are reliable national data on Caesarean sections and other interventions in England was 1985 (Figure 3.4). This was the last year of the Maternity Hospital In-Patient Enquiry (Department of Health and OPCS 1988), the predecessor of Maternity HES. Data about anaesthesia and analgesia, including the use of epidurals were collected in a recent national survey of pain relief in labour (Chamberlain et al. 1993). More recent but less detailed data should be available through Maternity HES but are unreliable (Middle and Macfarlane 1994).

Figure 3.4.   Trends in operative deliveries, England and Wales, 1955–85

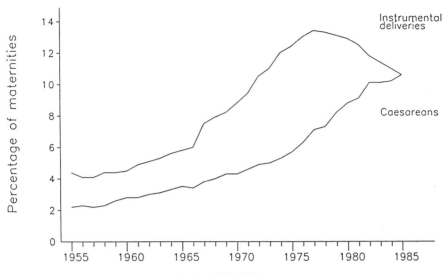

Source: Maternity Hospital In-patient Enquiry, Welsh Office

Even if Maternity HES was complete it would still have severe limitations. As its name suggests, it is an episode based system, with no identifier to link successive episodes of hospital in-patient care for the same woman. Thus it could tell us how many antenatal in-patient episodes there were in a given time period, but not how many women had one or more in-patient episodes during pregnancy. In addition, there is no routine linkage with records about care given in outpatient clinics, in the community or in general practice. This could be done if, as has been proposed, NHS numbers were included on all NHS records.

Until 1987, data collected about the work of community midwives in England and Wales included the numbers of deliveries they conducted at home and in hospital and the numbers of women to whom they gave postnatal care in the community. These are shown in Figure 3.5. Data were not collected about the women or their babies. The introduction of team midwifery and other new ways in which midwives work in both hospital and the community means that more appropriate data are now needed, but the change did not respond to this. Since 1988, only the total numbers of 'face-to-face contacts' have been collected, without any reference to what work these contacts involved.

Although Maternity HES should cover all registrable births, those outside NHS hospitals appear to be under-reported. The Scottish SMR2 system has always included some but not all births outside NHS hospitals. Since 1993, a determined effort has been made to ensure that data are collected about all of them. With the move to community based care, there is a need to expand the scope of each country's data collection system to ensure that births in places other than NHS

Figure 3.5.   The changing role of community midwives, England and Wales, 1949–87

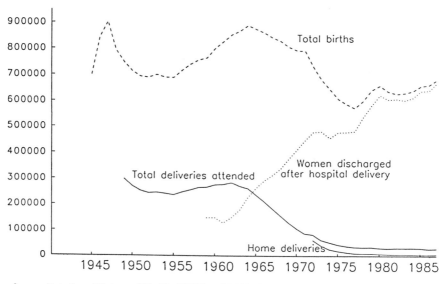

Source: Data from Ministry of Health, DHSS and Welsh Office publications

hospitals are included and classified appropriately. For example, distinctions should be made between planned and unplanned home births.

The need for a pregnancy based record has long been recognised (Thomson and Barron 1980). In Scotland, it may be possible to achieve this by record linkage. In England the plan to put NHS numbers on all NHS records offers the potential for linkage, but more is needed. Systems must be devised to link together episodes of care by doctors and midwives in hospital in-patient and outpatient settings, in general practitioners' surgeries, in people's homes and elsewhere. This will need the agreement of all the providers concerned as well as the appropriate technology and software. There are different ways of achieving this. In the short term, the potential for pregnant women to carry their own notes in electronic as well as paper form could be explored, as well as the possibility that the 'lead professional' could have a role in coordinating information.

Where can care be given?

Until recently, the four central government health departments kept lists of maternity units and the numbers of consultant and general practitioner beds in each. In England, the categories were extended in the late 1980s to include a third category of bed, to which both consultant obstetricians and general practitioners had access. Although they gave some indication of changes over time (Figure 3.6), the statistics did not show the extent to which the facilities may have been used by midwives for 'domino' deliveries or were provided in midwife-led units. Thus they were clearly in need of revision, but the change which occurred led to less rather than more detail.

With the introduction of the internal market in April 1991, however, the Department of Health stopped holding centrally the names and locations of individual units and the numbers of beds in each. Instead, it keeps only the names of providers of care and the total numbers of beds of each type they provide, on the grounds that 'beds within one unit may be on more than one site or in more than one hospital' (Sackville 1993). This makes it impossible to monitor the extent to which accessibility, in terms of the geographical distribution of maternity units of different types, is changing. It also means that there is no longer a central list of maternity units which can be used as a sampling frame for surveys. More generally, the Department of Health does not know how many hospitals there are in England (Sackville 1994).

With shorter lengths of postnatal stay in maternity units and the possibility that the numbers of women admitted for delivery only will increase, the use of the counts of beds as a measure of the capacity of a maternity unit should be reconsidered. Alternative measures of resources, such as the numbers of midwives per woman delivered can only be developed if reliable and consistent data are available about staff. In any case, more detailed information is needed about the extent to which facilities of different types are provided and about their geographical location. It is probably more appropriate to collect this through occasional surveys, such as that done in 1984 by the National Birthday Trust (Chamberlain and Gunn 1987) than through routine data collection systems.

Although the overall numbers of home births can be obtained from birth registration data, its function is to record the location of the event rather than the type of care or whether the birth occurred in the place which had been intended. This information should be recorded in the Maternity Hospital Episode System. Birth registration data have been used to plot Figure 3.7, which shows that after reaching an all-time low of 0.9 per cent of all maternities in the mid 1980s, the percentage at home rose marginally but steadily to 1.3 per cent by 1992. This does include births which took place at home unintentionally. These accounted for a third of births at home in 1979 and 1984 (Chamberlain and Gunn 1987; Campbell and Macfarlane 1994).

For whom are services provided?

Information about the people who use the services is needed both for planning and evaluation of services and for interpreting measures of outcome. Birth registration is the main source of social and demographic information about the baby's parents. Even this, which includes the parents' ages, occupations, and countries of birth, is limited. It does not include information about housing, unemployment, educational level or economic circumstances. As the proportion

Figure 3.6.   Numbers of maternity beds and maternity units, United Kingdom, 1980 and 1989–90

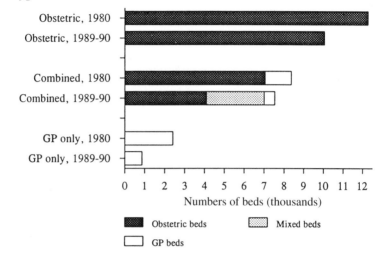

Numbers of beds in maternity units,
United Kingdom, 1980 and 1989–90

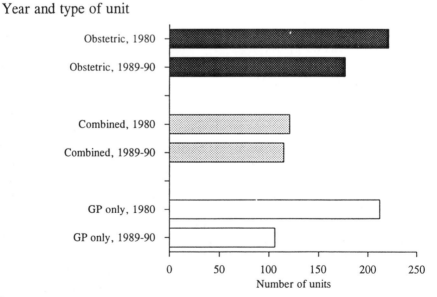

Numbers of maternity units,
United Kingdom, 1980 and 1989–90

Source: Hansard

Figure 3.7.   Percentage of deliveries at home, England and Wales, 1964–92

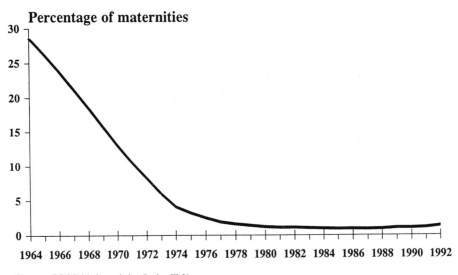

Percentage of maternities

Source: OPCS birth statistics Series FM1

of babies whose parents are living on means tested benefits and were therefore eligible for maternity payments from the Social Fund rose from 21 per cent in 1988–89 to 30 per cent in 1992–93 (Maternity Alliance 1993), the lack of fuller information about their circumstances is a major gap. Nevertheless, it may be more appropriate to collect more detailed socioeconomic data through surveys rather than through routine systems.

The socioeconomic data collected at birth and death registration are obtained directly from parents by Registrars of Births and Deaths. They are trained to ask specific questions and can usually obtain more accurate information about items such as occupations than most NHS staff.

For births outside marriage, even the majority which are jointly registered by both parents, parity is not recorded. For births within marriage, the definition of parity is restricted to 'previous live births by this or any previous husband'. A White Paper *Registration: Proposals for Change* (OPCS 1990) proposed that every woman registering a birth should be asked about any previous live and still births, irrespective of her marital status at the time. Unfortunately, this White Paper, which includes a proposal to specifically record mothers' occupations at birth registration, along with many other useful changes to the law about registering births, marriages and deaths appears to have been forgotten by the government.

In general, there is very limited personal information about the characteristics of the baby's parents in most NHS routine information systems at regional and national level, although this may be less true for Scotland. Fuller information may be collected locally in clinical notes or through birth notification, but there is considerable variation in the choice of data items collected, the way they are defined and their accuracy. Thus data about the parents held at national level are in a separate system from those about the care given and the place in which it is given. It has therefore been suggested that if the Maternity Hospital Episode System was improved, data from it could then be linked to OPCS' birth registration data. It would be appropriate also to link in the corresponding NHS data for Wales, which has been implementing a system with a similar minimum data set to Maternity HES. In Scotland, birth registration data are already linked to the SMR2 Maternity Discharge Record.

In the past, the mother's country of birth, which is recorded at birth registration, has been used as a proxy measure of ethnic origin. This is increasingly unsatisfactory as an increasing proportion of people from minority ethnic groups giving birth in the UK today were born here themselves. Because of this, it is intended that ethnic origin, classified as in the 1991 Census, be recorded on all NHS records. Interpreting these data may be problematic, however (Sheldon and Parker 1992). It will be interesting to see to what extent black women in the childbearing age range who have lived most or all of their lives in the UK choose to classify themselves as 'Black British', rather than choose descriptions such as 'Indian', 'Pakistani', 'Bangladeshi', or 'Black-Caribbean'.

The costs of care

A review of available data about the costs of care in different settings found that most of it was already old, although it called into question the assumption that care in small units cost less than that in larger units (Mugford 1990). Thus, as has been pointed out (National Perinatal Epidemiology Unit 1993) there were no contemporary data readily available to cost the changes proposed in *Changing Childbirth*. The assumption that adequate care can be provided in the community more cheaply than in hospitals has proved unfounded in other areas of health and social care. This makes it essential to have data available to cost plans for community based maternity care.

These data may prove to be elusive. The introduction of the internal market in April 1991 has led to sweeping changes in NHS financial systems and made redundant many financial returns which had been introduced following the recommendations of the Körner Committee. These changes have been driven by trusts' need to monitor the resources they buy and pay for, and to recoup the cost. Specialty costing, which was also recommended by the Körner Committee, has increasingly been developed in different ways in different places.

Although there may be more detailed financial data collected within units and trusts than in the past, less information is publicly available. The district health authorities, who purchase health care for their populations, have information about the prices they have to pay, but in their new role have less access to data about resources and their costs.

Figure 3.8.   Perinatal mortality rates for districts, England and Wales, 1990–92

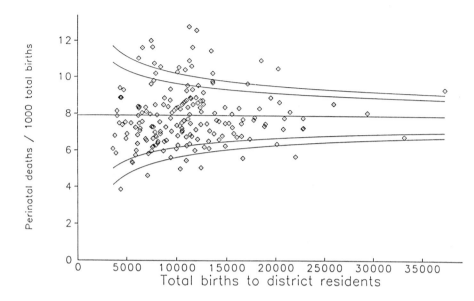

The outcome of pregnancy

Less than 1 per cent of babies are stillborn or die in the first week of life, but considerable efforts are put into collecting data about them through death registration and confidential enquiries. Although much has been written about the need to interpret data in relation to the characteristics of the populations giving birth (Macfarlane and Mugford 1984, Botting and Macfarlane 1990), it is depressing to see the extent to which crude stillbirth and infant mortality rates are still presented as measures of the health of the population as well as of the quality of the care it receives (Department of Health 1993d).

The method of presentation shown in Figure 3.8 is now used routinely by OPCS in its DH3 Monitor Series. Because the numbers of events in each district are small, aggregated rates for the years 1990–92 combined are plotted against total numbers of births in the district. The horizontal line is the England and Wales rate and the curved lines are the 95 per cent and 99 per cent confidence intervals based on the numbers of births in the district. Clearly more than 1 per cent of the districts have rates which lie outside the 99 per cent confidence intervals so the differences are not merely a consequence of random variation. Districts with exceptionally high rates tend to be those where a high proportion of fathers are in manual occupations or where a high proportion of mothers were born in the 'New Commonwealth'.

A similar approach can be used in monitoring trends over time. Figure 3.9 shows trends in two districts from the 1981 reorganisation onwards. One district claimed to have reduced perinatal mortality by centralising its maternity units, but mortality remained virtually constant. The other used to be singled out for its high mortality, which then fell. It may be difficult to continue these graphs beyond 1993, as Bradford district has merged with another. More generally, the continuing mergers of health authorities in England and the restructuring of its regions will make it difficult to monitor trends over time.

Data collected at death registration can be linked to data collected when the birth was registered. Figure 3.10 produced from these linked data is an update of a graph which was published in 1980 (Macdonald Davies 1980). The high reported mortality rate for births at home influenced the House of Commons Health Committee to conclude at the time that planned home births were unsafe. In doing so it ignored the fact that some of these births were not planned to occur at home and many of these were the ones with the highest risk of death (Campbell and Macfarlane 1994).

This is just one instance where it would be helpful to use birthweight specific mortality rates. Although birthweight is not itself a measure of morbidity, it is relevant to it as smaller babies are more likely to be stillborn or die shortly after birth or experience poor health in the neonatal period or later in childhood.

Birthweight is recorded on stillbirth certificates and since 1975 OPCS has been attempting to collect birthweight for all live births in England and Wales. It has done this indirectly, rather than by asking the parents. Birthweight is included on birth notifications sent by the birth attendant, usually the midwife, to the local health authority. Registrars of Births and Deaths have then obtained birthweight data from the health authority and added them to the information given by parents and recorded on the birth 'draft entry' which they forward to OPCS. When the information did not arrive in time, OPCS obtained the missing birthweights from the hospital or other place of birth. By 1983, birthweight data were virtually complete with less than 1 per cent missing, mainly for very immature babies who were not weighed. In 1989, OPCS stopped obtaining missing birthweights and nearly 4 per cent are now missing (Figure 3.11). OPCS has been investigating ways of collecting the missing data and alternative ways of collecting all birthweights, but it will need the resources to implement its conclusions.

There are few routine data about the morbidity of mothers and babies, except for in Scotland. In England, diagnostic data collected through Maternity HES about mothers and babies are very incomplete and of poor quality (Middle and Macfarlane 1994). In particular, they are much worse than those in its predecessor, the Maternity Hospital In-patient Enquiry. Child health computer systems contain a considerable amount of information about morbidity, but in England and Wales most are not organised in such a way that statistical information can be extracted from them. On the other hand, the North East Thames and South Western Regions, like Northern Ireland and Scotland have been developing the use of data from child health systems to collect data about the birth and the outcome of pregnancy.

Figure 3.9.   Monitoring crude perinatal mortality in two English districts, 1981–92

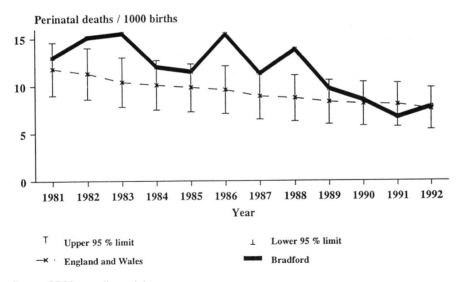

Source: OPCS mortality statistics

Figure 3.10.   Perinatal mortality by place of birth, England and Wales, 1975–91

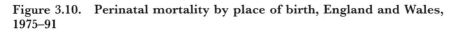

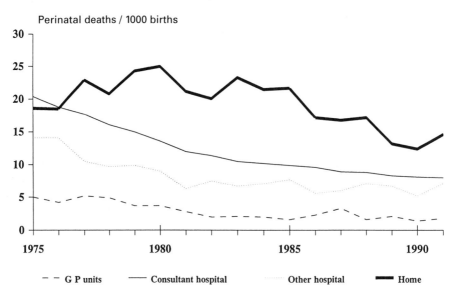

Source: OPCS mortality statistics, DH3

Figure 3.11.   Percentage of live birth registrations with birthweight missing, England and Wales, 1977–92

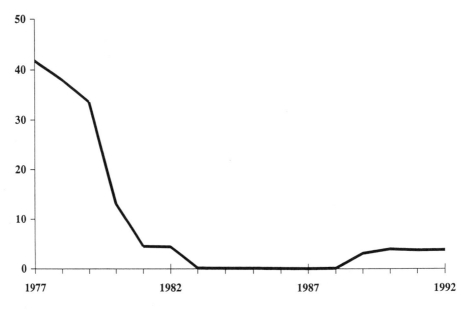

Source: OPCS

The Clinical Standards Advisory Group (1993) has commented on the poor quality of routine data about babies undergoing neonatal intensive care and of the problems in linking them with data about their mothers. Although there have been many follow-up studies of babies treated in particular units, population-based data about their health status later in childhood are even more difficult and expensive to collect. The Audit Commission has also recently drawn attention to the need for such data.

Conclusions

The quality, extent and completeness of routine NHS data in England have not improved over the past ten years and in many cases have deteriorated. There have been important developments in record linkage in Scotland, which also has NHS data of high quality. The creation of the internal market has led to some improvement in the availability of financial data within NHS trusts and units, but has greatly decreased the extent to which data are publicly available.

To monitor the introduction of community based care, existing systems need to be improved and modified. This includes linking data from different providers with demographic data. In order to achieve this, NHS trusts must share information which should be made publicly available. Arrangements are also needed to replace the information function of regions in England. Some more detailed recommendations are given below.

Recommendations

Improvements to existing routine data collection systems

1 Urgent action should be taken to improve the quality and completeness of data in the Maternity Hospital Episode System.
2 National NHS data collection systems should include data about all births and maternity care provided outside NHS hospitals.
3 Data about the facilities and resources of NHS trusts and other provider units, including the location, size and nature of facilities for maternity care and their costs should be made public and collected by central government.
4 Urgent attention should be given to making arrangements at subnational level in England to carry on and develop the information work currently done by regional health authorities.
5 Resources should be made available to OPCS to collect the birthweight data missing from birth 'draft entries' for England and Wales.
6 The government should legislate on the proposals in the White Paper *Registration: Proposals for Change*.
7 Methods developed in Scotland for linking data about care given to women and the subsequent care given to their babies in the first year of life should be adapted and extended for use in the other countries of the UK.

8 Population-based methods should be developed to collect information about the health status of children in childhood and relate it to information collected at or around the time of birth.

9 Fuller use should be made of data collected at birth notification and through child health computer systems. Scotland should be encouraged to maintain its child health data system and to implement the proposals to link it with data from pre-school surveillance. In England and Wales, data from birth notifications could be analysed at a national level and linked to data collected at birth registration.

Developing data systems for new forms of maternity care

1 A minimum dataset for a pregnancy based record should be drawn up, piloted and agreed. This could draw on the work already done for the Information Management Group in England to draw up a new contract minimum dataset.

2 Data items collected and classifications used in routine systems should be reviewed and changed, where necessary, to make them suitable for collecting data about new forms of maternity care. Clear definitions should be drawn up to increase the consistency with which data are recorded.

3 Fuller information should be collected about the care given by general practitioners.

4 Information systems should be developed to bring together data about care given to the same woman and her baby or babies in hospital, the community and general practice. These should allow caregivers access to full information about all the care being given to individual women and also allow anonymised data to be collated on a population basis. In the longer term this may be linked to the development of population registers which should be developed to bring together data about maternity care with data about other care given to individuals.

Acknowledgements
Thanks to colleagues in the National Perinatal Epidemiology Unit, the Government Statistical Service and elsewhere for help, information and advice in the preparation of this chapter. The author is funded by the Department of Health.

References

Audit Commission (1993) *Children First: a Study of Hospital Services*. London: HMSO

Barron, S.L. and Macfarlane, A.J. (1990) 'Collection and use of routine maternity data' in R.J. Lilford (Ed.) *Computing and Decision Support in Obstetrics and Gynaecology*, pp. 681–97. London: Bailliere Tindall

Botting, B.J. and Macfarlane, A.J. (1990) 'Geographic variation in infant mortality in relation to birthweight' in M. Britton (Ed.) *Mortality and Geography*, pp. 47–56. London: HMSO

Campbell, R. (1991) *Information Collected on Stillbirths and Infant Deaths in Northern Ireland*. Report to the Department of Health and Social Services

Campbell, R. (1992) 'Demographic statistics in Northern Ireland' in *Research Data on Northern Ireland*. Colchester: ESRC Data Archive

Campbell, R. and Macfarlane A.J. (1994) *Where to be Born? The Debate and the Evidence*, 2nd edn. Oxford: National Perinatal Epidemiology Unit

Central Statistical Office (1990) Guide to Official Statistics, No. 5. London: HMSO

Chamberlain, G.V.P. and Gunn P. (Eds) (1987) *Birthplace*. Chichester: John Wiley

Chamberlain, G.V.P., Wraight, A. and Steer, P. (1993) *Pain in Labour and its Relief*. London: Churchill Livingstone

Clinical Standards Advisory Group (1993) *Access to and Availability of Specialist Services*. London: HMSO

Department of Health (1993a) *Changing Childbirth*. Part 1: Report of the Expert Maternity Group. London: HMSO

Department of Health (1993b) *Managing the New NHS*. London: Department of Health

Department of Health (1993c) Data provided in letter to Audrey Wise MP

Department of Health (1993d) *Population Health Outcome Indicators for the NHS, 1993*, England. A consultation document. Guildford: University of Surrey

Department of Health and Office of Population Censuses and Surveys (1988) *Hospital In-patient Enquiry Maternity Tables, England, 1982–85*, Series MB4 No. 28. London: HMSO

Macdonald Davies, I. (1980) Perinatal and infant deaths: social and biological factors. *Popul Trends* **19**, 19–21

Macfarlane, A.J. (1990) 'Official statistics and women's health and illness' in H. Roberts (Ed.) *Women's Health Counts*, pp. 18–62. London: Routledge

Macfarlane, A.J. (1994) 'Sources of data' in M. Maresh (Ed.) *Audit in Obstetrics and Gynaecology*, pp. 18-49. Oxford: Blackwell Scientific

Macfarlane, A.J. and Chamberlain, G.C. (1993) What is happening to Caesarean section rates? *Lancet* **342**, 1005–6

Macfarlane, A.J. and Mugford, M. (1984) *Birth Counts: Statistics of Pregnancy and Childbirth*. London: HMSO

Maternity Alliance (1993) Born in poverty. *Maternity Action* **61**, 9

Middle, C. and Macfarlane A.J. (1994) Labour and delivery in 'normal' primiparous women, analysis of routinely collected data. Report for the Clinical Standards Advisory Group. London: CSAG

Mugford, M. (1990) Economies of scale and low risk maternity care: what is the evidence? *Maternity Action* **46**, 6–8

National Perinatal Epidemiology Unit (1993) *Response to 'Changing Childbirth'. The Report of the Expert Maternity Group*. Oxford: National Perinatal Epidemiology Unit

Office of Population Censuses and Surveys (1990) *Registration: Proposals for Change*. London: HMSO

Sackville, T. (1993) Written reply to parliamentary question from Dawn Primarolo MP. *House of Commons Official Report (Hansard) 17 May*, col. 26

Sackville, T. (1994) Written reply to parliamentary question from David Blunkett MP. *House of Commons Official Report (Hansard) 28 January*, col. 417

Sheldon, T.A. and Parker, H. (1992) 'The use of "ethnicity" and "race" in health research: a cautionary note' in W.I.U. Ahmad (Ed.) *The Politics of 'Race' and Health*. Bradford: University of Bradford and Ilkley College

Steering Group on Health Services Information (1985) *Supplement to the First and Fourth Reports to the Secretary of State*. London: HMSO

Thomson, A.M. and Barron, S.L. (1980) 'A Standard Maternity Information System' in I. Chalmers and G. McIlwaine (Eds) *Perinatal Audit and Surveillance*. London: RCOG

Chapter 4

Review and assessment of maternity services in the Netherlands

Martine Eskes and Dirk van Alten

Introduction

In 1818 the ministers of the King constituted a Public Health act on the 'Instructions for midwives in the Kingdom of the Netherlands: The midwife was only allowed to assist in the natural birth process, to perform some methods of operation without use of any instrument.'

In 1862 Thorbecke became Secretary of State. In the same year he introduced to the Parliament four Public Health Bills to regulate the State Health Inspectorate, the training required to qualify as a physician, pharmacist and midwife; the practice of medicine and the practice of pharmacy.

The decision to acknowledge the profession of midwife could be considered as a pragmatical one (no control required in numbers, cheaper than physicians, supervision of the State Health Inspectorate); however, Thorbecke's view was that maternity care concerns the normal pregnancy and labour in the healthy woman in the first place and therefore needed a different approach. Later Kloosterman postulated the 'Basic Philosophy of Dutch Obstetrics' which would have the approval of Thorbecke:

> In the Netherlands the principle is still adhered to that pregnancy and parturition are essentially normal events which as a rule require careful examinations and counselling, and medical intervention is only required if there is an indication. (Kloosterman 1978)

At the same time attention was paid to the training of midwives. Between 1861 and 1913 three midwife schools were founded. Until 1993 the training lasted three years, and currently is four years full-time after secondary school (GCE 'A' level equivalents in chemistry and biology).

Since the beginning of the twentieth century both the conditions of childbirth in hospital and at home have improved. Organisations were founded to train young girls to take care of a healthy woman and her baby during the lying-in period and in doing her household chores. In 1925 those activities were coordinated by the Government through the Maternity Home Help Organisation. Nationwide, trained maternity-aid nurses are available to assist at home deliveries.

The independent midwife, assisted by a maternity-aid nurse offers the healthy woman with an uncomplicated pregnancy the opportunity to choose between a delivery at home or in hospital. Pre-, intrapartum and postnatal care is performed by a midwife or sometimes by a general practitioner. Since 1945 the percentage of home deliveries has decreased continuously. In 1961 71.2 per cent of all deliveries took place at home, in 1978 35.8 per cent and in 1991 31 per cent.

General principles of the Dutch system

The prenatal, intrapartum and postnatal care for the uncomplicated pregnancy and delivery is performed by an independent midwife or general practitioner. If a midwife or general practitioner diagnoses a symptom or sign of pathology, they are expected to advise obstetric care by a specialist in a hospital. There are agreed criteria for referral to hospital and confinement.

Selection for place of delivery of the pregnant women is an important part of the basic philosophy of obstetrics in the Netherlands. Selection is necessary both to allow a woman to have her baby at home or in a local hospital, and to concentrate the high-risk patients in fully equipped obstetric departments of large hospitals.

The Dutch Goverment supports this organisation:

1 By taking care of the training of midwives in special schools.
2 By protecting the midwives economically. In districts where one or more midwives are practising, the midwife (not the general practitioner) is paid by the compulsory insurance of the Health Service for normal obstetrics.
3 By stimulating the 'Maternity Home Help Organisation', a nationwide organisation that provides well-trained maternity-aid nurses to help the mothers, and to assist the midwife.
4 By directing the system through compulsory and private insurance.

The current list of medical indications for specialist care during pregnancy, labour and the puerperium has existed since 1959, when it was drawn up after national consultation of the medical advisers of the insurance companies and Kloosterman. In 1982 the list of medical indications for specialist care during the puerperium was published by mutual agreement. This was an important event because of the great interest in the puerperium at home after the delivery at home as well as after the delivery in hospital. The composition of a new list of medical indications for specialist care during pregnancy and labour was published in 1987 and is under discussion. There is some criticism of the scientific basis of some of the indications and according to some, the obstetrician is not considered to be the obvious person to decide on the type of care provider in doubtful cases.

In the Netherlands, much discussion has taken place during the last two decades about the effectiveness of a system of care that is different from that of almost all other European countries and developed countries in the Western World, a system with a high percentage of home deliveries.

In 1991 31 per cent of the infants were born at home, which represents a slow decline from the 1986 figure of 35.9 per cent. In 1991 71.9 per cent of the births at home were conducted by midwives. Of all births 45 per cent were conducted by midwives, 46 per cent by the obstetricians and 9 per cent by the general practitioners (total number of births in 1991: 199 732) (Netherlands Central Bureau of Statistics 1993). Perinatal mortality in the Netherlands has not shown the same decline since 1982 as in some other countries such as Scandinavia. The figures (per 1000) were 9.8 in 1985, 9.7 in 1986, 9.4 in 1987, 9.6 in 1989 and 9.1 in 1991.

In 1991 the Caesarean section rate was 7.9 per cent, forceps and vacuum extractions 9.2 per cent (SIG 1992), low compared with many other countries.

Research information

Breyer and Stolk (1971) studied 3724 cases of stillbirth in 1961 and concluded that the indication for hospital confinement was ignored in a significant number. Smits (1981) describes a regional study (Enschede) in 1974. He concluded that the selection for place of delivery carried out by midwives, family doctors and obstetricians was not always correct. The study comprises 91 per cent of the children born in the study period. Doornbos et al. (1987) studied the under-registration of the perinatal mortality in 13 hospitals in Amsterdam. All cases with birthweight $\geqslant 500$ g and gestational age >22 weeks were considered. They found under-registration to be 14.3 per cent in 1981 and 1982. (Birthweight >1000 g and gestationed age >28 weeks: under-registration 7 per cent.) Hoogendoorn (1986) advocated: 'reconsideration of the delivery of Maternity Services and particularly to examine criteria for home vs hospital delivery'. Hoogendoorn did not speak at all about midwifery care. Treffers and Laan (1986) concluded from a study of regional perinatal mortality and hospitalisation at the delivery that the degree of hospitalisation was not a major factor in determining variations in regional perinatal mortality rates in the Netherlands.

In 1988 a study in the Nijmegen area was published of 1034 infants born to women of a low-risk population. The infants were neurologically examined in the neonatal period (Berghs and Spanjaards 1988): 62 per cent were attended during pregnancy and delivery by a midwife, 12 per cent by a general practitioner and 26 per cent by a specialist obstetrician. The neurological condition of the newborns showed no difference in the three groups. The main difference between the deliveries attended by specialist obstetricians and those attended by midwives and general practitioners was the significantly higher rate of intervention by the obstetricians.

In 1989 the results of the Wormerveer Study were published (Van Alten et al. 1989). This long-term prospective investigation focused on the effectiveness of care by independent midwives in a small suburb north of Amsterdam. The study comprised 7980 women consecutively booked at the midwives' practice during a period of 13 years (1969–83), with a complete follow-up of their pregnancies, deliveries and 8055 children. The chosen place of birth was at home or in the

Table 4.1.   Place of birth of the 8055 infants born in the study group of 7980 women and perinatal mortality (stillborn and early neonatal mortality)

Place of birth	Women n (%)	Infants n (%)	Perinatal mortality n (per 1000)	
Hospital after maternal referral				
Antenatal	1367 (17.1)	1430 (17.7)	74 (51.7)	
Intrapartum	623 (8.0)	637 (7.9)	7 (11.0)	} (2.3)
At home and in maternity unit	5981 (74.9)	5988 (74.3)	8 (1.3)	
Total	7980 (100)	8055 (100)	89 (11.1)	

The Wormerveer Study (van Alten *et al.* 1989)

small maternity unit at Wormerveer or in a hospital. An estimated 92 per cent of all nulliparous women in the catchment area of 40 000 inhabitants booked at the midwives practice and 79 per cent of all parous women.

One of the aims of the study was to evaluate the selection procedure by which midwives separate pregnant women into groups of high and low risk. Outcome variables were perinatal mortality (i.e. all stillbirths and all neonatal deaths within one week of birth with a birthweight $\geqslant 500$ g), infant morbidity (measured by admission rate to the hospital), and convulsions in the first week of life. In a subgroup of the total population of newborns (175 consecutive bookings in 1982), the umbilical artery pH was recorded and a neurological examination was performed, using strictly standardised methods.

Of the 89 perinatal deaths, 15 (17 per cent) occurred in the group of 6625 infants (82.2 per cent) born to the mothers selected as low-risk cases during pregnancy (Table 4.1). The remaining 74 perinatal deaths (83 per cent) occurred in the group of 1430 infants born to mothers selected as high-risk cases (17.7 per cent).

Convulsions in the first week of life occurred in 12 of these 8055 children (1.5 per 1000); in seven cases the convulsions occurred in term infants during the first 48 h after birth (0.9 per 1000) and 0.7 per 1000 in the group born under sole care of the midwife. Dennis and Chalmers (1982), who proposed this incidence of convulsions as a standard for measuring the quality of perinatal care, found in Great Britain an incidence of 4.2 convulsions per 1000 births and 1.7 per 1000 births in term infants within 48 h after birth. In an Irish study the incidence of convulsions was 3.0 per 1000 births (MacDonald *et al.* 1985).

The mean umbilical artery pH value in children born under the sole care of a midwife was 7.27 (Knuist *et al.* 1987), higher than the value found in another study of home deliveries and hospital-based deliveries (Eskes *et al.* 1981). Only one of the 45 first-born infants born under sole care of a midwife had a suboptimal neurological score, a very low incidence (Eskes *et al.* 1987). The admission rate to a paediatric department within a week of birth was 3.8 per cent in the group born

Table 4.2. Caesarean section and operative vaginal delivery rates by parity in the total group of 7980 and the selected group of 6613 women

| | | | Mode of delivery | | | |
| | | | Caesaream section | | Operative vaginal[a] | |
Parity	Total *n*	Selected *n*	Total *n* (%)	Selected *n* (%)	Total *n* (%)	Selected *n* (%)
0	4000	3092	80 (2.0)	21 (0.7)	344 (8.6)	230 (7.4)
⩾1	3980	3521	30 (0.7)	8 (0.2)	24 (0.6)	18 (0.5)
Total	7980	6613	110 (1.4)	29 (0.4)	368 (4.6)	248 (3.7)

[a]Includes forceps and vacuum extractions.
The Wormeveer Study (van Alten *et al.* 1989)

under sole care of the midwife. Most admissions were for observation only. A total of 23 (0.4 per cent) born under sole care of a midwife were admitted immediately after birth because of asphyxia, of which 21 were born in the period 1969–1976, and only two during the period 1977–1983.

These results were obtained in spite of a low rate of intervention. In the total group of 7980 women, 110 (1.4 per cent) had a Caesarean section. In the group selected as low-risk cases during pregnancy (6613 women), there were only 29 Caesarean sections (0.4 per cent) (Table 4.2).

The cases of perinatal mortality were studied by a panel of independent experts to assess non-optimal management. In 66 (75 per cent) of the 89 cases complete or near consensus was reached. In this group preventable factors were noticed in 29 cases (44 per cent). In 30 cases (45 per cent) the mortality was judged as inevitable. Preventable factors were mainly present in decisions made during the prenatal period by the midwife (or a general practitioner) and the obstetrician, and in care during labour and delivery and the postnatal period by the obstetrician and paediatrician. The care of the midwife during labour and delivery had little influence on preventable perinatal mortality. In the 29 cases with preventable factors, 12 cases concerned the skill of the obstetrician, seven cases the skill of the paediatrician, and seven cases the skill of the midwife. A further decrease of perinatal mortality may be achieved by analysis of the cases and continued education of all workers in perinatal care (Eskes *et al.* 1993).

The Dutch perinatal database

The perinatal data base of the Netherlands (LVR) was initiated with the voluntary participation of the gynaecologists in 1982. The midwives' participation started in 1985. Unfortunately the general practitioners did not join. In 1989 76 per cent of all deliveries cared for by specialists and 73 per cent of all those cared for by

Table 4.3.   Place of birth in the Netherlands 1988–1991 (Central Bureau of Statistics)

Born in the Netherlands	1988	1989	1990	1991
At home	64 114	63 397	64 008	61 949
	34.2%	33.4%	32.1%	31.0%
Hospital	22 893	125 979	134 392	137 097
	65.4%	65.8%	67.5%	68.6%
Abroad	678	703	704	686
Total	187 685	190 079	199 104	199 732

midwives were registered. In 1991 the percentages of participation were 81.4 per cent and 83.9 per cent respectively.

Place of birth

In 1991 199 732 infants were born in the Netherlands. A review of the place of birth is given in Table 4.3. Of the 61 949 births at home, 44 535 were attended by midwives (71.9 per cent) and 17 414 by general practitioners (28.1 per cent). In the following analysis facts from the annual report of 1989 are used, because more details about home deliveries were available for that year, especially about perinatal mortality and morbidity (van der Esch and van Alten 1993; Lems *et al.* 1994).

Choice for home delivery

In 1989 data were recorded of 44 164 women who chose home delivery (19 677 nulliparous and 24 487 parous women). During pregnancy 22.1 per cent of the nulliparous and 10.1 per cent of the parous women were referred to the obstetrician. Table 4.4 shows the reasons for referral during pregnancy. After the process of risk-selection, 15 326 nulliparous and 21 996 parous women started labour under the sole care of a midwife (selected group). During labour and delivery, 4758 (24.2 per cent) of the nulliparous and 1593 (6.5 per cent) of the parous women were referred to the obstetrician. The reasons for referral are given in Table 4.5.

Instrumental and operative deliveries: in the group of women referred during delivery the Caesarean section rate was 2.4 per cent for the nulliparous and 0.3 per cent for the parous women. Vacuum extraction was carried out in 1232 cases (8.0 per cent) in nulliparous and in 150 cases (0.7 per cent) in parous women. The figures for forceps deliveries were 480 (3.1 per cent) and 33 (0.2 per cent) respectively (Table 4.6).

Home deliveries (1989 LVR)

Home delivery occurred in 30 971 women who gave birth to 30 977 infants; six twins were born at home; 30 915 infants were born in vertex position, 45 in breech position (0.1 per cent). Of the infants born with a certain gestational age, 213

Table 4.4.   Home delivery: referrals during pregnancy (LVR 1989)

Referrals during pregnancy	Nulliparous women $n_1 = 19\,677$ (%)	Parous women $n_2 = 24\,487$ (%)
PIH	1041 (5.4)	259 (1.1)
Postmaturity	710 (3.6)	442 (1.8)
(Threatening) preterm labour	684 (3.5)	414 (1.7)
Malposition breech incl.	722 (3.7)	325 (1.3)
S.G.A.?	414 (2.1)	274 (1.1)
Diabetes of pregnancy	96 (0.5)	90 (0.4)
Multiple pregnancy	101 (0.5)	119 (0.5)
Vaginal bleeding after >20 weeks	143 (0.7)	140 (0.6)
Positive size – dates discrepancy	80 (0.4)	44 (0.2)
Fetal death	77 (0.4)	83 (0.3)
Placental abruption	24 (0.1)	13 (0.0)
Miscellaneous	72 (0.5)	96 (0.5)
Remaining problems	187 (0.4)	192 (0.8)
Total referrals	4351 (22.1)	2491 (10.2)

Table 4.5.   Home delivery: referrals during labour and delivery (LCR 1989)

Referrals during labour and delivery	Nulliparous women $n_1 = 19\,677$ (%)	Parous women $n_2 = 24\,487$ (%)
Malposition	237 (1.2)	171 (0.7)
Fetal death	8 (0.04)	8 (0.03)
Absence of labour 24 hours after rupture of membranes	785 (4.0)	450 (1.8)
Poor progress in first stage	1069 (5.5)	186 (0.8)
Meconium stained amniotic fluid	825 (7.2)	407 (1.6)
Poor progress in second stage	1436 (7.4)	203 (0.8
Signs of fetal distress	249 (1.3)	59 (0.2)
Blood-loss during labour	28 (0.1)	35 (0.1)
Need for analgesia	66 (0.3)	7
Placental abruption	4	6
Others	51	61
Total	4758 (24.2)	1593 (6.5)

Table 4.6.   Caesarean section and operative vaginal delivery rates by parity in the selected group of 15 326 nulliparous and 21 996 parous women who started labour at home

Parity n (%)	Primigravida n (%)	Parous n (%)
Caesarean section	362 (2.4)	71 (0.3)
Forceps	480 (3.1)	33 (0.2)
Vacuum extraction	1232 (8.0)	150 (0.7)

Table 4.7.   Infants born at home and gestational age (LVR 1989)

Weeks	n (%)	Weight (g)	n (%)
20–27	— ⎫		
28–31	1 ⎪	500–999	3 (0.01)
32–34	15 ⎬ 213 (0.7)	1000–1999	23 (0.07)
35	29 ⎪	2000–2499	264 (0.8)
36	168 ⎭	2500–2999	3437 (11.1)
≥37	28 573 (92.2)	3000 and >	27 218 (87.9)
unknown	2 191 (7.1)	unknown	32 (0.1)
Total	30 977 (100)	Total	30 977 (100)

were preterm (<37 weeks; 0.7 per cent) (Table 4.7). Infants with a birthweight <2500 g were recorded in 290 cases (0.9 per cent) (Table 4.7), infants born with a gestation >40 weeks and a birthweight <2500 g occurred in 18 cases (0.06 per cent). A total of 30 cases of perinatal mortality (≥22 weeks' gestation and/or ≥500 g birthweight) occurred in the group of 30 977 infants (0.97 per 1000) born at home.

Analysis of the second stage of labour showed that of the nulliparous women 80.8 per cent delivered within 60 min, 95.3 per cent of the parous women within 30 min.

The state of perineum was as follows: episiotomy 22.3 per cent, vaginal and perineal tears 32.4 per cent (complete rupture 0.4 per cent), intact perineum 43.2 per cent. The Apgar score was registered in 30 960 of the 30 977 infants (99.9 per cent). Apgar score <7 after 5 min was present in 123 infants (0.4 per cent).

Admission to a paediatric department was necessary for 935 infants (3 per cent); 369 (1.2 per cent) immediately after birth, 171 (0.6 per cent) during the first day of life and 395 (1.3 per cent) during the lying-in period of the mother (days 2–7). The most important reasons for referral immediately after birth were dysmaturity, asphyxia and respiratory problems, including meconium aspiration. During the first day after birth respiratory problems and jaundice were the most important

Table 4.8.   Perinatal death home-deliveries (LVR 1989)

Fetal death ($n=6$)	1 – second child of not recognised twin pregnancy, birthweight 900 g
	1 – small for date <2.3 centile
	4 – no further information
Apgar score 1–6 ($n=7$)	1 – Down syndrome
	1 – congenital heart malformation
	5 – no further information
Apgar score 7–9 ($n=6$)	2 – gastrocardiac syndrome
	1 – transposition of the great arteries
	1 – other congenital malformations cardiovascular system
	2 – no further information
Apgar score 10 ($n=11$)	7 – congenital heart malformation
	1 – gastrocardiac syndrome
	1 – spina bifida
	1 – infection with group B streptococcus
	1 – no further information

reasons, whereas during days 2–7 after birth jaundice and feeding problems were important.

Maternal referrals to specialist care after delivery was necessary in 352 nulliparous women (3.3 per cent) and 277 parous women (1.4 per cent). Postpartum haemorrhage (>1000 ml) occurred in 134 nulliparous women (1.3 per cent) and 117 parous women (0.6 per cent). Manual removal of the placenta was necessary in 85 nulliparous (0.8 per cent) and 89 parous women (0.4 per cent). A total of 133 (1.3 per cent) nulliparous women and 71 (0.4 per cent) parous women were referred because of an extensive perineal tear.

To gain more understanding of the perinatal mortality an anonymous enquiry was carried out of midwife deliveries. Perinatal mortality in the group referred during labour was 30 cases in 6351 infants (4.7 per 1000). This group comprises five preterm infants and 25 infants at term. In the infants at term 18 post mortems were performed: 11 infants had a birthweight <10 centile, in five cases placental abruption was the cause of death.

The 30 cases of perinatal mortality in the group born at home are described in Table 4.8. The perinatal mortality rate in this group was 0.97 per 1000. The proportion of infants with congenital heart malformations in this group is high and the proportion of infants with birthweight centile <10 is relatively small.

Perinatal mortality in the group selected for delivery at home was 60 cases in 37 328 infants, i.e. 1.6 per 1000.

Discussion

A complete perinatal data base is not yet available in the Netherlands. The data related to midwife delivery have been collated. Prenatal care starts in 75–85 per

Table 4.9. Obstetrical risk groups total pregnant population vs. at home

	National per 1000	LVR-I 1989 at home per 1000
Multiple births	12	0.2
Pre-term births	55	7.4
SGA-infants	23[a]	0.6[b]
Term breech deliveries	30	1.0
Perinatal mortality	9.4	1.0

[a] <2.3 centile
[b] >40 weeks <2500 g

cent of all pregnancies at the midwife's practice, and 45 per cent of all deliveries are conducted by them. Assessment of the selection criteria shows results are good (Table 4.9).

Perinatal mortality in the Netherlands, although not the lowest in the world, shows it to be low in infants born at home, and in hospital after referral during labour started at home. Results of the referrals during pregnancy are not available. Linking of the databases of midwives and gynaecologists needs to be accomplished as soon as possible.

The low Caesarean section rate is related to:

1 The confidence of the pregnant woman in the maternity services and midwife care.
2 The fact that in the Dutch system the responsibility for care of normal pregnancy and labour is in the hands of a profession not qualified to intervene in the normal sequence of events (Treffers *et al.* 1990).

The morbidity in the selected group is low as far as studied (Berghs and Spanjaards 1988; van Alten *et al.* 1989).

References

Berghs, G. and Spanjaards, E. (1988) De normale zwangerschap: Bevalling en Beleid. Nijmegen, The Netherlands, University of Nijmegen, Thesis

Breyer, H.B.G. and Stolk, J.G. (1971) Enkele beschouwingen naar aanleiding van een onderzoek over doodgeboorte in het jaar 1961 in Nederland. *Ned Tijdschr Geneeskd* **115**, 1638–46

Dennis, J. and Chalmers, I. (1982) Very early neonatal seizure rate: a possible epidemiological indicator of the quality of perinatal care. *Br J Obstet Gynaecol* **89**, 418–26

Doornbos, J.P.R., Nordbeck, H.J. and Treffers, P.E. (1987) The reliability of perinatal mortality statistics in the Netherlands. *Am J Obstet Gynecol* **156**, 1183–7

Eskes, M., Knuist, M. and van Alten, D. (1987) Neurologisch onderzoek bij pasgeborenen in een verloskundigenpraktijk. *Ned Tijdschr Geneeskd* **131**, 1040–3

Eskes, M., van Alten, D. and Treffers, P.E. (1993) The Wormerveer Study: Perinatal mortality and non-optimal management in a practice of independent midwives. *Eur J Obstet Gynecol Reprod Biol* **51**, 91–5

Eskes, T.K.A.B., Jongsma, H.W. and Houx, P.C.W. (1981) Umbilical cord gases in home deliveries versus hospital-based deliveries. *J Reprod Med* **26**, 405–8

Hoogendoorn, D. (1986) Indrukwekkende en tegelijk teleurstellende daling van de perinatale sterfte in Nederland. *Ned Tijdschr Geneeskd* **130**, 1436–40

Kloosterman, G.J. (1978) De Nederlandse verloskunde op de tweesprong. *Ned Tijdschr Geneeskd* **122**, 1161–71

Knuist, M., Eskes, M. and van Alten, D. (1987) De pH van het aterile navelstrengbloed van pasgeborenen bij door vroedvrouwen geleide bevallingen. *Ned Tijdschr Geneeskd* **131**, 362–5

Lems, A.A., van der Esch, L., van Alten, D. *et al.* (1994) De LVR en de perinatale sterfte. De LVR-cijfers van 1989 nader beschouwd (3). *Tijdschr v Verloskundigen* 10–14

MacDonald, D., Grant, A., Sheridan-Pereira, M. *et al.* (1985) The Dublin randomized controlled trial of intrapartum fetal heart rate monitoring. *Am J Obstet Gynecol* **152**, 524–39

Netherlands Central Bureau of Statistics (1993) Monthly Bulletin of Health Statistics.

SIG Zorginformatie (1992). Jaarboek verloskunde 1991. Utrecht

Smits, F. (1981) De doelstreffendheid van het selectiesysteem binnen de verloskundige zorg. Academisch proefschrift. Katholieke Universiteit te Nijmegen

Treffers, P.E. and Laan, R. (1986) Regional perinatal mortality and regional hospitalization at delivery in The Netherlands. *Br J Obstet Gynaecol* **93**, 690–3

Treffers, P.E., Eskes, M., Kleiverda, G. *et al.* (1990) Home births and minimal medical interventions. *JAMA* **264**, 2203–8

van Alten, D., Eskes, M. and Treffers, P.E. (1989) Midwifery in the Netherlands. The Wormerveer Study: Selection, mode of delivery, perinatal mortality and infant morbidity. *Br J Obstet Gynaecol* **96**, 656–62

van der Esch, L. and van Alten, D. (1993) Verwerking en interpretatie van LVR-cijfers (2). *Tijdschr v Verloskundigen* 484–8

Chapter 5

Place of birth: finding the next step forward

Julia Allison

On 24 January 1994, the Department of Health invited Regional Health Authorities to submit to the National Health Service Management Executive (NHSME) by 31 December 1994 their strategies for 'Changing Childbirth', including their timetable for implementation within the following five years. Their definition of a 'Changing Childbirth' service is one where:

1 Purchasers and providers are asking women what they want and testing levels of consumer satisfaction;
2 The service has the support of local women;
3 The service produces good clinical outcomes.

The ten key indicators of success which should be visible within five years are:

1 All women should be able to carry their own case notes.
2 Every woman should know one midwife who ensures continuity of her midwifery care – the named midwife.
3 At least 30 per cent of women should have the midwife as the lead professional.
4 Every woman should know the lead professional who has a key role in the planning and provision of her care.
5 At least 75 per cent of women should know the person who cares for them during their delivery.
6 Midwives should have direct access to some beds in all maternity units.
7 At least 30 per cent of women delivered in a maternity unit should be admitted under the management of the midwife.
8 The total number of antenatal visits for women with uncomplicated pregnancies should have been reviewed in the light of available evidence and the RCOG guidelines.
9 All front line ambulances should have a paramedic available to support the midwife who needs to transfer a woman to hospital in an emergency.
10 All women should have access to information about the services available in their locality.

The debate has ended, the job begun and we, the carers, must find the next step forward.

The national consensus conference on maternity services convened by the Department of Health on 4 and 5 March (Department of Health 1993) agreed that: 'continuity of care would best be provided by small teams of midwives with their own caseloads working between hospital and home'. However, we are still a long way from understanding how this type of care will be provided.

Over the past decade, a variety of new schemes, described as team midwifery, have been introduced to replace the fragmented systems of care which evolved following the implementation of the Peel Report (DHSS 1970).

Today's teams may be hospital or community based or provide a seamless service between hospital and community, whereas a few provide continuity of carer in a meaningful sense; many have been designed simply to produce 'a team' rather than choice and continuity of carer for women.

The IMS Report, *Mapping Team Midwifery* (Wraight *et al.* 1993), which was set up to: 'identify through a descriptive mapping exercise, what midwifery staff management practices are being carried out in England and Wales in the name of team midwifery', found that: 'few schemes are currently organised in ways which will improve continuity of care'.

Early in their report, Wraight *et al.* state: 'maternity care cannot return to the system in operation fifty years ago when continuity of care was simply provided by the woman's own GP and domiciliary midwife' (p. 12). This may be so, but no explanation is offered as to why, although at the conclusion of their study, they note that team midwifery:

> seems to demand a different style of working for the midwife, for example, flexible and on-call hours and total responsibility for a group of women ... these factors may cause difficulties to the midwife with dependants and to the newly qualified midwife seeking support and advice from her more experienced colleagues (pp. 125–6).

Since the centralisation of maternity care, it has become increasingly difficult for us to conceptualise how care used to be given. One way of looking at how to step forward is to look for clues in the past, to question how services were provided and to what extent they offered continuity of carer.

From my study of the work of district midwives in Nottingham, I offer the following example of the type of maternity services which were provided across England and Wales between 1948 and 1972 (City of Nottingham 1949–72). Nottingham lagged behind the rest of the country in moving towards hospitalisation of birth, due to a shortage of hospital maternity beds.

> National Health Service Hospitals – there were 76 287 hospital births to the City of Nottingham between 1948 and 1972. Eighty per cent took place in the maternity wards of the city's general and women's hospitals and twenty per cent at the only maternity hospital; women saw between nine and sixteen carers throughout their pregnancy; most were delivered by someone they had previously met.
>
> Home Birth by Local Authority District Midwives – the vast majority of home births were undertaken by city midwives, between 1948 and 1972, they carried out 62,444 home deliveries. Women were guaranteed continuity of carer, throughout the antenatal, intrapartum and postnatal period. All were delivered by their own midwife or her partner, whom they had met.

Private Nursing Homes – the number of births occurring in private nursing homes diminished over time, in 1950, 214 were recorded in an unspecified number of homes, whilst in 1967, the number had reduced to 26 in one. Some of these women had continuity of carer, others had part private and part NHS care.

Home Birth by Private (Independent) Midwives – the number of homebirths undertaken by private midwives diminished from twenty births by five midwives during 1950 to eleven births by one midwife in 1962, after which time there were none. All such women had continuity from one carer, all had homebirths.

Home Birth by Private Doctors – on rare occasions, home births were undertaken by private doctors; eight occurred in 1949 and one in 1956, after which no more appear to have taken place. These women may have had a private maternity nurse, some used the NHS district midwife in addition.

An interesting feature of these data is the way in which private (independent) practice by both midwives and doctors rapidly disappeared after the introduction of the National Health Service.

Is it without coincidence that the demand for independent practitioners arose again in the 1980s following the demise of a viable homebirth service.

Despite the shortcomings of the midwifery services of the past, there is evidence that most women in Nottingham received continuity of carer and most were satisfied with the service they received (Goodacre 1974), whether it was provided by the hospital service or the local authority domiciliary midwifery service.

By 1991, almost 100 per cent of births occurred in one of two central delivery suites and, in a 1991 survey of 1074 women, following delivery, 50 per cent said they wished they had been given information about domino birth and 27 per cent wanted information about home birth (Allison 1991, p. 53).

Interestingly, there has been a domino birth facility in Nottingham since the 1970s, with designated beds on the maternity units for GP and community midwife use, yet in 1990 there were less than 1 per cent home and domino births in the city.

As discussed by Flint (1993, pp. 75–8), the domino system, born out of the backlash to the Peel Report and greatly in demand by the consumer, is seldom available because it is so difficult and threatening to the majority of midwives and GPs (Allison 1991, pp. 39–43).

In a 1991 review of Nottingham's maternity service, I interviewed community midwives and GPs to try to understand why this service was used so little. The reasons listed below were given by carers for the decline in use of the domino scheme.

General Practioner Obstetrics

The few GPs who used the scheme, highlighted the fact that the unwillingness of the majority of GPs to be involved presented difficulties, especially with regard to 24 hour cover and equity of service.

The majority of GPs never used the scheme and suggested a number of reasons for their decision:

1 Lack of necessary experience
2 Lack of commitment to the underlying philosophy
3 Lack of financial incentive
4 Lack of peer support/cover
5 Pressure of other practice work
6 Did not meet the criteria of the GP Obstetric Committee

GPs who had once belonged to the scheme, but had since withdrawn gave the following reasons for their decision:

1 It was not a service offered to all suitable women
2 Any benefits conferred by the scheme, to either the GP or woman, were outweighed by the difficulties of running the service
3 Women who entered the scheme still could not be assured of the presence of a known carer at delivery
4 Difficulty in maintaining relevant skills when dealing with small numbers of women
5 Likelihood of increased Medical Defence Union fees to offset increased risk of litigation, where the GP is involved in the care of a number of women in the intrapartum period.
6 The terms of the scheme made the attendance of the GP during the intrapartum period imperative. This condition exceeded the requirement of GPs with regard to home birth and was difficult to comply with because of other practice commitments.

Midwives

Reasons for the decline of the scheme given by Community midwives who had been involved in the scheme were twofold. First, peer pressure not to book women under the scheme unless they were prepared to put themselves on 24-hour call. The midwives thought the reasons for this were:

1 Their colleagues felt uncomfortable delivering women they did not know, in unfamiliar territory.
2 Difficulty in covering the next day's work when one member of the team had been up all night and needed to sleep.
3 Midwives who worked with GPs who used the GP unit scheme were somehow seen as elitist and, in consequence were not always well supported by their colleagues.

Second, the midwives had ambivalent feelings about the scheme:

1 It did not make sense to book just a few women under this scheme, when it was well understood that many other women whose GPs did not subscribe to it also wished to be offered the same facility but were refused.
2 They encountered difficulties when trying to book their holiday, knowing that women whom they had booked would be transferred into hospital on the least pretext if they were not there to 'defend' them.

3 Some of them experienced a feeling of isolation as participants in such a little
used scheme.

Underlying the reasons given by midwives, it became apparent that lack of
ownership was an important issue in a variety of ways:

1 Because the scheme is dependent upon GP participation, midwives were unable
to accept women who approached them for domino birth unless they were
registered with a participating doctor or could persuade one who took part in
the scheme to give care during the pregnancy. (They expressed the view that
midwives were capable of selecting and giving care appropriately.)
2 Although the scheme was community orientated, the place in which the
community midwife was expected to deliver the baby was hospital territory.
Although community midwives acknowledged the friendliness and helpfulness
of their hospital colleagues, they also referred to being guests on someone else's
property. They had no room of their own to make telephone calls, write notes
or make a drink or snack. They relied entirely on the goodwill of hospital
midwives for everything they needed.
3 The layout of hospital delivery rooms is more clinical than aesthetic in appearance. Some community midwives felt that in their own rooms they could
have made decisions with the couple about the environment for birth.
4 The rooms available for domino births are integral to the delivery suite; some
midwives felt it was impossible to create a 'normal' atmosphere with the
background 'noise' of a delivery suite.
5 Some mentioned the discomfort they felt when attending to one client in labour
while hospital midwives were busy attending to two or three but, at the same
time, feeling ambivalent about the role they should adopt in such situations.
6 Supervision and management caused difficulties for some community midwives
who felt that they were practising on territory which was managed and supervised
by a different midwife manager. They felt this situation caused 'tensions'.

There has never been a time when midwives and GPs provided an equitable,
nationwide, seamless service between hospital and home. I suspect that if the
personalities and backgrounds of midwives who choose to work in a hospital
compared with those who choose to work in the community, there would probably
be some measurable differences between the two types, which are the very elements
which generally make them best suited to practise in the area they choose.

A key feature of midwifery education, during the period when homebirth was
the norm, was that in addition to gaining enough experience in both hospital and
home settings to ensure competency and confidence to practise in either, pupils
had sufficient experience of each type of care to help them decide where they
were best suited to practise on qualification.

It was well understood that some midwives were born to practise in hospital
and others 'made for the district', just as some doctors choose general practice
and some specialise in hospitals.

Some would argue that it is as inappropriate to expect *most* midwives to be able
to attend a Caesarean section in the morning and run a community based,

antenatal clinic in the afternoon as it is for a GP to perform a ventouse extraction occasionally or the obstetrician to come and take morning surgery.

It could be said that it is equally inappropriate to require a midwife to have two years' experience of working in hospital before she can apply for a community post; it is more likely that the hospital experience will defuse her confidence than improve her skills in preparation for domiciliary midwifery care.

A concern regarding some approaches to providing team midwifery is that it can become the only choice and place of entry to the maternity service if one area fails than to do the very thing it was set up for – to offer women choice.

In the past, there were two distinct services for women to choose from – home or hospital – both offering choice and continuity of carer to women and career choice for midwives. I do not suggest that this past example is a paradigm for maternity care for the future, but it is one way of examining how we might take the next step forward.

References

Allison, J. (1991) Report to the District General Manager Regarding the Future of the Midwifery Service. Nottingham Health Authority

Ball, J.A., Flint, C. and Garvey, M. (1992) *Who's Left Holding the Baby?* Leeds: Nuffield Institute, University of Leeds

Campbell, R. and MacFarlane, A. (1987) *Where to be Born.* Oxford: National Perinatal Epidemiology Unit

City of Nottingham (1949–72) Annual Reports of the Health Services. Medical Officer of Health, Wm. Dodd, MD

Department of Health (1993) *Changing Childbirth.* London: HMSO

Department of Health – Kings Fund (1993) Maternity Care, Choice, Continuity and Change: statement from the national consensus conference

DHSS (1970) *Domiciliary Midwifery and Maternity Bed Needs.* Report of the Standing Maternity and Midwifery Advisory Committee (Chairman Sir John Peel). London: HMSO

Flint, C. (1993) *Midwifery Teams and Caseloads.* Oxford: Butterworth-Heinemann

Goodacre, J. (1974) A Survey of Home and Hospital Confinements in Nottingham. Dissertation for Part 2 of the Degree of Bachelor of Medical Science (Honours). Department of Community Health, University of Nottingham

HMSO (1970) *Domiciliary Midwifery and Maternity Bed Needs.* London: HMSO

HMSO (1989) *Women's Experience of Maternity Care – A Survey Manual.* London: HMSO

HMSO (1979/1980) Social Services Committee – Perinatal and Neonatal Mortality, 2nd Report From the Social Services Committee Session. London: HMSO

Wraight, A., Ball, J. and Seccombe, I. (1993) *Mapping Team Midwifery.* IMS Report Series 242. Brighton: Institute of Manpower Studies

Chapter 6

Place of birth

Gavin L. Young

The proportion of births occurring at home in England and Wales has dropped from 85 per cent in 1927 to under 1 per cent in 1985. Over the same period perinatal mortality rate (PMR) has dropped from 60.8 to 9.8 per 1000. Some would argue that no further evidence is required; that the UK policy of centralising birth in specialist hospitals is entirely vindicated by the contemporaneous fall in perinatal deaths.

Childbirth has increasingly been viewed as dangerous and frequently requiring immediate medical help. This view is shared by lay people and professionals alike. However, it is, within the history of childbirth, very recent. In 1936 the British College of Obstetricians and Gynaecologists stated that: 'Adequate hospital provision for all cases could only be made at great expense: the results of domiciliary midwifery do not warrant such expenditure.' What brought about the dramatic shift in views? Was it scientific evidence?

One major influence was the creation of the National Health Service. Expectant mothers could afford to deliver in hospital, and many wished to do so. The number of hospital obstetricians increased in parallel. Penicillin became available, as did antituberculous drugs, and hospitals came to be seen as benign, problem-solving institutions.

The Government commissioned reports which recommended increasing the percentage of hospital births and ended by congratulating itself by declaring in 1984: 'The practice of delivering nearly all babies in hospital has contributed to the dramatic reduction in stillbirths and neonatal deaths and to the avoidance of many child handicaps' (Maternity Services Advisory Committee 1984). These reports, largely based on opinions of hospital-based professionals, have now almost achieved their ultimate aim: all women in the UK delivering in large specialist hospitals. The shift to hospital care over the past 40 years is one of the most fundamental changes in health care. Was there evidence to support this change?

Evidence of greater safety of hospital birth?

Three kinds of evidence provided suport for the idea that specialist hospital care was safer.

53

1 The fall in maternal and perinatal mortality coincided with an increase in deliveries under specialist care.
2 Transfer of patients from home or 'isolated GP units' was associated with high PMRs (Hobbs and Acheson 1966).
3 Personal experience of many obstetricians who saw and remembered vividly some of those transferred with problems.

This third category is a highly selective sample. One would not examine an orthopaedic ward in Zermatt to discover if skiing is an experience of acceptable safety.

Behind the evidence lay – and still does lie for many – the unshakeable belief that hospital must be safer. Commonsense would indicate that it must be safer to deliver where full facilities are available to cope with any possible mishap during or after delivery. Yet, commonsense also tells us that the sun goes around the earth.

Cochrane (1972) doubted the evidence for centralising maternity care: 'It is surprising how successive committees have been content to accept trends as something God-given which must be followed, instead of demanding a more rigorous analysis of causality.'

If all were happy with centralisation of birth there would be no need to question the policy. However, many women and some professionals are very unhappy: the former because they would like to have their babies at home and the latter because they have worries that encouraging reluctant women to deliver in hospital may be both an abuse of power and scientifically unsound.

Two recent surveys (National Council of Women of Great Britain 1990; MORI 1993) show that about one woman in eight would like to choose a homebirth. As only 1 in 100 achieves a home birth, it can probably be assumed that there is some heavy dissuading pressure put on nearly all women who ask for it. There is a wealth of anecdotal evidence held by the National Childbirth Trust to support this assumption.

As the wishes of a significant minority of women are being blocked by present policy, health professionals have a duty to carry out Cochrane's 'more rigorous analysis'.

Evidence against centralisation

Figures for home birth are difficult to interpret. A direct comparison with hospital should not be made as planned home births are, by and large, to low-risk women. Hospital tends to be the place of delivery for women predicted to be at high risk, e.g. diabetics, breech presentation. Nonetheless, it is reasonable to examine the figures for home birth to see if it can be considered 'safe enough'. Home birth figures have been misinterpreted. The Cardiff births survey revealed that by 1979 the number of unplanned home births in that survey exceeded births planned to occur at home. (Murphy *et al.* 1984). This shift has a huge impact on the apparent lack of safety of home birth. A survey of all home births in England and Wales in

1979 (Campbell *et al.* 1984) showed that the PMR for planned home births (67 per cent of total) was 4.1, but for births not booked at all (3 per cent) the rate was 196.6. Births booked for hospital but which took place at home (21 per cent) had a PMR of 67.5. (In 9 per cent intended place of delivery was not known.) Unfortunately, this survey was not able to discover the outcome for women moved from home in labour.

It is not only birth at home that has been vigorously discouraged – rural GP/midwife units have been closed down on the grounds of lack of safety. They came in for particular attack in the Short Report (Social Services Committee 1980). Such units are still being threatened with closure. Most will not have facilities for general anaesthesia nor for Caesarean section and will, therefore, offer few extra facilities beyond those available at home.

Nonetheless, the great majority of women served by such units choose delivery there rather than at home or in a specialist unit (unpublished data available from the author). It is not clear why, and it would be a useful piece of research to discover how a woman reaches her decision concerning choice of place of delivery. Data from such units are another source of information about births taking place at a distance from specialist help.

A postal survey of all isolated GP units (131 in number) in England and Wales in 1977 (89 per cent response rate) found the PMR to be 5.1 including the cases transferred in labour (Cavenagh *et al.* 1984). My own much smaller, but more detailed, survey of the isolated unit at Penrith in Cumbria (Young 1987) found a PMR of 4.7 for all women starting labour in Penrith. The above evidence conflicts with the opinions given to government committees by hospital specialists. The opinion of the Royal College of Midwives (RCM) was also against such units, and it is interesting that the RCM now appears to have moved away from the 'only the centre is safe' view. A variety of studies from other countries (Finland, Canada, New Zealand) has been examined by Rosenblatt (1987). All the studies suggest that outcomes for low-risk obstetric populations may be better in less technologically intensive settings.

It is this last finding that makes many (including women using maternity services) have doubts about the policy of centralisation. A five-year prospective study (Shearer 1985) of home births in Essex 1978–1983, using matched controls under specialist hospital care, found no perinatal deaths in either hospital group and an increased second-degree tear rate, despite a higher episiotomy rate. This finding of a higher intervention rate in low-risk women when under specialist care was repeated in a comparison of women booked under GP/midwife care in the integrated unit in Oxford as against a similar low-risk group booked under specialist care on the same unit (Klein *et al.* 1983). The most exhaustive study in the UK, analysing PMR by place of birth, was Marjorie Tew's analysis of unpublished data from the British Births 1970 survey (Tew 1985). An attempt was made to overcome the bias that specialist hospitals delivered difficult cases, by giving each woman an antenatal and labour weighting for risk, i.e. 'prediction scores'. Using these scores Tew found significantly lower PMRs in the GP units and at home as compared with specialist hospitals for all levels of risk except the very highest where the difference did not reach significance level. This study has been criticised because it may reveal that the prediction scores were invalid. However, until recently there has been almost no evidence pointing in the opposite direction to Tew's findings. A recent report (Sangala *et al.* 1990) matched low-risk women in Bath with similar women booked to deliver in rural GP units. This study found PMR in the central unit to be 2.8 and in the rural units 4.8. However, this included deaths before labour began. It was not, therefore, solely a study of the safety of birth in different units. PMRs after the onset of labour were 0.9 and 1.5 respectively, which does not reach significance level. This study has been given wide publicity and needs examining. It is in essence a study of low-risk urban Bath women compared with low-risk rural women. Most of the perinatal deaths occurred before labour and it is not clear in what ways these might have been avoided if the rural units had not existed. It is unlikely that specialist care would have affected these antenatal deaths. The chance of a baby surviving after an antepartum haemorrhage decreases with distance from the place of Caesarean section, i.e. rural women will fare less well whatever the facilities available. The PMR in the integrated (central) GP unit was zero by intended place of delivery at the time of onset of labour (or the time of diagnosis of intrauterine death).

In the triennium 1988–90 PMRs for the same groups in the Bath area were 2.6 for the consultant unit and 3.0 for the peripheral units (data available from Wiltshire Health Care Trust, St John's Hospital, Trowbridge, BA14 0QU). Once again, most of the difference of 0.4 per cent per 1000 consists of deaths before labour.

The evidence overall about safety and place of birth in the UK suggests that home and isolated units are as safe as hospital care for the women who choose such care. There are not now a large enough number of births in these settings for a proper comparison to be made. Campbell and MacFarlane's (1987) review of the evidence up to 1985 included this comment:

> It would have been possible to mount such a trial in the 1960s or early 1970s when substantially more women were giving birth at home and it is unfortunate that such an opportunity was missed by the successive committees who made recommendations about the place of delivery.

The Netherlands is now the only country in the developed world where such evidence can be made available. In 1988 36 per cent of Dutch women delivered at home. The PMR in the Netherlands is the same as in the UK. This information itself raises major doubts about the justification for the British policy of centralisation which is, however, shared by all other developed countries.

The Dutch experience

A very detailed study of 7980 women booking with midwives in and around Wormerveer, just north of Amsterdam, between 1969 and 1983 was published in 1989 (van Alten, Eskes and Treffers 1989). This study involved 92 per cent of the nulliparous women and 79 per cent of parous women in the catchment area. Of these women, 75 per cent had midwife-only care – either in a small maternity unit or at home. The PMR for these women, including those transferred in labour, was 2.3. The national figure over this period was 14.5. Though this study – as in all the previous studies cited – is not a randomised controlled trial, it does show that the great majority of women can give birth safely away from specialist care. It is unlikely that the PMR would have been better had they delivered under specialist care and there might have been more intervention. (The Caesarean section rate in the midwife-only group was 0.4 per cent.) Regional PMRs in the Netherlands do not correlate with the degree of hospitalisation (Treffers and Laan 1986).

The UK is not the Netherlands, yet the Dutch evidence cannot be ignored or, rather, it should not be. In the event, it has been ignored and it is striking even now, how those who make decisions about place of birth – be they health service managers, specialist obstetricians deciding health authority policy or general practitioners advising their patients – can continue to be so adamant that birth away from specialist care, particularly at home, is unsafe.

The evidence shows that place of birth does not have a significant impact on perinatal mortality. This should not be surprising, given that most perinatal deaths are a result of:

1 congenital malformation
2 preterm birth
3 unexplained death before labour (IUD)

None of these would be affected by women choosing to deliver away from specialist units once they had completed 37 weeks of pregnancy.

That women and their babies do as well away from big hospitals, may at first seem contrary to commonsense, but psychosocial factors in the woman may have a greater impact on the outcome of labour than we suppose. There is evidence from Guatemala showing that lay support can halve the length of labour, compared with women left alone in labour (Klaus *et al.* 1986). This says nothing about place of birth but it says a great deal about the effect of a sense of security in labour.

Mammalian evidence points to an overriding need for the pregnant animal to feel safe when she gives birth (Naaktgeboren 1989). Where a woman feels safest may not be where we believe she would be safest. We cannot decide for her where she will feel most safe. We can do our best to provide her with as unbiased information as we can – a difficult task. Feeling safe may go part of the way to being safe.

Perinatal morbidity

There is no evidence that perinatal morbidity would be influenced by place of birth. Obstetric technology appears unable to affect the incidence of cerebral palsy. A five-year follow-up of the Dublin trial found no difference in the incidence of cerebral palsy whether there had been continuous electronic fetal monitoring or intermittent auscultation (Grant *et al.* 1989). A review of two large studies – from Western Australia and the National Collaborative Perinatal Project in the USA –

came to the conclusion that in less than 10 per cent of cases of cerebral palsy was intrapartum asphyxia a factor (Nelson 1989).

Cost

If safety is not important in the debate about place of birth, is cost? The cost per case of small units can rise sharply if the number of deliveries falls. The reluctance of many GPs to book women for rural units (primarily because the great majority of GPs see care at birth as lots of trouble for very little reward) has led to the closure of many such units. Booking criteria can be so exclusive that rural units can become non-viable. Rural units have their advantages. The NHS Management Executive's (1993) report concluded that 'maternity services could learn much from the comfortable and user-focused environments often found in midwife and GP units', and saw no reason why their example should not be followed more widely.

With our present midwifery system split between community and hospital, and again, the reluctance of GPs to be involved, providing two trained professionals for a home birth is also expensive.

However, a change to an integrated midwifery service primarily based in the community, and encouragement and appropriate training for GPs, could alter the costs.

Conclusion

The overall evidence about safety and place of birth shows no significant differences in outcome (maternal mortality, perinatal mortality or morbidity) between home, primary care units and specialist hospitals.

It would be unthinkable that road travel between London and Edinburgh was phased out because the railway industry believed it provided a safer way of travelling between the two cities. Yet, in effect, a similar process has occurred with maternity care in the UK. Campbell and MacFarlane (1987), after the most extensive search of maternity statistics in the UK, conclude: 'There is no evidence to support the claim that the safest policy is for all women to give birth in hospital' and 'The policy of closing small obstetric units on the grounds of safety is not supported by the available evidence.'

The final words of their study are depressing: 'Perhaps the most persistent and striking feature of the debate about where to be born, however, is the way policy has been formed with very little reference to the evidence.' (Campbell and Macfarlane 1987)

In 1992 the House of Commons Health Committee chaired by Nicholas Winterton was impressed at the lack of evidence to support centralisation and suggested the government rethink its policy. This has now happened, and the Expert Maternity Group, chaired by Baroness Julia Cumberlege, reported in August 1993. The report *Changing Childbirth* (Department of Health 1993) accepted that there is no clear answer as regards safety, and suggested that: 'The job of midwives and doctors, therefore, must be to provide the woman with as much accurate and objective information as possible, while avoiding personal bias or preference' and that: 'The responsibilities accepted by midwives in caring for women who wish to have a home birth must be acknowledged. Obstetricians and GPs should ensure that they support the midwives, and that they make clear their readiness to give advice and help if needed.'

The unsatisfactory state of not having an answer is better than believing one had when one had not. It is more honest, if more uncomfortable.

Further research is being undertaken: the Northern Region has just completed a prospective survey of all women requesting home births whose babies were born in 1993, and the National Birthday Trust has just embarked on a national 1-year survey of home births. Neither study, however, has the methodology or size to give a definitive answer to the question of safety of birth away from a specialist centre. Therefore in the meantime, and probably for ever, we must tolerate uncertainty and live with doubt. We need:

1 staff trained to provide care as safe as possible in rural units and at home;
2 the training of midwives and GPs to be changed to allow them to be able safely to undertake care at birth, as at present large areas of the UK have no one competent to help a woman deliver her baby at home;
3 to have adequate ambulances and suitably trained staff to move women with complications in labour;
4 to be able to give fair, honest information, especially outlining what facilities are and are not available;
5 to respect the wishes of women who may make a decision with which we disagree – and to continue to care for them;
6 to make all maternity hospitals more welcoming, so that women can feel more 'at home' in them. This depends more on familiar faces than on wallpaper and curtains and may require the establishment of midwifery units within specialist units;
7 informed purchasers who are able to decide what level of 'choice' is affordable;
8 to stop being obsessed about place of birth and concentrate on more important issues in health care.

References

British College of Obstetricians and Gynaecologists (1936) Outline of a scheme for a national maternity service. London: RCOG

Campbell, R. and MacFarlane, A. (1986) Place of delivery: a review. *Br J Obstet Gynaecol* **93**, 675–83

Campbell, R. and MacFarlane, A. (1987) Where to be born? The debate and the evidence. Oxford: National Perinatal Epidemiology Unit

Campbell, R., MacDonald Davies, I., MacFarlane, A. *et al.* (1984) Home births in England and Wales, 1979: perinatal mortality according to intended place of delivery. *Br Med J* **289**, 721–4

Cavenagh, A.J.M., Phillips, K.M., Sheridan, B. *et al.* (1984) Contribution of isolated general practitioner maternity units. *Br Med J* **288**, 1438–40

Cochrane, A.L. (1972) *Effectiveness and Efficiency: Random Reflections on the Health Service*. London: Nuffield Provincial Hospitals Trust

Department of Health (1993) *Changing Childbirth*. London: HMSO

Grant, A., Joy, M., O'Brien, N. *et al.* (1989) Cerebral palsy among children born during the Dublin randomised trial of intrapartum monitoring. *Lancet* **ii**, 1233–6

Hobbs, M.S.T. and Acheson E.D. (1966) Perinatal mortality and the organization of obstetric services in the Oxford area in 1962. *Br Med J* **i**, 499

Klaus, M., Kennell, J., Robertson, S. *et al.* (1986) Effects of social support during parturition on maternal and infant morbidity. *Br Med J* **293**, 585–7

Klein, M., Lloyd, I., Redman, C. *et al.* (1983) A comparison of low-risk pregnant women booked for delivery in two systems of care. *Br J Obstet Gynaecol* **90**, 118–22

Maternity Services Advisory Committee (1984) *Maternity Care in Action*. Part II: Care during childbirth. London: HMSO

MORI (1993) *Changing Childbirth*. London: HMSO

Murphy, J.F., Dauncey, M., Gray, O.P. *et al.* (1984) Planned and unplanned deliveries at home: implications of a changing rate. *Br Med J* **288**, 1429–32

Naaktgeboren, C. (1989) 'The biology of childbirth' in I. Chalmers. M. Enkin, and M.J.N.C. Keirse (Eds) *Effective Care in Pregnancy and Childbirth*, Vol. 2, pp. 795–805. Oxford: Oxford University Press

National Council of Women of Great Britain (1990) Are we fit for the 90s?, p. 5. London: NCWGB

National Health Services Management Executive (1993) A Study of Midwife- and GP-led Maternity Units, p. 10. London: HMSO

Nelson, K.B. (1989) What proportion of cerebral palsy is related to birth asphyxia? *J Paediatr,* **112**, 572–3

Rosenblatt, R. (1987) Perinatal outcome and family medicine – Refocusing the Research Agenda. *J Fam Pract* **24**, 119–22

Sangala, V., Dunster, G., Bohin, S. *et al.* (1990) Perinatal mortality rates in isolated general practitioner maternity units. *Br Med J* **301**, 418–20

Shearer, J.M.L. (1985) Five year prospective survey of risk of booking for a home birth in Essex. *Br Med J* **291**, 1478–80

Social Services Committee (Chairman, R. Short) (1980) *Perinatal and Neonatal Mortality*. Second Report from the Social Services Committee, Session 1979–80. Vol. 1, Cmnd. 663–1. London: HMSO

Tew, M. (1985) Place of birth and perinatal mortality. *J R Coll Gen Pract* **35**, 390–4

Treffers, P.E. and Laan, R. (1986) Regional perinatal mortality and regional hospitalisation at delivery in The Netherlands. *Br J Obstet Gynaecol* **93**, 690–3

van Alten, D., Eskes, M. and Treffers, P.E. (1989) Midwifery in The Netherlands. The Wormerveer study: selection, mode of delivery, perinatal mortality and infant morbidity. *Br J Obstet Gynaecol* **96**, 656–62

Young, G. (1987) Are isolated maternity units run by general practitioners dangerous? *Br Med J* **294**, 744–6

Chapter 7

Choice: Discussion

Spencer: May I ask Dr Eskes? Do the women in fact have a choice in the Dutch system? Is the provision of community or domiciliary care for home birth to the 30 per cent a choice, or is it an imposition by the system which in fact has an obstetrician at the head of the recommendations?

Eskes: It is really a choice. If the woman is healthy and she has no complications in her obstetric history, she has free choice. She can go to the midwife and together with the midwife she can make her choice for home or hospital delivery. There are perhaps some midwives who themselves have some preference. Some years ago when there was a shortage of midwives, the midwives had problems covering home confinements. It takes much longer to look after a home birth and more women were persuaded to go into hospital, but in general there is free choice.

Spencer: Initially the woman can go to a midwife or to a GP. Is that an open choice or does the woman only have the choice to go to a midwife who can then decide what the subsequent choices are? Does the woman have the choice to see a consultant obstetrician?

Eskes: She has the choice but if there are no medical grounds to go to an obstetrician, she must pay for the consultation and the care herself.

Cumberlege: It sounds as though she has direct access to a midwife and after that it is almost compulsory. Is that right?

Eskes: It is.

Lewison: In the field of maternity care there are a lot of women who are having to exercise negative choice. Gavin Young said that if we made hospitals friendlier places where women had more autonomy, perhaps fewer of them would be choosing home births. Certainly in the National Childbirth Trust we find that women are making decisions which are perhaps not their first choice of care because of previous bad experiences or stories they have heard from friends and relatives.

I know of independent midwives who are being approached to provide care at home by women who have had previous Caesarean sections, by women who are relatively old and who are perhaps expecting their fourth or fifth babies. These are women who all of us would assess as being at the high end of the continuum of risk and we have to ask ourselves what is happening to these women that they should be making these negative choices. What can we do to end negative choice and to enable women to make more positive choices?

Hall: If a high-risk woman in Holland chooses a home confinement, can she have it? We do have some women here who inadvisedly choose home birth and they do have a right to have a home birth. Even if we advise against it they can still choose to have it. What would happen to a high-risk woman in Holland who would normally be excluded by the Klostermann criteria but who chooses to have a home birth?

Eskes: The midwife would send her to the obstetrician. It would be very rare. I cannot say it does not happen but most midwives would not take responsibility for a high-risk pregnancy.

Hall: Which points up a difference between the Dutch system and our system. The Dutch midwife can refuse to take on for care a woman that she does not think is suitable whereas midwives in the UK have a statutory responsibility to look after women irrespective of whether the choice the woman has made is thought to be wise or not.

Eskes: The midwife in Holland is independent and is on her own responsibility; she can explain why she does not want to take on the care.

Zander: I was concerned about what Alison Macfarlane was saying about the reduction in data which are now available to us in research. Where should pressure be put to reverse this deteriorating situation? Should it be the Department of Health? Is it due to the reorganisation of the NHS? Does it come from the Treasury? Is there any constructive move that a group like this can take to reverse something which does seem to be very worrying in the light of trying to plan maternity care?

Cumberlege: Those were thoughts I had when I was listening to the presentation. Researchers always do want more data and it is never quite in the form that they would really like. But clearly what was said was right, when we have got these enormous changes coming, it will be much more difficult to follow trends if we are without information. I take the point about purchasers and providers, and merging of health authorities.

I think improvement is not insuperable and the problem needs addressing. I am not sure, particularly in this field, that that has been done perhaps as vigorously as it might.

Modle: All the data held on patients in the National Health Service are to be converted into electronic form over the next two to three years and will then be more easily manipulated, used for statistical purposes and passed from one part of the service to another.

Cumberlege: There are other initiatives that are coming forward, not necessarily in this field. In terms of evaluation, for some things like maternal death rates, we have always had very full information; it has been done extremely vigorously by the professionals. Medical audit is likely to improve the information.

Purchasers will want that information, so in some ways outcomes and how we achieve them are likely to be much more sought after than they have been in the past.

Coats: It seems that to progress appropriately, we need accurate meaningful information, and it seems that from a group like this there ought to be some real force towards organising and orchestrating that so that it is tuned to precisely what we are trying to put into place.

I should like to ask Alison Macfarlane how would she like the data collected for the purposes that we have in mind – particularly for changing childbirth?

Macfarlane: There is a whole series of things which need to be done, some of them simple and some of them complex. Scotland has always been proud of its data collection systems and justifiably so; a number of the items on my shopping list of recommendations are already happening in Scotland. Scotland has managed to implement the internal market without this loss of information, so that is something that England can learn from Scotland.

In terms of the detailed points, I had a page and a half of them. It is not that the data are not there, there is audit and there are a lot of data generated at local level, but coordination is important because although people are collecting more data at local level, they are collecting it in a number of different ways so that it cannot be compared with what is happening in other places. This is not deliberate but often people are unaware of definitions or definitions have not been put forward.

The Körner Committee made several recommendations about what data should be collected but did not cover how they should be collected and used. A lot more thought needs to be put into how data are collected to make them consistent with other similar data that are collected elsewhere.

The hardware and the software are very much developed piecemeal. The data should connect to other systems.

Scotland is about the same size as an NHS Region, it is a manageable population, and the steps being taken in Wales and in Northern Ireland show that that is a reasonable size. I am concerned that the documents about changes in the NHS

Regions did not mention the information functions of Regions. This is a gap that needs to be attended to urgently, because people with knowledge are going.

Cumberlege: There is a focus group at the Department that is looking specifically at information and its needs.

Chapter 8

The use of risk factors in predicting possible consequences of changing patterns of care in pregnancy

Susan K. Cole and Gillian M. McIlwaine

In both Scotland (Scottish Office Home and Health Department 1993) and England (Department of Health 1993) the government departments responsible for the health services have explicit policies of increasing choice in different types of care for pregnant women, laying emphasis on midwife-led care in a range of settings. The implications of a major change from nearly all deliveries in obstetrician-led units to a substantial proportion of home delivery and increasing use of general practitioner and midwife led units, have given rise to some anxieties. There are legitimate concerns that the undoubted gains made in neonatal and maternal mortality over the past 30 years could be halted, or even reversed. It would be ideal to be able to predict which women could safely expect to have a normal pregnancy and to remain under the care of her midwife and general practitioner without experiencing a sudden emergency that might threaten her life or that of her baby. Although that goal will never be realised, analysis of the Scottish maternity data, and annual surveys of stillbirth and neonatal mortality can help to minimise adverse consequences of a change in patterns of care that otherwise has broad support.

Data sources

For 20 years, Scotland has had the advantage of a highly clinical data set (form SMR2) designed by clinicians and covering some 97–99 per cent of deliveries (Cole 1980). Recent quality assurance studies which have involved blind recording of a sample of SMR2 from each hospital (ISD unpublished) show that the data are on the whole, remarkably accurate and thus may be used with some confidence to predict consequences of changing practice. The SMR2 is an episode record of inpatient and hospital day cases. Since 1980 it has been linked by probability matching (Kendrick and Clarke 1992), giving episodes within pregnancy linked to the delivery. Successive pregnancies in the same women are also linked.

Since 1979, perinatal deaths (with the addition from 1985 of late neonatal deaths) have been subjected to individual scrutiny and the causes of death classified systematically by a single observer (McIlwaine *et al.* 1979; Scotland Annual Reports

1986–90). In the present chapter these causes have been aggregated to produce three groups: lethal congenital abnormality, antepartum stillbirth; and 'other'. Neither of the first two groups is affected by care given during labour, but the third, which includes immaturity and asphyxia related disease, is profoundly associated with perinatal care.

Risk factors

Clinical practice at booking clinics has always involved the use of risk factors in planning antenatal care and to forecast likely problems at delivery. In our analysis we used explicit risk factors from a current trial of antenatal care in low risk women (P. Howie, personal communication) and approximated the SMR2 data to them (Table 8.1). Other indicators of disorders arising during the course of pregnancy were added.

The SMR2 data relate to deliveries in 322 543 women during 1986–90. Table 8.2 shows the distribution of risk factors in primiparous and multiparous women, delivering at term (gestation >36 weeks) and graphically illustrates the heavy dependence placed on the track record of previous pregnancies when assessing prospects for the current pregnancy. The additional risk factors of antenatal episodes and predelivery length of stay were selected to indicate problems arising during the index pregnancy, and are probably very crude, given the increasing frequency of antenatal admissions for monitoring, but although these factors may place actual low risk women in the high risk group, it is unlikely that women with significant obstetrical illness would be wrongly missed and thus included in the low risk group.

However, even these imperfect indicators of high risk, all of which would be known before the onset of labour, can differentiate between women who received some kind of medical care during labour and those who did not, and therefore indicate which women would be likely to require transfer from general practitioner or midwife to consultant obstetrical care.

Results

In Scotland, 45 per cent of the pregnant population are primiparous (Table 8.3), and only 4 per cent of them have risk factors at booking, compared to 26 per cent of multiparous women who have one or more risk factors. Table 8.4 shows the actual events that occurred in pregnancy in low-risk women and although the 'need' for interventions such as induction or assisted delivery (Caesarean section or assisted vaginal delivery) is debatable, they indicate the maximum percentages that would require transfer from 'normal' care to consultant-based care.

On the assumption that only women with the clinical factors indicating high risk would be booked or transfer to consultant-led care, it can be seen that 60 per cent of outset low-risk women in their first pregnancy would need to be transferred from midwife or general practitioner care. Transfers during labour (for assisted

Table 8.1. Risk factors

Antenatal trial	SMR2
Past obstetric history	
Previous stillbirth or neonatal loss	Previous perinatal death
Previous 3 or more consecutive spontaneous abortions	Previous spontaneous abortions (3+)
Last baby preterm delivery (before 34 weeks)	Last baby preterm (<37)
Any previous baby BW <2500 g	Last baby BW <2500 g
Last pregnancy severe proteinuric pre-eclampsia	——
Previous surgery on reproductive tract	Previous Caesarean section
General medical	
Insulin-dependent diabetes mellitus	[a]Diabetes (1)
Essential hypertension (including diastolic BP >90 mmHg at booking)	[a]Essential or other pre-existing hypertension (2)
Renal disease	[a]Renal hypertension (3)
Cardiac disease	[a]Heart disease (congenital or acquired) (4)
Known substance abuse	[a]Drug dependence (5)
On medication/or other severe medical disease	——
Weight <45 kg or >100 kg	——
Other severe illness	[a]Epilepsy (6)
Current pregnancy	
Age <16 or >35 years	Age <16 or >35
Iso – Imm	——
Diagnosed multiple pregnancy	Multiple pregnancy
Hb <100 g/1	——
	Other risk factors acquired during pregnancy
	2 or more antenatal admissions
	Predelivery stay >3 days
	Breech presentation at start of labour

[a] ICD 9 Codes   (1) 250.-648.0; (2) 642.0-642.2; (3) 642.1; (4) 648.5-.6, 745–747, 390–398, 410–459; (5) 648.3, 304; (6) 345.

delivery) are potentially urgent, because the indication may be fetal distress and it is a matter of concern that 17.4 per cent of this group have assisted delivery after going into spontaneous labour. This may be a rather high proportion because it is likely that the proportion of women with assisted delivery (with a ratio of

Table 8.2.   Scotland 1986–90; Term deliveries. Percentage with risk factors by parity; SMR2 risk factors

Risk factor known at booking	Para 0	Para 1+
Previous perinatal death	—	3.5
Previous Caesarean section	—	12.9
3+ previous spontaneous abortions	0.3	1.1
Age <16 or >35 years	2.3	7.0
Last baby preterm	—	2.0
Last baby BW <2500 g	—	2.3
Existing hypertension	0.3	0.3
Diabetes	0.3	0.4
Pre-existing heart disease	0.2	0.2
Other (drug dependence, epilepsy)	0.3	0.3
Known during pregnancy		
Multiple pregnancy	0.5	0.7
2+ AN episodes	12.4	10.3
Predelivery stay >3 days	8.1	5.4
Breech presentation	3.7	2.8
% of women with any risk factor	24.3	36.4

Table 8.3.   Scotland 1986–90: parity and risk

	All parities		Para 0		Para 1+	
	n	%	n	%	n	%
All pregnancies	322 543	100%	144 435	44.8	178 108	55.2
High risk at booking		16.1		4.0		25.9
Low risk at booking		83.9		96.0		74.1

3:7 Caesarean section: assisted vaginal delivery) is inflated by those having epidural analgesia during labour, which would not be available to those delivering outside consultant units.

Low-risk multiparae being booked for delivery outwith a consultant unit would have lower transfer rates, with 64 per cent delivering spontaneously at term and only 3 per cent having assisted delivery. Women who transfer in either parity group to higher levels of care for reason of (a) premature labour, (b) high-risk factors emerging during pregnancy, or (c) induction, would not be placed at

Table 8.4. **Events requiring possible transfer to medical care**

	Para 0 Low-risk women %	Para 1+ Low-risk women %
At booking	100.0	100.0
Preterm delivery	6.7	4.4
Term delivery		
Acquire risk factor in pregnancy	19.9	14.5
'Need' induction at term	15.2	14.0
Spontaneous labour		
'Need' assisted delivery	17.4	3.0
Spontaneous delivery	40.7	64.1

additional risk above that incurred currently, because there would be the same kind of delay before admissions to a consultant unit as there is at present.

Perinatal mortality

The most important outcome measure to monitor during a period of change such as that currently proposed, is perinatal mortality. Lest there is any question that women in preterm labour require consultant care, during 1986–90, perinatal mortality in preterm deliveries was 99.5/1000, 14 per cent due to lethal congenital anomalies, 45 per cent to antepartum stillbirths and 40 per cent to other conditions, mainly immaturity and birth asphyxia. This is in marked contrast to the low rate of 3.3/1000 in deliveries after 37 weeks when 25 per cent were due to congenital anomalies, 50 per cent to antepartum stillbirths and 25 per cent to other conditions, mainly birth asphyxia.

At term, primiparous women in both high- and low-risk groups show no significant difference in perinatal mortality, unlike multiparous women, among whom the high-risk group have a significantly higher perinatal mortality rate than in the low-risk group (Table 8.5). This higher rate is largely due to death associated with lethal congenital anomalies. The high-risk factor of relevance in these cases may well be the past obstetric history of previous perinatal death.

At present, the intrapartum care for all women gives similar rates of death during labour and in the first week of life in first and subsequent pregnancies and in both risk groups. However, in another analysis of the same data set, submitted for publication elsewhere, there is a suspicion, based on small numbers, that the intrapartum stillbirth rate in GP units may be around 1/1000 compared to 0.5/ 1000 in consultant units. If this observation is true, then it is most important that

Table 8.5.   Perinatal mortality rate/1000 by parity risk and cause at term

| | Para 0 | | | | Para 1 + | | | |
| | High risk | | Low risk[a] | | High risk | | Low risk[a] | |
Cause	Rate	(95% CI)	Rate	(95% CI)	Rate	(95% CI)	Rate	(95% CI)
Perinatal mortality	4.3	(3.6–5.0)	3.6	(3.2–4.0)	3.9	(3.4–4.4)	2.6	(2.3–2.9)
Congenital anomaly	0.9	(0.5–1.3)	0.7	(0.5–0.9)	1.2	(0.9–1.5)	0.6	(0.5–0.7)
Antepartum stillbirth	2.2	(0.7–2.7)	2.0	(1.7–2.3)	1.6	(1.3–1.9)	1.4	(1.2–1.6)
Other	1.2	(0.8–1.6)	0.8	(0.6–1.0)	1.0	(0.7–1.3)	0.6	(0.5–0.7)

[a] Includes women with induction of labour.

Table 8.6. Perinatal mortality in low-risk multiparous women with spontaneous onset of labour at term

Cause	Assisted		Spontaneous	
	Rate	(95% CI)	Rate	(95% CI)
Perinatal mortality	8.7	(5.8–11.6)	1.7	(1.4–2.0)
Congenital anomaly	2.7	(1.1–4.3)	0.4	(0.3–0.5)
Antepartum stillbirth	1.0	(0–20)	0.9	(0.7–1.1)
Other	5.0	(2.9–7.1)	0.4	(0.3–0.5)

this category of asphyxia-associated deaths in normally formed infants is monitored closely in any new system of devolved care during labour.

The proportion of onset low risk multiparous women who require assisted delivery is low (3 per cent), or 4.5 per cent of those who go into spontaneous labour. These numbered just over 4000 women in the five years analysed. They experienced a perinatal mortality rate of 8.7/1000 (Table 8.6) with an 'avoidable' rate of 5.0/1000 which could rise to 10/1000 if the observed excess of intrapartum mortality in GP units is a true excess and not a statistical chance finding.

Summary

Analysis of data in Scotland between 1986 and 1990 shows that about 40 per cent of all pregnant women are multiparous and have no risk factors at booking. Such women could well be considered for antenatal care and delivery outwith a consultant-led obstetrical unit. About one third of this group might need transfer to a higher level of care by reason of preterm labour (4.4 per cent), conditions arising during pregnancy (14.5 per cent) or the need for induction of labour (14.0 per cent). A further 3 per cent may need emergency transfer during labour, leaving 64 per cent of the group (or a quarter of all pregnant women) who would deliver spontaneously. The perinatal mortality rate in this quarter of the population is currently 1.7/1000 with a potentially preventable perinatal mortality of 0.4/1000.

References

Cole, S.K. (1980) 'Scottish Maternity and Neonatal Records' in I. Chalmers and G. McIlwaine (Eds) *Perinatal Audit and Surveillance.* Proceedings of the Eighth Study Group of the Royal College of Obstetricians and Gynaecologists. London: RCOG
Department of Health (1993) *Changing Childbirth.* London: HMSO
Kendrick, S. and Clarke, J. (1992) The Scottish record linkage system. *Health Bull* **51**, 72–9

McIlwaine, G.M., Howat, R.C.L., Dunn, F. *et al.* (1979) The Scottish Perinatal Mortality
    Survey. *Br Med J* **ii**, 1103–6
Scotland Annual Reports Information and Statistics Division (1986–90). Stillbirth and
    Neonatal Survey. Common Services Agency of the Scottish Health Service
Scottish Office Home and Health Department (1993) *Provision of Maternity Services in Scotland:
    A Policy Review.* Edinburgh: HMSO

Chapter 9

Selection of women for community obstetric care

Michael J. V. Bull

General practitioner obstetricians are a declining breed; a recent survey undertaken by the Electoral Reform Ballot Services on behalf of the General Medical Services Committee of the British Medical Association (ERBS/GMSC 1992) found that 32.5 per cent of general practitioner (GP) principals claimed that they personally provided intrapartum care for their patients, although an earlier study (Smith and Jewell 1991) had shown that, in 1988, only 5.9 per cent of hospital maternities were in GP care whereas approximately 1 per cent more occurred at home. A generation ago, almost all GPs would have undertaken some intrapartum work since 40 per cent of cases still occurred at home then (DHSS 1970). A number of factors seem to have contributed to GP disenchantment with obstetrics: a falling birthrate, the drift away from domiciliary midwifery, the advent of policies for active management of labour and the increasingly complicated technology associated therewith, increasing media interest in safer childbirth and fear of litigation. Poor remuneration for obstetric care and problems with duty rosters in group practices have probably also played a part.

The Cranbrook Committee, set up in 1956 to review the provision of maternity services in the United Kingdom and reporting in 1959 (MOH 1959) recommended that only 'normal' cases should be delivered in GP care but did not specify the requisite criteria in detail. In 1967, however, the Ministry of Health published a pamphlet for GPs, hospital medical staff and midwives (MOH 1967) based on four triennial confidential reports on maternal deaths and defined high risk groups of women as follows:

1 Any woman whose general physical state is unsatisfactory
2 Any woman pregnant for the fifth or subsequent time
3 Any woman over 35 years of age or over 30 years if a nullipara
4 Any woman with an abnormal obstetric history
5 Any woman known to have rhesus antibodies

They advised that: 'Patients in these groups should be referred to a specialist unit' and further suggested that, for a confinement to take place in the home or in a GP maternity unit, the following criteria should apply:

Table 9.1.   Criteria for selection of women for community-based obstetric care

An uncompromised medical and obstetric history	
Nulliparae:	Age less than 30 years at booking
	Stature greater than 152 cm
Multiparae:	Age less than 35 years at booking
	Parity less than 4

1 As far as can be ascertained, the woman's general physical state is unimpaired
2 She is pregnant for the second, third or fourth time, the previous pregnancies labours and puerperia having been normal and she is under 35 years of age or, if a nullipara, she is under 30 years of age
3 She is known to have no rhesus antibodies
4 Her home conditions are suitable

Although still somewhat non-specific, these requirements (but now including suitable nulliparae) have formed the basis for criteria for booking women for GP obstetric care to this day (Table 9.1)

The Peel Report, in 1970 (DHSS 1970), recommended that, on the grounds of assumed increased safety, at least 70 per cent of births should occur in designated maternity units and that small, isolated obstetric units should be replaced by larger combined consultant and general practitioner units situated in general hospitals. In the event, mainly due to geographical considerations, this did not prove possible and around 65 isolated maternity units without direct specialist cover, still exist within England and Wales (Smith and Jewell 1991). GPs booking their patients in such units as well as those still undertaking domiciliary midwifery and, to a lesser extent, those attending mothers in integrated units in hospitals with specialist cover, will thus be concerned to select women of low obstetric risk and those who are most likely to deliver without operative intervention. With the emergence of midwife-led maternity care the same booking considerations should apply.

But how can women of low obstetric risk effectively be identified? Risk scoring systems have been developed in the past (Haeri *et al.* 1974; Chamberlain *et al.* 1975; Boddy *et al.* 1980), but these have primarily been designed with reference to the chance of fetal perinatal death rather than the probability of uncomplicated pregnancy and delivery. There is, of course, no such thing as a 'no-risk' pregnancy (Newcombe 1985) but it is possible, with careful assessment of women at booking and during the antenatal period, to reduce the chance of perinatal losses for patients in GP care to very low levels and to maximise the expectation of spontaneous vaginal delivery appropriate to community care (Bull 1985).

By far the most effective predictor of normality is past obstetric history. A woman who has had one or more previously uncomplicated pregnancy and has spontaneously deliverd a child of reasonable birthweight (say, >3000 g) has something like a 95 per cent chance of doing so again and can usually be booked with confidence for community obstetric care. Nulliparae, with no such track record,

Figure 9.1.   Nulliparae: mode of delivery by maternal stature (Scotland, 1977).

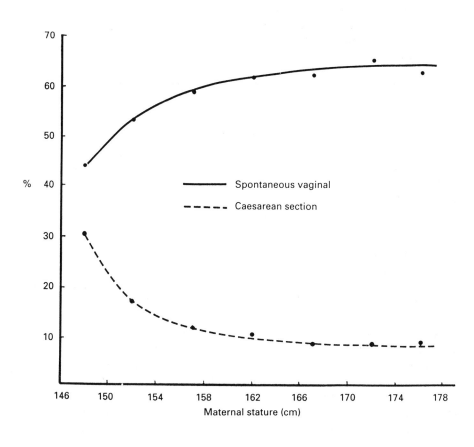

(Reproduced with permission of the editor, *Maternal and Child Health.*)

are more difficult to assess but there are a number of reliable predictive factors on which to base a booking decision. Possibly the most important is stature; small women tend to have a small pelvis. Data derived from the Scottish Perinatal Mortality Survey (McIlwaine *et al.* 1979) show that women less than 152 cm tall have a significantly increased risk of abdominal delivery which increases inversely with their height (Figure 9.1). Traditionally, small feet also have been associated with a small pelvis and Haddad *et al.* (1986) showed that women with a shoe size of 5 or less had a threefold increase in the risk of cephalopelvic disproportion. Maternal stature, nevertheless, is probably the more reliable indicator. Maternal youth in nulliparae is also a predictor of spontaneous vaginal delivery in the

Figure 9.2.   Nulliparae: spontaneous delivery rate by age group

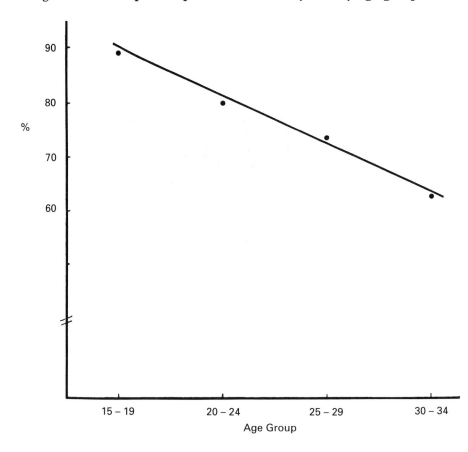

(Reproduced with permission of the editor, *Maternal and Child Health.*)

absence of other adverse factors. Figure 9.2 demonstrates this in a cohort of low risk women booked into GP care in Oxford during the 1970s, a finding later confirmed in a larger study (Reynolds and Yudkin 1987).

Reynolds *et al.* (1988) in the same Oxford unit, looked at other factors including marital status, maternal weight at booking, social class, and smoking habit and found that all, apart from marital status were low grade predictors of complication especially in nulliparae but no one factor had a strong enough influence to alter booking criteria for the unit. Of any, excessive maternal weight at booking was the most significant factor outside the original criteria for the unit.

But how should success in booking low-risk women for community care be measured? Perinatal mortality is a poor indicator for two reasons: first, the number of bookings (the denominator) in most GP units is so small that even a single loss, expressed in terms of events per thousand births in a given year, will give a value that is improbably high and, second, the causes of perinatal loss such as extreme

Figure 9.3.   Transfer of care: Oxford GP Unit; 1968–77. All cases.

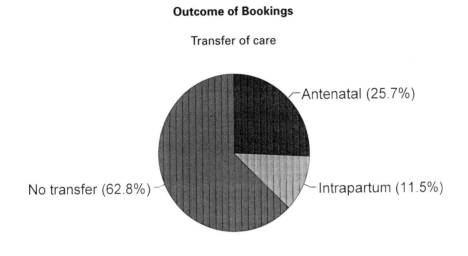

Outcome of Bookings

Transfer of care

Antenatal (25.7%)

No transfer (62.8%)

Intrapartum (11.5%)

($n = 7562$). (Reproduced with permission of the editor, *Maternal and Child Health.*)

preterm delivery, fatal congenital abnormality, antepartum haemorrhage and intrauterine death of unknown origin cannot usually be foreseen or remedied and can thus be regarded as unavoidable. On the other hand, losses due to intrapartum asphyxia or trauma during operative delivery are more suggestive of suboptimal practice.

Transfer rates, however, either before or during labour, from community to specialist care may be a more significant marker for selection policies. Figure 9.3 shows transfer rates over a ten-year period in the Oxford GP Maternity Unit (Bull 1983) when roughly one quarter of low-risk bookings developed problems before labour and one-eighth during parturition. Furthermore, one baby in fifty needed transfer to the special care baby unit. However, when the women were subdivided by parity a very diverse picture appeared; nulliparae (Figure 9.4) had transfer rates double that of multiparae (Figure 9.5) emphasising the difficulties in predicting the performance of women without previous obstetric experience.

Mode of delivery is another indicator of effective selection policy. GPs and community midwives will try to anticipate spontaneous vaginal delivery since, in most units, they have neither the skills nor the facilities for instrumental intervention. Figure 9.6 compares spontaneous deliveries in the Oxford GP unit with those in specialist care in the same hospital. The respective spontaneous delivery rates of approximately 90 per cent in the former with 70 per cent in the latter suggests reasonable selection for community care. During more recent years data have been published which seem to show that universal hospital confinement is not necessarily safer (Tew 1978) and that women can be safely delivered without

Figure 9.4.   Transfer of care: Oxford GP Unit; 1968–77. Nulliparae.

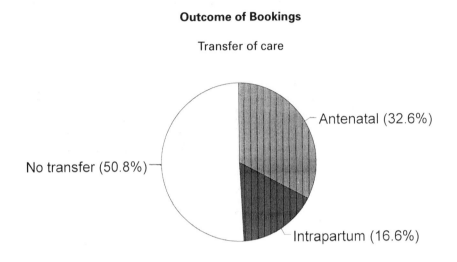

Outcome of Bookings

Transfer of care

Antenatal (32.6%)

No transfer (50.8%)

Intrapartum (16.6%)

(*n*=3614). (Reproduced with permission of the editor, *Maternal and Child Health.*)

Figure 9.5.   Transfer of care: Oxford GP Unit; 1968–77. Multiparae.

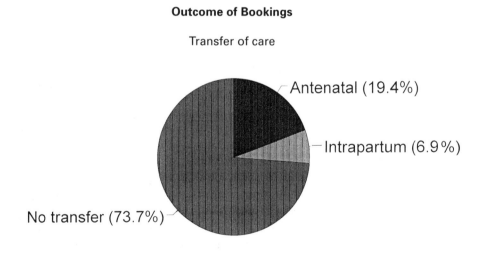

Outcome of Bookings

Transfer of care

Antenatal (19.4%)

Intrapartum (6.9%)

No transfer (73.7%)

(*n*=3948). (Reproduced with permission of the editor, *Maternal and Child Health.*)

Figure 9.6.   Spontaneous delivery rates: GP Unit and Specialist Unit; Oxford

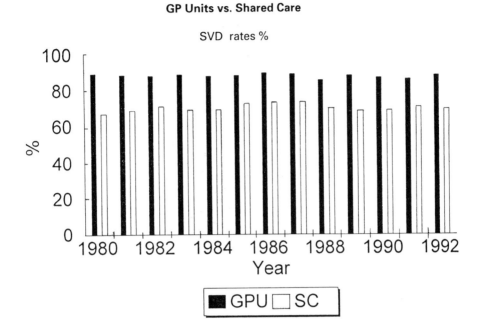

excessive intervention (Klein *et al.* 1983a,b; Tew 1986). Moreover, two recent government reports (House of Commons 1992; DOH 1993) have advocated more choice for mothers and a return to community maternity care. Thus there might yet be renewed interest by GPs in intrapartum care for low-risk women as well as further development of midwife-led facilities. Two ventures in the latter category have been reported (Street *et al.* 1991; MacVicar *et al.* 1993) and it is interesting to note that, although criteria for suitable women were broadly similar to those used in the Oxford GP unit, transfer rates both before and during labour were considerably higher. One implication of this observation could be that the GP obstetrician still has an effective role in community obstetric care.

In conclusion, if the recommendations of the Winterton and Cumberlege reports (House of Commons 1992; DOH 1993) are to be implemented, it seems that women could be selected for community care with a fair degree of confidence, parous women on the strength of an unblemished obstetric history and nulliparae on the basis of stature, age and absence of concurrent medical conditions. In view of the much higher incidence of unforeseeable complications during both pregnancy and labour in nulliparae, it might well be wise not to book these women at home or in isolated maternity units without immediate specialist support.

Summary

- Normality in obstetrics is essentially a retrospective judgement.
- Formalised risk prediction systems based on perinatal mortality rates in large cohorts are of limited value in the case of individuals.
- Past obstetric experience is the best predictor of future performance.
- In nulliparous women, small stature and advancing age increase the prospect of operative delivery
- Defined risk status should be tightly linked to planned place of delivery.
- A progressive system for risk detection and problem management should be associated with routine antenatal care.
- Excellent results can be achieved by an appropriate community-based obstetric care team approach.

References

Boddy, K., Parboosingh, I.J.T. and Shepherd, W.C. (1980) *A Schematic Approach to Prenatal Care*. Department of Obstetrics and Gynaecology, Edinburgh University

Bull, M.J.V. (1983) Obstetrics: selection of patients for GP care. *Matern Child Health* **8**, 84–90

Bull, M.J.V. (1985) 'Selection of patients for general practitioner care' in G.N. Marsh (Ed.) *Modern Obstetrics in General Practice*. Oxford: Oxford Medical Publications, Oxford University Press

Chamberlain, R., Chamberlain, G., Howlett, B. *et al.* (1975) *British Births 1970*. Vol 2: Obstetric care. London: Heinemann

DOH (1993) *Changing Childbirth*. London: HMSO

DHSS (1970) Report of the Standing Maternity and Midwifery Advisory Committee (Chairman: Sir John Peel). *Domiciliary Midwifery and Maternity Bed Needs*. London: HMSO

ERBS/GMSC (Electoral Reform Ballot Services/General Medical Services Committee) (1992) *Your Choices for the Future: a Survey of GP Opinion. UK Report*. London: Electoral Reform Ballot Services

Haddad, N.G., Beazley, J.M. and Chia, K.V. (1986) Shoe size and outcome of labour: a prospective anthropometric study. *J Obstet Gynecol* **7**, 97–9

Haeri, A.D., South, J. and Naldrett, J. (1974) A scoring system for identifying pregnant patients with a high risk of perinatal mortality. *J Obstet Gynecol Br Cwlth* **81**, 535–8

House of Commons (1992) Health Committee Second Report. Session 1991–2. *Maternity Services* (Chairman Lord Winterton). London: HMSO

Klein, M., Lloyd, I., Redman, C.W.G., Bull, M.J.V. and Turnbull, A.C. (1983a) A comparison of low-risk pregnant women booked for delivery in two systems of care: shared care (consultant) and integrated general practice unit. I. Obstetrical procedures and neonatal outcome. *Br J Obstet Gynaecol* **90**, 118–22

Klein, M., Lloyd, I., Redman, C.W.G., Bull, M.J.V., and Turnbull, A.C. (1983b) A comparison of low-risk pregnant women booked for delivery in two systems of care: shared care (consultant) and integrated general practice unit. II. Labour and delivery management and neonatal outcome. *Br J Obstet Gynaecol* **90**, 123–8

MacVicar, J., Dobbie, G., Owen-Johnstone, L. *et al.* (1993) Simulated home delivery in hospital: a randomised controlled trial. *Br J Obstet Gynaecol* **100**, 316–23

McIlwaine, G.M., Howat, R.C.L., Dunn, F. and Macnaughton, M.C. (1979) The Scottish Perinatal Mortality Survey. *Br Med J* **ii**, 1103–6

MOH (Ministry of Health) (1959) *Report of the Maternity Services Committee*. London: HMSO

MOH (Ministry of Health) (1967) *Safer Obstetric Care*. London: HMSO

Newcombe, R.G. (1985) 'A statistical review of risk factors' in G.N. Marsh (Ed.) *Modern Obstetrics in General Practice*. Oxford: Oxford Medical Publications

Reynolds, J.L. and Yudkin, P.L. (1987) Changes in the management of labour: 2. Perineal management. *Can Med Assoc J* **136**, 1045–9

Reynolds, J.L., Yudkin, P.L. and Bull, M.J.V. (1988) General practitioner obstetrics: does risk prediction work? *J R Coll Gen Pract* **38**, 307–10

Smith, L.P.F. and Jewell, D. (1991) The contribution of general practitioners to hospital intrapartum care in maternity units in England and Wales in 1988. *Br Med J* **302**, 13–16

Street, P., Gannon, M.J. and Holt, E.M. (1991) Community obstetric care in West Berkshire. *Br Med J* **302**, 698–700

Tew, M. (1978) 'The case against hospital deliveries: the statistical evidence' in S. Kitzinger and J.A. Davis (Eds) *The Place of Birth*. Oxford: Oxford University Press

Tew M. (1986) Do obstetric intranatal interventions make birth safer? *Br J Obstet Gynaecol* **93**, 659–74

Further Reading

James, D.K. and Stirrat, G.M. (1988) *Pregnancy and Risk: the Basis for Rational Management*. Chichester: John Wiley

Chapter 10

Risk limitation in obstetrics

Brian J. Capstick

A simple approach to reducing the financial risks of obstetric practice comprises three elements:

1. the identification of risks by means of claims audit and untoward incident reporting.
2. the reduction of accidents by improving those areas of practice identified as unusually vulnerable to error.
3. the limitation of losses arising after an accident has occurred, by the efficient management of poor outcomes and claims.

Identification of obstetric risks

The identification of risks is the subject of Chapter 9. Suffice it to say in the present context that, in the United Kingdom, most large obstetric claims are brought on behalf of people afflicted with cerebral palsy. The number of such claims made nationally is thought to have risen from about 70 in 1984 to about 200 in 1989 and perhaps as many as 600 in 1990 (Acheson 1990). The incidence of cerebral palsy itself has remained constant, despite improvements in other obstetric outcomes, at about one in 400 live births, or 1500 cases a year.

Studies of these claims show that a small number of risks arise with unerring regularity (Capstick and Edwards 1990; Ennis and Vincent 1990; Ennis *et al.* 1991 and, in America, Julian *et al.* 1985). They concern the adequacy of the assessment of fetal well-being on the labour ward and the response to any abnormalities which are revealed. The usual allegation is that the records disclose evidence of fetal distress which was not acted upon, either at all or in time to prevent the alleged damage.

Risk control

There are two elements in the control of risks. The first relates to the prevention of accidents by the provision of adequate resources and improvements in clinical practice. The other aims to reduce the number of false positives in which unmeritorious claims succeed because of poor record keeping or other failures on the part of hospitals to collect the evidence they need to defend themselves.

Accident prevention

Training

Training is required in the lessons to be learned from the analysis of large series of claims and any untoward incidents that come to light locally (for a summary, see Edwards *et al.* 1993).

A particular objective should be to improve the use and interpretation of electronic fetal heart monitoring (EFM) by medical and midwifery staff on the labour ward. Quite apart from those cases where there may be legitimate differences of opinion about the interpretation of the CTG trace, many claims continue to arise in circumstances where the picture is obvious and the omission to do anything about it is a gross error. Staff should be made familiar with the main abnormalities which can be revealed and how these should be interpreted within the overall clinical picture in respect of the particular labour. If such training encourages good quality notes, including observations of the CTG trace and the appropriate response, the prospects of avoiding disasters would be enhanced and a number of legal claims avoided. Case studies are appropriate material for the modern, more participative style of training which removes much of the weight from the trainer and etches the message that much deeper than traditional methods.

Supervision

A common feature of the claims is that avoidable delays occur in reacting to markers of fetal compromise because insufficient supervision is available from senior obstetric staff. All too often, any shortcomings on the part of the midwifery staff in appreciating fetal distress are compounded by the inability of the junior doctor to take appropriate action. In some cases, midwives may find themselves in a situation where they have to accept the interpretation and instructions of a junior doctor who has considerably less experience of labour ward practice than they do.

Clinical directors should therefore review the lines of communication within their units to ensure that, in appropriate circumstances, midwives will be able to make contact through the Sister in charge of the labour ward with the duty registrar or consultant. Clear guidelines should be introduced for those circumstances in which personal involvement by a consultant is essential (Clements 1992).

A related issue is the amount of time that consultants spend on the labour ward. A study group convened by the Royal College of Obstetricians and Gynaecologists to consider the problems of litigation concluded that consultants do not spend sufficient time in the labour ward (Chamberlain *et al.* 1985) and health authorities have been instructed under HC(90)16 to review the work programmes of their consultants.

Staff levels and turnover

The ideal staffing arrangements would permit one midwife to one woman and ensure that student midwives should not have individual responsibility for any women in labour. Junior staff should have adequate supervision from more senior colleagues. In practice, staffing levels often militate against such arrangements, but the resource requirement has to be assessed against the background that a single obstetric disaster could result in the loss of 2 million from the health care budget.

A high turnover of staff is destructive of quality in any service organisation and its reduction is a priority in many obstetric departments in the national health service. Locum doctors, agency staff and trainees on short-term appointments are not subject to the same standard of selection as permanent staff and, if they are only on short-term appointments, will inevitably be an unknown quantity for much of the time, thereby increasing the risk of accidents.

Adequacy of resources

In obstetric practice, a lack of resources may be reflected in a number of ways: for example, whether there is sufficient consultant cover to support junior staff with difficult traces, whether fetal scalp blood sampling is available to give a more accurate diagnosis than EFM, whether, if the decision is made to intervene surgically, there is an unreasonable delay in doing so because facilities are inadequate. All these are resource issues and management's task is to identify the point at which lack of resources exposes the hospital or the doctor to unacceptable risks.

Once a hospital has undertaken to provide treatment, the courts will not accept lack of resources as an excuse for an inadequate standard of care. In the leading case (*Bull* v. *Devon Area Health Authority* 1989) the allocation of resources had led to a split site for the hospital's obstetric and gynaecological activities. In these circumstances, there was an inherent risk that an experienced obstetrician would not be able to attend within a reasonable time whenever required to do so. Despite the fact that the administrative arrangements were determined by the availability of resources, the Court held that the delay in arrival of a qualified obstetrician was unreasonable and the cover arrangements negligent.

Record keeping: decisions to 'wait and see'

Clinicians are exhorted to maintain better records frequently enough for the point not to be laboured here, except in one specific context that constitutes a greater risk of litigation than is generally appreciated.

It relates to the situation where clinicians prefer to wait and see how a labour progresses in the face of possible alarm signals before coming to any decision to intervene. Since the majority of claims comprise allegations that the medical team did not respond quickly enough to signs of fetal distress, there is a conflict between such decisions and legal pressure for earlier intervention, or a higher proportion of Caesarean deliveries.

Clinicians therefore have to document decisions to 'wait and see' in the face of abnormal or equivocal traces. If the signs of possible distress are recorded at the time, perhaps automatically by a machine, but the decision to 'wait and see' is not documented, the image of events that will appear in the rear view mirror of legal proceedings is that the warning signs were there, but that nothing was done about them.

The solution is to maintain a clear record of any indications of potential fetal compromise, and to record decisions that were made in the light of them, even if the decision was only to maintain an appropriate level of monitoring. Where fetal scalp blood sampling is available, that should be used where clinically indicated to give a more precise assessment of fetal condition than is possible with EFM.

Limitation of losses

The limitation of losses after an accident has occurred by the efficient management of poor outcomes and claims is the area which, in the short term, is likely to result in the greatest financial savings. In summary, the available means are as follows.

Outcome reporting

The average interval between the date of birth and a hospital being notified of a claim is over five years, with 25 per cent taking more than seven years (Capstick and Edwards 1990). The purpose of outcome reporting in obstetrics is therefore to permit the identification of and preparation for litigation claims as soon as possible after the birth, which means that hospitals have to learn to identify potential plaintiffs.

The likelihood that a person will become a plaintiff in an obstetric claim is determined mainly by the size of the potential damages award. The diagnosis of cerebral palsy in a baby is therefore likely to give rise to a claim. However, in the neonatal period, it is difficult to identify all of the babies who may suffer lasting physical or mental impairment, as it may take up to a year before brain damage is diagnosed.

The result is that some other marker has to be used as the indicator for a potential claim. Paediatricians now recognise that encephalopathy in the first 72 hours of life is the most accurate marker of clinically significant asphyxia at birth (Hall 1989). There would appear to be a consensus that infants who later show signs of brain damage but who did not have moderate to severe encephalopathy as neonates did not suffer their brain damage as a result of birth asphyxia. In cases where babies subsequently develop some sort of chronic disability (including cerebral palsy) neonatal encephalopathy is likely to be sufficiently severe to produce fits, impaired consciousness, abnormal neurological function and renal dysfunction.

By no means all infants who show signs of fitting will turn out to be brain damaged, but the number is not so great as to make a review of the obstetric management of all of them impracticable. Every case of moderate to severe neonatal encephalopathy should be reported and investigated as a potential claim, particularly where it appears that the baby was born in poor condition, perhaps with low Apgar scores requiring resuscitation and admission to SCBU.

The objective of an outcome reporting system is to ensure that, if there is a bad outcome, a thorough review of the obstetric management is carried out and the evidence which may subsequently be necessary to account for a particular course of obstetric care is not lost. The body of evidence thus gathered should be used for the purpose of obtaining legal advice and case planning against the possibility of a claim.

This requires proper documentation of the intrapartum and neonatal care, including statements from the midwives and doctors involved. An accurate diagnosis should also be sought which, apart from its clinical value, may also help to establish whether the infant's condition was caused by any shortcomings in the obstetric management. Details of the infant's condition at birth may be of considerable evidential value, so it is important to ensure where possible that such evidence is preserved during the neonatal period. In particular, it would be valuable to have an indication of whether the baby suffered from birth asphyxia, although this is not always easy to diagnose unequivocally.

Outcome reporting and its ensuing investigations should be standard practice in cases of moderate to severe neonatal encephalopathy. The procedure should be documented and should identify clearly who has responsibility for making and receiving reports, for following them up and securing appropriate legal advice.

Privilege and disclosure

An important consideration for doctors and hospital managers is whether the documents that are generated in the course of an outcome reporting procedure are liable to be the subject of a court order for compulsory disclosure to a potential plaintiff. Such documents can be protected from disclosure if the procedure complies with the appropriate formalities and a protocol will be produced in the next few months.

Claims management

The main activities consist of outcome reporting (above), gathering evidence, and choosing and handling lawyers.

Many cases are difficult or impossible to defend because the requisite evidence is missing, not because the obstetric management was at fault. Hospitals should therefore ensure that evidence relevant to the defence is gathered or, at least, not lost. The original medical records should be secured and a copy made for clinical use if necessary. The records should be checked for completeness, in particular that the CTG trace is not lost, and to identify who made them, as signatures are often illegible.

Choosing and handling lawyers

Once an accident has happened, the principal factor within the hospital's control that will influence how much it costs will be the skill with which a claim is defended by its legal and medical experts. This will affect issues not only of liability but also of quantum, or the amount of compensation which the hospital is required to pay if a claim cannot be successfully defended. Huge variations routinely occur between the cost of claims that are handled well and those that fall victim to inexperience or inertia.

Subjective factors inevitably play an important role in making an assessment of various solicitors' firms, but there are objective factors which should not be disregarded. The first consideration is that of size, where a client should be concerned not with the overall size of the firm but the extent of the obstetric claims experience, where a firm with less than four full-time equivalents practising in the field would have difficulty keeping up with the body of knowledge required to handle major obstetric claims.

Evidence of professional expertise is difficult to assess directly. Publications, even a few, are a sign that a firm is sufficiently up in its field to make some contribution to its development and their quality is easily assessed. Likewise, prospective clients can ask for details of the training which the firm offers its staff. Some firms give training sessions to clients or other lawyers and this too is a healthy sign.

It is also important to try to assess the depth of the organisation. The quality of a law firm's assistant solicitors is a good guide to the quality of the service that will be delivered to the client and prospective clients should ask to meet the individuals who will deal with their cases. The quality of assistants is also an indicator of the quality of the firm as a whole, as it is difficult for indifferent firms to attract or retain the best staff.

Having instructed a firm, it is important for clients to manage their cases by means of regular review with the solicitors. An initil assessment of the likely cost of the claim, including legal costs and experts' fees, will identify the large claims as the management of a small claim will be different from that of a claim in which hundreds of thousands of pounds are at risk. The next step is to make an early assessment of liability, a task that will be a great deal easier if an outcome or incident reporting procedure has captured the evidence soon after the event.

Having made an assessment of liability and cost, small claims that cannot be successfully defended should be settled early in order to save costs. In the case of large claims that cannot be defended, the assessment of compensation is a substantial and skilled activity and, in choosing solicitors and managing claims, hospitals often overlook the fact that it is at the point of analysing such demands and negotiating a compromise that the greatest savings in the overall cost of claims is likely to be made.

References

Acheson, D. (1990, 1991) William Power Memorial Lecture to the Royal College of Midwives, 5 December 1990, reprinted in *Hospital Doctor* 10 and 17 January 1991

Capstick, B. and Edwards, P. (1990) Trends in obstetric malpractice claims. *Lancet* **336**, 931–2

Chamberlain, G.V.P., Orr, C.J.B. and Sharp, F. (1985) *Litigation in Obstetrics and Gynaecology.* Proceedings of the 14th Study Group of the Royal College of Obstetricians and Gynaecologists. London: RCOG

Clements, R.V. (1992) 'Obstetric litigation' in *Advances in Obstetrics and Gynaecology* 5. Abingdon: The Medicine Group (Education) Ltd.

Edwards, P., Mason, D., and Capstick, B. (1993) *Litigation – A Risk Management Guide for Midwives*. London: Royal College of Midwives

Ennis, M. and Vincent, C.A. (1990) Obstetric accidents: a review of 64 cases. *Br Med J* **300**, 1365–7

Ennis, M., Clark, A. and Grudzinskas, J.G. (1991) Change in obstetric practice in response to fear of litigation in the British Isles. *Lancet* **338**, 616–18

Hall, D.M.B. (1989) Birth asphyxia and cerebral palsy. *Br Med J* **299**, 279–82

Julian, T.M., Brooker, D.C., Butler, J.C. Jr *et al.* (1985) Investigation of obstetric malpractice closed claims: profile of event. *Am J Perinatol* **2**, 320–4

Chapter 11

Balancing risks and choice: Discussion

Opening remarks by Lesley A. Page

Pregnancy as rite of passage

'Pregnancy is a long and very special journey for a woman. It is a journey of dramatic physical, psychological and social change; of becoming a mother, of redefining family relationships and taking on the long-term responsibility for caring and cherishing a newborn child.' We are reminded in the foreword to the report *Changing Childbirth* (Department of Health 1993, p. ii) that pregnancy and birth is a rite of passage, a social and psychological preparation for taking on the task of parenting. Any discussion about the rights of the family to make decisions about the birth of their baby, must be put into this context.

This transition, into one of the most demanding roles of adult life, that of parent, is affected by a complex interplay of social and cultural factors, psychological and physical change. The mother especially, and often the father too, live with the consequences of care provided for the rest of their lives. It might also be safely assumed that in most situations nobody cares more for, or has more influence over, the child than the mother and her family. Parents will need to make decisions about risk and health for their child for many years to come.

We are aware of the meaning of pregnancy and the birth of child as a rite of passage, and are aware that childbirth must have an impact on the psychosocial development of the woman. But, as Simkin (1991) reminds us, the understanding is elusive because the complexities of human personality make it difficult to isolate the impact of childbirth from other influences in her life. Simkin explored the long-term impact of the birth experience in a group of 20 women who were part of a natural childbirth class. She found that the women with the highest long-term satisfaction ratings were those that felt that they accomplished something important in giving birth, that they were in control, and that the birth experience contributed to their self-confidence and self-esteem. This was a small study. Nonetheless, it is worth considering that the ability of the woman to feel in control is associated with improved satisfaction and increased self-esteem. Given that positive self-esteem is an important component of effective parenting, this idea seems worthy of respect.

The demand for more choice and control

There are convincing arguments and ethical imperatives for respecting the autonomy of the mother and enabling her to make choices in her care. There is also considerable evidence that women and their families want more control, more choice, in their care.

The House of Commons Health Select Committee (1992) reported that they 'received much evidence in support of the case for providing more choice for women'. A 1993 MORI survey similarly found that at the entry point to the maternity services discussion about the choice of service for both antenatal care and the place of birth was limited.

Users of the maternity services are asking for the right to choose, but how ready are professionals to support women and their families in taking responsibility and making informed decisions? There is a commonly held view that when women want to make their own decisions their actions are selfish and endanger the health of their baby. Giving women the right to make choices about their care might result in some risk, yet there might be greater risk in preventing parents from taking the responsibility for decisions about care. Midwives and doctors do have specialised expertise and knowledge which is of great potential benefit to the family making choices about their care, and this expertise should be recognised. But in using this expertise we must work with parents to help them make informed choices, while avoiding paternalism and maternalism in our relationships, and coercion and persuasion in our communications.

The meeting of helper and helped is popularly referred to as a partnership between professionals and parents, a partnership where each has a strong and important contribution to make, but where the parents themselves should always be the ones to make the final decision.

One of the most important preconditions for work within this partnership is an acceptance of the uncertainty of our knowledge. Unfortunately the track record of midwives and doctors for discriminating between what is sound evidence and what is opinion or ritual, is not good. The importance of interventions in producing safer outcomes has often been overemphasised (Tew 1990), and some important interventions have been ignored (Chalmers *et al.* 1989). There are many areas in which parents can make choices about their care where the approach is unlikely to make a difference, and decisions should be based purely on their values.

Should there be limits to choice?

Are there any situations in which the personal autonomy of the mother should be ignored in order to protect the unborn child? How many clinical situations are there in which the refusal of treatment puts the child's life at risk? There are actually few. Thornton (1993) describes the examples of cord prolapse in the first stage of labour, a very severe degree of fetal distress, or uterine rupture. Yet, as he reminds us, these are not usually the situations in which maternal professional conflict occurs.

It is difficult to justify refusing the mother's wishes (for example if she wishes to have her baby at home, or to have a trial of labour after Caesarean), when the risks to the fetus, if present at all, are small.

Supporting and enabling informed choice

It seems then that there are few clinical constraints on the mother's right to make decisions about her care, where she should have her baby, who should attend her, and her treatment. But decisions about care, place of birth and professional attendant are likely to make a great difference to the interventions used and the parent's perception of the birth of their child. Genuine involvement in decision making is very likely to have a psychologically positive effect. The central question is how can we help the individual mother and her family decide what is best for them, and how can we create services where families are enabled to make decisions about their care?

For parents to be able to make genuine choices options have to be available. Home birth, small birthing centres, domino delivery or group practice, and the option for low technology care are important options for many women.

The provision of information which is based on research evidence, for parents and professionals, in regularly updated forms such as that provided in the *Cochrane Pregnancy and Childbirth Database* (Cochrane Collaboration 1993) is essential for enabling parents to make truly informed choices.

The basis of care which supports parents and helps them in deciding what is best for them is the development of trusting relationships. It is not only effective and caring communications, but also an appropriate organisation of care which will support the development of this trust and support.

Some decisions are complex, and depend on weighing up risks and personal values. Decision analysis is a method of breaking complex problems into manageable component parts, analysing these parts in detail, and then combining them in a logical way to indicate the best course of action (Thornton *et al.* 1992). Models such as these remove the emotion and avoid well-recognised biases in making decisions, and go a long way in helping clinicians and parents to make the decisions that are best for them.

One of the great challenges is to develop practice where we recognise the individual needs of parents, and take these into account together with sound evidence in helping parents to make up their own minds about the birth of their children. Such care might well be a crucial factor in the development of families where pride and self confidence in parenting lead to greater health in the future.

Discussion

Page: What do we mean by choice? What are the implications of that word?

Spencer: At this point I would like to suggest what it is not. It is not a choice to take responsibility for the risks because most women are not capable of doing that without sufficient empowerment with knowledge and skills.

Perhaps at this stage it is to be involved with the process: the choice is to be involved. There are some women whom we all deal with who do not want to be involved and we had an example of that: 'You are the midwife, you are the doctor, you are there to make the decisions.' There are many people who want that.

When expectations are not fulfilled, someone has to take the rap. If something goes more seriously wrong, we have to bear the burden of some of the responsibility for that. We cannot pass that on to the women by saying, 'Well, it was your decision.' So I hope that it is not that we expect them to take responsibility. We should wish them to share it, but not take it. I would like to suggest it is being involved with the process; then we can work on what that process should be and that may differ in different parts of the world.

Kroll: To take that one step further, it must include communication. Communication has been brought up as one of the new Cs as though we have not used it before. But in antenatal education we have seven months, and a lot longer postnatally. Involvement becomes a lot easier if women are seeing the same professional regularly, building up a relationship, so that the woman can be helped to make a choice. We cannot expect them to learn and to know about the things that have taken us ten, twenty, thirty years to understand. Suddenly, because they are pregnant for the first time, they are expected to know what it means to make a choice of a home delivery. Women are very emotional in the early days of pregnancy when we first meet them, and choice becomes very difficult then because they may come to us with subjective views of what they think their choice is. Hence the building up of the relationship and communication becomes extremely important.

Page: Is it so wrong to take women's subjective views on board? It seems to me that there is an argument in helping families make choices and being in control of the birth of their own babies, that a lot of those choices should be made on the values of the family. For one family their personal freedom and personal autonomy might be great enough that they wish to have their baby at home and that could outweigh any kind of possible risks that there might be.

Kroll: It is important because we cannot ask women to get rid of the feelings that they have. The problem is we rely a lot on women talking to one another. It always amazes me how many women tell me that a friend up the road had a home delivery and they know we can do it. Alternately, a friend up the road was told she could not have a home delivery and I have to explain it is because she lives in a different health authority area, but that in my area if the woman wants a home delivery we can discuss it.

One of our problems is that we see a disproportionate number of older mothers. The age of our primiparous women is quite a lot higher than Michael Bull's. We have many women aged over 35 coming with their first pregnancy. When a woman walks into the surgery for the first time saying she wants a home delivery and that is her first choice, that choice is based on what she feels at the time and what she has heard. If by the end of her fifth or sixth month of pregnancy she still wants that home delivery, after we have spent time talking about it and finding out what is behind it, I think that request for a home delivery is telling me something. It is not automatically only saying that she wants the baby delivered at home, but she is telling me that she wants to stay out of that hospital because she knows that when she walks through that door she will have lost control. She is petrified that when she goes into hospital somebody will take control away from her. Working with women for the last 17 years, I understand what they are saying, and I think that is part of the communication. If in the end home delivery is what they want, and they understand the circumstances, they understand the risks, they understand the benefits, fine. But just accepting home delivery and saying, 'Yes, we do it; the midwives will do it for you', we forget what else is happening.

Page: So communication should delve into what they really want and we have to invest time in that communication, get to know the women, and help women explore for themselves.

Kroll: And that is where continuity of care is so important for all those things develop from that.

Allison: One issue not covered yet has to do with choice, risk factors, and the relation of risk factor to social disadvantage. These are women who have a very high perinatal death risk even if they do not necessarily have medical or obstetric risk factors; these women are those with whom it is most difficult to communicate because often they do not present themselves for care. What should carers be considering when they are talking to women who are in the high-risk group because of social disadvantage, the women who have bad housing, who are unsupported or who may be drug addicts? Perhaps our wisdom in the past has been to lump this group of women together and to say that the safest thing for them is hospital birth with a longer postnatal stay.

I believe that there is a great deal to be said for supporting the woman to have whatever sort of birth she wants and to work with her to improve her social situation, rather than keeping her in hospital for a long while and then returning her to that same social situation. If we can improve her social situation at home we have improved it for the growing child also; this may then reduce the rate of infant mortality.

Zander: John Spencer made an important point in saying he does not believe in choice but he certainly agrees with involvement. There is a fundamental difference whether we actually do give value to choice. Ms Kroll went on to ask how can we make sure this choice is as good as we can get it but it was quite a different point she was making. We need to challenge John Spencer's statement, because he quite clearly said he did not believe in choice.

I believe that as professionals we need to decide whether we do believe in choice, and if so, then how to make it better with communication issues following on from that.

I should like to underlie what Professor Page has said. The title for this discussion should not be 'Balancing Risk and Choice' because some might assume that choice will create more risk. Choice is the issue and then we have to balance risk and benefit. What Professor Page said is very important, because of the social and psychological benefits. We need to recognise that there are real benefits to be derived from giving choice, which is to be balanced with risk.

Newburn: I believe in choice and women without any doubt should be able to make the choice. The bottom line is that they should be able to make a choice about what happens to them and their body and their baby.

Having said that that is the bottom line, most of the time I do not think there is a lot of conflict. Because everybody wants a happy, healthy outcome, and because that is not a problem in most cases, we should not be too worried by that. Everybody makes decisions on the basis of a subjective understanding because nobody can ever know everything there is to know and balance all the risks and all the benefits. People's interpretation of research, even when it is very thorough, will be different. As an example: we have been troubling ourselves about vitamin K and its appropriate form for prophylaxis postnatally in terms of choice and the information given to parents. It has been suggested that health professionals have a responsibility to guide parents, because they have a professional understanding of the issues. I would absolutely agree with that. It would be a very sad state of affairs if we expected all parents to have all knowledge, and many frequently will seek the guidance of health professionals and be very happy to go along with that. However, there are some who for whatever reason will want to do things differently, whether it is a cultural reason, whether it is because they know the research literature themselves quite well, or whether they are just bloody minded. Women should be able to make choices.

Downe: I want to pick up on the issue of responsibility. Choice means responsibilty. I absolutely believe that women will take responsibility in many areas if they are given the information. What has happened in the past is that they have not been given that information and therefore it has been hard for them to accept re-sponsibility for the choices they make. I am not saying that women should be blamed if things go wrong. This happens when we make choices and we do not necessarily blame ourselves. We have to accept that in saying to women that choice is acceptable, we have also to say to them that this means a degree of responsibility that they bear for themself and their child. I do not think women would find that difficult. Once the baby is born we have no problem with accepting that women have responsibility for their children, so why should it be different when they are pregnant?

There are other more subtle areas to this. I am not saying this to countermand what I have just said but there are things we should bear in mind. There are times when we use the word 'choice' when the choice is a non-choice, e.g. antenatal screening. If a woman is bound to have a baby with a problem, the choice to be made is a non-choice between terminating a baby she wanted and going ahead with a pregnancy which will have a known bad outcome at the end. It is a different paradigm of choice. Sometimes we present choices to a woman that society itself has not made decisions about; they become very difficult and women are left very isolated in those circumstances. In general, we are paternalistic if we believe that women cannot accept responsibility for themselves and their babies at that moment in time when they can for the rest of the child's life.

Spencer: We were asked what was the choice that women should be making; some women, perhaps even a majority, are ill prepared or are not capable of taking the responsibility that the last two or three contributors have exemplified. Those that can and those that wish to should be given the opportunity to do so.

Capstick: We see very few cases in which things go right but quite a number in which things go wrong. It has certainly become more frequent in the last few years that there are altercations between the woman who may want one particular pattern of care and the midwife or obstetrician who thinks she should have a quite different one. For example, it may be medically advisable to have a Caesarean section and the woman may not want one, or may not want one yet, and time is lost while this is debated; this is becoming an increasingly frequent part of the litigation experience. It is evident from that that carers are thrown into the debate with very little understanding or training in how they should cope with situations where a mother is determined to exercise her rights and the carers who still have a responsibility to see that she gets a satisfactory level of medical care.

This conflict cannot be resolved by weasel words that try to get the best of both worlds. It is only fair to tell the patients and the people who are expected to care for them exactly what the guidelines are and who does have control of this process. Otherwise it will have to be sorted out in the courts, which is a very expensive way of doing it.

Page: Who would a lawyer say has control of that process at the end of the day?

Capstick: The woman has a right to say no, she has a right to refuse treatment. But at the end of the day it is the hospital that is responsible for any financial consequences of a bad outcome. One can go to court and one can argue these cases, but the woman remembers very vividly everything that happened and the carers cannot remember the details at all. The result is that the version of events that comes out after a few years is very different from what actually happened at the time. So, any assessment of the situation will not be just and accurate, but will inevitably be skewed.

Page: So there is some conflict between enabling women to have some control of their care and then not accepting advice.

Capstick: It is the very situation that Mr Spencer has identified. Women can be given an involvement, a right to partcipate and to be consulted in what is happening to them, but at the end of the day the clinical responsibility that in this situation such-and-such ought to happen regardless of what the mother says she wants, cannot be ducked. That is the issue. How the professionals resolve it is a matter for them.

McGinley: The view has been expressed that perhaps the women we should be listening to are those who have a voice or those who are able to express the choices. I would argue with that. I believe that those who most need access to empowerment are those who have the least voice. It is very important therefore that in designing a new maternity service we give time and consideration to creating a system that will ensure that those who do not currently have a voice will have one. It is very often those who are marginalised that are processed through the system; instead of empowering women and making childbirth a very positive experience for them, it just detracts from their feeling of self-worth. In looking at a maternity service we have to think about giving these women the opportunity to form the relationships that enhance the childbirth experience. I do not think that our maternity system does that.

Smith: Speaking as a general practitioner, I would like to make two points. First, this question of autonomy. I do not see why childbirth should be a particularly special case. As GPs we advise patients every day on various treatments and interventions which we think they should or should not have.We supply them with information so that they can make decisions and provide informed consent. In my experience some patients wish to be involved and others do not. What is important is that they should be given the opportunity to exercise their autonomy and they should also be given sufficient information to make an informed choice about the type of care they want.There is no valid reason why childbirth should be any different from the rest of primary care.

Second, I have great sympathy with midwives seeing women for the first time who say they want home delivery and they are desperate not to go near that hospital. The point has been made that it takes time to sit down with such a woman and to build a relationship to find out what she really wants.It is sometimes forgotten that GPs have known these women for many years beforehand and have a good idea of what they may or may not want. I frequently discuss future childbirth, also contraception and other aspects of their health long before pregnancy and I hope I have some insight into what they might want when they finally become pregnant. Some GPs – not all – take a similar approach and their contribution to trying to help women achieve what they want, should not be forgotten.

Hall: I wanted to agree about making sure that the women who are not articulate or demanding have access to choice. I want also to raise the question about whether there should be any restriction of choice.

My particular interest is the woman who asks for more intervention than is indicated medically. If, for example, a woman asked for a Caesarean section for which there were no medical indications whatever, what situation would the professional be in then? No doctor would do an appendectomy on someone who had no medical indications; should an obstetrician do a Caesarean section on a woman who has no medical indications? There are hardly any absolute indications for a Caesarean section, just a spectrum of conditions. There is no difficulty with discussion when there is some indication for a section, but if there are no medical indications whatever for a section, should we agree to such a request?

Page: Dr Hall has raised a question at the heart of a modern-day dilemma. A lot of women ask for an elective Caesarean section; I am not sure how I shall deal with that when I next face it. It is a provocative question that gets us to the heart of some of the issues.

Chamberlain: There is a very good paper on this from the Swedish literature (Ryding 1993). I have great sympathy with the women who ask for Caesarean sections. They are making a cry for help just as much as if there is a physical problem; it is a mental problem, in their minds they want it. In many cases it is easy; for example they have had a bad time previously, with a difficult forceps delivery, and so one agrees at the beginning of pregnancy – this is when it should be said. The question should be asked and answered at the beginning of the pregnancy so that the woman knows then and will go through a happy pregnancy.

The more difficult decisions are the women who have never had a pregnancy before and they are just as much requesting help as the women who have an obvious indication. They deserve consideration. If the centre has good anaesthesia, good surgeons, good midwives, and good care, the risks of elective Caesarean section are not much greater than vaginal delivery. It is then a simple question of risk-benefit. I would talk to the woman and often I would say yes.

Young: I am concerned about the possibility of electronic fetal monitoring and whether it is being considered an absolute need or else there might be litigation. I should like some clarification from the group that none of us, I hope, would support anyone who claimed there was insufficient monitoring just because an electronic monitor had not been used.

We have got ourselves into this mess, not the lawyers. I remember an editorial about four years ago entitled 'Cerebral palsy, intrapartum anoxia and a shot in the foot', which pointed out that one of the mistakes we have made is in misinforming women at how good we are at our job (Anon. 1989). We are not perfect at detecting fetal distress, nor at avoiding cerebral palsy. I should like to hear some views on whether we genuinely should be informing women that electronic fetal monitoring does not protect from cerebral palsy.

Page: The recommendations that have been published by the RCOG on this are quite clear and this is a good time to publicise them (Spencer and Ward 1993).

Macfarlane: Having commented that Dr Bull's list of risk factors is the list of the 1950s and 1960s, we must accept that often the lst of selection factors for home delivery was drawn up from data available in the 1950s andthe 1960s for allocating scarce hospital places. These data have now been turned round the other way and taken as selection factors for low-risk care.

From a statistical point of view we see two different types of indicator, those that apply to the woman herself with her particular conditions, and those that are based on groups of women such as age and parity. Statistical analysis can show that women in certain age groups and parity groups have a higher risk of maternal or perinatal death but tells us nothing about the individual woman. It seems important to take another look at this and to question the population-based factors, the demographic considerations, as indicators for the initial booking.

Might I suggest that the reasons to change booking after discussion is re-examined; a high transfer rate in the antenatal period is not necessarily something adverse. We would want to know more about the reasons for change. If changes are made, is this following full discussion with women exercising different choices, or do women make an initial choice and then change because of some very specific clinical indication? It may be that a high antenatal transfer rate is a measure of a service in which real choices are being made.

I would suggest that this is another crude statistic that needs to be broken down to become more useful in monitoring the extent to which we are seeing choice in one direction. It may be a better detector of possible complications to avoid transfer in labour, something everyone wants to avoid.

Cumberlege: I am conscious that we shall be taking forward the proposals in *Changing Childbirth*. I know that for these to be successful depends very much on all those people working in the field and in that I do include statisticians and researchers as well as obstetricians, GPs and midwives.

I am absolutely convinced that we do have to move forward. I have listened very carefully to the whole issue of choice. Some of the women now who are much older when they have their first baby are leading very different lives. Many are in control of their lives, they are in control of other people's lives, they are career women. They are a tiny minority, but like the praetorian guard, they are leading the way forward and in their wake are a whole lot of other women who are inarticulate, who are struggling and who are finding it very difficult to just live a normal family life. Their needs are just as great, their aspirations are considerable, and although they find it more difficult to express their views, I suspect that they want to share many of the same ideas about choice.

Editors' note
The editors recall a discussion that took place between Professor Chamberlain, Dr Marion Hall and Dr Rubin, about the relative safety of elective Caesarean section compared with vaginal delivery. Professor Chamberlain contended that a woman had the right to ask for an elective Caesarean section. If she understood the risks of that method of delivery, the obstetrician should consider her request and its psychological effect, just as in other circumstances he would judge the wishes for a physical induction. Doctors Hall and Rubin felt that there was still an increased risk of Caesarean section even in the best hands over vaginal delivery and therefore should not be done.

We could not find this on the tapes of the discussion but have handwritten notes; we feel it should be recorded for completeness.

References

Anon. (1989) Cerebral palsy, intrapartum care, and a shot in the foot (editorial). *Lancet* **ii**, 1251–2

Chalmers, I., Enkin, M. and Keirse, M.J.N.C. (1989) *Effective Care in Pregnancy and Childbirth*. Oxford: Oxford University Press

Cochrane Collaboration (1993) *Cochrane Pregnancy and Childbirth Database*. Cochrane Updates on Disk, 1993, Disk Issue 2. Oxford: Update Software

Department of Health (1993) *Changing Childbirth*. London: HMSO

House of Commons Health Select Committee (1992) *Second Report on the Maternity Services*. London: HMSO

MORI (1993) Maternity Services Summary Report prepared for the Department of Health.

Ryding, E.L. (1993) Investigation of 33 women who demanded a cesarean section for personal reasons. *Acta Obstet Gynecol Scand* **72**, 280–85

Simkin, P. (1991) Just another day in a woman's life? Women's long-term perceptions of their first birth experience. Part 1. *Birth* **18**, 203–10

Spencer, J.A.D. and Ward, R.H.T. (Eds) (1993) *Intrapartum Fetal Surveillance. Proceedings of the RCOG 26th Study Group*. London: Royal College of Obstetricians and Gynaecologists

Tew, M. (1990) *Safer Childbirth? A Critical History of Maternity Care*. London: Chapman and Hall

Thornton, J.G., Lilford, R.J. and Johnson, N. (1992) Decision analysis in medicine. *Br Med J* **304**, 1099–103

Thornton, J.G. (1993) Are there proper limits to women's freedom of choice in pregnancy? Paper to consensus conference on Britain's Maternity Services. March 1993, unpublished

SECTION II
PROVISION OF SERVICES: WHAT AND HOW?

Chapter 12

Prepregnancy care: genetic risk assessment and counselling

J. Michael Connor

Improvements in control of many environmental agents have resulted in an increased relative importance of genetic diseases. These diseases are now the commonest causes of childhood handicap and mortality and they often carry high recurrence risks for parents and other family members. Hence their recognition is vital but this task is complicated by the large number of distinct conditions which have now been described (Table 12.1).

For the obstetric team the chromosomal disorders, single gene disorders and congenital malformations due to multifactorial inheritance are most relevant (as most other multifactorial disorders and somatic cell genetic disorders occur after childhood). Table 12.2 (see overleaf) indicates the factors evident either before or during a pregnancy which serve to indicate an increased risk for one of these conditions.

Identification of the at-risk pregnancy

Factors identifiable prior to a pregnancy

Elevated maternal age

The commonest identifiable risk factor prior to a pregnancy is elevated maternal age and in the UK about 7 per cent of mothers will be 35 years or older at their

Table 12.1. Classification of genetic diseases

Type	No. of subtypes	Combined frequency in livebirths (%)
Chromosomal disorders[a]	>600	0.7
Single gene disorders	>5000	1
Multifactorial disorders	>100	25
Somatic cell genetic disorders	>100	30

[a] Including disorders of mitochondrial chromosomes.

103

Table 12.2   Identification of pregnancies at increased risk for fetal abnormality

	Chr	SGD	MCM
Factors identifiable prior to a pregnancy			
Elevated maternal age	+	−	−
Parental consanguinity	−	+	+
Ethnic origin	−	+	(+)
Positive family history	+	+	+
Maternal illness or medication	−	(+)	+
Population carrier screening	−	+	−
Factors identifiable during a pregnancy			
Abnormal ultrasound appearance	(+)	(+)	(+)
Maternal serum screening	+	−	(+)
Maternal exposure to teratogens	−	−	+

Chr: chromosomal disorders; SGD: single gene disorders, MCM: major congenital malformations
+ =associated, (+)=may be associated, − =not associated

estimated date of confinement. Elevated maternal age is related to the incidence of several chromosomal abnormalities including autosomal trisomies (21, 18 and 13) and 47,XXX.

Parental consanguinity

Parents often do not realise the importance of consanguinity and will not volunteer that they are blood relatives unless directly questioned. Consanguinity results in an increased frequency of autosomal recessive disorders and multifactorial congenital malformations. If the family history is otherwise negative, the couple can be advised that the risk of a major congenital malformation is 4 per cent (as compared with the general population risk of 2 per cent) and that the added risk for autosomal recessive conditions is about 1 per cent. No special screening is indicated before a pregnancy unless indicated by other factors, such as ethnic origin, but during a pregnancy detailed ultrasound scanning for malformations might be considered. Consanguinity *per se* is not an indication for fetal chromosomal, DNA or biochemical analysis.

Table 12.3.   Ethnic associations of genetic diseases

Disease	Populations at risk	Carrier test
Alpha-thalassaemia	Chinese, Thais	Red cell indices
Beta–thalassaemia	African blacks, Chinese, Cypriots, Egyptians, Greeks, Turks	Red cell indices, Hb electrophoresis
Cystic fibrosis	North Europeans	DNA analysis
Gaucher disease	Ashkenazi Jews	Serum beta-glucosidase
Sickle cell disease	African blacks, Arabs, West Indians	Sickledex test
Tay–Sachs disease	Ashkenazi Jews	Serum beta-N-acetylhexose aminidase A

Ethnic origin

Certain ethnic groups have high carrier frequencies for particular autosomal recessive conditions (Table 12.3). Hence, if a couple belong to one of these ethnic groups, screening for carrier status should be considered.

Positive family history

The traditional question, 'Is there a family history of tuberculosis, diabetes or epilepsy?' is completely inadequate if a serious attempt is to be made to identify high-risk pregnancies. Conversely, the construction of a detailed pedigree would be impractical for every patient in a busy antenatal clinic and a compromise would be, in addition to the standard medical and previous obstetric history, to ask about the above points (maternal age, parental consanguinity and ethnic origin), about malformed and/or handicapped children in the immediate or distant family and whether or not any condition seems to run in the family.

Correct interpretation of a positive family history may be straightforward or be a difficult challenge. Difficulties most frequently arise when the diagnosis in the affected individual has not been adequately documented or is unknown, and where genetic conditions are clinically similar or identical (genetic heterogeneity). In view of the potential consequences of faulty advice, referral to a clinical geneticist should be considered if any doubts exist or if more distant family members are at increased risk.

Table 12.4. Common lay misconceptions about heredity

Absence of other affected individuals means that a disorder is not genetic and vice versa

Any condition present at birth must be inherited

Upsets, mental and physical, of the mother in pregnancy cause malformations

Genetic diseases are always untreatable

If only males or females are affected in the family this indicates sex linkage

A 1 in 4 risk means that the next three children will be unaffected

Maternal illness or medication

Maternal illnesses such as insulin dependent diabetes mellitus, epilepsy, spina bifida and congenital heart disease carry an increased risk for fetal abnormality and many drugs have been implicated as teratogens.

Population carrier screening

At the present time population carrier screening is confined to ethnic groups with particularly high frequencies for certain autosomal recessive disorders and screening for cystic fibrosis is being considered for the general population in the UK (Table 12.3).

Factors identifiable during a pregnancy

There may be no clues to an increased risk of fetal abnormality until it is signalled during the pregnancy by an abnormal ultrasound appearance, an abnormal result on maternal serum screening or exposure to a teratogen.

Genetic counselling

Identification of an at-risk pregnancy from the preceding approaches will necessitate counselling for the couple. Adequate time in an appropriate setting is essential and in general 30–45 minutes is required for a new family in order to take the medical history, construct the pedigree, examine key family members, consult appropriate records and counsel the family. Precision of diagnosis is the cornerstone of medical genetics and hence counselling should be deferred until all data from specialised investigations and/or evaluation of medical records or other family members are available. Ideally both parents should be counselled and neither the corner of a hospital ward nor a crowded clinic room is adequate.

Counselling needs to include all aspects of the condition and the depth of explanation should be matched to the educational background of the couple. Generally geneticists consider a risk of more than 1 in 10 as high and of less than 1 in 20 as low but the risks have to be considered in relation to the degree of disability. Couples often feel very guilty or stigmatised and it is important to recognise and allay these and other common misconceptions (Table 12.4). Counselling must be non-directive; the aim is to provide the couple with a balanced

Table 12.5.   Pitfalls in genetic counselling

Incorrect or incomplete diagnosis

Genetic heterogeneity (genetic mimics)

Non-penetrance (clinically normal gene carriers for autosomal dominant traits)

Variable expression (clinical variation of dominant traits)

Unstable mutations (with consequent variable severity in different family members)

Gonadal mosaicism (mutation confined to the gonad – hence high risk to offspring for an autosomal dominant trait or chromosomal disorder despite clinically normal parents)

Inadequate knowledge of the literature

Previously undescribed disease

version of the facts which will allow them to reach a decision with regard to their reproductive future. There are several pitfalls for the unwary in this area and the commonest is an inaccurate or incomplete diagnosis (Table 12.5).

Assessment and counselling can often be accomplished in one session and many geneticists follow this with a letter to the couple which summarises the information given and invites the couple to return if new questions arise.

Further reading

Connor, J.M. and Ferguson-Smith, M.A. (1993) *Essential Medical Genetics* (4th edn). Oxford: Blackwell Scientific

Harper, P.S. (1994) *Practical Genetic Counselling* (4th edn). Bristol: John Wright

Nuffield Council on Bioethics (1993) *Genetic Screening: Ethical Issues*. London: Nuffield Council on Bioethics

RCP (1989) *Prenatal Diagnosis and Screening*. Community and Service Implications. London: Royal College of Physicians

Chapter 13

Prepregnancy care

Lindsay F. P. Smith

Introduction

The idea that care before the commencement of pregnancy can improve the outcome of a subsequent pregnancy is attractive both for the providers of health care and to its consumers: pregnant women and their partners. Prevention of ill-health is quite fashionable at present but we, as carers, must be certain that we can indeed prevent the problem that our intervention is designed to, i.e. the intervention must be of proven efficacy. The gold-standard of such proof is the randomised controlled trial (RCT).

But, unfortunately, there is little evidence from research that changing any aspect of a woman's prepregnancy medical, social, psychological or spiritual well-being can effect such an improvement in outcome. With one major exception, the prepregnancy advice that will be discussed here is not supported by any evidence from RCTs and must therefore be viewed with some scepticism.

I would accept that some of the following prepregnancy care and advice may eventually be proven to be of benefit in terms of improved pregnancy outcome. But until then we have an obligation as providers of prepregnancy care to fully inform women that such care is unproven but pragmatic. Only then will women and their partners be in a position to make enlightened choices and give informed consent (or refusal) to the care that we are offering.

Folic acid and neural tube defect

There is clear evidence from randomised clinical trials that if women increase their intake of folic acid in the month before conception and for the first 4–12 weeks of gestation then their risk of conceiving a child with a neural tube defect (NTD) is significantly reduced. This reduction in risk holds true for both women who have never conceived such an affected fetus and for those who have been unfortunate to so do.

The Medical Research Council Vitamin Study (1991) was an RCT which enrolled 1817 women who had had at least one pregnancy with a neural tube defect. Of 1195 women with known pregnancy outcome, six (1.0 per cent) of 593 who had received folic acid supplementation suffered a neural tube defect compared to 21 (3.5 per cent) of 602 controls. Thus the relative risk of having an affected pregnancy was 0.28 (95 per cent confidence interval (CI) 0.12–0.71). The dose given was 4 mg from randomisation to 12 weeks gestation.

Two subsequent studies have supported the hypothesis that supplementation with folic acid can also prevent a first occurrence of neural tube defect. In an RCT (Czeizel and Dudas 1992), Hungarian women were given either multivitamin (which included 0.8 mg folic acid) or trace element tablets daily for at least one month pre conception to at least the second missed period. There were no neural tube defects among 2104 women in the vitamin group compared to six among the 2052 who received the trace-element supplementation ($p = 0.029$). In a case-control study (Werler et al. 1993) 436 North American women with first neural tube defect were compared with 2615 control with other major malformations. The prevalence of use of multivitamins was compared in women belonging to these two groups after excluding women who knew of the folic acid NTD hypothesis. For daily use of multivitamins containing folic acid the relative risk of conceiving an affected fetus was 0.4 (95 per cent CI 0.2–0.6). For those taking exactly 0.4 mg the relative risk was lower at 0.3 (0.1–0.6). Vitamins had been taken for at least 28 days before conception to at least 28 days after the last period.

There is thus clear evidence that periconceptual supplementation with folic acid can prevent occurrent and recurrent NTDs. This has been accepted by an Expert Advisory Group of the Department of Health (1992) and all women planning pregnancy should now be advised to increase their folic acid intake to at least 0.4 mg daily from the time of starting to try to conceive until 12 weeks gestation. Those women with a previous NTD pregnancy should have a higher intake of at least 5 mg per day for the same time period.

Rubella

Women who are not immune to rubella and who contract the disease in pregnancy are at high risk of congenital malformation (Smith 1993). Immunisation at the age of 12 for all girls has been Department of Health policy for some years but some girls remain non-immunised. The more recent introduction of the combined mumps–measles–rubella vaccine and its administration to all 13 month olds should improve herd immunity and reduce this problem. In the meantime, all women and teenagers need to be counselled about the risks of rubella infection in pregnancy, tested to check that they are immune, immunised if not and again checked that they have seroconverted. There is some evidence that clinical audit can detect those women at risk and successfully immunise them against rubella (Somerset Medical Audit Advisory Group, personal communication).

Smoking

There is good evidence that smoking in pregnancy is associated with adverse outcomes. These include miscarriage, intrauterine growth retardation, premature delivery, placenta praevia, abruptio placentae and premature rupture of the membranes. Several RCTs have attempted to reduce women's smoking during pregnancy with varying results. The most successful interventions have emphasised how to give up smoking rather than simply giving women information about the effects of smoking. Both of these RCTs (Sexton and Hebel 1984; Windsor *et al.* 1985) demonstrated that telling women how to give up significantly reduced the probability that women would continue to smoke during pregnancy (Odds Ratios of 0.19 (CI 0.07–0.54) and of 0.14 (CI 0.10–0.21)).

Furthermore, there is evidence from primary care that patients can be effectively advised to discontinue smoking. One RCT (Imperial Cancer Research Fund General Practice Research Group 1993) of 1686 (929 women, mean age 42.6 (SD 10.0)) heavy smokers (mean 24/day) demonstrated the effectiveness of nicotine transdermal patches. They found in 19 general practices that, compared to placebo, 12 weeks treatment with nicotine patches resulted in a 7.6 per cent (95 per cent CI 4.2–11.1) greater abstinence at the end of the intervention. Russell *et al.* (1993) also found in a RCT of 600 (367 women, mean age 39.3 (SD 9.2)) heavy smokers (>15/day) in 30 general practices that 18 weeks transdermal nicotine patches with brief advice and support were better than placebo in producing prolonged abstinence at one year (9.3 per cent vs 5 per cent). At present nicotine patches are not licensed for use in pregnancy, and these trials have included few women of child-bearing age.

However, there are no RCTs which have intervened in women who smoke and who are planning to conceive to determine if advice given to this group pre-pregnancy will either reduce the prevalence of smoking or if subsequent pregnancy outcome is improved. This would be an ideal area for a multicentre primary health care study. In the meantime it seems prudent to advise women to stop smoking before they become pregnant, and particularly to advise them on how to give up.

Alcohol

It has been known for all of this century that alcohol has harmful effects on pregnancy. These include spontaneous abortion, intrauterine growth retardation, mental retardation, a dysmorphic congenital syndrome ('fetal alcohol syndrome') and neonatal irritability. However, there is uncertainty about whether there is a safe lower limit for alcohol consumption so it is difficult to advise women whether they should abstain or not. One prospective population study (Lumley *et al.* 1985) found that women who drank less than two standard drinks per day had no excess risk of adverse pregnancy outcome.

It is possible to identify women in a primary care setting whose alcohol intake is hazardous. The AUDIT questionnaire (Saunders *et al.* 1993) has been found in the USA to have high sensitivity (92 per cent) in detecting harmful alcohol intake and high specificity (94 per cent) in excluding those with low levels of intake. A meta analysis of RCTs of brief intervention in people with raised alcohol consumption (Effective Health Care Bulletin 7 1993), has shown that such intervention can reduce alcohol consumption by 24 per cent (95 per cent CI 18–31 per cent). Brief intervention usually comprised an assessment of the individual's alcohol intake, being informed of the risks of excess alcohol intake, and an information booklet. No RCTs of intervention to reduce alcohol intake either during pregnancy or prepregnancy have been reported.

Inheritable disorders

Although there is no effective intervention (apart from abortion which I would not classify as an effective treatment) to improve the pregnancy outcome of most inheritable diseases, women should be made aware of any particular risks that they would have in a pregnancy. Thus carers should be aware of those women who are at especial risk and either advise them or refer them to clinical geneticists for formal counselling.

Over 100 uncommon inborn errors of metabolism can now be detected by DNA testing but prepregnancy diagnosis is possible for only some of these disorders. Cystic fibrosis is the commonest inheritable gene defect carried by the United Kingdom population. The risk of carrying a defective gene is 1:25. Several gene mutations can lead to cystic fibrosis in homozygous babies. Diagnostic testing for carriers of known mutations which cause the disorder can be performed prepregnancy.

Certain ethnic groups are at especial risk of bearing children with inherited disorders. Ashkenazi Jews are at increased risk of bearing children with Tay–Sachs disease and thus should be screened for carrier status (1 in 27 carry the abnormal gene). Sickle-cell trait should be screened for in those of African stock (carrier rate up to 25 per cent). Screening for beta-thalassaemia (up to 17 per cent) should be offered to Italians, Greeks and others of Southern European ancestry, and for alpha-thalassaemia to individuals from Southeast Asia and Filipinos.

Nearly all chromosomal abnormalities affecting fetuses increase markedly with maternal age, especially after 30. Thus older women need particular counselling. Finally those women who have already had a pregnancy or child with an inheritable disorder should receive particular counselling.

Chronic maternal disease

Increasingly disorders such as asthma, diabetes, hypertension and epilepsy are being managed totally in primary care. It would seem sensible that such women are counselled prepregnancy about the possible adverse outcome that might result from poor disease control. It is also likely that they would wish to discuss any possible effects of their medication on pregnancy. There is some evidence that if insulin dependent diabetics attend a prepregnancy clinic they have a better pregnancy outcome than control women who do not attend (Steel *et al.* 1993; Gregory and Tattersall 1992), but there have been no RCTs to support this view.

Indeed there is little published evidence from RCTs that prepregnancy care for any chronic maternal disease improves pregnancy outcome.

Other advice

It would seem sensible that women should stop all medication before trying to conceive. Those medications which are absolutely contraindicated can be found by reference to standard texts such as the British National Formulary. For other drugs the aim to avoid theoretical fetal damage has to be balanced against any necessary treatment, e.g. for asthma or epilepsy; these judgements can be difficult. There is very little evidence that changing diet, exercise or occupation affects pregnancy outcome. Practically nothing is known about any aspect of paternal health or well-being in respect of pregnancy outcome (Lumley and Astbury 1989).

Prepregnancy clinics

There have been no published RCTs of the ability of prepregnancy clinics to improve fetal outcome. Cox *et al.* (1992) were able to improve the pregnancy outcome of those women that they saw with chronic maternal disease (240, 22.3 per cent) in that their subsequent live birth rate improved to 81 per cent from their previous rate of 42 per cent (95 per cent CI 29–55 per cent). The subsequent live birth rate was not improved for women referred because of previous miscarriage, previous fetal abnormality or for other problems. Steel *et al.* (1993) were similarly able to lower the incidence of congenital abnormality in subsequent pregnancy among 143 insulin dependent diabetics seen in their prepregnancy clinic (2/143 vs. 10/96 in controls). Both these studies are flawed because of the selection of control groups. It is also not possible to say whether the women would have faired as well if properly cared for by appropriate physicians outside of a prepregnancy clinic. Thus there is some evidence that prepregnancy clinics improve pregnancy outcome for women with chronic medical disease.

Disadvantages of prepregnancy advice

There are side-effects of prepregnancy advice for both women and their caregivers. The latter may delude themselves that they can, through their advice, affect various pregnancy outcomes in a positive way when in fact no such causal relationship exists. If the woman subsequently suffers an adverse outcome it can become very easy to 'victim-blame', suggesting, for example, that she must not have followed the carer's advice. The woman may be falsely reassured that specific outcomes can be improved. She may also become less self-confident, or reliant on her own capabilities. She may suffer heightened anxiety about the pregnancy or increasingly guilty about failure to follow advice, e.g. inability to stop smoking.

Where and who should provide advice

It would seem sensible that women at high risk of adverse pregnancy outcome are seen by the relevant specialists if there is a proven effective treatment or intervention for their particular problem. Thus women with diabetes should receive consultant care which may be best given in prepregnancy clinics. Those 2–3 per cent of women with inheritable disorders (Royal College of Physicians 1989) may be best served by seeing a clinical geneticist prepregnancy.

However, for the majority of women (those at 'low' risk of adverse pregnancy outcome) prepregnancy advice could be given opportunistically by the primary health care team. Practices should have an agreed policy on whom to advise and when. Over two-thirds of people visit their general practitioner every year (RCGP 1986) and women of child bearing age visit more frequently than average. Women can easily be counselled when they register with the practice, at contraceptive checks, when cervical smears are performed, in well-women clinics, or when they attend with their children. Advice could be given by the general practitioner, health visitor or practice nurse. Other community sites where advice might be given are family planning clinics and child welfare clinics.

Conclusion

Women could be divided into those at low risk of adverse pregnancy outcome and those at high risk; the advice (intervention) that they receive should depend on the group to which they belong. All women should receive advice about the need to take folic acid and be immunised successfully against rubella. It seems reasonable that all women are advised to reduce their smoking and their alcohol intake, although such intervention to improve pregnancy outcome has yet to be proved effective in a RCT. Such advice is probably best given in primary care (at least two thirds of women see their general practitioner each year) by each general practice having an agreed policy on advice. All women should have a family history taken to detect inheritable disorders.

Certain women are at high risk of adverse pregnancy outcome. These include those 2–3 per cent with inheritable disorders and those with previous adverse pregnancy outcome or with chronic maternal disease. There is some evidence that pregnancy outcome for the latter group can be improved by particular prepregnancy care in specific specialist prepregnancy clinics although confirmation of this from RCTs, and for which chronic diseases this holds true, is required. Adverse pregnancy outcome may be avoided for those with inherited disorders by pre-pregnancy counselling if this results in avoidance of pregnancy or subsequent screening and selective termination of affected pregnancies.

References

Cox, M., Whittle, M.J., Byrne, A., Kingdom, J.C.P and Ryan, G. (1992) Prepregnancy counselling: experience from 1075 cases. *Br J Obstet Gynaecol* **99**, 873–6

Czeizel, A.E. and Dudas, I. (1992) Prevention of the first occurrence of neural–tube defects by periconceptional vitamin spplementation. *N Engl J Med* **327**, 1832–5

Department of Health (1992) Report from an Expert Advisory Group. Folic acid and the prevention of neural tube defects. London: Department of Health

Gregory, R. and Tattersall, R.B. (1992) Are diabetic prepregnancy clinics worthwhile? *Lancet* **340**, 656–8

Imperial Cancer Research Fund General Practice Research Group (1993) Effectiveness of a nicotine patch in helping people stop smoking: results of a randomised trial in general practice. *Br Med J* **306**, 1304–8

Lumley, J. and Astbury, J. (1989) 'Advice for pregnancy' in I. Chalmers, M.Enkin, M.J.N.C. Keirse (Eds) *Effective Care in Pregnancy and Childbirth*. Oxford: Oxford University Press

Lumley, J., Correy, J., Newman, N. and Curran, J. (1985) Cigarette smoking, alcohol consumption and fetal outcome in Tasmania, 1981–2. *Aust NZ J Obstet Gynaecol* **25**, 33–40

MRC Vitamin Study Research Group (1991) Prevention of neural tube defects: Results of the Medical Research Council Vitamin Study. *Lancet* **338**, 131-7

Royal College of General Practitioners, OPCS, DHSS (1986) Morbidity statistics from general practice. Third national study 1981–2, series MB5, No.1.London: HMSO

Royal College of Physicians (1989) Prenatal diagnosis and genetic screening. Summary and recommendations of a report of the Royal College of Physicians. *J R Coll Phys* **23**, 215–20

Russell, M.A., Stapleton, J.A., Feyerabend, C. *et al.* (1993) Targeting heavy smokers in general practice: randomised controlled trial of transdermal nicotine patches. *Br Med J* **306**, 1308–12

Saunders, J.B., Aasland, O.G., Babor, T.F. *et al.* (1993) Development of the alcohol use disorders identification test (AUDIT): WHO Collaborative project on Early detection of persons with Harmful Alcohol Consumption. *Addiction* **88** (suppl), 791–804

Sexton, M. and Hebel, J.R. (1984) A clinical trial of change in maternal smoking and its effect on birth weight. *J Am Med Assoc* **251**, 911–15

Smith, L.F.P. (1993) Infection and pregnancy. *Practitioner* **237**, 857–62

Steel, J.M., Johnstone, F.D. Hepburn, D.A. and Smith, A.F. (1993) Can prepregnancy care of diabetic women reduce the risk of abnormal babies? *Br Med J* **301**, 1070–4

Werler, M.M., Shapiro, S. and Mitchell, A.A. (1993) Periconceptional folic acid exposure and risk of occurrent neural tube defect. *J Am Med Assoc* **269**, 1257–61

Windsor, R.A., Cutter, G., Morris, J. *et al.* (1985) The effectiveness of smoking cessation methods for smokers in public health maternity clinics: a randomised trial. *Am J Public Health* **75**, 1389–92

Chapter 14

Appropriate use of technology

Philip J. Steer

What is technology?

Technology comes from the ancient Greek word for 'art' or 'skill'; their word for carpenter came from the same root. Latterly, the word technology has come to mean the 'science and history of the mechanical arts, as distinct from the fine arts' (Wyld 1936). The systematic use of technology is what separates humankind from other animal species; essential features in its development are manipulative hands and the ability to accumulate information by transferring it between individuals and generations (speech and memory).

Technology surrounds us in everyday life; everything from the roof over our heads, the clothes we wear, our transport to work, and the word processor on which this was written. Even the supply of food necessary to support our burgeoning population depends on technology. Small groups of people (Australian aboriginals, Bushmen in the Kalahari, Amazonian Indians) still live in a self-sustaining closed ecosystem, but they now make up less than 1 per cent of the world population. The rest of us depend on technology for our existence. Technology has given us such an enormous advantage that the growth in numbers of the human species now threatens the stability of the planetary ecosystem.

Should technology be appropriate for the species or the individual?

From a simplistic viewpoint, it could be argued that the most appropriate technology for the survival of the human race is contraception. However, it is widely believed that a central requirement for the successful implementation of birth control is a low perinatal, infant and child mortality. When this is achieved, couples can limit their reproduction confident in the likelihood that their genes will be perpetuated (the concept of the 'selfish gene': Dawkins 1992).

The selfish gene provides a powerful explanation for the development of Medicine. Natural selection, left to itself, would steadily improve the human race by weeding out (for example) diabetics, hypertensives, and poor reproducers. But the urge to duplicate our own genes (rather than support those less closely related) means that we try to overcome our own defects (and thus perpetuate them in future generations) by technology (insulin, antihypertensives, in vitro fertilisation (IVF)). Thus the driving force behind technology in perinatal medicine is improved survival of the individual. Mothers will ask for intensive care for their 23 week gestation infant, despite a chance of survival of less than 5 per cent and a handicap rate of 50 per cent. Many question whether on cost/benefit grounds this is an appropriate use of technology, but such is its emotional content that few dare argue against it.

Technology for comfort

A major driving force in evolution is the efficiency imperative – to do more (gather food, reproduce) with less use of scarce resources (food). The more successful you are at this, the more you outnumber your rivals. Thus we plough the fields with tractors, and drive to the shops when we could easily (and more healthily) walk. Many women see Caesarean section in this light – an 'easy option'. It is certainly quicker and more efficient for the obstetrician. There is an increase in risk for the mother, but only a very few suffer serious consequences, and there is the balancing consideration that for most babies, the risk is reduced (the selfish gene effect again). Pain is a mechanism which makes us avoid danger – we take our hand from the fire, and our foot from the pin. But pain only works as a protective mechanism because it is so unpleasant that we will go to great lengths to avoid it or relieve it. Pain in labour certainly makes the mother look for a safe and comfortable place in which to seek refuge, a major advantage when the baby is born. But does pain serve a useful function once the mother is in her den? It makes her bear down harder in the second stage of labour, which is probably why epidural anaesthesia is prone to increase the proportion of instrumental deliveries. In other respects, however, pain in labour seems to serve no essential function, and it seems both reasonable and humane to use technology in its relief.

Technology for safety

The Dublin trial is often quoted as showing that intermittent auscultation is as effective a method of fetal surveillance in labour as electronic fetal monitoring (EFM) (MacDonald *et al.* 1985). However, the converse is also true, and in situations where it is not possible for there to be a trained midwife with the woman at all times, EFM is a cost-effective alternative to auscultation. It may also reduce the incidence of neonatal convulsions by half (MacDonald *et al.* 1985), a significant cost saving in terms of neonatal care, not to mention anxiety to the parents. In a setting where intervention rates were traditionally low, it did not significantly increase intervention. In Riverside Health Authority (London), where team midwifery and intermittent auscultation are the norm for low risk women, intervention rates are at an all time high. Recent data (Harding and Steer, in preparation) in our unit suggest that this is due to increasing willingness on the part of professionals to support women's choice, even when this involves using technology/intervention, rather than forcing a non-intervention policy upon them. The majority of inductions of labour, for example, are social and performed at the behest of the women rather than for any medical indication. The slight increase in risk does not deter women from asking for induction, as they perceive the advantages of likely success to outweigh the small chance of failure. Their choice is similar to that of a family who value the advantages of driving to Edinburgh from London (convenience, a high degree of control and relative privacy) even though travelling by train is ten times safer.

Technology as a choice

In developed countries, childbirth is very safe because of technologies that many take for granted (and even fail to think of as technology), such as antibiotics, blood transfusion, anaesthesia, and surgery. Arguments tend to occur around the margins of technology, such as EFM, pain relief, and induction of labour. This may have more to do with fashion than science. For example, waterbirth is commonly represented as part of a 'natural childbirth' package, and yet there is clearly nothing natural in humans labouring or giving birth in water. The temperature of the water has to be controlled accurately between 35°C and 37°C, which is just as demanding as topping up an epidural. On the other hand, substantial sums of money are paid in the private obstetric sector to ensure continuity of care despite the known links with high intervention and Caesarean section rates.

We should therefore perhaps distinguish between technology for safety, and technology for convenience. The latter needs to be reasonably safe, but does not necessarily have to confer a specific medical (as opposed to social) advantage. A good example is antenatal diagnosis. Detection of fetal anomaly does not safeguard the woman's health directly, and in most cases it cannot benefit the fetus. However, the woman can (if she chooses termination) avoid the subsequent pregnancy, and the social and financial implications of the birth of an abnormal child. Many women request repeated scans during pregnancy, not because of a medical need, but because they like to 'see the baby'. Whether this is appropriate will depend on the risk of ultrasound (probably very small) and the financial implications (it might be inappropriate if the taxpayer is expected to pay for what is essentially a recreational activity, but appropriate if the woman herself is prepared to pay).

When should choice be limited?

Technology in medicine is growing faster than the ability of most people to pay for it. Choices (for example, length of stay in hospital postdelivery) may need to be curtailed because of economic factors. In some areas this has already happened; for example in Riverside the level of risk of Down's syndrome at which the woman is entitled to a 'free' (paid for by the taxpayer) amniocentesis has been raised from one in 400 to one in 250, in order to limit cost. In addition, technology is offering choices which may pose threats to the nature of the species. Gene therapy is easily seen to be justified in cases of disease such as cystic fibrosis, but what of manic depression? Sex selection is another choice which could strike unpredictably at the roots of our society.

Summary

Many technologies (antibiotics, blood transfusion, anaesthesia and surgery) have made major contributions to the safety of childbirth. These technologies are usually seen as appropriate. In developed countries there will be continuing pressure for improvement, which will come more from the individual than from the needs of society. Further developments in technology are likely to centre around individual choice ('consumer convenience') as much as around medical priorities. Choice will be limited by cost (and the ability of the 'consumer' to pay) but might also need to be limited in the interests of the stability of the species. Only when the implications of technologies such as gene therapy are more fully understood will we be in a position to decide if they are appropriate or not.

References

Dawkins, R. (1992) *The Selfish Gene* (2nd edn). Oxford: Oxford University Press

MacDonald, D., Grant, A., Sheridan-Pereira, M., Boylan, P. and Chalmers, I. (1985) The Dublin randomized controlled trial of intrapartum fetal heart rate monitoring. *Am J Obstet Gynecol* **152**, 524–39

Wyld, H.C. (1936) *The Universal Dictionary of the English Language*. London: Herbert Joseph Ltd, Selfridge and Co. Ltd.

Chapter 15

Support: emotional and education

Gillian Halksworth

The focus of health and the care within maternity services, from all the health professionals involved, is primarily based on issues of mortality and medical outcomes rather than on the social and qualitative dimensions.

Self-esteem

Women are the pivotal point of our maternity services, yet as Rivers *et al.* (1979) said:

> . . . studies of women have repeatedly shown disturbing patterns: lack of self esteem, an inability to feel powerful or in control of one's life; a vulnerability to depression; a tendency to see oneself as less talented less able than one really is.

Women appear to be central to our family life and yet are often the the most vulnerable members, self-esteem frequently being the most crucial issue. Self-esteem can be affected in many ways in childbirth, from the changing body image of pregnancy to the financial implications and change in lifestyle that the baby will have on the family. Yet, it is in this area that support from health professionals is often lacking.

General Practitioners care for women and their families from 'the cradle to the grave': a potentially privileged position to facilitate both the provision of maternity services and emotional support to meet individual needs. Obstetricians and midwives, in theory, only appear for nine months at a time, through the lives of women. Yet, it is an intensive nine months that can be utilised to the full, given the time and resources, to work with GPs to address problems and facilitate the growth of an individual.

Studies have questioned the value of the antenatal care programmes in existence and the suggestion has been made that women are often 'overnatalled'. Recommendations of changes in the current practices have been made, suggesting that a pattern of nine visits for primigravidae and six for multigravida women would be appropriate, (Hall *et al.* 1980; RCOG 1982). This may be appropriate from a physical or medical perspective but provision is needed for the social and psychological support antenatally. Often issues are interpreted as medical problems, for example, depression is treated as an illness rather than a reaction to isolation or lack of support (Nicolson 1986). Similarly, there is often a link between depression and the domestic environment (MacArthur *et al.* 1991).

Studies have shown that six weeks after delivery mothers who had received enhanced social and psychological support during pregnancy were less likely than controls to be feeling physically unwell (Elbourne *et al.* 1989; Oakley *et al.* 1990); and there were fewer health problems in babies (Oakley *et al.* 1990).

Although often social class differences are highlighted in the health care scene in Britain in terms of birthweight and survival of babies there are also differences in the psycological, social and educational support needed between the social classes.

'The new mother culture'

Johnson and Johnson (1980) suggested that 'a competing cultural directive of motherhood has emerged'. Lewis (1991) suggests that there is a change in the common ideology depicting women as being the centre point of the family and home life, with men responsible for the issue of paid work. The culture change is creating a new breed of 'superwoman'. An image which suggests that women should not be confined to the domestic duties of the home but should also excel in a career combining the dual role of motherhood and career woman with success and vitality. Yet often this 'superwoman' is unable to define herself in a clear distinctive way. This threatens her self-esteem as she is faced with the dilemma of comparing herself with non-employed mothers (suggested to be better parents) and with female workers with no family commitments (who are suggested to be better workers).

Awareness and anticipation of this changing role antenatally, with the help of the health professionals concerned, will prepare a good foundation to build upon during the postnatal period.

In a similar way, career moves and the nuclear family structure, can leave women isolated from family and close friends at a time when they are feeling vulnerable and insecure. The support needed from the health professionals for these clients may be different from that needed by those who are socially disadvantaged.

Socially disadvantaged

Pregnancy and the ensuing childcare is known to be stressful. The stress of parenting in poverty has also been associated with higher rates of child abuse (Blackburn 1991).

Studies have shown that clinics which offer continuity of care and are sensitive to the social circumstances and the needs of their clients result in a reduction in the incidence of suspected child abuse or neglect as well as a reduced incidence of repeat pregnancies by eighteen months. Hence, it is suggested that increased support from caregivers may have important benefits for low income mothers and their children (Hodnett, 1993a).

Drugs

The stresses of poverty may lead women to abuse drugs or alcohol and to postpone obtaining health care. Similarly, pregnant women who use drugs may be worried about the legal ramifications of detection such as the possibility of removal of children (Kalmuss and Fennelly 1990). Continuity of caregiver for this client group facilitates the development of trust and sharing of information which enhances care. A harm reduction programme can be initiated at an early stage of pregnancy with resultant benefits (NHS Drug Advisory Service 1993).

Ethnic groups

Ethnic groups are also a vulnerable group. Maynall and Foster (1990) found that women who had been in the United Kingdom less than ten years felt the lack of mothers and sisters. Migration being responsible for cutting off the sources of support and advice and increasing the effects of isolation and lack of emotional support.

Smoking

Health behaviour is central to the current debate about the nation's health, smoking being one particular issue.

The recent press reports indicated that 'midwives are not doing enough to discourage pregnant women from smoking' (survey conducted by the RCM and the Health Education Authority). Also, Lumley (1993) stated that, 'Obstetricians and midwives should ensure that information on self – help behavioural strategies for quitting smoking, prepared specifically for pregnant women, are available and accessible to all women in their care.'

It is easy to tell women about the health problems of smoking. It is all to easy to question the rationale behind spending money on cigarettes when low income families have adopted a strict budgeting strategy in an attempt to make ends meet. It is not so easy to see why spending on tobacco becomes an item of necessity rather than an item of luxury. Graham (1990) found that when interviewed, women reflected on the priority of tobacco in their lives. Respondents suggested that a cigarette was associated with breaks from caring and a way of coping: giving them time and space to rest and gather momentum for the ensuing demands of the children. Similarly, others find smoking a calming influence in stressful situations.

Graham (1990) postulates that:

> ... cigarettes offer moments when the experience of relative poverty is suspended
> ... in such circumstances smoking can be both necessity and luxury: a necessity
> that enables a woman to maintain her role as family health-keeper and a luxury
> that symbolises her participation in the lifestyle of the other society.

Similarly, studies relating to budgeting for household expenditure, have revealed that priority is given to 'the bills' and that spending on other resources directly related to health and child development including food, clothes and shoes etc. is restricted. It is the food budget that is most clearly affected, smoking often being used as an appetite depressant (Graham 1990).

Hence, professionals need to be aware of a woman's reasons for smoking. It may be necessary to address these issues before an attempt is made to modify her health behaviour.

Education

Education obviously begins in the schools and health professionals can play an important role in this environment. However, persuading school governors of the advantages of the educational input health professionals can have is often difficult.

Once pregnant, classes are organised within the maternity services to facilitate the education of the woman and her partner on the varying aspects of parenting skills. However, Nicolson (1986) questions, whether there is a professionalisation of motherhood which is taking away the natural instinct of being a mother. Many of the problems experienced by mothers are not covered in these education classes and often advice is sought and given from family and friends when the health professionals are not present. The scheme in Scunthorpe where sessions were run to update grandparents could be extended to include relatives or friends who may well form the support network (Department of Health 1993). Similarly, a study by Olds et al. (1986) involved 'significant others' in a social support scheme in the community, with positive results.

Other schemes around the country are fundamental to improving the psychological wellbeing of women using the maternity services, such as: drop-in centres; social groups, structured parentcraft education classes; teenage groups; educational classes which include such issues as 'making the most of yourself' and 'cooking on a budget' are equally beneficial.

Postnatal support groups and postnatal exercise sessions both have educational elements incorporated within them.

Exercise

Apart from the physical benefits of muscular development and fitness, exercise also enhances a sense of wellbeing and improved self-esteem (Sibley et al. 1981; Mellion 1985; Wallace et al. 1986; Artal and Artal Mittlemark 1991). Hence, it is an important area that can be developed to improve a woman's self-confidence at an emotionally vulnerable time.

One study of a group of women exercising in pregnancy, revealed statistically significant results in terms of higher self-esteem and lower physical discomfort scores than in a control group of non-exercising women. Similarly, by enhancing the psychological status, one study demonstrated the beneficial physical results of exercising by women being more prepared for labour and delivery (Hall and Kaufmann 1987). Mellion (1985) suggests that exercise is an effective therapy for people who are anxious or depressed: 'exercise produces a sense of mastery and control, and the positive effects of being successful in an exercise programme spill into other realms of life.'

Continuity of caregiver

Continuity of caregiver is defined by Hodnett (1993b) as 'the actual provision of care by the same caregiver or small group of caregivers throughout pregnancy, during labour and birth, and in the postpartum period'. This concept allows for personalised care and therefore a more sensitive maternity service.

The building of a relationship between health professional and client allows the appropriate support to be given as well as meeting the individual educational needs. The South Manchester family worker project (Spencer *et al.* 1989), although showing no significant statistical difference in the mean birthweight, indicated that the family workers increased the subjective wellbeing of the clients. This and other such studies indicate the importance of continuity of caregiver in improving maternal satisfaction (Kowalski *et al.* 1977; Shear *et al.* 1983; Flint and Poulengeris 1986; Watson 1990; Hodnett 1993b).

Conclusion

The science of obstetrics and midwifery plays a vital role in ensuring the health of mother and baby. However, alongside the medical aspect of obstetrics there are the social dimensions affecting our clients. Continuity of caregiver is essential to the notion of giving support and facilitating the educational needs of each individual. It is questionable whether a hospital is the most suitable environment in which to build and develop a trusting relationship and thereby provide the necessary support. Care within the community or within a woman's home, has the advantage of being in a familiar territory. The resources to undertake this care and support are limited and equally dependent on the attitude, skill and flexibility of the professional involved. Ballantyne (1914: cited by Oakley 1986) postulated the following in reference to technology used in maternity services; however, I feel it is also pertinent to the psychological side of caring for women:

> ... when the potter ... fashions a vessel upon the wheel he may feel his work marred not only by reason of some inherent defect in the clay from which he makes it, but also on account of faults of handling, of turning, of drying, of firing, of glazing and of decorating: the expert workman may do much even with an inferior

material whilst in the hands of the bungler the finest substance may be fatally spoiled.

It may be idealistic but there is a school of thought that suggests given the time, resources and flexibility, the team involved in maternity services can work together to provide seamless care. The woman and her individual needs, both medical and social, are therefore the pivotal point around which maternity care must revolve. How to achieve this remains the burning issue. It is questionable whether the ideals of continuity of carer, increased social support and seamless care can be achieved under the present restrictions in resources.

References

Artal, M. and Artal Mittlemark, R. (1991) 'Emotional aspects of exercise in pregnancy' in R. Artal Mittlemark, R.A. Wiswell and B.A. Drinkwater (Eds) *Exercise in Pregnancy.* Baltimore: Williams & Wilkins

Ballantyne, J.W. (1914). 'Expectant motherhood: its supervision and hygiene' in A. Oakley (Ed.) (1986) *The Captured Womb*. Oxford: Basil Blackwell

Blackburn, C. (1991) Poverty and Health: Working with Families. Buckingham: Open University Press

Department of Health (1993) *Changing Childbirth*. London: HMSO

Elbourne, D., Oakley, A. and Chalmers, I. (1989) 'Social and psychological support during pregnancy' in I. Chalmers, M. Enkin and M.J.N.C. Keirse (Eds) *Effective Care in Pregnancy and Childbirth*. Oxford: Oxford University Press.

Flint, C. and Poulengeris, P. (1987) The 'Know Your Midwife' report. London.

Graham, H. (1990) 'Behaving well: women's health behaviour in context' in H. Roberts (Ed.) *Women's Health Counts*. London: Routledge

Hall, M. H., Chng, P. K. and MacGillivray, I. (1980) Is routine antenatal care worthwhile? *Lancet* **ii**, 8185: 78–80

Hall, D.C. and Kaufmann, D.A. (1987) Effects of aerobic and strength conditioning on pregnancy outcomes. *Am J Obstet Gynecol* **157**, 1199–203

Hodnett, E.D. (1993a) 'Support from caregivers for socially disadvantaged' in M.W. Enkin, M.J.N.C. Keirse, M.J. Renfrew and J.P. Neilson (Eds) *Pregnancy and Childbirth Module.* Cochrane Database of Systematic Reviews: Review No. 07674, 16 April 1993. Published through Cochrane Updates on Disk. Oxford: Update Software

Hodnett, E.D. (1993b) 'Continuity of caregivers during pregnancy and childbirth' in M.W. Enkin, M.J.N.C. Keirse, M.J. Renfrew and J.P. Neilson (Eds) *Pregnancy and Childbirth Module*. Cochrane Database of Systematic Reviews: Review No. 07672, 16 April 1993. Published through Cochrane Updates on Disk. Oxford: Update Software

Johnson, C. C. and Johnson, F. A. (1980) 'Parenthood, marriage and careers: situational constraints and role strain' in F. Pepitone-Rockwell (Ed.) *Dual Career Couples*. London: Sage

Kalmuss, D. and Fennelly, K. (1990) Barriers to prenatal care among low income women in New York City. *Family Planning Perspectives* **22**, 215–18

Kowalski, K., Gottschalk, J. and Greer, B. (1977) Team nursing coverage of pre-natal-intrapartum patients at a university hospital. An innovation in obstetric nursing. *Obstet Gynecol* **50**, 116–19

Lewis, S. (1991) 'Motherhood and Employment: the impact of social and organisational values' in A. Phoenix, E. Lloyd, and A. Woolett (Eds) *Motherhood Meanings, Practices and Ideologies*. London: Sage

Lumley, J. (1993) 'Strategies for reducing smoking in pregnancy' in M.W. Enkin, M.J.N.C. Keirse, M.J. Renfrew and J.P. Neilson (Eds) *Pregnancy and Childbirth Module*. Cochrane

Database of Systematic Reviews: Review No. 03312, 27 April 1993. Published through Cochrane Updates on Disk. Oxford: Update Software

MacArthur, C., Lewis, M. and Knox, E.G. (1991) *Health after Childbirth*. London: HMSO

Maynall, B. and Foster, M.C. (1990) *Child Health Care: Living with Children, Working with Children*. Oxford: Heinemann Nursing

Mellion, M.B. (1985) Exercise therapy for anxiety and depression. 1: Does the evidence justify its recommendations? 2: What are the specific considerations for clinical application? *Postgrad Med* **77**, 59–98

NHS Drug Advisory Service (1993) *Services for Problem Drug Users in The Mid Glamorgan Health District*. London: Department of Health

Nicolson, P. (1986) 'Developing a feminist approach to depression following childbirth' in S. Wilkinson S (Ed.) *Feminist Social Psychology*. Milton Keynes: Open University Press

Oakley, A., Rajan, L. and Grant, A. (1990) Social support and pregnancy outcome. *Br J Obstet Gynaecol* **97**, 155–62

Olds, D.L., Henderson, C.R., Tatelbaum, R. and Chamberlain, R. (1986) Improving the delivery of prenatal care and outcomes of pregnancy: a randomized trial of nurse home visitation. *Paediatrics* **77**, 16–78

Rivers, C., Barnett, R. and Baruch, G. (1979) *Beyond Sugar and Spice: How Women Grow, Learn and Thrive*. New York: Putnam's Sons

Royal College of Obstetricians and Gynaecologists (1982) Report of the RCOG Working Party on Antenatal and Intrapartum Care, Appendix 2. London: RCOG

Shear, C.L., Gipe, B.T. and Mattheis, J.K. (1983) Provider continuity and quality of medical care. A retrospective analysis of prenatal and perinatal outcome. *Med Care* **21**, 1204–10

Sibley, L., Ruhling, R.O., Cameron-Foster, J., Christensen, C. and Bolen, T. (1981) Swimming and physical fitness during pregnancy. *J Nurse Midwifery* **26**, 3–12

Spencer, B., Thomas, H. and Morris, J. (1989) A randomised controlled trial of the provision of a social support service during pregnancy: the South Manchester Family worker project. *Br J Obstet Gynaecol* **96**, 281–88

Wallace, A.M., Boyer, D.B., Dan, A. and Holm, K. (1986) Aerobic exercise maternal self-esteem and physical discomforts during pregnancy. *J Nurse Midwifery* **31**, 255–61

Watson, P. (1990) *Report on the Kidlington Midwifery Scheme*. Oxford: Insitute of Nursing

Chapter 16

Provision of services: what?　Discussion

Allison: We should now be discussing the issues of this session, what the maternity services should be providing. There are two aspects to this discussion: issues that have been raised by the speakers, and what the group may feel that they want to add to these issues.

Page: A comment, and a fear that I have, about prepregnancy care; any such care that we provide should be based on evidence. My concern with prepregnancy care is the great danger there is of controlling the lives of women without there being any cause to do so. We have already done this in pregnancy. We have given a lot of advice which has not been based on strong evidence. I have heard many, many people over the last five years preach the gospel of what is often called preconception care and my concern is when does professional support become social control.

Smith: I also share those concerns. I did not have the time to discuss what I would view as potential adverse outcomes or adverse effects of prepregnancy counselling but there are potentially adverse outcomes for both the carers and the women. Women can be caused unnecessary anxiety if they are unable to follow advice such as giving up smoking; they can be caused to lose their self-confidence, or self-reliance on their own abilities to decide what to do and what is best for them. From the point of view of the carers, if we arenot careful and if we do not look at the research evidence, we can delude ourselves that we are affecting pregnancy outcome when there may be no causal relationship at all; then we subsequently blame the woman for adverse outcome when it is not their fault. Often there is not the evidence there to support what we are suggesting.

Hall: There is a much bigger problem. It is an illusion to think that most pregnancies are planned. A great many women get pregnant when they were not expecting to get pregnant. There are other women who may very much want to become pregnant and who are taking all the right advice but may turn out to be infertile.

126

Quite apart from whether the interventions might be beneficial, identifying a population of women who are planning to get pregnant seems to be an insuperable problem. We would do better to do what we are now advised to in terms of reducing the risk of coronary artery disease, to try to raise the health of the whole population, rather than try to target women who are likely to get pregnant.

Chamberlain: Prepregnancy care was started to look after women who already had an illness and wanted to know what was the likely effect of that illness on the pregnancy and vice versa. Diabetes, heart disease and kidney disease and are good examples. In its original meaning prepregnancy care encompassed those who knew they were likely to become pregnant and had a medical illness but in the last fifteen years the concept has grown into something else.

Downe: We have been talking about the impact of prepregnancy care on women, but surely men should be involved. The obvious issue is smoking and passive smoking, but there is also the issue of quality of sperm, which is often associated with prepregnancy advice and men smoking. If we are to proceed with this philosophy we should not forget that men should be involved as well.

Styles: Dr Smith has made a useful contribution, coming as it does from general practice. But we should remember that for the last two or three years we in general practice have been undertaking a whole series of health promotion and preventive aspects in our practices of doubtful value. Coming from that background, we can understand why he is saying that if we are to get into prepregnancy care, then can we be involved in those procedures that have been shown to be of some value. We do not want to have to repeat this exercise in relation to pregnancy that those of us in general practice have been through in terms of other aspects of health promotion.

When discussing prepregnancy care, which pregnancy are we discussing? I assume we are discussing the immediate pregnancy, but there will be pregnancies in the generations to come. I would hope that any studies that are set up will be longitudinal.

Zander: I am anxious about some of the issues that Professor Connor touched on. Linking with what Professor Steer says, if we look five to ten years down the road I wonder if we shall really be able to screen for a whole range of conditions that are certainly not life threatening. Professor Steer mentioned the manic depressive conditions. The conditions we are screening for now we could argue are non-controversial, although there are certain issues. But just around the corner we shall be into a different scene about what we are screening for.

Connor: No one would disagree. The technology that already exists is already putting up problems; over the next ten years these problems will just get wider and we shall move from conditions that are relatively clear cut to less and less clear issues.

Geneticists have been extremely conservative about how this technology should be used. That has driven quite a number of working groups looking at the ethics of this area – whether this should be used for life insurance, for job selection, and what should be made compulsory. This is being aired. To an extent many of the genetic tests are driven by the public and possibly this is what the public wants. We have seen quite substantial shifts in what people are demanding. The future will depend on what a person wants and that will have to be geared with education. The technology is coming to make a lot possible that is not possible at this moment and this will only escalate as a problem.

Zander: We are moving into a completely different approach of acceptability of normality. In certain areas pregnancies are being terminated because of the sex of the fetus; the anxiety is that we are about to get into a similar situation with any sort of abnormality.

Connor: This will obviously be linked in with gene therapy. Take a condition like cystic fibrosis: if an effective treatment can be found then the issues of screening, of prenatal diagnosis and of population screening disappear immediately. There would be no point. We could screen neonatally and treat from the word go. There are changes coming in this whole area. The technology can be equated to a gun which can be used for good or bad, but those decisions should be made by public discussion. We are involved in trying to provide the information and we are often involved in generating the technology but at the end of the day it should be driven by public opinion.

McKinlay: Most of us will be aware of couples who have only conceived when they have thrown away the thermometer. Making too great a focus on doing everything right is probably inhibitory. But it is not all negative. It seems that gene therapy in the future will have positive corrections. At the moment we can only offer termination, which is a very negative option, but in the future there will be potential cures for this abnormality through gene therapy and this will involve a major role for GPs in primary care in the future. We shall have to become much more skilled in genetic counselling and Hilary Harris in Manchester has demonstrated that genetic screening and genetic counselling from primary care is highly acceptable to the consumer (Harris *et al.* 1993).

Allison: We have teased out some issues about prepregnancy care but I am not sure that we have the answers. But what about the two other areas in the appropriate use of technology and support.

Spencer: Would Professor Steer comment on his feeling about choice for some of the technologies. If a woman has a normal pregnancy and low risk, it is appropriate that she chooses to have a CTG for her management of labour?

Steer: I cannot imagine why not. Choice is choice.

Spencer: Are there any technologies that – as a service provider – he would be very cautious about continuing in current practice?

Steer: I was trying to get across that I think we have gone beyond the stage when we need to look at technology always in terms of safety or in terms of survival of the species. Maternal mortality is now at a relatively low level and we no longer regard it as a public scandal, as was the case early this century, and we are moving into an era where people see technology as an aid to convenience. It surrounds our daily lives. Microprocessors control so many things, why not childbirth?

There are the group of women who like to do everything completely unaided just like there are some men who like to walk across Antarctica. I do not happen to share that view, I hate the winter and I like to stay indoors in my thermostatically controlled environment.

In my experience there are substantial numbers of women who have similar feelings about childbirth. It is a broad church, there is a wide spectrum of opinion and if we are giving people choice and giving them the service that they want we should be equally prepared to support women at either end of that spectrum without fear or favour.

It is just as important for midwives to appreciate that some women like technology, and in their view a simple pain-free, well-organised birth, as it is for some obstetricians to understand (particularly male obstetricians) that some women like to yell and shout. If that is the way they want to do it then I am all in favour. It is a matter of respecting the other person's point of view.

Newburn: Some of these issues are difficult to answer once we start pushing to the boundaries. Professor Steer raised the issue, but did not answer it, of the woman who wants to have repeated scans – what he described as a leisure activity rather than for the purposes of monitoring, and whether that was acceptable. We would be interested in his answers. Personally I am unsure. When I said that choice was the bottom line I should have said informed choice. It needs clarification and none of these things is really simple.

Steer: I can answer that from my own point of view. We have first to consider the risk, whether these repeated scans are dangerous. There is no real evidence that they are and in terms of current knowledge I would never tell a woman that she must not have another scan because it is too dangerous. My inclination is that if she likes seeing the baby, if it is increases bonding and she is happy, she should have it. But, as the Director of Maternity Services in my District, I have to find the funds for that. If every woman wanted an extra scan in the third trimester we would be talking about hundreds of thousands of pounds a year that I could not justify. This raises a further issue, namely why deny women the opportunity if they want it purely for financial reasons? Perhaps we should say they are perfectly free to have it, but they must find the economic price of having that scan. Is that a reasonable alternative? People may say that we should try to provide an equal service, but life is not equal. Should we in the maternity services be trying to provide a social service, and revolutionise society, and all sorts of other things? I do not think we can. Our job is to do what we can with the resources we have.

We do not pay for triple screening because currently we cannot fund the extra scans that are involved, but we give women advice about where they can get it done and we help them to understand the results if they choose to have it done; my view would be the same for the third trimester scan. If they want it and can afford to pay for it, then I would be happy to arrange it.

These issues need to be discussed and there will be more and more of them in the next ten or fifteen years.

Smith: There has been a lot of work from North America suggesting that social support in labour is beneficial to women but that antenatal social support probably is not. No one has looked at the type of support that is provided by the British midwife antenatally, through labour and then postnatally, to see if that has any effect in more objective outcome terms. This social support should not be neglected but it is an area which doctors tend to ignore because it is seen as falling within the remit of the social scientists and not something which we as doctors should be dabbling in. However the continuity and the benefits the women see from it, may be connected with the social support the midwives give which may be lacking from their other support networks.

McGinley: The randomised controlled trial in Glasgow is looking at continuity and we hope to be able to answer some of the questions in relation to what they feel about the care they received and whether or not they benefited from the continuity. By 1995 that trial should have some answers.

Walkinshaw: Professor Steer has raised two issues, one of which I agree with, and one of which I do not – which is about power. We have now begun to grasp the money aspect which we have all studiously ignored for most of the day. If we begin to look at choice, and choice in terms of technology, and choice in terms of what women want, there is little doubt that perhaps more resources will be needed rather than less. That is not how the Health Service runs and his analogy with ultrasound brings that home. But we must address the issue of if there is technology available now which increases intervention, for example electronic monitoring would be one and epidural analgesia would be another, then perhaps within the system we have to address that issue. Would society wish that we throw away some of our monitors, sack some of the anaesthetists and employ more midwives so that we can deliver one-to-one care? That is one of the issues that we may have to grasp within the new structure.

Reference

Harris, H., Scotcher, D., Harley, N. *et al.* (1993) Cystic fibrosis carrier testing in early pregnancy by general practitioners. *Br Med J* **306**, 1580–3

Chapter 17

Purchaser and provider contracts

Percy M. Coats

> We are tranferring power to the users of public services by providing real information about the performance of the providers of public services. ... In brief, we are privatising choice. (Prime Minister 1993)

Introduction

The procedure of contracting for health care is at the heart of the recent changes in the National Health Service and is the most crucial to affect the National Health Service since it began. By placing financial resources in the hands of the purchasers it ought to lead the providers to compete for funds and develop effective, efficient and discriminatory services. The best possible implementation of those services benefits all. Separating those who hold the funds from those who provide the service is fundamental to the process. The quality, quantity and cost of service specified makes the providers accountable for their performance. Achievement of Contracts or NHS service agreements allows the process to evolve while concurrent evaluation influences the shape of future contracts.

In reality these ideals of employing a business model are difficult to effect. In the National Health Service opportune and refined information upon which to make decisions is largely lacking. There is also a natural reservation by many members of staff to change long-standing workable and effective practices. Health services always demand more of a nation's resource than is obtainable; separating the purchaser of the service from the provider is expected to contain expenditure.

The market concept

Alain Enthoven, the American economist, introduced the idea of applying an internal market to health care. It was the Conservative government who introduced this into the National Health Service with the NHS and Community Care Act of 1990. It is through this principle that competition is expected to act as the essential driving force to achieve the highest quality of care possible for the money spent.

The contracting process

The mechanism used to achieve value for money purchasing is the contracting process. Establishing an NHS contract should not be approached as a legalistic or adversarial exercise but as an opportunity to discuss and agree how improvements to patient care can be secured and over what time; appropriate professional staff must be involved (DOH 1990). The purchaser has to understand how money spent effectively will maximise health benefits for their population. This aspect of buying health care requires a detailed understanding of how pound for pound one service compares with another. Limited information exists in this area of health economics but one approach to evaluating cost-effective purchasing is to split health provision into disease groups and care groups.

Agreement is needed to establish 'best practice' or at least to narrate which choices are acceptable to all involved in the setting of contracts. Through expert discussion with clinical advice a solution is reached on the proper service to buy. These discussions are complex and without a clear scheme to follow may be fruitless. Effective, efficient cost-effective choices can only be made when the full facts are available. Cost-benefit analysis is probably the only truly comprehensive method of economic evaluation of health care (Robinson 1993). There is an enormous research area ripe for study perhaps using procedures such as decision analysis to provide meaningful approaches by which choices can be made in health services.

The contracting year

The contracting year begins when contracts are signed and preparation must then begin to plan for the following year. A rolling process starts with evaluation by the purchaser and by the provider of the effects of the previous contract. A District Health Authority will have issued a commissioning plan that usually represents the next twelve months of its five year strategy for service. Such plans are drawn up within a framework set out by the National Health Service Management Executive (NHSME) and Regional Health Service (RHA) guidelines that include National priorities. A RHA programme is followed (Table 17.1) and moderates the discussions (Communications Directorate 1993).

Forms of contract

There are three forms of contract which District Health Authorities (DHAs) consider:

(a) *The block contract* specifies the provision of facilities that may include work load agreements and patient activity targets within agreed limits. Funding is provided by regular instalments from the DHA irrespective of the actual usage of the facilities. It is not easy for a DHA to fix the service requirements or monitor

Table 17.1.   The 1993/4 contracting timetable

RHAs planning guidance issued	June–July 1993
DHAs and GPFHs purchasing intentions issued	September 1993
RHAs issue contracting guidance	September 1993
Preliminary provider prices issued	November 1993
Purchasing plans finalised	December 1993
Providers finalise their prices	December 1993
Contract negotiations	December 1993/ March 1994
RHAs issues resource allocations to DHAs	December 1993
RHAs issues final budgets to GPFHs	December 1993
Contracts signed	March 1994

Table 17.2.   The benefits of cost and volume contracts

	Purchaser advantage	Provider advantage
Output to facilities specified	√	
Flexible use of resources		√
Payment linked to activity	√	
Funding matched to workload		√

the quality achieved. It is up to the provider to ensure that the contract is fulfilled in good order. Such a contract has the benefit to the provider of flexibility in handling unexpected fluctuations in the number and type of clinical problems treated. Already many contracts for maternity services fall into this group.

(b) *The cost and volume contract* specifies the level of service required by the purchaser. Payment is linked to agreed activity levels.

Resources committed by the purchaser for work not done would be wasteful and hence a maximum volume is specified to the provider as this allows operating within cash limits. Capacity not filled with work would also be wasteful for the provider and a threshold of cases is set to ensure against this. Providers can effectively plan for the future.

Fixed prices are paid up to a volume threshold and a price per case paid up to a volume ceiling. It is negotiations that will set the threshold securing funding for the provider while cost per case to a ceiling contains the costs for the purchasers.

There are advantages and disadvantages for the purchaser and the provider (Table 17.2). (Provider units will be able to link payments with work load and deploy resources more flexibly.) This type of contract is open to negotiation and is the most popular with purchasers and providers. In maternity services a cost and volume contract is attractice as there is ample room for negotiation. Quality issues are considered (DOH 1993a) and outcome measures evaluated (McColl and Guilliford 1993).

(c) *The cost per case contract* specifies the cost of each patient to the purchaser, that reflects the severity of the illness or health problem. Evaluation of this is an expensive process and may only be used in a few non-emergency cases. Generally maternity contracts absort their more expensive cases although if home deliveries become a larger part of maternity services the cost per case may be considerable particularly when up to two midwives attend the delivery.

Elements of a contract document

Each contract agreement will be different according to local needs and expectations. The requirements of the mother and her baby in maternity services are central to any formulation of the service. The purchaser and provider must therefore take notice of the views of those concerned with the development of the service. The pregnant woman, her family doctor, her midwife and her obstetrician and paediatrician all contribute to shaping the contract and evaluating it. This task is complex and can only be facilitated by involving all those interested, professional groups, women themselves and and statutory groups such as Maternity Liaison Committees (Maternity Services Advisory Committee 1985). This is an enormous task for managers of the service to harmonise. Purchasing authorities need guidance and some initial direction is available (Malone and Akehurst 1991) but year-by-year contract review is probably the most effective way of improving service provision.

A typical contract may take the following format:

Introduction
A summary of the service containing an explanation of what is to be contracted for and with which provider.

The aims and objectives often idealise the well-being of the mother and child in the antenatal, intrapartum and postnatal periods. References should be made to the physical and emotional needs of childbirth.

The precise population to be served is identified and a demographic profile stated using data from the Office of Population Censuses and Surveys, forecast of population trends are also important.

Direction setting at this stage permits rational future service planning. The substance of the action points, set out in Changing Childbirth will constantly have to be considered (DOH 1993b, c).

Volume in a maternity contract states the number of women who are likely to give birth in the health district and the number expected to deliver outside the district. A projection of the birth rate can be useful for planning over the ensuing three years. Contracts have in the majority of instances been set as a 'block' but for the future these will probably become cost and volume.

The term of any contract is generally for a set period, usually one year.

Payment is agreed to be phased over the year and can be set through the bargaining process. Withdrawal of patient from the contract would be very unusual in a maternity contract although if alternative services were available then the Health Authority may choose to exercise the option. It would only be appropriate if a pregnant woman had not already booked with a provider.

Termination of a contract would likewise be very unlikely to happen since a Health Authority has an obligation to guarantee a maternity service to its population but a threat of withdrawal may well arise if the terms of the contract were not being met; this is unthinkable.

Quality guidelines apply to all contracts but there are those specific to maternity services. The Health Authority usually agrees special indicators that it will wish to monitor and to use in future discussions when new contracts are set. Perinatal mortality, Caesarean section rates, forceps rates and perhaps maternity mortality are examples of such indicators. The availability of pain relief and epidural rates can also be used as monitors of quality. Much more difficult to measure are other outcome dimensions reflecting satisfaction of the mother and family with the service. Audit may be part of the contract setting. To what extent minor changes in these measures realistically modify future purchasing intentions is difficult to know, many provider units are the preferred provider because of their geographical position. This is made all the more pertinent in some health districts where there is a rationalisation of numbers of hospitals providing services.

Professional supervision of midwives with current arrangements presents its own problems applied to a 'seamless' service when a mother lives in one district and through choice decides to deliver in another. Monitoring the quality in this situation is difficult with the majority of antenatal and postnatal care given in the one district and intrapartum care occurring in another. Contracting for this has to be sophisticated and quality monitoring needs special arrangements. Quality monitoring is an enormous task and extends across all aspects of maternity and obstetric care. It is difficult for the purchaser alone to have a comprehensive understanding of the subject and advice must be forthcoming from the professionals who are usually the providers. The key to effectiveness in this will surely be a collective understanding among the health professionals. 'Changing Childbirth', in particular, is probably the best opportunity we could have to develop a truly multidisciplinary approach to maternity and obstetric care.

Specific quality issues should be set and will include those of the 'Patients Charter' (DOH 1991b).

Patient satisfaction surveys gathered by both purchasers and providers need to be available for discussion when quality issues are deliberated upon. Adherence to sensible waiting times in antenatal clinics will be mandatory to the purchaser; this will often become easier to achieve with the majority of low risk antenatal care being provided in the community.

Quality can be summarised overall as effectiveness, appropriateness, equity, accessibility, acceptability and responsibility.

Monitoring required

Arrangements will be set up to fix the frequency and means by which the purchasers are to be kept informed of how close to contract, providers' activities appear. It is obvious that this whole process of quality control can only be achieved at extra cost to the service and it can only be paid for out of the resource allocation that the provider holds. It remains to be seen whether this is beneficial to patient care and curtails waste thereby allowing more effective use of scarce resources.

In the contracting process Health Authorities will seek access to the provider's place of work, the extent of this should be agreed. Concern will be expressed for professional integrity and patient privacy.

Each obstetric unit and maternity service will be expected to have its own internal quality assurance process.

Monthly contract performance should be available with agreed topics for evaluation. Information will range from consultant episodes derived from patient administration systems (PAS) to birth numbers often collected in a department. These crude data will be elaborated upon perhaps with easily available data from the maternity service such as the number of babies entering special care or intensive care, Caesarean section rate, perinatal mortality, and less specific information of complaints received. All this must be considered in the context of the population served.

Outcome indicators

Every effort has to be made to establish meaningful indicators of the effectivenss of changes in the way a health service provides for its users (DOH 1993d).

Arbitration

Resolution of discordance may be needed when there is disagreement about the terms of an established contract not being met or cover the terms of a potential contract not achieved. Regional Health Authorities provide a conciliation service the decision of which is binding on the purchasers and providers, no compromise in arbitration is permitted.

Initiatives influencing Maternity Services Contracting

Among all the NHS reforms (DOH 1991a) 'Changing Childbirth' is the most important to consider when contracting for maternity care (Table 17.3). Midwives, family doctors, obstetricians and paediatricians need to be involved in developing contracts for maternity care. Every effort should be made by those to work together to achieve appropriate services for their patients.

Table 17.3. The list of 'Changing Childbirth' initiatives which influence contract setting

Safety	Meeting individual needs
Trusted and familiar faces	Access to maternity unit beds
Review antenatal care	Choice of the place of birth
Emergency services	Care in labour
Postnatal care	Role of the GP
Role of the midwife	Role of the obstetrician
Role of the SHO	Assess local needs
Lay representatives	Communication and information
Uptake of service	Women with disabilities
Making best use of the services	Education and training
Strategic plans	Monitoring contracts
Research and audit	Evaluation of new patterns of care
Use of resources	

Conclusions

A whole new industry of health care economics is in the process of development. It will probably become as big a cost to the health care budget as any new developments in medical science; it has yet to be seen whether this tool will deliver a more effective as well as a more cost-effective Health Service.

Political intervention is almost inevitable since ministers will be unable to avoid involvement in the outcome of their constituents' local health services thereupon constraining the competitive incentives promised.

References

Communications Directorate (1993) *South West Thames Briefing*. J. Thompson. South West Thames RHA

DOH (1990) *Working for Patients*. London: HMSO

DOH (1991a) *The Health of the Nation*. London: HMSO

DOH (1991b) *The Patient's Charter*. London: HMSO

DOH (Ed.) (1993a) *The A–Z of Quality*. London: NHS Management Executive

DOH (1993b) *Changing Childbirth* I: *Report of the Expert Maternity Group*. London: HMSO

DOH (1993c) *Changing Childbirth* II: *Survey of Good Communications Practice in Maternity Services*. London: HMSO

DOH (1993d) *Population Health Outcome Indicators for the NHS*. Guildford: Institute of Public Health, University of Surrey

Malone, S. and Akehurst, R. (1991) *Cost Effective Purchasing of Maternity Services*. University of York: Health Economics Consortium

Maternity Services Advisory Committee (1985) *Maternity Services in Action*. London: HMSO

McColl, A.J. and Guilliford, M.C. (1993) Population Health Outcome Indicators for the
    NHS. London: Faculty of Public Health Medicine, United Medical and Dental Schools
    of Guy's and St Thomas' Hospitals
Prime Minister (1993) Fifth Carlton Lecture. Carlton Club, Carlton Club Political Com-
    mittee
Robinson, R. (1993) Cost-benefit analysis. *Br Med J* **307**, 924–6

Chapter 18

Contributions of the professions

Andrew A. Calder

Interprofessional relationships

In July 1992 the Presidents of the three Royal Colleges participating in this study group produced a document entitled 'Maternity Care in the New NHS – A Joint Approach' in which they described our three disciplines as representing the three sides of an equilateral triangle with the expectant mother in the middle. Perhaps because of a slight fear that she might be inclined to feel 'hemmed-in' and uncertain which way to turn I would prefer to regard the three lead professionals in the maternity service (the obstetrician, the general practitioner and the midwife) as providing the three legs of a tripod for the support of mother and baby. There are in addition at least a dozen other professional groupings whose contributions are vitally important. These include anaesthetists, neonatologists, radiologists and radiographers, parentcraft teachers, physiotherapists, specialist nurses in neonatal care, laboratory workers of a variety of different types, dieticians, clerical officers, medical records officers, managers and administrators.

In the musical 'Annie Get Your Gun' Irving Berlin included the song entitled 'Anything you can do I can do better'. However enjoyable that musical contribution might have been it clearly does not apply to the maternity services. We should take as the starting point for building the best kind of maternity service a mutual acknowledgement of a crucial interdependence of those specialists. Figure 18.1 offers a scheme to illustrate the structure of interdependent components on which the service should be built. The midwife brings emotional support to the mother, often acting as her spokeswoman or even her advocate. Her midwifery skills are important in following the course of the pregnancy and then delivering the baby when everything is normal.

The family doctor makes special contributions in continuity of care, in understanding the broad family situation of mother, father and baby and also in bringing very extensive general medical skills.

The obstetrician has skills to recognise complications of pregnancy and labour and the surgical and other operative skills which may be required when such complications arise.

Figure 18.1: Scheme showing the structure of the interdependent components of the maternity services

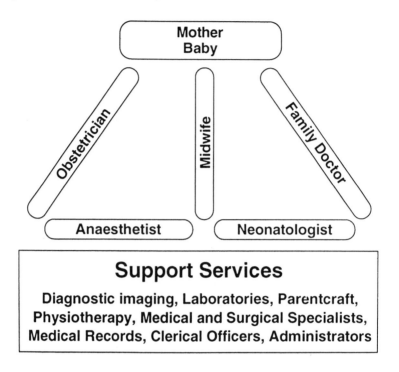

The anaesthetist can offer pain relief in labour and anaesthesia for operative procedures. Furthermore, where the mother should become particularly sick, the anaesthetist often has a very special role to play in critical care.

The paediatricians on whom we all rely so heavily are there to 'pick up the pieces' in the case of the very premature and sick babies and have made enormous strides in neonatal intensive care.

A simple sequence of support has the baby dependent on the mother, cared for by the midwife with the support of the obstetrician and other medical and ancillary professionals. The wider range of skills provide the 'underarching' support for cases where complications arise (Figure 18.2).

Current problems

In theory, this may all seem fairly straightforward, but the reality is often very different. Nowadays we increasingly find ourselves under criticism for deficiencies in the service we provide. Although we may often claim to be hindered by outmoded facilities, very often our attitudes are equally outmoded. There is often a shortage of resources but we may be guilty of using scarce resources with less than optimal care and efficiency.

Figure 18.2: Simple sequence of support for mother and baby

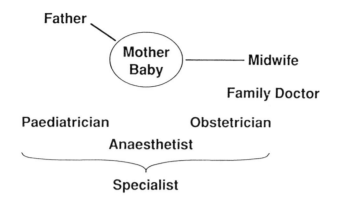

There is also an ever present danger of conflict of interests between the different professional groupings. All groups have engaged in territorial disputes and when we start fighting over our own territory from the basis of self interest, the best interests of our client are likely to suffer. Disputes can involve any of the specialist groups but when they concern the three main components of the tripod of midwife, family doctor and obstetrician, the consequences are likely to be the most serious.

External criticism

Professionals are not good at heeding criticism. When the media or organised pressure groups disparage our work or our service we are usually, and understandably, very resentful. No group relishes having its professional judgement or skill impugned. In the mid 1970s some newspapers and television documentaries began to pour criticism on obstetricians who at the time responded with particular resentment. With hindsight it is clear that some of these criticisms were valid and undoubtedly led to obstetricians taking more account of the feelings and interests of the consumers and in particular of the need to explain and discuss interventions with the mothers and their partners.

Internal divisions

Of much greater importance, however, has been the recent tendency to see a wedge being driven between midwives and doctors (Figure 18.3). This has probably arisen from a number of sources, some of them external, but many of them created amongst and between ourselves. Obstetricians (happily perhaps those of the older generation) have sometimes regarded the midwives as their handmaidens, there to do their bidding! Such an attitude has clearly caused difficulties in the past and has no place in the modern service. The midwives themselves have not been blameless and have too often proved intransigent, narrow of outlook or inclined

Figure 18.3: The wedge between midwives and doctors

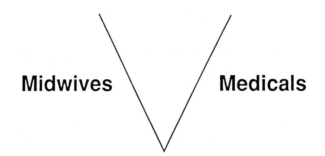

Figure 18.4: A mutually supporting arch

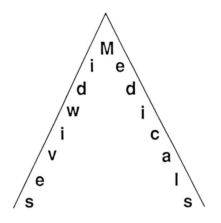

to overdo their efforts to reassert themselves. The concept of the independent midwife, if this implies a total self-sufficiency in the care of expectant mothers, is unlikely to find enthusiastic support from those other professionals working in the maternity service.

It would seem more appropriate that the wedge of Figure 18.3 should be turned upside down to become the mutually supporting arch of Figure 18.4 which recognises the need for midwives and medical staff to rely upon one another. We have to communicate effectively and work together. It is crucially important for us all to recognise that as well as possessing skills (often unique to our own specialty) we have major limitations and must rely heavily on other specialists to meet the needs in those areas of expertise which we may lack.

A framework for progress

Effective progress in improving the maternity services will depend on appropriate interaction between different professional groupings. General practitioners must

Figure 18.5:   The ladder of risk assessment

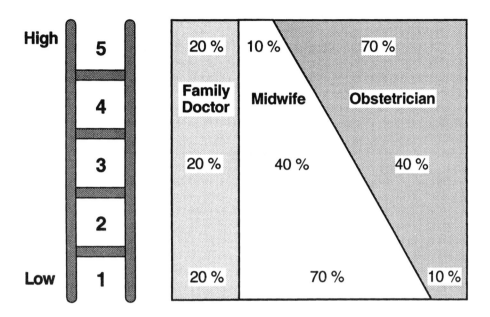

interact with midwives and specialist obstetricians in planning the obstetric care for each expectant mother, beginning with a process of risk assessment which takes heed of a careful review of the information available to us. We must perfect a system in which our different categories of professional can acknowledge the need for a greater or lesser involvement depending on the needs of the particular case: that it will often be appropriate to stand aside and yield ground to midwife or doctor as required but never to the exclusion of either.

There is much to commend compiling a care-plan in early pregnancy but it may be a dangerous over simplification to suggest that women fall neatly into low and high risk categories. Figure 18.5 suggests the application of a ladder of risk assessment. This recognises, firstly, that 'risk' occupies a spectrum and, secondly, that through the course of any particular pregnancy the mother and her baby can move across the spectrum in both directions or rather up and down the 'ladder of risk'. One mother might start the pregnancy at very low risk but become very high risk during its course. Perhaps she is a healthy primagravida but develops fulminating pre-eclampsia at 30 weeks' gestation. Another might begin the pregnancy perceived as being at very high risk on account of a strong history of previous preterm deliveries. By the time the pregnancy in question has reached 34 weeks' gestation the risk from that source may have receded almost completely and she may thereafter remain low risk for the rest of the pregnancy. Some mothers may remain at low risk throughout a pregnancy, others may be at high risk throughout while the remainder may move up and down the ladder of risk as circumstances change.

Throughout this process it is necessary to maintain a friendly dialogue with access to immediate lines of communication with our colleagues in the other disciplines especially the midwives and general practitioners. The three lead professionals should be prepared to vary the degree of involvement depending on the placement of the individual mother on the ladder at any given point in the pregnancy. At the bottom rung of the ladder the care can be vested very largely in the midwife with little or no involvement of the obstetrician, whereas at the top the reverse applies. The role of the family doctor might be considered to vary rather less and remain fairly constant at all rungs of the ladder except perhaps where the mother is admitted to hospital.

Professionals' views of each other

During the summer of 1993 a study was conducted by an Edinburgh medical student engaged on a summer project which tried to address the question of relationships between different groupings in the hospital. In the Simpson Memorial Maternity Pavilion in Edinburgh we look after around 5500 women each year. During her summer project the medical student did two things. First of all she sought the opinions of the different people working in the labour ward as to what they felt about the activities of their colleagues. To do this she interviewed 35 members of staff of whom 20 were midwives and 15 were medical staff. In essence the view of the 20 midwives was firstly that there were too many doctors and secondly that they didn't appear to understand the role of the midwife. She then interviewed 15 medical staff and their broad view was that there were too many midwives and that they did not take enough responsibility. From this unpromising start she then proceeded to study the interactions that take place within the labour ward on a day-to-day basis.

Over a four-week study period she examined 377 labours. The case notes for each labour had a sheet attached to the front on which every interaction between midwives and medical staff was recorded. The reasons for the consultations were put down as was the outcome of the labour. In order to preserve good relations and allow uninhibited expression of views a special pen was used which was invisible on the assessment sheets, which could only be read under ultraviolet light. Both the referring midwife and the responding obstetrician were asked to write down their comments as to how they felt about the consultation process. During the period of the study there were 204 cases which were considered to be 'midwifery only' supervised cases and 173 which were considered to be at higher risk due to medical or obstetric complications. The latter group included all the inductions.

Of the 204 midwifery cases a doctor was consulted during the course of the labour in 44 per cent and the average rate of consultation was just over two per case (Table 18.1). Perhaps not surprisingly in 95 per cent of the medical cases the midwives sought obstetric advice at some point and there were slightly more episodes of consultation in those cases. The common reasons for seeking a medical

Table 18.1.   Intrapartum interactions

	4 week study period – 377 labours	
	Midwife cases	Medical cases
Number	204	173
Advice sought	44%	95%
Poor progress	33%	48%
Fetal distress	25%	23%
Analgesia	23%	14%
Other (inc bleeding)	17%	15%

Table 18.2.   Assessment of performance: midwives' view of obstetric responses (529)

	Percentage
Poor	1
Average	4
Good	18
Very good	77

Table 18.3.   Assessment of performance: obstetric views of appropriateness of requests (479)

	Percentage
Unnecessary	1
Dubious	6
Necessary	21
Very necessary	72

opinion were poor progress in labour, fetal distress, and the need to decide about analgesia (Table 18.1).

During the course of the study there were 1008 consultations of which approximately half were recorded in invisible writing. The midwives' views as to how they had been responded to (whether this was useful or whether they felt they had not received good support and advice from the obstetric staff) is shown in Table 18.2. It was judged to be poor in only 1 per cent, average in 4 per cent, good in 18 per cent and very good in 77 per cent. This tends slightly to belie what the preliminary study would have predicted. Another finding was that the grade of the midwife concerned seemed to be an important determinant in that the more junior grades of the midwives tended to be the more critical.

Table 18.3 shows the views of the doctors giving their assessment of the appropriateness of the requests for consultation. Again 1 per cent gave the lowest rating of unnecessary, 6 per cent of dubious, 20 per cent of necessary and 72 per cent of very necessary. As with the midwives the more junior the staff concerned the more critical they seemed to be.

These findings seems to show fairly clearly that the professional groups were interacting satisfactorily but perhaps highlight the problem of inexperienced midwives coping with junior obstetric staff and vice versa. Doctors who are only in post for perhaps six months or a year at the most may find it hard to command the respect of inexperienced midwifery colleagues. What needs to be emphasised is the need for mutual understanding and respect.

Conclusions

This highly personalised view undoubtedly demonstrates a bias from the obstetric viewpoint but a number of responsibilities are evident. The first of these is for professionals to recognise the boundaries of their own role in the maternity service and to operate effectively within these. Secondly it is necessary to acknowledge the special contributions of fellow professional groupings with whom we work towards the achievement of our common purpose. Lastly and perhaps most importantly is the need to work together to foster a happy working relationship. Good human relations, kindness and consideration are essential to effective co-operation. No government nor even any interdisciplinary working party of Royal Colleges can legislate for such a thing and it remains for the individual professional to be constantly aware of his or her responsibilities in this regard and to work effectively and happily with colleagues in other disciplines.

Acknowledgement
I am grateful to Dr Euan Wallace and Miss Claire McIntosh for permission to reproduce the data from their study.

Chapter 19

The contribution of the general practitioner to maternity care

Luke I. Zander

Introduction

When considering the contribution that general practitioners can make to the provision of maternity care it is important to relate this to their role in the overall system of health care delivery.

The characteristics which distinguish general practitioners from other providers of health care are that they are responsible for providing personal, continuing and comprehensive medical care to both individuals and families. As a result they acquire an extensive knowledge about, and play a significant role in many aspects of their patients' lives. The existence of an established and ongoing relationship between a woman and her doctor is an important factor in encouraging a person-centred or holistic approach to care, and in ensuring that her pregnancy is placed in its appropriate biopsychosocial context. It is from this that their particular expertise and role in pregnancy care is derived.

For the general practitioner the management of a woman's pregnancy forms part of his/her continuing care for that person; care which predates conception and extends beyond birth and the immediate postnatal period into the stages of motherhood, parenting and child care which follow. In this way it reflects the nature of pregnancy itself, which is not an encapsulated event to be considered in isolation, but an integral part of the life experience not only of the mother but also of those closest to her.

The general practitioner and the primary health-care team

In the UK today over 85 per cent of general practitioners work in partnerships or group practices. A direct result of this has been the development of the primary health care team consisting usually of GPs, midwives, health visitors and district nurses, but occasionally including also social workers, counsellors, psychologists and others. When considering the role of the general practitioner in pregnancy care one should therefore be thinking of this in terms of his/her contribution to the services provided by a closely integrated group of professionals with differing and complementary expertise and experience.

Support for the concept of the health care team is based on the belief that care provided by a group of professionals with differing training and perspectives working together and in co-operation enables individuals to achieve objectives which they could less easily or completely achieve by working separately or individually.

The question of how to achieve appropriate interdisciplinary working is a central issue in the present debate concerning the delivery of maternity care, and much thought, mutual understanding and willingness to change is required if the potential of the team concept is to be realised.

The relationship between primary and secondary health care

The basic structure on which health care in Britain has been built is that the primary health care services should to a large extent determine the utilisation of specialist secondary care provision, in the belief that this is likely to ensure the most appropriate and cost effective utilisation of available resources. In the provision of maternity care the situation has been rather different and it has been largely the specialist services which have not only made the decisions as to how pregnant women, even those with no apparent abnormality, should be cared for, but have in fact undertaken a major part of that care itself. This situation is now changing and there is general recognition that benefits are to be derived from shifting the responsibility for much of primary obstetric care to the community-based midwifery and general practitioner services.

The general practitioner in antenatal and postnatal care

Most general practitioners are involved in pregnancy care, but the great majority restrict this to its antenatal and postnatal phases. It is therefore appropriate to consider their role in this aspect of care separate from that in intrapartum care.

This can be summarised as follows:

1 To ensure that their patient receives the type of care that she needs, from whatever resource and in whatever way is considered to be most appropriate.
2 To ensure that the services delivered by the different providers of care are appropriately co-ordinated.
3 To facilitate the appropriate functioning of the primary obstetric care team.
4 To ensure that appropriate facilities are provided for the provision of antenatal and postnatal care.

These responsibilities, which are inherent in the GP's role as the woman's personal doctor, do not in themselves predict the actual activities that s/he will undertake in any individual case. These will appropriately be dependent on the many variables which will characterise each situation.

It has recently often been stated that the general practitioner's contribution to antenatal care should be restricted to the initial physical assessment of the woman, and the monitoring and management of any aspects of care which relate directly to clinical pathology. This would be an unnecessary and inappropriate restriction of his/her provision of care, and one which would deprive many women of what might be a much valued aspect of continuity of care. Reid and McIlwaine (1981) studying consumer opinion about antenatal care found that when women were asked whom they would consult if they had worries about their pregnancy the most commonly mentioned person was their general practitioner.

The opinion has also been strongly stated that if general practitioners are not prepared to provide intrapartum care they should not be involved in antenatal or postnatal care, as this will result in an inappropriate fragmentation of care. This view is largely based on the objective of achieving continuity of care and carer. The arguments against such a position are as follows:

1 The antenatal and postnatal aspects of pregnancy care fit very well into the framework of general practice, and it is well within the competence of a conscientious practitioner to maintain his knowledge and skill at an adequate level. This is in sharp distinction to intrapartum care.
2 At present it is often the general practitioner who provides the greatest amount of continuity of personal care. This is likely to remain the case until such time as midwifery teams providing personalised care throughout pregnancy, birth and the postnatal period become the rule rather than the exception.
3 In the studies in which women were asked whether they would like continuity of care and carer from their midwives, they understandably responded very positively. They were not asked, however, whether they positively did not wish also to be seen by their general practitioners.
4 Choice is one of the cornerstones of the plan for a new approach to maternity care as stressed by the Cumberlege report. If this is to be available it will be necessary to take account of the possibility of women wishing to receive care from their own doctors.

When considering the role of the general practitioner in maternity care it is relevant to consider not only the services the GP can provide, but also what would be the effect if general practitioners cease to provide such care.

1 If midwives are to be totally responsible for antenatal care where is this to be provided, and what would be the cost and service implications?
2 It is difficult to see general practitioners undertaking vocational training similar to that being planned at present if they are not to provide maternity care.
3 Practitioners would not be able to make a meaningful contribution to the general debate about how maternity care should be delivered and developed if they were not involved in its provision.

There is, however, a need to take account of situations in which the general practitioner is unprepared or unwilling to undertake any form of pregnancy care, or if a woman indicates a wish to have her care provided entirely by midwives;

the possibility for midwife-only care should be one of the options available to women.

The general practitioner and intrapartum care

Over the past 30 years there has been a steady decline in the involvement of general practitioners in intrapartum care. The reasons for this trend are varied but a central influence has been the shift in the place of confinement from home to hospital, and the dramatic increase in the technology and sophisticated methods of management that have been introduced into obstetric practice. Few general practitioners would now have the expertise to employ many of these techniques, or even interpret their results, and their introduction has played a major part in encouraging the attitude among many family doctors as well as their specialist colleagues that the management of childbirth is something best left to the 'experts'.

Few gave serious consideration to the advantages that intrapartum care undertaken by the general practitioner/midwife might have over that of specialist obstetric care because of a difference in the nature of the care provided.

Studies of general practitioner involvement in intrapartum care that provide reliable and meaningful information are difficult to undertake. The numbers of deliveries looked after by any one general practitioner, or in any single GP maternity unit, will inevitably be small. There are problems in achieving compatibility between the groups to be studied, and the resources required for such an undertaking are not readily to be found in the setting of primary care.

In spite of these difficulties many studies auditing and evaluating the nature of general practitioner intrapartum care have been undertaken in different settings and as a result certain clear relationships have become apparent between the involvement of general practitioners in childbirth and the nature and outcome of the care provided. A search of the available literature (Klein and Zander 1989) showed that intrapartum care provided by general practitioners and midwives has been shown to be both fully justified on grounds of safety, and to have certain inherent benefits with regard to intervention rates and maternal saisfaction scores. Also, these benefits appear to be independent of whether this care is provided within GP maternity units, integrated or associated with obstetric units, independent or isolated from the main obstetric hospital, or in the woman's own home.

The care of a delivery in the home involves managing the physiological process of birth and detecting deviations from the norm which might indicate the need for obstetric intervention. When these arise, transfer to the hospital is almost always the appropriate course of action. The home is a place for the practice of midwifery, and the principal professional involved is the midwife; it is not the place for the practice of obstetrics.

The role of the general practitioner

The role of the general practitioner willing to be involved in intrapartum care at home, is to act as a support to the midwife – a midwife facilitator – rather than to be considered as an extension of the obstetric team. This means s/he must accept responsibility, with the midwife, to ensure that the quality of care is appropriate, be able to detect deviations from the norm that might indicate the need for specialist help, and be adequately skilled to undertake the appropriate care for mother and baby until further help is available.

The activities s/he undertakes in any individual situation will depend on the needs and concerns of his midwifery colleagues. Until recently GPs were usually called on to undertake perineal repairs and the setting up of IV infusions, but increasingly these have become part of normal midwifery. At present it is the practitioner who does the initial baby check, but it is quite possible that these will also soon be recognised as being within the compass of the midwife, as recommended in the Winterton Report (House of Commons Health Select Committee 1992).

The essence of the GP's role is to enable the patient to give birth in the place of her choice, if that is considered appropriate, to ensure that the care she receives is appropriate, and to respond to any request for his presence should it be made.

With intrapartum care in a maternity unit, the situation is different, as the amount of intervention that might be considered appropriate will inevitably be greater. In such a setting the general practitioner may need to be able to provide a level of service more appropriate to the title of GP obstetrician. To undertake this role appropriately it will be necessary for him/her to maintain his obstetric skills at a higher level of expertise.

Many general practitioners do not feel inclined or able to undertake any personal involvement in the provision of intrapartum care, which is a decision that they are perfectly entitled to take. But in their capacity as their patient's personal doctor they still have an important role to play with regard to responding appropriately to their patient's wish as to the place of birth. This will be to ensure that she is given the appropriate advice as to where she might receive such care.

Conclusion

General practitioners wishing to contribute to maternity care face some uncertainty concerning their role. Much of this focuses on a lack of clear distinction and demarcation between their role and that of midwives. All too frequently this is seen negatively as a disadvantage or problem; the differing providers of care being seen as competitors, each inhibiting the activities of the other, and solutions suggested which aim at establishing appropriate spheres of activity for each member of the obstetric team.

Rather than focusing attention on the 'territories' of the providers of care with the inherent danger of fragmentation and interdisciplinary tension, a more constructive approach is to concentrate on the care itself. There is a clear identity of objectives between the GP and the midwife concerning the nature of the care which they are endeavouring to provide, and there is likely to be general agreement between them about the criteria for seeking specialist advice and assistance. Rather than being in competition, they should view each other as colleagues, and allies in their attempt to achieve the provision of a form of care with which they both essentially agree.

References

House of Commons Health Select Committee (1992) *Second Report on the Maternity Services*, pp. xcv, 1. London: HMSO

Klein, M. and Zander, L. (1989) 'The role of the family practitioner in maternity care' in I. Chalmers, M. Enkin and M.J.N.C. Keirse (Eds) *Effective Care in Pregnancy and Childbirth*. Oxford: Oxford University Press

Reid, M.E. and McIlwaine, G.M. (1981) Consumer opinion of ante-natal clinics. *Scott Sci Med* **14a**, 363–5

Chapter 20

Tunafanya nini – what business are we in?

Debra Kroll

I have entitled this chapter 'Tunafanya nini' which is a literal translation from Swahili and means 'What business are we in?'

The reason for this choice of title will become clear as I move on but suffice it to say that I believe that it is time we seriously looked at the business we are in and how we wish to run it. The interprofessional rivalry and squabbling that has dominated the maternity service for so long has meant that the business of providing effective maternity care, which meets consumer rather than professional needs, has gone astray.

The issue of birth and power is one which arouses strong emotions, because birth is a profoundly moving experience for all those who participate in the event, whether as the person who should be at the central point, the pregnant woman, or as the person who should be in the supporting role, the midwife or the doctor (Savage 1986).

My colleague, John Spencer, addresses the issue of working together in Chapter 21. I will, therefore, confine myself as much as possible to the contribution of midwifery to the maternity services. However, midwives cannot work in isolation so reference to obstetricians and general practitioners is vital.

There have been momentous changes and improvements in the delivery of maternity care in all industrial countries in the last 50 years. There are many midwives who would support Tew (1990) in her assertion that in the revolution in the provision of maternity care the philosophy and methods of the obstetric profession have triumphed. For many midwives this has meant a loss of professional status and an ongoing struggle to maintain their role in the care of healthy pregnant women. This revolution in obstetrics is of course no bad thing as it has brought with it the subsequent major improvement in the safety of childbirth. Unfortunately it has also led to resentment, rivalry and territorial protection between the three main professional groups involved in the provision of maternity care rather than the cooperation that is so urgently needed to ensure the provision of effective care.

However, much has changed. There are two main issues which I want to address. First, midwives have been fighting back to win control over what many of us see as our rightful place in the care of women experiencing a normal physiological process. Second, the needs and demands of consumers, who are so much more vocal, has meant we all have to sit up and take note. This was clearly demonstrated by the evidence taken by the House of Commons Health Committee (1992) in its review of Maternity Services. These, together with the resource constraints on the provision of health care and the uncertain future of the National Health Service, as we know it, requires that professional rivalries are forgotten and we sit down and seriously consider what business we are in and how we are going to provide a safe and effective maternity service.

What business are midwives in and what contribution do we wish to make to the maternity services?

Women have told us what they want. But what is it that we want? What do we as a group of professionals want to do and how will we marry the two?

As a midwife and a midwife manager I have thought a lot about the changes that are needed, the obstacles which are in the way of bringing about change and the contributions that are required from all professionals involved.

The nature of health care provision in the United Kingdom is changing radically. None of us can be immune to the impact of the new purchaser/provider contracts and the effect this has had on our services. The provision of maternity care has not escaped the changes. It has also become highly complex and expensive. I believe the organisation of maternity care needs radical restructuring.

The future market leaders in pregnancy care will, in my opinion, undoubtedly be those who can either offer, for low risk women, a package of community-based care with continuity of care, backed up by a good hospital-based secondary care service or a midwife-led service in the maternity unit of their choice. This will leave the hospital-based teams of obstetricians and midwives to care for those women with medical and obstetrical complications.

(It is important I think to clarify why I have included a hospital-based midwife service as an option for low-risk women. The clientele who come to the unit in which I work come from a large number of Health Authorities. Only 40 per cent of the women live locally. Of the 60 per cent from outside many are low-risk and have made a choice to come to our unit. Not all midwives wish to work in the community and not all women choose to have care based in the community. Neither should be excluded from low-risk hospital-based care.)

To achieve this model midwives and general practitioners (GP) have to come to an agreement and I know what I would like that to be. I believe that midwives have to be the central professional pivot around which maternity services revolve. Only in this way can we maintain the physiological normality of pregnancy as a life event. Boundaries between the roles of midwife, obstetrician and general practitioner have to be better defined and the considerable degree of overlap in the respective roles and responsibilities of these three professionals must stop.

Midwives are trained to care for women with healthy pregnancies, to assess risk factors and deviations from the norm. We do not wish to prevent women from getting the care that they need and we are aware of the importance of continuity of care. It will make it so much easier for midwives to know that when they refer a client to an obstetrician, continuity of care would still be a priority.

What about GPs? I know there will be GPs who will be extremely unhappy with my suggestions. I have heard their arguments before. However, as stated earlier, midwives cannot work in isolation. If community-based care is to be effective, interprofessional cooperation and communication is vital. As more care is moved into the community, midwives become important members of the primary health care team. Unlike other members of the team midwives spend a large amount of time in the hospital and therefore form an essential link between the primary and secondary health care teams. This not only ensures good communications but also ensures an effective use of resources.

I would argue, somewhat pessimistically, that it will prove very hard to achieve real collaboration if the hierarchical way in which the maternity service is organised is not addressed. At a local level the politics of health care is greater than the individual can hope to deal with adequately and as long as there is disparity at a national level, in the pay and status of midwives and doctors, disagreement about who should be responsible for which group of women, and differing forms of assumed and real responsibility, the achievement of real collaboration is going to be difficult.

The politics of the current organisation of maternity care affects the ability of midwives and GPs to collaborate effectively because of two factors. First, the continual disagreement over maternity payments and the resulting, and frequently misunderstood, degrees of assumed responsibility that go with these payments. Second, the power of the medical fraternity over the midwifery profession within the organisation of the Health Service. The latter manifests itself in two ways. Many GPs still feel the need to refer their pregnant patients directly to another medical practitioner, i.e. an obstetrician. Their mistaken belief that referrals cannot be made directly to a midwife comes from the lack of knowledge that many medical practitioners have about the autonomy and sphere of practice of the midwife.

Obstetricians are far more likely to know their midwife colleagues, their training and the policies and procedures that govern their practice than to know all the GPs that offer antenatal care. Yet many obstetricians seem more willing to trust shared antenatal care to these GPs, with little knowledge of their maternity experience, than to assist midwives in their endeavour to reorganise care locally. This must change.

Another area of contention between GPs and midwives is their individual perceived ability to provide continuity of care. Wall (1981) describes the nature of continuity of care as an attitude as well as an action. Of the many dimensions of this concept, duration and intensity, are two important factors (McWhinney 1982). GPs offer continuity because of the long-term relationship that is developed with the family. By the nature of their work and the duration of pregnancy, on the other hand, midwives can only offer short-term continuity. Nevertheless, most midwives believe that the intensity of the care that they offer can be just as valuable as the long-term care provided by GPs, particularly if GPs and midwives communicate about the organisation and nature of care needed. In fact, these two aspects of continuity are not mutually exclusive and women who are the object of intended continuity can benefit from both. Keirse (1989) argues, with some justification, that vague terms such as 'holistic' care, superior knowledge and continuity of care are used more to defend professional prerogatives than to improve care. It is certainly the case that there are still GPs who feel there is no role for midwives in their surgeries, since they are capable of providing the care themselves. The nature of the GPs' work is changing and their workload is increasing. Surely it would make sense to trust a specific section of their work to colleagues who they know well, work closely with and who they trust to give their clients the best service possible. And this trust and cooperation is essential. Every GP should have a named local midwife to whom clients are referred as soon as they are pregnant. Whether that midwife holds weekly antenatal clinics in the GP surgery, the local health centre or even in the hospital is irrelevant. It is the nature of cooperation and communication that is so important.

Hospital-based care similarly needs a radical review. The fact that in the majority of units in the country healthy pregnant women are still booked under a named consultant even if they are receiving midwifery care demonstrates the point. There is no dispute that obstetricians should have overall responsibility for women with medical or obstetrical complications. However, the responsibility for low-risk care needs to be addressed urgently. In the current confusion everyone suffers but the people who suffer most are women using the services who become the recipients of poor care which is laundered with confusion and contradictions.

Effecting change

The first booking interview, which is probably the most important visit of all, is the time where the initial decisions about the type of care should be made. We need nationally accepted risk factors similar to the system used in the Netherlands. At the booking visit the midwife using these (something I believe most midwives already do) can assess whether the woman should be receiving midwife or obstetrician-led care. Even GPs should be using these to guide their referrals. Woman should then be booked either under a named consultant or a named midwife/team of midwives and that professional will then be the lead practitioner responsible for her care.

At the initial visit the plan for care must be clearly documented in the notes as well as any changes that occur along the way. This will provide an important means of auditing practice.

Accepting change and working with it

Accepting the view advocated by the House of Commons Health Select Committee Report (1992) that midwives may be the best qualified professionals to give care to healthy women with problem-free pregnancies is a cultural change of such enormity that it appears, in my view, to be the major stumbling block in the way of change. This is not just a problem for GPs and obstetricians, it is also a difficulty for many midwives whose training and education in a climate of medicalisation of childbirth has led them to lose their skills, expertise and confidence in the management of normal childbirth alone. Midwives have to work hard to educate their medical colleagues and the public about the role of the midwife.

One of the ways of doing this is to follow the House of Commons Health Select Committee Report (1992) recommendations to implement multiprofessional education for GPs, midwives and obstetricians. This would enhance interprofessional collaboration, trust and respect at a time when change in the role and responsibility of all three groups is likely to occur. It is well known that understanding the roles and responsibilities of different health professionals begins in the educational system (Opoku 1992). Yet, to date, there does not appear to be a concerted effort by medical and midwifery educators (or their professional bodies) to address the traditional methods whereby each group receives its education in isolation. The education of those involved in maternity is further flawed in the fact that primary health care professionals, midwives and GPs, receive the majority of their training in the institutionalised setting, steeped in the medical model of care. This does not prepare them well for the care of childbearing women in the community and family setting. This will continue as long as the medical model predominates, and midwives, medical students and Senior House Officers (SHO) are exposed largely to high risk obstetrics in hospital. Midwives need to make a greater contribution to the education of medical students and SHOs' working patterns need to be more closely linked to those of the midwifery staff running the unit.

Conclusion

Purchasing health care on behalf of a local population is still a relatively new activity. In maternity care, purchasers have tended to use historic demand as a basis for contracting (NHS Management Executive 1993). There can be little doubt that women will receive a better quality of care from persons who are experienced in, and committed to, the principles of primary care and who understand what the pregnancy signifies to the pregnant woman and her family. Those requiring specialised care will also benefit from individualised specialised care from clinicians which are not overburdened with caring for women who would do better to have care from midwives supported by GPs. We are in the business of providing a safe, effective maternity service which is both responsive to the needs of the clients and the professional development of those who provide the care. It is time to stop talking and to start making changes.

However strong the need and desire to reorganise maternity care, change is never easy. The perceived personal losses usually outweigh the potential declared benefits. Yet the ongoing changes in the National Health Service will undoubtedly have a major impact on the provision of maternity services. This climate of resource management, greater efficiency and cost–benefit analysis is here to stay and the implications for maternity care mean that the current duplication of care and inefficient use of available resources cannot be ignored.

Study groups are a major recognition of the need to change. However, we have to make a greater effort to work with all our colleagues in hospitals and the community to convince them of the urgency with which this issue has to be tackled.

References

NHS Management Executive (1993) *A study of midwife- and GP-led maternity units*. London: HMSO

House of Commons Health Select Committee (1992) *Second Report on the Maternity Services*, Vol. 1. London: HMSO

Keirse, M.J.N.C. (1989) 'Interaction between primary and secondary care during pregnancy and childbirth' in I. Chalmers, M. Enkin and M.J.N.C. Keirse (Eds) *Effective Care in Pregnancy and Childbirth*. Oxford: Oxford University Press

McWhinney, I. (1982) Continuity of care. *J Fam Pract* **15**, 847–8

Opoku, D. (1992) Does inter-professional co-operation matter in the care of birthing women? *J Interprofessional Care* **6**, 119–25

Savage, W. (1986) *A Savage Enquiry. Who controls birth?* London: Virago Press

Tew, M. (1990) *Safer Childbirth? A Critical History of Maternity Care*. London: Chapman and Hall

Wall, E. (1981) Continuity of care and family medicine: definition, determinants and relationship to outcome. *J Fam Pract* **13**, 655–64

Chapter 21

Working together

John A. D. Spencer

Introduction

The recent report of the Expert Maternity Group *Changing Childbirth* (Department of Health 1993) suggested a number of changes to the provision of maternity services. That women should be at the centre of decisions about their care is not a new idea but the report implies that the present organisation of maternity services leaves much to be desired. Working together, professional groups need to reorganise the service so that it focuses upon the need and wishes of women rather than their own preconceptions. By working together with each pregnant woman, professionals will be able provide care that is safe, effective and satisfying.

The present problem

Over the last ten years or so midwives have assumed an increasing degree of responsibility in the management of normal pregnancy. The reasons for this include dissatisfaction with large hospital antenatal clinics by patients and an increasing recognition of the potential capabilities of midwives as responsible practitioners. However, the pace of change has been difficult for the many consultant obstetricians 'brought up' to assume direct, personal, responsibility for all women throughout pregnancy and labour. Accepting the role of the midwife as a trained practitioner capable of responsibility for normal pregnancy has been shown to improve community obstetric practice (Street *et al.* 1991).

Hospital medical staff have lost the support previously provided by midwives who have rejected the role of 'obstetric handmaiden' in antenatal clinics. No longer are midwives prepared to take blood pressures and test urine samples for doctors. Consultant obstetricians need to adapt fully to the specialised role considered appropriate to their skills and training. This means less direct involvement in uncomplicated pregnancies and a greater willingness to be consulted about suspected problems, without the satisfaction of routinely following-up on their decisions.

Changing Childbirth suggests that women be allowed to choose their lead professional. Many consultants are concerned that the option to choose consultant unit care either will not be made clear or will not be possible if resources are limited. General Practitioners also need to clarify their role in pregnancy care. Their contribution should complement that of midwives, particularly in the community. Many GPs feel that their contribution to the care of pregnant women has been usurped by midwives eager to assume full responsibility of women in the community. Unfortunately, a number of GPs remain stubbornly opposed to 'sharing' care with midwives, insisting upon a named consultant obstetrician and personal feedback about each woman – normal or otherwise. This possessive atitude is a barrier to choice and, not surprisingly, is perpetuated by many consultants afraid of losing potentially valuable links with GPs.

A particular area requiring clarification is the management of labour in General Practitioner Units where midwives, employed by the local trust and working under 'consultant unit' management guidelines, have shared responsibility for women considered to be 'under GP care'. The question of who is responsible for what needs to be clearly established in the form of agreed written guidelines.

Effecting change

Changes need to be formally incorporated into the management strategy of local maternity services if a uniform standard of care is to be achieved. In order that pregnant women be offered appropriate choices, all professionals need to work together and this will require agreement on basic rules or guidelines. It is appropriate that the three professional groups concerned with provision of maternity care recognise their respective roles. The contribution to care from GPs is likely to vary in different parts of the country and according to their training. Input from midwives and obstetricians is likely to be, by the nature of their training, consistent but the balance should vary, primarily as a result of the (objective) needs and (subjective) wishes – choice – of the woman.

Planning local maternity services

Local arrangements need to account for each GP, each midwife and each obstetrician when it comes to planning the service. Strategic planning must account for the contributions from all parties concerned and allow full midwifery responsibility. By contributing to the overall planning of the local service, obstetric consultants will continue to share in the overall responsibility for maternity services, including the care given by midwives to women who do not need to, or choose not to, see a consultant.

Major difficulties exist where neither consultant obstetricians nor GPs agree about the service to be offered. The Maternity Services Liaison Committee (MSLC), with its ability to influence Purchasing Health Authorities, should assume sufficient power in the future to persuade providers, possibly through contracting arrangements, to ensure an agreed consultant policy. However, whether the MSLC will be able to exert such control over GPs remains unclear but the proposed merger between their controlling body, the Family Health Services Authority (FHSA), and the local Health Authority will help ensure that GPs contribute appropriately to the changing shape of maternity services.

Training and supervision

The training of medical students requires experience of normal pregnancy and birth. All professions will need to accept that hospital-based medical school training confined to the obstetric department is inappropriate for the needs of future GPs. As suggested in *Changing Childbirth*, midwives will need to contribute to the teaching of medical students and postgraduates in the community.

The need for different professional groups to understand better both their own roles and that of others means that training and education will need to be modified. The involvement of user representatives will be a useful addition to the training process by helping to maintain the focus on the needs and wishes of pregnant women. It will take some time before aspects of the education of different professionals can be undertaken at one time but an agreed syllabus of core knowledge, available to all groups during their training, would be a good start.

Regular meetings between obstetricians, midwives and local GPs will be essential if continuing education and cooperation is to be effective. This will be necessary at all levels, national, regional and local. The respective colleges have the opportunity to lead the way and this volume is a good example of how future discussions might proceed. Variations in standards of ability are inevitable without adequate coordination and supervision of the provision of maternity services in each area.

Guidelines for care

Written guidelines for the management of all situations arising during pregnancy will ensure the dissemination of appropriate information and will act as the focus for continuing discussion and debate about management. The only guarantee that each woman will be given the same opportunities within a local service is the availability of a comprehensive and clear guide. This should be incorporated into an appropriately designed maternity record which can be carried by each woman. She will be able to select from options available within local resources and, with professional help, construct and document her own individual care plan. Alterations may be appropriate in the light of recorded progress, observations and test results. Thus, according to her circumstances at any time during the pregnancy, and regardless of the influence of any particular group of professionals, each woman will have available to her the information necessary to make appropriate choices for subsequent care.

Naturally, it would be expected that all professional groups, together with user representation, participate in the design of an appropriate maternity record. Such a written record should prevent conflicting advice being given by different professionals in the absence of a change in circumstances.

Audit and quality

Given the potential complexities of the management of individual pregnancies by different parties at the local level, specific management objectives should be regularly audited. In Camden and Islington, the MSLC has set up an Effective Care Group. Using evidence of research-based practice, standards of clinical management will be agreed and the three preferred Provider Units will be encouraged to show that their own practice guidelines concur. Subsequent audit will then be expected to show compliance with the standard. Some guidelines are already available, such as the use of steroids in preterm labour (RCOG 1992) and management of massive obstetric haemorrhage (Chief Medical Officer 1994), and it is increasingly likely that such standards will be incorporated into local contractual arrangements.

Outcome objectives should also be identified and audit of these will enable the quality of care to be monitored. The MSLC has an important role in this area, particularly in view of the opportunity it offers for direct discussions between user representatives, professionals and officers from the purchasing Health Authority. The quality standards now expected by Camden and Islington Health Authority resulted from discussions at the MSLC. Assessing the ability of the three main Provider Units in Camden and Islington to achieve the proposed targets will also be undertaken by the MSLC. User satisfaction surveys are likely to provide an important contribution and may, in themselves, become an important outcome measure.

Unnecessary duplication of provision is not cost-effective but the ability to offer a degree of choice will mean the cost will rise. Therefore, increased choice must be seen to equate with increased quality of the service and thereby justify the cost. Whether or not the standard outcome measures of childbirth will be improved by such changes remains to be seen but outcome measures that specifically reflect the quality of provision will be appropriate for the future.

Working together

Entry to maternity services

Most women who are likely to have uncomplicated pregnancies will first see their GP or a community midwife. Each woman should receive consistent, unbiased, advice about the maternity services available, and a written guide will ensure the uniform dissemination of information. Similarly, the options available to each woman, according to her circumstances and those of her pregnancy, should also be available. The evaluation of each pregnancy will also need to be standardised and the agreed local maternity record will contain guidelines and checklists. Each woman will be allowed to choose whom to see and when to see them, and no individual group of professionals should necessarily 'expect' to be the favoured option.

Routine assessment and screening

The rationale for, and methods of, assessment and screening of maternal and fetal health and well-being during pregnancy should be agreed, particularly with regard to who does what. The RCOG (1993) recommends that all pregnant women be advised to see a medical practitioner, preferably her GP, at least once early in the pregnancy. Obstetricians should not be excluded from the care of normal pregnancies by the assumption that 'they are not needed'. Some women will choose full hospital obstetric care. Most routine screening for fetal normality during the second trimester involves tests usually available at the local hospital. Local maternity services will need to have identified and agreed mechanisms for counselling, performing tests, dissemination of results and discussion of problems arising from them. Visiting the hospital for any such tests provides a potential opportunity to see hospital-based professionals.

Subsequent antenatal care

Women differ in their expectations of, and in their interactions with, different professionals. Pregnancies without risk factors or complications are likely to have a number of care options available to them. Women need to be able to choose a lead professional and a pattern of care, according to local available options, that suits them best. Private care, either by obstetrician or independent midwife, is the only means by which total continuity of care by a chosen professional can be guaranteed. Such care within the service is, at present, beyond available resources but small teams incorporating 'named' lead/link professionals are now common. Amalgamation of hospital and community midwives into 'cross boundary' teams based at the University College London Obstetric Hospital has further improved continuity of care by allowing the same team midwife to continue care during labour even when, as a result of complications, responsibility is transferred to the obstetric unit medical staff.

Complications arising during pregnancy will be one indication for referral to the local obstetric unit with its expertise. Guidelines for referral will ensure efficient and consistent service provision by the Day Assessment Unit and Ultrasound departments. All parties concerned, including the women themselves, should have access to management protocols which may offer agreed options in some circumstances. The maternity record will allow modification of care plans according to such changes in circumstances. Clear documentation of the reason for any change and the option selected will be available to all professionals within the service.

Some women will start pregnancy with a pre-existing medical disorder. Greater supervision by obstetric staff may be appropriate, together with a physician if indicated, but midwifery input remains essential for the complete preparation of the woman for birth and parenthood. Just as midwives must be available for women attending medical staff clinics, so medical staff need to be available for women attending midwives' clinics. At the University College London Obstetric Hospital, for example, diabetic women always see one of two specialist midwives at each visit, as well as the physician or a nurse specialist, but do not see an obstetrician every time whilst observations and investigations remain within agreed management guidelines. Such teamwork exemplifies trust in the skills and abilities of the respective groups of professionals contributing to the provision of care.

Care in labour

Ideally, a midwife should always be available to provide support throughout labour. Problems are likely when responsibility is not clearly defined, both within hospital and the community. Once it is agreed and established that an uncomplicated pregnancy and normal labour be managed by a midwife, she remains immediately responsible (within the local service guidelines) until she transfers that responsibility to a doctor when a complication arises. Consultations during labour with a GP in the community, or with obstetric staff in hospital, must produce a clear result in terms of any action required and who remains responsible for the subsequent management. Usually, this will depend on the reason for and nature of the consultation, but a clear record should be made of each consultation and its consequences. The role of GPs in labour remains a matter for much discussion (Sangala *et al.* 1990) but it is generally agreed that a minimum per year is appropriate if experience is to be maintained. In the obstetric unit, liaison with anaesthetic and paediatric staff is also necessary in a number of circumstances.

Support for midwives, in terms of consultation with senior obstetric and paediatric expertise needs to be agreed, as appropriate, both before, during and after labour. Consultant obstetricians may ask, or be asked, to 'approve' a request by individual women who wish a home birth. However, if local guidelines contain clear criteria for home birth requests then the option to see a consultant should be the woman's choice. Consultant obstetricians must not withdraw from joint overall responsibility for the service just because they no longer see all pregnant women. They must continue to contribute to the planning of the service in order to agree referral arrangements and options. Arrangements for the support of labour at home, usually in terms of recommending immediate transfer to hospital when problems develop, should be well understood by all concerned, including the woman herself.

Postnatal care

Much of the recent squeeze on resources in the Health Service has resulted in reduced provision of adequate postnatal care. It seems as though safe delivery is the end point of the service whereas, in fact, it is just the beginning of parenthood. Satisfaction relates closely to understanding and support, and the opportunity to discuss events, even those which professionals consider normal, is often requested by couples. Long-term follow-up is required. The roles of GP and midwife need to be clarified in this under resourced area. A single check-up at six weeks is probably not adequate and the transition of care from midwife back to GP is an area worthy of particular attention. Feedback sessions, possibly in the form of informal groups at regular intervals, with senior members of all professional groups, may be an appropriate means by which recent users of the service communicate and share their experience.

Conclusion

Neither the organisation of maternity services nor the care of individual women should be subject to vested interests or power struggles between professionals. Nor can care continue to be based on unwritten, historical, precedents. Prospective organisation involving representatives of all professionals, as well as user representatives, will ensure a planned and coordinated service. Each group of professionals should clarify their respective roles and agree the options available in a particular district. Written guidelines are essential to ensure a consistent, auditable, standard of practice. Identified outcome measures should be monitored. The development of a locally designed and agreed maternity record, to be carried by each woman, has the potential to act both as a catalyst for change at local level and a tool for improving care for each individual woman.

References

Chief Medical Officer (1994) *Report on the Confidential Enquiries into Maternal Deaths in the United Kingdom 1988–1990*. PL/CMO(94)1. London: Department of Health

Department of Health (1993) *Changing Childbirth*. Part 1: Report of the Expert Maternity Group. London: HMSO

RCOG (1992) Corticosteroid administration and neonatal respiratory distress syndrome. *The President's Letter*, December

RCOG (1993) Response to the Report of the Expert Maternity Group on Changing Childbirth. London: Royal College of Obstetricians and Gynaecologists

Sangala, V., Dunster, G., Bohn, S. and Osborne, J.P. (1990) Perinatal mortality rates in isolated general practitioner maternity units. *Br Med J* **301**, 418–20

Street, P., Gannon, M.J. and Holt, E.M. (1991) Community obstetric care in West Berkshire. *Br Med J* **302**, 698–700

Chapter 22

Balancing technology with non-intervention: Discussion

Opening remarks by William McN. Styles

Balancing technology with non-intervention in maternity care is a dilemma that daily faces those who have responsibility for looking after pregnant mothers, and for ensuring the safe delivery of their babies. On the one hand, pregnancy and birth are natural processes that usually proceed in uncomplicated ways; on the other, each can be associated with not-uncommon hazards to the health and life of the mother, as well as to the well-being and survival of her baby. The prime aim of maternity care is to recognise these dangers as early as possible so that they might be avoided, or at the very least, so that their deleterious effects can be lessened. In this way, the outcome of a healthy baby and healthy mother can be better assured. The traditional rituals of antenatal care are directed towards this:

1 The checking of blood pressure so that those at risk of pre-eclampsia and fetal growth retardation can be identified;
2 Urinalysis to identify the prediabetic mother;
3 Palpation of the uterus as a crude indicator of fetal growth.

Recent and more sophisticated techniques, such an amniocentesis and fetoscopy, have enabled monitoring to be undertaken more reliably, and to be extended into the prenatal diagnosis of a number of hazardous conditions.

Similarly, in labour, traditional techniques, such as the well-timed episiotomy to promote the speedy delivery of the distressed baby, can be supplemented by sophisticated technology, such as the cardiotocograph and the fetal blood sample, so that the state of the fetus can be closely monitored, and prompt delivery ensured.

When necessary, the benefits of technology have extended after the birth, into the special care baby unit through techniques for the constant monitoring of acid–base balance, biochemistry, heart rate and breathing.

Undoubtedly, the development of these techniques has made a considerable contribution to the decrease in maternal and perinatal mortality rates that has been steady in recent decades. Most of us would recognise that such reductions owe as much to improved social conditions and the consequent healthier nutritional state of today's mothers, as they do technological advances. Nevertheless, as a general practitioner, throughout the last 25 years I have been able to witness for myself through my work, some of the tremendous

166

benefits that the introduction of technology into maternity care has brought. Let me give you a few examples.

I am always pleased to see Jane White, who some 21 years ago was the sole survivor of her mother's six pregnancies. Her mother developed Rhesus immunisation in her first pregnancy, which ended in the first of her two neonatal deaths. Jane's survival would have been impossible without two intrauterine transfusions, and three exchange transfusions after birth. She graduates from Southampton University later this year.

And more recently, I marvel whenever I see Emma, a five year old whose bladder neck obstruction was diagnosed on ultrasound in the last trimester. Subsequent postnatal surgery dealt successfully with a problem that otherwise would have resulted in chronic renal failure and an early demise.

And then, in my practice of 13 000 patients, there are at least a dozen babies who are successful graduates of the special care baby unit – children who 20 years ago would have been unlikely to survive, or if they had, would have been physically and/or mentally damaged. Now, we expect all our three-pound babies to thrive and eventually to attend normal schools.

So why do we need to balance technology at all? If it has brought such tremendous improvements to perinatal survival in the last few decades, why not just import it wholesale to ensure positive outcomes from all pregnancies?

To adopt such a view is to overlook an aspect of pregnancy that is of fundamental importance: the fact that pregnancy and childbirth are natural life events. They are products of a caring and positive human relationship, and as a consequence each carries considerable emotional overtones. It overlooks the fact that for most pregnancies and births, the application of sophisticated medical technology is totally inappropriate. It underestimates the powerful emotional feelings that are part of every pregnancy. Feelings that are established between a mother and her unborn baby, with its father and with its siblings, and with the whole processes of pregnancy and birth. For many, pregnancy and birth will be the most fulfilling experiences of their lives. Experiences to be savoured and enjoyed; experiences that must not be compromised in any way through needless interference.

Sadly, for many mothers, the increase in the use of technology in maternity care has been at the cost of diminishing the emotional experience of a major life event. Some have complained that their experience with technology has made them feel less than human, has given them a sense of exclusion and loss of control, and for some has resulted in considerable physical and emotional discomfort. Those who have resisted the trend and who have tried to retain the initiative in the natural processes in pregnancy and childbirth, have sometimes been made to feel guilty for their efforts. Yet the case for those who have questioned the need for technology is strengthened by the inconsistent ways in which some techniques are applied. Not least of these must be the tremendous variations that are reported in the rates of episiotomy, for forceps delivery and for Caesarean section between obstetric units throughout the country. Variations that are difficult to sustain in terms of quality of care and improved rates of perinatal survival. If such well-established techniques as episiotomy and Caesarean section are applied in such haphazard ways, can we be confident that the latest technology is not being similarly abused?

There is a great need for us to be able, not only to use modern technology to the benefit of mothers and babies, but also to be able to demonstrate the selective way in which we achieve this. We have to be accountable to patients and to colleagues for our practice, and to be able to justify all that we do. If we fail in this, then there is the risk of even greater rejection by mothers of the benefits of new technology, and this would not be in their best interests, nor that of their babies.

The priority must be to help mothers to recognise the benefits of modern technology in maternity care, and to explain to them on an individual basis when its application is necessary, so that they can be involved in any decisions that are made. They must not feel that they are abandoning control to the medical and midwifery professions. Our aims must be to make the application of modern technology as bearable as possible in both the physical and emotional sense.

At the same time, we must understand that natural disquiet for technology is healthy. It is not a threat to the professional integrity of midwives or doctors. Nothing could be worse for us all than an acquiescent, dependent, non-challenging patient population that is afraid to voice its views or to ask for reasonable explanations about the plans for their pregnancies, and for the safe delivery of their children.

Discussion

Styles: We have opened up earlier the area of team working, of professionals working together, of cooperation, and perhaps more important, some of the issues of interprofessional rivalry. It seems to me that an occasion like this provides an opportunity for us to address these in some detail.

We have heard some excellent and courageous contributions from people who have put their feelings and thoughts fairly and squarely before us. I suggest that we react to them and perhaps take them a stage further.

Page: Today has been very encouraging, but one of my fears is that we end up being so politically correct that we get into what I call pink and fuzzy communications. Although there is a great need for agreement and for working together, particularly in our management structures and in the clinical environment, between people who trust each other and who work together, there has to be room for disagreement too. Midwives, or rather midwifery, brings a different perspective to care, than does obstetrics.

I think that we have to trust each other and work together well enough that we can disagree at times but continue to work together. My own first mentor was an obstetrician; we had terrible disagreements but he respected me as a clinician and I respected him as a clinician. I would hate us to leave this meeting thinking that we could not disagree with each other. Professor Klostermann has said that it is the job of the midwife to disagree with the obstetrician and perhaps there has to be room for that kind of debate as well.

Patel: What are the implications of changes alluded to by Mr Coats in terms of cost?

Coats: At the moment we do not know the answers. There are various approaches being looked at. There is the suggestion that proper cost–benefit analysis brought into medical care may be of value but it is in its infancy. We are all talking about introducing these changes without knowing clearly what the costs are likely to be.

There is no doubt in my mind that much of the business of contracting and apparently producing better value for money is itself in doubt because of the costs involved in setting up the system which is necessary to effect that. I simply do not have the answer.

Bull: We have heard a lot about teamwork and so I was rather disappointed by Ms Kroll's proposals for the organisation of maternity care. These perfectly exemplified the power struggle between professionals to the exclusion of the GP, alluded to by Professor Calder. I can illustrate it with a parable. I have a high hedge around my garden at home, 15 ft high at least, which needs trimming every year. My neighbour has an A-frame ladder with three legs and this enables me to stand on the top step and to use a dangerous electrical hedge trimmer with complete safety. This year when I borrowed the ladder I found that the third leg had broken off. It became an extremely dangerous contrivance and I refused to use it. I think this is the situation with maternity care if one of the lead professionals should be excluded.

McGinley: What is clear from the discussion is the need for integrated care. The woman will move during a period of nine months from community through to hospital and back to community. There is no doubt that the care will have to be integrated and the role of the midwife is such that she is able to provide care in all three areas. The time has come for us not to look for demarcation lines. Much of the discussion we have had is about moving from high risk to low risk being seen as success or failure. That is not the way we should be looking at it. It is a continuum of care. Professor Calder's ladder which allowed women to move according to clinical need was a lesson and something we should go back to. We should be working as a team, yes, but there has to be recognition that all the members in the team are equal. If midwives are to take on the responsibility and the autonomy they have to be supported by their colleagues. They do not have to be forced into a position where they are trying to defend what they do. There needs to be trust, and the recognition of the midwife as an equal member of the team. Only if the midwife is so empowered will she be able to empower women and allow them to exercise the choice that we are all saying is so essential.

We need integrated care, care which is a continuum, care which allows the low-risk and the high-risk to be cared for according to the women's needs at the time and a system of care which offers the women choice. No demarcation lines.

Downe: I am not an expert in physics but it seems to me that a four-legged chair is more secure than a three-legged one. I would suggest that that fourth person is the woman. In our local health authority, we have, between the purchaser and the provider, devised a strategy for future maternity services on which a specification is being built. There is to be a minimum that each professional provides: medical care from the GP, obstetric care from the obstetrician if necessary, and midwifery care from the midwife. If the woman chooses the GP as a lead professional, she has the GP as a lead professional. If she chooses the midwife, she has the midwife, and if she chooses the obstetrician she has the obstetrician. To me the important facet of that system is that the basic skills of each of those groups is provided, but on top of that the woman's choice of lead professional is also provided for. If I might say something about the risk factors. I agree with Dr Spencer that the difference between risk and complication is important. The trouble with risk assessment is that we do not know what we are assessing. Is it important that we assess some method of delivery when we know that the clinician's preference may dictate that and not the necessity for the woman of that delivery? Is it important that we look at outcome and what dictates that outcome? Are transfer rates a negative outcome or not? We simply do not know.

One of the basic problems we have in all of these areas is a lack of research, and particularly in the risk area. We do not know what the risk of iatrogenic morbidity is in attributing risk to people who may have a very small chance of having an abnormal outcome.

I would make a plea that one of our recommendations is for more time and more money to be spent on research into these areas, or we cannot move forward.

Jenkins: The environmental culture within the NHS leaves us in the position as professionals of remaining very disparate. We all come with our own professional baggage and our own professional socialisation, which is why we are here today. But we all work in the NHS, and the NHS to my mind is one of the most divisive of environments because it creates a hierarchy in every one of its sections. Yet I have not heard that word mentioned. I want to offer some solutions that we could look at to try to break down hierarchies.

Hierarchies do not just operate between professionals. They are the main reason why we see the obstetrician at the top and the midwife at the bottom, but they are also the main reason why midwifery has the G-grade midwife at the top and the E-grade midwife at the bottom, and ne'er the twain shall meet, let alone discuss or debate. Perhaps what we should positively discriminate against is all hierarchy. Perhaps we should put the chair of the Maternity Services Liaison Committee with an E-grade midwife if she has got those skills, the chair of the audit committee with a good SHO if he or she has got those skills. If we could look at some of that we might create a melting pot in maternity that would tell some of the other services how to get rid what I think is the most pervasive element of disruption that sits in the NHS today.

McKinlay: Whenever there is a discussion of professional territories I always think that it is not like this at ground level. I get on very well with my own midwife.

I was interested in something that was said earlier by Mrs Allison, that there are philosophical and personality differences between community midwives and hospital midwives. The difference is not in the relationship between the community midwife working in a primary healthcare team and the GP, but in the interface between primary and secondary care. Community midwives and GPs will work well together when they define their own roles within a primary care team, but we need to focus on where the patient crosses the divide between primary and secondary care and what are the criteria for that. Also we need to examine how the patient can move back down Professor Calder's ladder and recross from secondary care to primary care when that is appropriate. So we are perhaps looking at the wrong divides.

Smith: I am not sure if a woman has to be looked after by a midwife or to see a midwife to enable her to have choice. With suitable education GPs should be able to offer choice. I know midwives who are very against home deliveries as I know doctors who are for home deliveries. We should not push people into boxes, that all midwives think home delivery is wonderful and all GPs think it is dreadful; there is a danger of that happening.

We can debate why GPs have given up intrapartum care and why there will be few of us doing it in ten years time, indeed whether any of us will be doing any obstetric care at all in ten years time, antenatal or postnatal. If pregnant women as a group within society decide that they want to have the midwives provide low-risk care and the obstetricians provide the high-risk care and that there is no role for the GP, then so be it. GPs refer patients to surgeons for appendectomy, they refer them to physiotherapists for back problems, we can refer women to midwives for maternity care. There is no *a priori* reason why GPs have to provide obstetric care. We may enjoy it, we may argue that it is a part of the core of general practice, but the core of general practice is not well defined and we do not know what core services are. Just as GPs have adapted to challenges such as incentives for minor surgery and incentives for child health surveillance, if there was the political will to change things such that it was seen as right and proper that the GPs do more maternity care and more intrapartum care, and if the incentives were put in place, then I am sure the GPs would educate themselves to provide that service.

Styles: Is it suggested that in future the GP, rather than being the provider of maternity services might be the commissioner or the purchaser of primary care maternity services from midwives?

Smith: Fundholders may have to make that decision at some stage in the future.

Styles: General practitioners ought to be involved in commissioning even if they are not fundholders.

Smith: It depends on whether maternity services are defined as a core part of general medical services. I am not sure that that has been decided by the powers that be. That is a large part of what we are discussing today.

Zander: One has a responsibility within the contract. Whatever one says, we have a contract with our patients, which is different from anybody else, that we will actually provide care. We have to be there 365 days of the year. There are implications if we do not understand what this responsibility is. We may well within the confines of our own practice say that we do not personally have to be involved in that care at all ourselves. But supposing women who are registered with us (I shall not speak of 'my patients' any more than I shall speak of 'my midwives'; they are patients who are registered with the practice), find they do not actually get on with the alternative, whether it is obstetrics, whether it is midwifery, I have a responsibility to try and make that good. I am sure it is not the detailed care of the doctor that we are discussing, but it is what I feel very strongly is inherent in the concept of a personal doctor. We may go away from this system as a healthcare system in this country but we have got to be aware of what we might be losing. It is a system which seems to have served fairly well. But fundholding and the contract will just be another compounding factor and may catalyse change.

Lewison: I do not want to produce a red herring but I should like to pick up on what Dr Smith said about GP fundholding.

The government response to the Health Select Committee Report said that there would be no GP fundholders buying maternity services until there had been full consultation. The National Childburth Trust has not been consulted and as far as I am concerned, until it has there has not been full consultation.

I was glad that Dr Styles invited us to look at the conflicts between the different professionals. Listening to the debate I feel a bit like a woman in labour with the midwife trying to keep the doctor out of the delivery room. We as a group really must address the conflict and try to go through some sort of process where we come to resolution and agreement and only then can we trust each other to start the work that needs to be done.

It is not right to say that everything in the local garden is lovely. It is just not right. From my experience of talking to user representatives from all over the country there are conflicts everywhere – at local, at regional, and at national levels. Where at local level things are good, it is because the different groups, perhaps with users as the oil in the system, have gone through a process where they have looked at the difficulties and have come through and found a way to acknowledge each other's contribution to the service, to agree, and to provide women with the care that they need.

I would suggest that focusing on the needs of the individual and keeping that in the forefront might help the professions to look very carefully at their roles. I can feel the GPs struggling; I do not know whether they are or they are not under a different system. I have read what is said in *Changing Childbirth* about the GPs being responsible for seeing that care is provided but not for providing that care. Maybe that is wrong and maybe that needs to be looked at, but the money will have to come from somewhere. The Executive letter saying that *Changing Childbirth* is government policy made it very clear that there are no extra resources, so where are the extra resources that Mr Coats said are needed for setting up new systems of care to come from? Perhaps duplication of payment is one of the first places that that could come from.

I suggest that unless this group takes the lead there will be no change for the better, and we shall struggle, and at the end of the five years that has been given to the implementation of *Changing Childbirth*, nothing may have been achieved.

Spencer: I was disappointed to hear that Dr Bull was disappointed with Ms Kroll's presentation. I think we are suffering from the problems of differences that we already experience in our own locale. There is no question that somebody like Dr Bull when he was practising would ever have been ousted from the service that he was giving at the time. But this is all down to what local guidelines, local provision and resources would allow. If there are general practitioners locally who are capable, considered to be capable, then they are part of the resource that is available locally. We have no GPs in our locale offering intrapartum care and we have precious few doing what Ms Kroll would consider reasonable antenatal care, although we have a number who wish to perpetuate doing antenatal care.

Dr Bull's point was not really relevant to what Ms Kroll was suggesting. We have solved the issue of the midwife linking primary and secondary care because the teams are no longer concentric circles. There is not a team of midwifery in the community that is different from the team that is within the hospital. They actually radiate outwards. We have four teams, we have consultants linked on the inside with a group of midwives that go out and link to a group of general practitioners, but the fundamental problem we have is precious little input from general practitioners.

Hall: The Winterton Report [House of Commons Health Select Committee 1992] stated that fundholders should not commission maternity care yet recently I noticed an announcement that four fundholders were to commission everything, including maternity care. I wonder if there is not a conflict, a tension, or a vested interest. I am not sure if there is such an interest that it will be resolved in the way we might think, with fundholding practices keeping antenatal care to the general practitioners; it is much more likely that they will see economic advantages in having the midwives do it. But there is a conflict between the general practitioner as provider and as quasi-purchaser.

Reid: I was intrigued by Professor Calder's study of staff attitudes. It struck me that while we have a number of studies of consumer views, we have very few of staff attitudes. To quote from Cumberlege: 'We are convinced that the most fundamental change that needs to occur is one of attitudes on the part of some of the care givers' (Department of Health 1993).

Attitudes of staff are vital for moving the service forward and yet we do not have many studies of what is thought at grass roots level. That should be one of our recommendations, to find out what professionals of all kinds and perhaps of all grades think about the involvement of other staff, and what they think about the kind of care that they are giving. It could be very revealing.

McKinlay: The perception of general practice seems to be that of a generic GP but there is no such thing. General practice in the Orkneys is very different from general practice in Inner London which in turn is very different from general practice in Clitheroe. No one solution will do for everything. Perhaps more worrying is that the system Mr Spencer has described is one of outreach with the obstetrician at the centre and the midwives going out from the great ivory tower to deliver care in the community.

McGinley: That is a very good point, and it is why Ms Downe advocated, and I would support, the idea of there being a lead professional. Part of the problem is that there is this grey area where the general practitioner thinks he is in charge, the obstetrician thinks he is in charge, the midwife would like to be in charge and the woman does not know who is in charge.

There is a fundamental need not just in terms of professional teamwork to recognise who is leading the band. There is also the need from a medicolegal point of view for it to be very clear who the lead provider is. If that was identified clearly on whatever woman-held record exists, everybody would know who the lead provider was and, professional accountability would be vested in that person. Ideally that person would ensure that the relevant inputs to care were given – whether by the lead provider or by whichever other professional was deemed necessary. But there is this grey area that exists at the moment.

Downe: To take that forward and to pick up on what Mr Spencer and others have been saying, we need the development of guidelines. To build on the purchaser-provider system, we may now be reaching a point where the professional groups, with the women, and the pressure groups can, both nationally and locally, get together. We should look at a way of devising guidelines and ways of dealing with certain risk groups that may vary up and down through the pregnancy state. The time has come for us to look seriously at the development of guidelines and guidance in these areas at all levels, so that we can have something agreed which we can audit and monitor across the country in moving towards 'Changing Childbirth' targets and all the other areas we want to change.

Chamberlain: Following the first discussions on the Cumberlege Report (Department of Health 1993) the Royal Colleges of Midwives and of Obstetricians with consumers have set up a group which is already looking at guidelines to advise NHSME on good guidelines. We should try and do it in about six to eight months.

Styles: It is quite clear that tribalism still rules and that it will be difficult – but not impossible – to move on. I suppose that it is a product of our professional socialisation. We have all grown up through the system and it is very difficult when one has been brainwashed in the ways that we all have through our past experiences to get off some of the rails that we are all running on.

It does seem to me that one of the keys is in education and training. The more that we can undertake training activities together, then the more quickly we shall break down some of the divides that there are between us and achieve a greater understanding of each other's roles. Professor Calder highlighted the need for us not only to understand our own roles within the system, but those of the other professional groups with whom we work.

The next sections will discuss quality, and the important subject of education and training. I am sure that within these areas are the keys to successful future co-operation between our professions.

References

Department of Health (1993) *Changing Childbirth*. London: HMSO
House of Commons Health Select Committee (1992) *Second Report on the Maternity Services*. Volume 1: Report. London: HMSO

SECTION III
ACHIEVING QUALITY

Chapter 23

Effective practice in obstetrics

Michael J. A. Maresh and Richard J. Lilford

One of the cornerstones of obstetric audit is that clinical interventions should only be chosen as a quality control standard if they are of established benefit or disbenefit to the mother or baby. Information from randomised controlled trials is the most powerful source of information on effective procedures and in obstetrics it is fortunate that such a source exists both as a book (Chalmers *et al.* 1989) and as a computerised database (Enkin *et al.* 1993). The latter is more valuable as it is regularly updated and software with the latest revisions is released every six months. In addition to standards derived from controlled trials a number of other interventions have such large effects that their value has been established by means of observational studies, e.g. rhesus negative mothers without antibodies should be given anti-D post-delivery if their baby was rhesus positive (see Table 23.5). Yet other practices do not require controlled trials as there is consensus about their use, for example women with massive obstetric haemorrhage should be treated with intravenous volume expansion or that blood pressure should be measured antenatally.

Despite the ready availability of information on effective practices many busy clinicians seek advice from the Royal College of Obstetricians and Gynaecologists' (RCOG) Audit Unit about suitable topics for audit. If such contact is not made or if they cannot immediately think of an appropriate topic there is a possibility that nothing will be done or that they will simply embark on yet another small observational study. Thus, one of the functions of the Audit Unit of the RCOG is to provide clinicians with suitable topics for audit. Accordingly, a one-day workshop was held with five participants to agree a suitable list of clinical topics. These were derived mainly from the Cochrane database (Enkin *et al.* 1993), the whole of which was carefully reviewed. Selected topics are applicable to all maternity units, with the possible exception of prenatal diagnosis (Table 23.1). For covenience the different practices and procedures are tabulated by stage of pregnancy and are listed in Tables 23.1–23.5. The selected topics were first reviewed by the Audit Committee and subsequently approved by the full Council of the Royal College for publication (RCOG 1993).

Some obstetricians may not be in a position immediately to audit a particular subject as it may not be part of their routine practice and they may lack the

179

Table 23.1.   Prevention of malformations and prenatal diagnosis

1 Folic acid (0.4 mg/day) should be offered to all women before and immediately after conception. Women who have had a previous pregnancy associated with a neural tube defect should receive 4 mg of folic acid for a minimum of 1 month prior to conception and until at least 8 weeks' gestation.

2 Chorionic villus biopsy should not be performed under ten weeks' gestation.

3 As chorionic villus biopsy carries an increased risk of miscarriage in comparison to amniocentesis, counselling for the procedure should take particular care to include an assessment of the risk of the procedure; this can take into account outcome in that particular unit.

4 All obstetricians/midwives should have an agreed policy on the screening and diagnosis of Down syndrome, e.g. all women >37 years at delivery offered amniocentesis or all women offered serum screening. Adherence to this policy should be audited.

Table 23.2.   Routine antenatal screening and management

1 Rubella immunity testing should be performed in all pregnancies.

2 Rhesus status should be determined in all pregnant women. Rhesus negative women should be screened at least twice in pregnancy for antibodies.

3 If syphilis screening is carried out it should be performed as early in pregnancy as possible and women who are believed to be infected should be treated as soon as possible.

4 Haemoglobinopathy screening should be offered to those at risk. Clear guidelines should be available in all units and adherence to them audited.

5 Bacteriuria in pregnancy should be routinely screened for and actively treated.

6 Antismoking advice and intervention should be offered to all women who smoke in pregnancy.

7 Ultrasound scan findings should be visually demonstrated to all woman unless they decline.

necessary skills, e.g. external cephalic version of breech presentation at term (Table 23.3). In these cases it would be necessary for units to arrange for at least one person to be trained to perform the procedure effectively.

It is proposed that this list will be updated on a regular basis. A similar list is being prepared for gynaecology audit. This list deals mainly with technical procedures – medicines and procedures. The Audit Committee is aware of the importance of counselling and organisation of services in maternity care. To this end, separate committees (including midwives, obstetricians, public health directors and non-clinical advisers) have been formed to see if a consensus can be reached on minimal auditable standards in these areas.

Table 23.3.   Antenatal management of pregnancy complications

1 Multiple pregnancy should not be routinely managed by cervical cerclage.

2 Diabetic control in pregnancy should be tight, aiming for normoglycaemia.

3 If betamimetic (IV) therapy is given to delay preterm delivery the intravenous fluid should be restricted and a detailed protocol be available.

4 Betamethasone or dexamethasone should be given prior to preterm delivery when there is a significant risk of hyaline membrane disease, even in the presence of ruptured membranes. Chorioamnionitis is a contraindication and careful monitoring is required if there is prolonged rupture of the membranes, insulin dependent diabetes or severe hypertension.

5 For breech presentation at term a skilled service for external version should be available and offered.

6 Inverted and non-protractile nipples should not be managed by antenatal exercise and preparation.

Table 23.4.   Labour and delivery

1 Detailed written protocols should be available on the delivery unit. In particular, these should cover severe hypertension/eclampsia, major haemorrhage, investigations for unexplained perinatal death.

2 Women who have had one previous Caesarean section should be actively considered for a subsequent vaginal delivery.

3 Women who are known to have had group B streptococcus isolated from the genital tract, or a mid stream urine sample, should be given antibiotics if they present with pre-labour rupture of the membranes.

4 Clinical evidence of intrauterine infection should be treated as soon as diagnosed (rather than waiting until post-delivery).

5 Induction of labour in primiparous women with an unripe cervix should be managed by prostaglandins rather than artificial rupture of the membranes and oxytocin.

6 Induction of labour, or increased surveillance, should be offered by 42 weeks' gestation in an accurately dated pregnancy.

7 The ventouse should be the first choice as the method for instrumental delivery.

8 Antacids should be administered prior to general anaesthesia.

9 Prophylactic antibiotics should be used for intrapartum Caesarean section (and probably also for elective operations where the relative risk reduction is the same, albeit from a lower absolute level).

10 Perineal trauma should be avoided if possible.

11 Polyglycolic acid suture material should be used for perineal repair.

12 An oxytocic drug should be offered to all women for the third stage of labour as it reduces blood loss.

13 An injectable prostaglandin preparation should be available on all delivery units for intractable post-partum haemorrhage.

Table 23.5. Puerperium

1 Post-delivery rhesus negative women (without antibodies) should be given anti-D if their baby is not rhesus negative.
2 Women who are susceptible to rubella should be offered vaccination in the puerperium.
3 Mothers who have had a perinatal death, late miscarriage, or had a late termination of pregnancy, must be warned about milk production and suppression treatment offered.
4 Such mothers and fathers should be offered an opportunity to see the baby and a photograph obtained.
5 Non-hospital based carers (midwife, general practitioner) should be informed of pregancy outcome.

References

Chalmers, I., Enkin, M. and Keirse, M.J.N.C. (Eds) (1989) *Effective Care in Pregnancy and Childbirth*. Oxford: Oxford University Press

Enkin, M.W., Keirse, M.J.N.C., Renfrew, M.J. and Neilson, J.P. (Eds) (1993) *Pregnancy and Childbirth Module*, Cochrane Database of Systematic Reviews. Published through Cochrane Updates on Disk. Oxford: Update Software

RCOG (1993) *Effective Procedures in Obstetrics Suitable for Audit*. London: Royal College of Obstetricians and Gynaecologists

Chapter 24

Setting standards

Rosemary Jenkins

Past success?

In 1984, I was invited to join a small working group set up by the Welsh Office, which was to develop a manpower package for use in Wales. One of the first tasks of the group was to determine the standards of care that should be expected in any maternity unit before applying methods for deciding on the levels of staffing required. The subsequent handbook on Standards of Midwifery Care (Welsh Office 1985) was published as a stand-alone publication and commended for use by maternity services in Wales. To encourage its use, the first edition was followed up with a series of local conferences for midwives, to discuss its implementation. The group of five who were involved in preparing the document were confident of the relevance and acceptability of the standards which had been loosely based upon the Donabedian model of assuring quality-assessment of the structure, process and outcomes of activity (Donabedian 1980). We were also pleased with the innovative approach we had taken in formulating standards which were outcome-driven and based on statements about the needs of women. An example from the section on labour shows one of these standards:

> The mother is admitted to a safe, welcoming environment which promotes mother/midwife communication and interaction.

The book was widely circulated and there was considerable interest shown in it from within and outside Wales. However, although there were local discussions about its use, the project in its implementation was singularly unsuccessful. For the first part of this chapter, I shall discuss some of the reasons why I think this happened.

The 'standard setters'

Although the standards written were based on outcomes of care and women's needs, the group, five of us, were all professionals; four midwives and a health visitor. In 1984, it did not occur to us to invite a recent user of the services to our group. We did not consult the consumer groups and, although we did extensive reading, this was largely directed around professional research. Those who had children had had them some time ago when different expectations and conditions prevailed. Most of the outcomes were based, therefore, on assumptions. Some of them were little more than 'truisms' – worthy generalisations – and took little account of the cultural and social mix that makes up most of the local populations in the United Kingdom.

The top-down approach

The standards for midwifery care in Wales were imposed upon midwifery units from a group working at the Welsh Office. There is a proper place for the development of long-term, broad strategy at this level, and indeed Wales has since led the way in its programme of Strategic Direction and Intent, in the introduction of this approach and this will be discussed later. The setting of detailed standards of care should properly rest with the service and professionals most directly concerned with patient contact. This was not fully understood at the time.

Monitoring and evaluation

Our Welsh document failed to incorporate any measurable indicators or future time scales for evaluation which may have concentrated the minds and the activities of health service managers and professionals at clinical level. They were simply handed over on the somewhat naive understanding that something would happen. This indeed was also very much the case with the other great experiment in national standard setting, the three reports of the Maternity Services Advisory Committee (HMSO 1982–1985). Although the maternity services have clearly changed since their publication, it is very unclear whether improvements were the result of the Committee's recommendations or whether they stemmed from improvements in professional training, the continuing pressure from consumer groups and individual users of the services and media pressure. What is now certain, after the publication of the Winterton Report (House of Commons Health Select Committee 1992) and *Changing Childbirth* (Department of Health 1993), the maternity services still fall well below the standard expected by women and their families who use them.

Ensuring standards in the future

National standard setting

The United Kingdom is in a state of experimentation regarding the place for and implementation of national standards for health care and it is impossible to know at present whether the different formulae now being introduced will have any greater effect than before. There are, however, certain characteristics about the new approaches that are worth noting. They may be the answer to the problem of achieving stated standards which are then fully implemented.

Consumer involvement

Wales was the first of the UK countries to publish the current 'round' of national standards for maternity care. Under its general planning approach – the Strategic Direction and Intent – the Welsh Office published a series of protocols, one of which covered maternal and early child health (Welsh Health 1991). The content of the protocol was guided by three equal groups, a professional group, a resource group and a lay group. The latter was chaired by an influential national figure, and its report to the Welsh Office had a fundamental effect on the focus of the final protocol. In his evidence to the House of Commons Health Select Committee (1992), Dr Morton Warner, Director of the Welsh Health Planning Forum said: 'We have begun with the needs of the people, but then crucially we do not accept that the interventions that we have always done are necessarily the best ones'.

In England, we all know that the team of advisers that influenced the eventual content of *Changing Childbirth* (Department of Health 1993) was a mixture of lay and professional members. Again, the influence of the lay members in that expert group is easy to see. 'Women should be involved in the monitoring and planning of the maternity services to ensure that they are responsive to the needs of a changing society. In addition, the service should be effective and resources used effectively.'

Measurable targets

The Health Select Committee was impressed with the approach of the Welsh Office in suggesting targets for improvement and called for a 'national protocol which identifies the targets of maternity services in terms of health care' and stated 'local services must of course be responsive to local needs, but it is the duty of the centre to initiate the development of a coherent strategy for meeting those needs'. We now have those targets in England which reflect the national view of the strategic standards that should be met, the Indicators for Success listed in *Changing Childbirth*. Their measurability is easy: 30 per cent, 75 per cent, 100 per cent. The means by which these levels of activity will be achieved are not, however, outlined. This is left to local negotiations between purchasers and providers.

National to local standards: bridging the gap

Other chapters in this volume examine the detailed arrangements that exist in the NHS, and therefore there will be no expansion here on the potential place of the purchaser/provider mechanism. But the ideas of this chapter would not be complete if attention were not drawn to the opportunity presented by purchasing contracts for bridging the gap between nationally set standards and local implementation – a system not available to us when working on the standards of care for Wales. The Welsh protocol, the English *'Changing Childbirth"* and the recent report on maternity services in Scotland all rely heavily on references to the role of purchasing authorities' specifications as the driving force for change.

The UK is at the beginning of new approaches to national standard setting – consumer input, measurable target setting and the use of the NHS contract. In five years' time, attention may be drawn to another failed grand plan – I hope not and I am optimistic enough to believe that we are edging closer to some of the right solutions.

Setting standards locally

National activity must be put into context. It can only go so far. I am at present an adviser to the Romanian Government on its Human Resources Policies. Our aim is to assist them to put in place a framework of staffing policies that will drive higher standards into the service. On a recent visit there I heard of a UK national who had been admitted to hospital and was deeply concerned when receiving oxygen therapy, to be attended by a nurse who was smoking. To me, the gap between what is said nationally and what happens locally is not so horrifying here, but it still exists. I have been fortunate, however, to explore, through workshops with the World Health Organisation, a possible framework by which local standards may be set (WHO 1992). I want to use this framework, which I have called 'A Quality Circle Approach to Setting Midwifery Standards' (QAMID), to discuss some of the concepts of local standard setting (Figure 24.1).

Getting consumers' views

The first stage in this model draws upon expressing a standard solely in terms of the people who use the service. Those working in maternity services are now all aware of the wealth of written material on what women want. The health services have not yet fully exploited the techniques of market research to test the needs of service users. Purchasing authorities are now required to do this on a large population basis. The opportunity for the maternity services to incorporate such techniques when setting standards should be fully explored. It may not be easy to answer hypothetical market research questions on desirable standards of care for possible future coronary artery by-pass surgery; most of us would prefer not to think too deeply about it. But to ask young women, randomly, what they would like of their future maternity care – where would you like to have your baby? Would you like a doctor or midwife to look after you? – is a rational approach. They may not be pregnant at the time, but most young women would anticipate at some time having a baby.

The professional input

Putting women in the forefront when setting standards does not diminish the responsibility of the professionals. In two fundamental respects, their input is crucial to achieving standards that are acceptable, effective and efficient. They are the custodians of professional knowledge, research and audit. And they know what can be achieved within a given level of available resources.

The second stage in this quality cycle is the professional scrutiny which must be applied to the criteria set by the consumer. These criteria should be compared with current known research. Where they should be clearly modified in the light of research findings this should happen in consultation with women's representatives.

Figure 24.1. QAMID: a quality assurance model for midwifery

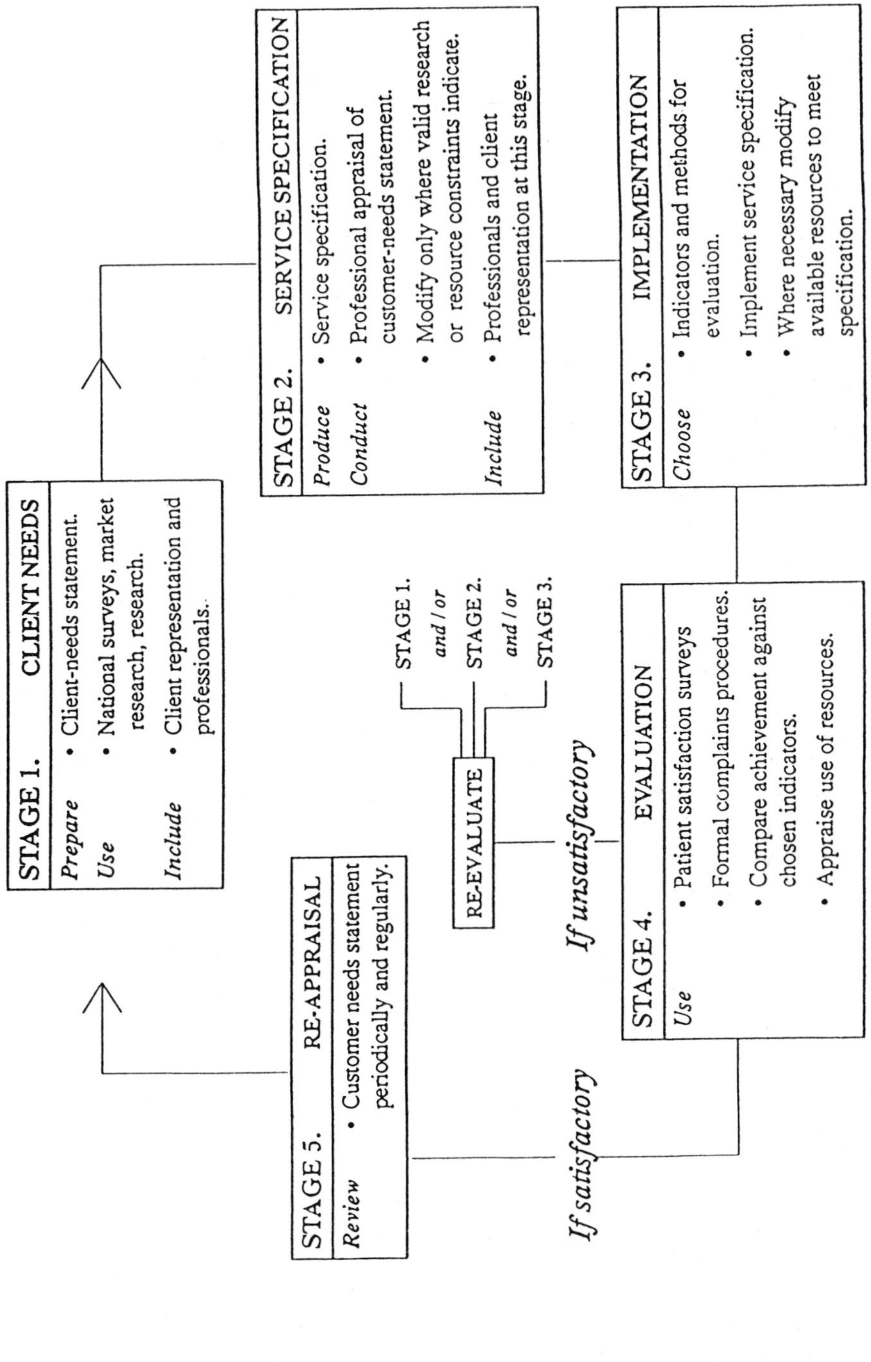

STAGE 1.	CLIENT NEEDS
Prepare	• Client-needs statement.
Use	• National surveys, market research, research.
Include	• Client representation and professionals.

STAGE 2.	SERVICE SPECIFICATION
Produce	• Service specification.
Conduct	• Professional appraisal of customer-needs statement.
	• Modify only where valid research or resource constraints indicate.
Include	• Professionals and client representation at this stage.

STAGE 3.	IMPLEMENTATION
Choose	• Indicators and methods for evaluation.
	• Implement service specification.
	• Where necessary modify available resources to meet specification.

STAGE 4.	EVALUATION
Use	• Patient satisfaction surveys
	• Formal complaints procedures.
	• Compare achievement against chosen indicators.
	• Appraise use of resources.

STAGE 5.	RE-APPRAISAL
Review	• Customer needs statement periodically and regularly.

RE-EVALUATE

STAGE 1.
and / or
STAGE 2.
and / or
STAGE 3.

If unsatisfactory

If satisfactory

Where there is no clear research, the standard set by the first stage in the process should prevail.

A more contentious issue, but one that is essential if standards are to be achievable, is the assessment of available resources. It is no good accepting that each bed in a hospital should have access to a personal television, or that 50 per cent of women can have a home birth if there are insufficient resources, or they are in the wrong place or the staff are not currently trained to provide a service. It may be possible to state long-term goals towards an agreed standard over a period of time. Some standards will always remain unattainable. The idea that standards may need modification because of resource restriction is one that few professionals feel comfortable with, but it is equally unacceptable to define standards of care that will never be met. Vuorni (1985) suggested that optimal rather than maximal care should be the goal of the health professional. In fact, he suggested that to seek the very best care may be counter-productive and he gives an example taken from a paper by Brook *et al.* (1976).

Evaluation

Finally, this model indicates the automatic principle of evaluation and appropriate modification of all standards. If a system is to remain dynamic and responsive to needs, standards must be consistently and continuously reviewed. The quality circle approach as this model demonstrates allows for the adoption of a continuous improvement approach, appropriate to the local environment.

Is local standard setting achievable?

Without resources, the answer to this question has to be no. It requires meetings, information services, medical library back-up and, above all, staff commitment. To be effective in a maternity setting, it also needs a multidisciplinary approach. It is not enough, however, to accept that standards cannot be set because they cannot be resourced. There is too much at stake. There is no point in introducing audit if there is no standard against which audit findings can be measured. Agreement on and the application of acceptable standards of practice may be the most powerful of the risk management techniques available to protect against medical litigation.

Conclusion

The process of change which has been started with the publication of the *Changing Childbirth* Report should itself be monitored so that an assessment of positive and negative influences on the change process may be identified. We should try to learn some lessons about how national norms can be translated into local activity. The opportunity should not be lost to learn lessons about replicability and generalisability so that other parts of the health services can benefit from us.

We should commend and support the use of a structured approach to local standard settings.

We should examine ways in which the consumer voice can be incorporated into the local standard-setting process in the same way that it has been in the setting of national norms.

We should look at ways by which resources in respect of back-up facilities, information services and professionals' time can be negotiated to enable full, informed involvement in the standard setting process.

References

Brook, R. H., Williams, K.N. and Avery, A.D. (1976) 'Quality assurance in the 20th century: will it lead to improved health in the 21st?' in R. H. Etgdahl and P. Gertman (Eds) *Quality Assurance in Health Care*. Germantown, MD: Spen Systems Corporation

Department of Health (1993) *Changing Childbirth*. London: HMSO

Donabedian, A. (1980) *The Definition of Quality Assurance and Approaches to its Measurement*. Ann Arbor, MI: Health Administration Press

HMSO (1982–1985) Maternity Services Advisory Committee. *Maternity Care in Action*, Parts 1, 2, 3. London: HMSO

House of Commons Health Committee (1992) *Second Report on the Maternity Services*, Volume 1. London: HMSO

Vuorni, H. (1982) *Quality Assurance of Health Services*. Copenhagen: WHO

Welsh Office (1985) *All Wales Standard of Midwifery Care*. Cardiff: Welsh Office

Welsh Health (1991) *Planning Forum Protocol for Investment in Maternal and Early Child Health*. Cardiff: Welsh Office

WHO (1992) *Midwifery Quality Assurance*. Report of a Workshop EUR/ICP/HSR342/2), Copenhagen: WHO

Chapter 25

Audit

Marion H. Hall

Audit should be relatively straightforward in pregnancy as it is a self-limiting condition in which the baby(ies) can be seen as the outcome. However, it is now recognised that there are a number of conditions which can be identified only long after the actual birth, e.g. cerebral palsy in the infant, hypertension and heart disease in adult life relating to obstetric factors, or maternal backache following epidural anaesthesia. Nevertheless, it is possible in the short term to perform useful audit, often by identifying intermediate outcomes.

Audit should normally incorporate intervention to improve the standard of practice, but interventions need to be rigorously evaluated (Grimshaw and Russell 1993). In the obstetric field, although a great deal of information is available about effective care (Chalmers *et al.* 1989) both in book form and as an electronic database, knowledge and utilisation of this among clinicians is limited (Paterson-Brown *et al.* 1993; Stocking 1993) and maximum benefit has not yet been achieved.

Because structure has already been fully discussed in this volume it will not be considered here except to express the hope that moves to decentralise care do not lead to fragmentation. Audit should be clinical or woman-specific – we do not need to know whether each professional group is satisfied with the care they administered, but whether the total care offered to the woman met her needs, even if in a complicated pregnancy she had to cross professional, hospital, district or regional boundaries. Purchasers need also to consider not just whether care is effective, but whether it is efficient (Mooney and Ryan 1992).

When audit is being performed it is essential, if provider units are being compared with each other, with national norms, or with their own performance in previous time periods, to adjust for case mix. A great many factors could be considered depending on the topic in question, e.g. (a) maternal age; (b) parity; (c) previous obstetric complications; (d) maternal height; (e) deprivation; (f) gestational age distribution; (g) birthweight distribution. Also, multiple pregnancy should be analysed separately.

In this brief chapter, three main issues will be discussed as examples: maternal mortality enquiries, a form of adverse outcome screening; Caesarean section (CS) where it is generally agreed that unnecessary operations should not be done, but not how to achieve this as there are very few randomised controlled trials; and

190

Table 25.1. Rates of direct maternal mortality per million pregnancies; England and Wales 1979–90

Cause	Year			
	1979–81 (n = 178)	1982–84 (n = 138)	1985–87 (n = 121)	1988–90 (n = 136)
Pulmonary embolism	9.0	10.0	9.1	8.0
Hypertension	14.0	10.0	9.4	8.6
Anaesthesia	8.7	7.2	1.9	1.0
Amniotic fluid embolism	7.1	5.6	3.4	3.5
Abortion	5.5	4.4	2.3	2.4
Ectopic	7.9	4.0	4.1	5.2
Haemorrhage	5.5	3.6	3.8	7.3
Sepsis	3.1	1.0	2.3	2.1
Ruptured uterus	1.6	1.2	1.9	0.7
Other	7.5	8.4	7.5	8.3
Total	70.0	55.0	45.6	47.1

Table 25.2. Case fatality rate by mode of delivery

Mode of delivery	n	Direct deaths	Rate per million cases
Vaginal	2 081 809	37	17.8
All CS	278 500	57	204.7
Elective CS	128 110	19	148.3
Emergency CS	150 390	38	252.7

screening for fetal malformation, where it is not really clear what the goals of programmes are.

Maternal mortality

Maternal mortality has been the subject of audit in England and Wales since 1952 (Department of Health 1994). Every single maternal death (thus 100 per cent threshold) is the subject of confidential enquiry by expert professionals and care is assessed as to whether it was substandard and whether there are lessons for future care. The most recent triennial report (Table 25.1) shows that the overall rate of direct death did not continue its previous decline in the years 1988–1990. For two specific causes, ectopic pregnancy and haemorrhage, there were actually increases in death rates and guidelines for practice are proposed which seem eminently sensible. The data can also be used to estimate case fatality rates for different modes of delivery (Hall 1994). Table 25.2 shows that although elective

CS is apparently safer than emergency CS, it is still associated with a mortality rate considerably higher than vaginal delivery. Nevertheless, this form of audit is unsatisfactory in that as much as six years may elapse before the reporting of some events so that it would be very difficult to be sure whether the process had resulted in benefit. Also there are no denominator data – we do not know how many women had similar clinical features and management, but did not die. There is a need, therefore, for current criterion audit at local level, using as intermediate outcomes events less severe than death, such as blood transfusion, or audit of third-stage oxytocic use (of proven value).

Caesarean section (CS)

International (or even interhospital) differences in CS rates are surely excellent examples of *unjustified* variation, as it is impossible for case mix or biological factors to explain more than a very small proportion of the variation, and good outcomes can be achieved with low intervention rates. It is not, however, known which individual sections are unnecessary. Basic monitoring requires that data should be population based, so that *rates* can be calculated and that an agreed classification of indications for intervention should be used thus allowing scrutiny of questionable indications. There is a reasonable consensus based on prospective studies that most women with a previous CS should be allowed to labour (American College of Obstetricians and Gynecologists 1988; Lomas and Enkin 1989) and a threshold of 50 per cent has been recommended by the Joint Commission on Accreditation of Health Care Organisations (1990) with the expectation that of those, 60 per cent would succeed. Other indications for CS have been scrutinised and the need for a second opinion and for objective corroboration of the diagnosis has been identified (Myers and Gleicher 1993).

　　Because practice is determined not only by rational analysis of risks and benefits, but also by obstetricians' characteristics, cultural factors, remuneration, litigation, etc., change has been very difficult to achieve even where there is academic consensus. National guidelines had only a modest effect in Canada (Lomas *et al.* 1989) but influencing 'opinion leaders' was more successful (Lomas *et al.* 1991). Myers and Gleicher (1993) describe an effective programme within an individual hospital where all the staff had agreed to participate, and a very low CS rate (by American standards) was sustained. Selection bias may be a problem, however.

Screening for fetal malformation

Screening programmes should of course have clear goals, which may include provision of information and reproductive choice for parents (Mooney and Lange 1993) as well as reduction in birth prevalence of malformations. Even with the latter rather limited goal, it is often inappropriately taken for granted that popular and widespread programmes can achieve this, but when random allocation to routine or selective scanning was evaluated (Ewigman *et al.* 1993), this proved not

Table 25.3.   Outcome in pregnancies with major fetal anomaly by routine two-stage (187) or selective (163) ultrasonic scanning (Ewigman et al. 1993)

	Detected				Not detected	
	<24/52		≥24/52			
	Routine	Selected	Routine	Selected	Routine	Selected
Termination	9	4	0	0	0	1
Perinatal death	4	3	2	3	4	8
Severe morbidity	2	0	3	1	21	30
Moderate morbidity	3	0	5	2	14	18
No adverse outcome	13	1	24	4	83	88

to be the case (Table 25.3). Although a slightly higher proportion (35 per cent) of major malformations was detected in the screened group than in the controls (11 per cent) there was no difference in mortality or morbidity. A more complete assessment of the quality of a screening programme would have to address the questions detailed by Hall (1993) and would include the coverage of the population offered and accepting the test, the information given to parents and their understanding of it, the quality of counselling and of technical services such as testing and laboratory procedures, and the precision of corroboration of diagnosis after delivery or miscarriage. Surveys of parents will be needed in addition to case record review and could be based on the seminal work of Green et al. (1992) and Marteau et al. (1988).

It goes without saying that some selection must be made among all the topics that could be audited and that scientific principles are as important in audit as in health services research (Russell et al. 1993).

References

American College of Obstetricians and Gynecologists (1988) Committee Opinion: Guidelines for vaginal delivery after previous caesarean birth, ACOG. Washington DC: ACOG

Chalmers, I., Enkin, M. and Keirse, M.J.N.C. (1989) *Effective Care in Pregnancy and Childbirth.* Oxford: Oxford University Press

Department of Health (1994) Report on Confidential Enquiries into Maternal Deaths in the United Kingdom 1988–1990. London: HMSO

Ewigman, B.G., Crane., J.P., Frigoletto, F.D. *et al.* Radius Study Group (1993) Effect of prenatal ultrasound scanning on perinatal outcome. *N Engl J Med* **329**, 821–7

Green, J., Statham, H. and Snowdon, C. (1992) 'Screening for fetal abnormalities: attitudes and experiences' in T. Chard and M.P.M. Richards (Eds) *Obstetrics in the 1990s: Current Controversies.* London: MacKeith Press

Grimshaw, J.M. and Russell, I.T. (1993) Effective clinical guidelines on medical practice: a systematic review of rigorous evaluations. *Lancet,* **342**, 1317–22

Hall, M.H. (1993) Audit of antenatal care. *Fetal Maternal Med Rev* **5**, 17–27

Hall, M.H. (1994) Maternal mortality higher after caesarean section (Letter). *Br Med J* **308**, 654–5

Joint Commission on Accreditation of Health Care Organisations (1990) Examples of monitoring and evaluation in obstetrics and gynaecology, 1. Renaissance Boulevard, Brook Terrace, Illinois 60181

Lomas, J. and Enkin, M. (1989) 'Variations in operative delivery rates' in I. Chalmers, M. Enkin and M.J.N.C. Keirse (Eds) *Effective Care in Pregnancy and Childbirth*. Oxford: Oxford University Press

Lomas, J., Anderson, G.M., Domnick-Pierre, K. *et al.* (1989) Do practice guidelines guide practice? The effect of a consensus statement on the practice on physicians. *N Engl J Med* **321**, 1306–11

Lomas, J., Enkin, M., Anderson, G.M. *et al.* (1991). Opinion leaders vs audit and feedback to implement practice guidelines: delivery after previous caesarean section. JAMA, **265**, 2202–7

Marteau, T., Kidd., Cook, R. *et al.* (1988) Screening for Down's syndrome. *Br Med J* **297**, 1469–70

Mooney, G. and Lange, M. (1993) Antenatal screening: what constitutes benefit? *Soc Sci Med* **37**, 873–7

Mooney, G. and Ryan, M. (1992) Rethinking medical audit: the goal is efficiency. *J Epidemiol Community Health* **46**, 180–3

Myers, S.A. and Gleicher, N. (1993) The Mount Sinai caesarean section reduction program: an update after 6 years. *Soc Sci Med* **37**, 1219–22

Paterson-Brown, S., Wyatt, J.C. and Fisk, N.M. (1993) Are clinicians interested in up-to-date reviews of effective care? *Br Med J* **307**, 1464

Russell, I., Grimshaw, J. and Wilson, B. (1993) Scientific and methodological issues in quality assurance. *Proc R Soc Edin* **101B**, 77–103

Stocking, B. (1993) Implementing the findings of effective care in pregnancy and childbirth in the United Kingdom. *Milbank Q* **71**, 497–521

Chapter 26

Audit as an agent of change

Susan M. Downe

Introduction

It is becoming increasingly clear that, as the rate of innovation in medical technologies gains pace, the temptation to introduce change without prior evaluation is almost irresistible. At the same time, it is becoming clear that many of the interventions historically implemented in medicine have never been subject to rigorous examination. Despite the fact that maternity care has had a long record of self-audit via the maternal mortality reports, many techniques used in maternity care are open to dispute, and applied with apparently illogical variation. Oakley and Houd (1990) illustrate this point in a fascinating series of snapshots of maternity care in Europe, demonstrating the lack of consensus on the best approach to a variety of situations, both between countries, and between professional groups. In recent years, the resolution of uncertainty about the relative effectiveness of different approaches to medical care has become a government priority. The development of audit has been a prime response to this.

Development of audit in the NHS

The Department of Health (DoH) white paper *Working for Patients* (DoH 1989a) set out a radical new agenda for the NHS. Its associated working paper No. 6, entitled *Medical Audit* (DoH 1989b), marked the onset of a growing understanding within the NHS of the power of audit to identify and promote new systems of care, or to eliminate current non-effective activities.

Since 1989, £200 million has been spent by the Department of Health on audit. However, it was always clear that this was temporary pump-priming money: as the Trent RHA medical audit implementation plan stated in March 1990: '... funding for audit will eventually become part of the cost of running a service of good quality. As such, it will have to be refunded from income from contracts.'

The Department of Health is now committed to the view that, although some unidisciplinary audit will continue, the bulk of work should be undertaken on a multidisciplinary basis, as clinical audit, to reflect truly the integrated nature of health care. The recent policy statement by the Clinical Outcomes Group defines clinical audit as:

> ... the systematic and critical analysis of the quality of clinical care, including the use of procedures used for diagnosis, treatment and care, the associated use of resources, and the resulting outcome and quality of life for the patient ... (it) embraces the audit activities of all health care professional, including nurses, doctors and other health care staff. (DoH 1993a, p. 4)

In pursuit of this strategy, the Department is allocating a small amount of funds to Regions to pump-prime clinical audit projects for the period Jan–Dec 1994. After this allocation, from financial year 94/95, funding will cease to be ring-fenced. Although there is as yet no official declaration on the method of distribution of monies for audit in future, it is likely to be through the contracting process.

Targeting health gain

Measurement, and improvement of, outcomes of health care is increasingly seen as being vital in ensuring maximum health gain for the population. Frater (1992), in discussing questions about the effectiveness of interventions used to generate health outcomes, goes so far as to state:

> ... the answers to these questions are not a simple matter of testing hypotheses; they need to overcome a complex system of health care, which has come to rely on anecdote, best guesses and tradition as the underlying reasons for many interventions and which assumes that doctors' values are a proxy for patients' values ...

The latter point is essential to bear in mind when making decisions about what to audit. Two prime illustrations of this point are the use of artificial rupture of membranes (ARM) in labour, and the implementation of prenatal fetal screening programmes.

The research evidence on ARM is somewhat equivocal, but it seems to indicate that the technique speeds up labour. However, do women want their labour speeded up? Literature on the subject appears to take it for granted that they would; however, this is by no means proven, and any decision to audit the use of ARM should certainly assess the opinion of women on the subject.

Antenatal fetal screening offers more obvious opportunities for the exploration of complex ethical and psychological dimensions. Outcomes assessment in terms of accuracy of diagnosis and reduction in undiagnosed fetal abnormalities is easy. Despite this, an assessment of health gain in this situation is extremely difficult. White-van Mourik et al. (1992) assessed a small sample of women and partners undergoing termination for fetal abnormality, and found that, at 2 years post-termination, 20 per cent of the women still complained of regular crying, feelings of sadness, and irritability; 12 per cent of couples separated for a while, and one couple divorced. This was an uncontrolled study, and it is not clear what the outcomes would have been had the couples gone on to have a handicapped child.

However, it does illustrate the point that the implications for the kind of choice offered to women and their families in this situation are not the same as for other choices offered in maternity care, and that any audit of this technology cannot be complete without the application of long-term health status measures.

Audit as an agent for change

Purchasers are increasingly being vested with the power to influence change in pursuit of cost-effective health gain (NHS Management Executive 1993). In exercising this power, they are beginning to set clear targets based on good evidence. The role of research and of audit in informing this process is of increasing interest to the government. These purchasing priorities will inevitably influence clinical practice through the auditing systems set up to ensure their achievement.

It is in this context that audit can be seen to be a primary agent of change in moving the service towards the indicators of success in *Changing Childbirth* (Department of Health 1993b). An overview of the activity in Trent Region and Southern Derbyshire Health Authority may serve as an example of this process.

The Trent Regional Health Authority (1990) R&D Outline Strategy stated:

> The results of research can indicate where new things can cost-effectively be done, development work tries new things out in practice, and puts the new data with what is known, modifying what is perceived as good practice. Purchasing then offers a way of saying what *should* be done, while audit and quality systems find out whether what is done measures up to that expectation, and, by their analysis of observed variations, pointing the way for future R&D work.

In taking this philosophy forward, Trent RHA produced a draft 'Health Gain Investment Programme' for pregnancy and childbirth in 1992. This was based on currently available research evidence, and, primarily, on data from the database of meta-analyses set up in Oxford, which resulted from the publication *Effective Care in Pregnancy and Childbirth* (ECPC) (Chalmers *et al.* 1989).

In December 1992 Southern Derbyshire HA seconded a midwife from the major local maternity services provider unit to work on their behalf to create a strategy for the future of maternity services in conjunction with the provider unit and the Family Health Service Authority (FHSA). This work was based on the regional document, ECPC and the Cochrane Centre database, government publications, and an audit of local need based on the OPCS instrument, *Women's experience of maternity care* (Mason 1989). The resulting strategy demonstrates the value of good purchaser/provider relations, balanced with the use of objective evidence. *Changing Childbirth* came out soon after the strategy was completed. There was very little fundamental difference between the two documents.

The strategy forms the basis of a service specification currently being negotiated between purchaser, providers and the local FHSA. The major provider has set up a comprehensive maternity and clinical auditing system to allow for audit of the jointly agreed specification. The first end-product of the system has been the creation of an antenatal protocol, agreed between all professionals providing care. The uptake and application of this document, and the ability of women to obtain flexible care within it, will be audited over the next year, and the results will inform future contracting and service developments.

The system outlined above for generating strategic developments is a first step towards breaking down historical assumptions about the value of particular types of care. However, it is possible that, once outcomes have been thoroughly explored, the importance of processes will reassrt themselves, since, in a service which is increasingly interested in cost-effectiveness, the use of expensive processes to achieve the same outcome as a cheaper process will not be acceptable. It is in this context that audit of the processes employed in bringing about the targets of *Changing Childbirth* will be essential.

Systems standardisation

Beyond the issue of linking strategic developments and outcomes locally, a particular area of debate exists around the need to develop a method of standardising data to enable comparison between clinicians, hospitals, and regions (Kings Fund 1990; Paterson *et al.* 1991). This will be particularly so in pursuit of universally applicable targets, such as those in *Changing Childbirth*. The achievement of such universality will require comprehensive and effective information technology systems. These are the very systems needed both in hospitals and in the community to implement community-based care, since routinely collected data should be the bedrock of any process and outcomes auditing systems (McKee 1993). However, despite the fact that moves towards resource management over the last few years have led to some hospitals collecting comprehensive databases relating to clinical care, there is little evidence in the literature that this is being used for audit – as Yudkin and Redman (1990) pointed out following their analysis of the use of computerised obstetric data in Oxford: 'Routinely collected computerised data enable ongoing clinical audit, but it becomes a reality only when clinicians agree on standards of practice, and have a flexible attitude towards change'.

The ideal auditing system would be flexible and relational, accommodating audit of various interlocking areas at both a general and a specific level with the minimum of secondary data collection. The system should be linked both to the strategic direction of the service and to the requirements of purchasers (based on population need). Standards, protocols, guidelines and principles should be as simple as possible, and should cover a range of areas, such as those defined by Maxwell (1984) (access to services, relevance to need, effectiveness, equity, social acceptability, and efficiency and economy).

Once the audit has been undertaken, the results should be reviewed and action plans drawn up to remedy shortfalls. The standards and protocols on which the audit is based should then be reviewed, adjusted as necessary, then reaudited.

Conclusion

Audit is still a relatively new concept in the NHS. It is, however, a fundamental element in the assessment of health technologies and the creation of a quality-based, cost-effective service. The experience of multidisciplinary maternity audit in Derby so far has led to the belief that the following criteria should be fulfilled in order to achieve successful audit, and, as a consequence, quality assessment and assurance:

Auditing systems must be:

1 based on objective evidence/external targets as far as possible;
2 powerful enough to have a direct impact on practice (usually through the involvement of managers at the highest possible level);
3 simple enough to be used;
4 applicable to, and applied to, all those employed in the relevant area;
5 able to encourage innovation as well as ensuring maintenance of agreed standards;
6 as integrated as possible into current systems (both of data collection, and of the organisation).

Audits of the outcomes of implementation of the *Changing Childbirth* targets are essential, both to ensure that it delivers clear health gain, particularly from the perspective of the women and family involved, and to ensure that the many advantages of current systems are not lost as its disadvantages are overcome.

Our experience is that it is possible to create a comprehensive auditing system which ensures health gain for the women and families in our care, fulfils the purchasers' requirements, meets the business plans of our organisations, enables us constantly to challenge out-dated practices, and which improves our expectations of ourselves.

References

Chalmers, I., Enkin, M. and Keirse, M.J.N.C. (1989) *Effective Care in Pregnancy and Childbirth*. Oxford: Oxford University Press

Department of Health (1989a) *Working for Patients*. London: HMSO

Department of Health (1989b) Working Paper 6: *Medical Audit*. London: HMSO

Department of Health (1993a) *Clinical Audit*. London: HMSO

Department of Health (1993b) *Changing Childbirth*. London: HMSO

Frater, A. (1992) Health outcomes: A challenge to the status quo. *Quality in Health Care* 1, 87–8

Kings Fund (1990) *Organisational Audit Project: A summary of the first phase, Spring 1989 – Autumn 1990*. London: Kings Fund

Mason, V. (1989) *Womens Experience of Maternity Care – a Survey Manual*. London: HMSO

Maxwell, R. (1984) Quality Assessment in Health. *Br Med J* 288, 1470–2

McKee, M. (1993) Routine data: a resource for clinical audit? *Quality in Health Care* 2, 104–11

NHS Management Executive (1993) *Purchasing for Health: A framework for action*. Leeds: NHSME

Oakley, A. and Houd, S. (1990) *Helpers in Childbirth: Midwifery Today*. WHO, New York: Hemisphere Publishing Corporation

Paterson, C.M., Chapple, J.C., Beard, R.W. *et al.* (1991) Evaluating the quality of the maternity services – a discussion paper. *Br J Obstet Gynaecol* **98**, 1073–8

Trent Regional Health Authority (1990) *Medical Audit Implementation Plan.* Trent RHA

White-Van Mourik, M.C., Connor, J.M. and Ferguson-Smith, M.A. (1992) The psychosocial sequelae of a second-trimester termination of pregnancy for fetal abnormality. *Prenat Diagn* **12**, 189–204

Yudkin, P.L. and Redman, C.W.G. (1990) Obstetric audit using routinely collected computerised data. *Br Med J* **301**, 1371–3

Chapter 27

Achieving quality: Discussion

Kroll: One previous discussion was who should be delivering maternity care, particularly the role of GPs. But listening to Ms Downe's address it occurred to me that possibly this is the best way to decide at local level what is good in that area.

Recently I had a discussion with our purchasers about whose responsibility it is to audit. I wondered whether it should become a joint purchaser-provider responsibility to audit what should be good standards for that area with the knowledge of the professionals and the systems in place in that area.

Downe: Obviously I would agree – being involved. The Family Health Service Authority was also involved and the GPs are involved in the system we have set up.

Spencer: I would entirely agree with that concept. The Maternity Services Liaison Committee (MSLC) provides the ideal opportunity to get involved with these activities. The MSLC was not mentioned and I wondered why not for they contain representatives of all the groups involved. Perhaps it is better to be specific rather than to assume that everybody knows that they are all on the MSLC. This is an up and coming issue.

On our MSLC we have taken the initiative to look at the Cochrane database, Oxford and decide what standards are appropriate. We have decided to examine one or two processes; we will have a small group, called an effective care group, get the standard agreed, go to the respective purchasers and ask them to what extent they agree with that standard. The group would come back, and by to-ing and fro-ing try to get an agreement. The purchasers are a party to that through the MSLC and are looking at influencing them by putting what we want into their purchasing requirement so that they ask us to provide what we want them to provide.

Smith: As far as standard setting is concerned we do not need to reinvent the wheel. There is much published work from Holland and the UK on the various characteristics of successful standard setting an audit should have. One of those

201

characteristics is local ownership of local standards. One of the reasons why national standards perhaps do not work is that there is no sense of ownership. Those professionals to whom the standards are to apply should be involved in standard setting, whether it is the MSLC or the local Medical Audit Advisory Group. For those who are involved in standard setting, there is already published work on those factors which facilitate uptake and implementation of standards (Haber 1991; Grol 1993).

Page: I wondered what implications Dr Hall's data have for the information that we are giving when women are wanting to make choices about elective Caesarean section without a clinical indication.

Hall: Having started that, I rather regret doing so because it really is not the case that we are besieged by women looking for unnecessary Caesarean sections. The potential increase in maternal mortality is one of the factors to be discussed with a woman for whom a Caesarean section was being proposed and it must be discussed. The risk of maternal mortality is still very low and it may not be a critical determining factor for the woman.

Styles: It is important if we are to give the woman the opportunity to make an informed choice that we are well informed ourselves.

Steer: Mrs Jenkins used *women's needs* and *women's wants* interchangeably and that misrepresents the situation. We can have nationally agreed standards of what we believe women need on safety, but the wants of women vary from one woman to another, from one area to another and from one generation to the next. We have not had enough discussion on how we meet those wants, where the funding should come from, and whether there should be greater input from the individual who chooses particular aspects of care which are not needed on purely medical grounds.

Page: Often we confuse needs and wants, and I think quite rightly because what we label as *women's wants* are often deep psychological *needs*. In the past we have tended to regard women's choices as being selfish yet there might be some psychological determinant. Although I accept the different definition between *wants* and *needs*, in maternity care they do overlap in many ways.

Lilford: I would agree. I see no distinction whatever between wants and needs. The distinction that is drawn by other people is paternalistic and quite harmful both in purchasing and resource distribution and in clinical care.

If a woman is fully informed of the risks and says that she would like a Caesarean section then she should have it. If a woman is fully informed of the risks and says she would like to have a home birth, then she too should have it. To quote from Shakespeare's Hamlet: 'There is nothing either good or bad but thinking makes it so.' [Shakespeare: *Hamlet*, Act 2, Scene 2]

Young: Professor Lilford is probably right. However, it will create real problems if we say all wants are needs and must be fulfilled. What of the general practitioner whose patient aged 20 comes in and demands sleeping tablets for the rest of their life because of insomnia? Do we respond to that and say we accept this as a need? There are real problems if we say every *want* is a *need*, resource problems let alone ethical problems, and I am slightly more on Professor Steer's side here.

Lilford: The exception would be if fulfilling somebody's needs interfered strongly with fulfilling somebody else's. That would be the exception to my libertarian stance.

Jenkins: I believe there is a clear role for professional mediation in women's stated wants and needs. That should be at the very minimum, and kept at the minimum, but we do have knowledge that we need to impart with full information, we do know what resources are or are not available. If every woman wants a home confinement we are the people who would know that we do not have the staff to do it.

   If we can with the help of women make a structured approach to standard setting that puts that very clear professional mediation in, we have no difficulty in using the words *wants* and *needs* absolutely interchangeably.

Macfarlane: I should like to reiterate what we saw. The implication is that audit is done locally but it is important that people have data that relate to their locality. It is essential to have a common core of data so that audit can also be done within larger areas, such as Scotland, or Regional Health Authorities in England. Those data need to be collected consistently. We have heard that the data collected about Caesarean sections in England did not distinguish between elective and emergency operations. They do, by their definitions, but they are collected in such an appallingly bad and incomplete way that they are not usable.

   It is important to be aware of what the common core of data are, and the extent to which they need to be changed; to design systems that are flexible and that will collect the common core of data while at the same time enabling people to change local and sub-national data items accordings to the particular concerns at the time and the particular concerns for that area.

McClure: I have missed any discussion on how needs are determined – I assume by some form of survey. But if we believed the surveys, we would all be driving Sinclair cars and Neil Kinnock would be in 10 Downing Street. They depend on what questions are asked, of whom, by whom and when. The science of surveying is poor indeed and if we go ahead on maternity services believing in surveys we will be building our house on sand.

Smith: I disagree with Professor Lilford. The impression I get is that he is suggesting we give women all the information in terms of advantages and disadvantages in terms of information and then let the woman make her decision about what she wants; then we fulfil that want. I do not believe, as a GP, that this is a tenable position ethically. We can give them the information, but we are patients' advocates and we have a responsibility to guide them. We cannot just give them all the information and sit back and say, 'Over to you, tell us what you want and we will do that for you.' We do not give sleeping tablets to people for thirty years at age 20 just because they have decided to sleep every night. Similarly if a woman aged 18 came in, having decided that she did not want the risk of breast cancer and asked to have both her breasts off, would Professor Lilford operate? He cannot truly believe that and perhaps he would come back on that point.

Spencer: There may be a difference in the doctors' approach from that of the midwife. Do the doctors generally want to retain some degree of responsibility for their doctor/patient interaction? Having given them full information and allowing them to partake in the decision making, is there a difference between the doctors taking this approach? Are midwives approaching this differently, giving all the information to the woman and then saying that she is responsible for the final decision? I need to have that clarified.

Lilford: The argument is over limits on autonomy and there is a lot been written on this by philosophers and others. People have addressed the issue of the limitations on people's autonomy, and in what circumstances is it legitimate and appropriate to overrule someone's autonomy. Various arguments may be given, some of them more important than others. One is the availability of the option. If there is no option for a home birth then clearly a home birth cannot take place, one cannot do it if one is doing something else. So one limitation is availability.

The second is whether in exercising her autonomy a woman is stopping somebody else from exercising their autonomy; that opens the whole question of resources.

The third legitimate level of someone's autonomy is the issue of competence. If somebody is not competent to exert their autonomy, they need to do something about it. We may say that if someone climbs up to the top of the London Business School and threatens to jump off, should we respect their autonomy and let them jump or should we try and dissuade them? The answer is that we would try to dissuade them on the basis that it is quite likely that their competence to make that decision may have been temporarily impaired.

The fourth limit is that imposed by beneficence, that one of us can decide for a competent woman that it is not in her interests to seek her own autonomy. It is that notion that I totally reject and it is in that sense that I believe that needs and demands are identical. In the end the best person to know what her values are is that individual woman. Should midwives or doctors be involved in that? It does not matter; whoever is involved should give that woman the maximum chance to reach autonomy. I have measured the values of different groups of people concerning the issue of prenatal diagnosis, in care providers and care receivers; they are very similar. There are those who would not contemplate termination of a pregnancy for Down's syndrome while there are others who would do a termination of pregnancy. There are people of that kind amongst doctors, amongst midwives and amongst patients. And it is for that reason that we cannot use our own values to subsume our patients' values.

Styles: The problem I have is how do we judge somebody's competence to be autonomous?

Lilford: One must do according to one's own conscience and best faith as best one possibly can.

Hall: It might be useful to reiterate that we are not besieged by women wanting unnecessary interventions; most of the evidence is that women do not want to have unnecessary interventions and that they think that some of the interventions we are offering them are unnecessary. It should be absolutely clear that women should not have to have interventions that they do not wish to have. What is not quite so clear is whether they should be able to demand completely ineffective interventions that are bound, because of their use of resources, to influence adversely some other woman's chances of getting an effective intervention.

References

Grol, R. (1993) Development of guidelines for general practice care. *Br J Gen Pract* **43**, 146–51

Haber, A. (1991) Setting up consensus standards for the care of patients in general practice. *Br J Gen Pract* **41**, 135–6

**SECTION IV
EDUCATION**

Chapter 28

Obstetric training of general practitioners

W. J. David McKinlay

The present

Although currently well under 15 per cent of general practitioners (GPs) are involved in intrapartum care, an obstetric component to vocational training is still sought after and 93 per cent of the applications for a Joint Committee Certificate included obstetric and/or gynaecology experience in 1991 (RCGP/RCOG 1993). Many obstetric posts are tied in to three-year vocational training schemes and Reeve and Bowman (1989) found:

> Our results show that trainees on these Schemes were more likely to complete a post in obstetrics and gynaecology or paediatrics, though little educational advantage seems to have been gained as they did not receive more teaching and had similar difficulties obtaining study leave as trainees on self constructed schemes. Surprisingly, they were also less likely to consider the teaching they did receive as being orientated towards general practice, although this may be because their expectations were higher. This is a sad state of affairs!

Studies in other regions (Kearley 1990; Smith 1991) confirm the unsatisfactory nature of current hospital-based training to prepare for general practice obstetrics – but practices require prospective partners to be eligible for the obstetric list, therefore trainees seek obstetric experience. Increasingly rigorous joint hospital visiting and the revised guidelines published jointly by the RCGP/RCOG (1993) will hopefully improve training. The RCGP visitors now assess the educational potential of posts against rigorous quality criteria (RCGP 1993). Kearley's (1990) important study identified topics perceived as most useful for a GP and noted how many were not addressed in the hospital post (Table 28.1). Kearley described her findings as 'support for the view, widely articulated among trainees, that in its present format the hospital component of vocational training for general practice is educationally of questionable value'.

In the North Western Region I have asked trainees at the start of the GP practice year to complete a questionnaire about their hospital jobs (Table 28.2) which points to little improvement in the years 1991–1993.

Tait (1987) suggested that hospital consultants and general practice trainers should meet at local level, and an example of a core curriculum agreed by the Blackburn

Table 28.1.   Topics perceived as most useful for a general practitioner, in order of frequency mentioned = 21 respondents and topics of which at least one respondent* and at least five respondents** felt were not addressed in the hospital post

Paediatrics
**   Minor self-limiting illness (infectious disease; ear, nose and throat)
       Recognising a sick child
**   Developmental surveillance
       Dealing with children
*   When to refer/working with the hospital
*   Chronic diseases (e.g. asthma; eczema; handicapped)
*   Care of the newborn
*   Behavioural problems
*   Prevention/education (e.g. immunisation)
*   Teamwork with allied professionals
       Acute illness (e.g. gastroenteritis; meningitis)
*   Outpatient experience
*   Family problems (e.g. non-accidental injury)
*   Communication
       Diagnosis and examination
       Therapeutics

Gynaecology
**   Family planning
*   Cervical cytology
       History and examination
*   Vaginal discharge/sexually transmitted diseases
*   Outpatient experience
       Menstrual disorders
*   When to refer
*   Therapeutics
       Infertility
       Abortion/ectopic pregnancy
*   Psychological factors
       Familiarity with hospital treatment
       Pelvic pain
*   Psychosexual problems
       Menopause problems
       Natural history of common diseases

Obstetrics
       Antenetal care
       Postnatal care
       Recognising problems/emergencies
       Intrapartum care
*   Psychological factors
*   When to refer
       Anticipation of risk
       Understanding of hospital investigations

From Kearley (1990).

Table 28.2.   North Western Region Survey: Obstetric SHO Posts

At the start of the practice year, on the Day Release Course, trainees are asked to complete four questionnaires (in optically read format) – one for each six month post in the previous two years.

For obstetrics –   1991–18 returns, about 9 districts
                        1992–54 returns, about 14 districts
                        1993–66 returns, about 16 districts

In 1991 all questions were YES/NO format.

All figures have been expressed as percentage and only 'YES' answers listed.

1) Was the experience relevant to general practice?

1991 – Yes – 56

	VERY	QUITE	LITTLE	NIL
1992	19	52	22	0
1993	26	55	15	0

2) How much teaching did you receive?
   (1991 – was teaching adequate?)

		A LOT	ENOUGH	INSUFFICIENT	NONE
A-Formal	1991	Adequate – Yes 33			
	1992	11	13	62	15
	1993	10	30	33	23
B-Informal	1991	Adequate – Yes 33			
	1992	7	30	0	0
	1993	15	50	0	0
C-GP Orientated	1991	Adequate – yes 17			
	1992	2	13	0	0
	1993	5	26	0	0

3) How much support did you receive?
   1991 Was there adequate support – from consultants Yes 61
                                  – from juniors Yes 72

		A LOT	ENOUGH	INSUFFICIENT	NONE
From tutor/	1992	22	35	35	37
consultant	1993	26	35	35	4
From other	1992	9	41	0	0
consultants	1993	12	26	0	0
From juniors	1992	24	50	20	0
	1993	30	53	11	0

4) How much feedback on your performance did you receive?
   1991 Did you receive feedback? – Yes 28

		A LOT	ENOUGH	SUFFICIENT	NONE
Positive	1992	11	19	46	24
(encouraging, useful)	1993	11	29	44	16
Negative	1992	2	20	31	41
(destructive,	1993	6	30	30	30
retribution)					

continued

Table 28.2. *continued*

5) What was your on-call rota?

		1:2	1:3	1:4	1:5	1:6	1:6
With prospective	1992	0	6	39	6	0	0
	1993	2	9	35	6	0	0
No prospective	1992	0	39	19	2	0	0
	1993	2	35	6	6	2	2

6) Please estimate your average weekly hours:

	60	60+	65+	70+	75+	80+	85+	90+	95
1992	0	2	6	11	28	39	9	4	2
1993	2	0	5	6	14	36	23	5	2

7) Was there an introductory assessment of your learning needs?
Yes 1991 – 11 1992 – 9 1993 – 8

8) Were you helped to develop a learning plan or log?
Yes 1991 – 6 1992 – 11 1993 – 11

9) Were you given an introduction to the units working routine?
A talk: Yes 1991 – not asked 1992 – 54 1993 – 50
A booklet 1991 – not asked 1992 – 26 1993 – 9

10) Have you had problems getting Form VTR2 after this job?
Yes 1991 – 24 1992 – 15 1993 – 8

11) Were you able to attend minor specialties in this job?
Yes 1991 – 22 1992 – 20 1993 – 38

12) Did you receive enough outpatient experience?
Yes 1991 – 83 1992 – 76 1993 – 86

13) Were you taught to communicate with General Practitioners?
Yes 1991 – 18 1992 – 15 1993 – 23

14) Did you request study leave?
1991 – 44 1992 – 57 1993 – 58
Did you get it? 1991 – 39 1992 – 54 1993 – 56

15) Did you get enough antenatal clinics?
Yes 1991 – 100 1992 – 81 1993 – 61

16) Did you get enough postnatal clinics?
Yes 1991 – 72 1992 – 50 1993 – 47

17) Did you get good labour ward teaching?
Yes 1991 – 44 1992 – 39 1993 – 35

18) Did you learn to:

	1991	1992	1993
Fit ring pessaries?	83	65	65
Fit coils?	39	28	30
Take cervical smears?	89	64	67
Do a pelvic examination?	—	74	68
Do a neonatal resuscitation?	56	30	35

Trainers' Workshop with the local consultants is appended. This serves as a learning log for the trainee as well as a tool to assess both the trainee and the educational qualities of the post. (It is produced in Filofax form.)

Ennis (1991) in a study of SHOs in obstetrics in four teaching hospitals and three district general hospitals found that 23 (58 per cent) thought they were inadequately prepared for the work expected of them both at one month and six month interviews, stating, 'recognition at all levels that the SHO grade is a training grade is called for, with more comprehensive and intensive training that concentrates on these aspects of practice in which problems commonly arise'. The management changes in the NHS increase the tension between service and training and the New Deal for doctors' hours risks a move towards shift and partial shift arrangements, especially in acute 'front line' specialties like obstetrics. Shift systems mediate against protected teaching time, a team identity and the trainee and consultant working closely together.

Smith (1992) found hospital vocational training in obstetrics increased the perceived competence of trainees but failed to encourage them to use obstetric skills and as many (25 per cent) trainees felt a six month post reduced their confidence to provide full obstetric care as felt it encouraged them. Smith perceptively stated, 'the underlying problem with vocational obstetric training is that the aim of training is unclear' and until we have a clear vision of the future of general practice obstetrics, it will be difficult to provide relevant training.

These problems are not peculiar to general practice trainees. Blunt (1991) in an editorial concerning recruitment problems in obstetrics and gynaecology, stated, 'training is defined almost entirely in terms of time rather than experience, so that juniors tend to be overexperienced but undertrained'.

The future

In spite of the consumer backlash and the lack of evidence that the medicalisation of labour improves outcomes in low risk pregnancies, it is unrealistic to believe general practitioners will resume the role they played in intrapartum care 20 years ago. In 1986 discussions were advanced between the GMSC, RCGP and RCOG for a two-tier obstetric list. Most general practitoners were expected to opt to provide antenatal and postnatal care only. Those wishing to be GP obstetricians and be involved in intrapartum care would have required satisfactory initial training and appropriate experience and/or a refresher course to maintain their skills. It was suggested that a three-month hospital post would be adequate for the non- intrapartum list, but even with job-sharing arrangements such a short post would not be popular with obstetricians who would get relatively little 'service return' for their educational input. Smith (1991) suggests shared-care-only training can be provided by community midwives and general practitioner trainers. Those trainees wishing to give intrapartum care would be trained by experienced general practice obstetricians, midwives and hospital consultants.

This system has great attractions as a means to make general practice obstetric training more relevant if the safeguard of an agreed core curriculum is in place.

The work of the Joint Working Party (RCGP/RCOG 1993) and the Royal College of Obstetrics and Gynaecology DRCOG Working Party (RCOG 1993a) has defined curricula which can be adapted to local needs similar to the Blackburn example (Appendix). Certainly the rigour and frequency of appraisal visits to training practices are at least the equal of joint visiting and general practice is the main provider of family planning advice. The teaching of intrapartum care of low-risk mothers during general practice training will demonstrate the aspects of continuity and patient autonomy not experienced in busy hospital units. In another study Smith (1992) concluded:

> ... most general practitioner trainees believed that both midwives and general practitioners have important roles in maternity care. Exposure of trainees to the provision of full obstetric care while in their training practice resulted in a more positive attitude towards the provision of such care by general practitioners.

The old 'back door' to the obstetric list (Department of Health 1992) whereby GPs could attend hospital antenatal clinics, 20 normal and 10 abnormal deliveries as a substitute for an obstetric post was rightly critised as inadequate training for the full range of intrapartum care. A similar arrangement may be very appropriate for doctors who are only to be approved for shared and/or low-risk care and who are getting valid training in a community setting with midwives and the training practice. Most training takes place in group practices, an average general practitioner will have about 28 new births per annum, so that in a practice of four a trainee will have access to a pool of 100 pregnancies with which to gain experience of general practice obstetrics, and 60 per cent will be normal deliveries (Fry 1993).

Currently many of our highly trained and skilled midwife colleagues are reduced to the 'weigh, wee and BP at the ANC' role which belittle their skills and frustrates; a prominent role in the training of GPs will help their morale. Community midwives and GPs have had their skills atrophy with disuse, a baby-boom or a crisis similar to the gastroenteritis outbreak in Teeside (which shut down a maternity unit) could make community intrapartum care of low-risk mothers a necessity again as beds are reduced.

However, a major shift of general practice training in obstetrics to a community setting will have serious consequences for obstetric manpower. There is a mismatch in calculations of the number of obstetric SHO posts occupied by career obstetricians and general practice vocational trainees. The RCOG Hospital Visiting Working Party (RCOG 1993b) quotes the RCOG Fourth Annual Manpower Report as stating 868 of 1499 (58 per cent) of posts are occupied by trainee GPs. However, Joint Committee Certificate applications in 1991 were 2128 of which 1970 (93 per cent) included obstetric experience. Even allowing for experience in other countries and over a wide period of time this discrepancy must mean that many SHOs considered to be in career posts subsequently apply for certificates to become principals in general practice. These are the 'closet' GPs who are either constructing their own vocational training scheme or have a change of career intention.

The DRCOG Working Party (RCOG 1993a) and the Joint Working Party (RCGP/RCOG 1993) have addressed clearly the standards and needs of education for GPs in hospital posts. For those who wish to undertake intrapartum care with high risk pregnancy such training is vital.

However, with few GPs involved in intrapartum care for community obstetrics the critical relationship is between GPs and midwives rather than GPs and obstetricians. The question remains – is hospital based training relevant at all? The importance of training for GPs in gynaecology must not be forgotten, but this may also be best acquired in training practices and/or outpatient attachments.

A political recognition of the status quo (i.e. a two-tier obstetric list with stated opt out of intrapartum care for those who wish it) is necessary if trainees are to stop training for what they will not do and train better for what they will do.

References

Blunt, S.M. (1991) Training in obstetrics. *Br Med J* **303**, 1416

Department of Health, Welsh Office (1992) Criteria for admission to the obstetric list: paragraph (vi) of paragraph 31/schedule 2 of Statement of Fees and Allowances Payable to General Medical Practitioners in England and Wales from 1 April 1990

Ennis, M. (1991) Training and supervision of obstetric Senior House Officers. *Br Med J* **303**, 1442–3

Fry, J. (1993) *General Practice: the Facts.* Oxford: Radcliffe Medical Press

Kearley, K. (1990) An evaluation of the hospital component of general practice vocational training. *Br J Gen Pract* **40**, 409–14

RCGP (1993) *The Quality of Hospital-based Education for General Practice.* London: Royal College of General Practitioners

RCGP/RCOG (1993) *General Practitioner Vocational Training in Obstetrics and Gynaecology.* London: Royal College of General Practitioners

RCOG (1993a) *Report of the DRCOG Working Party.* London: Royal College of Obstetricians and Gynaecologists

RCOG (1993b) *Report of the Hospital Visiting Working Party.* London: Royal College of Obstetricians and Gynaecologists

Reeve, H. and Bowman, A. (1989) Hospital training for general practice: views of trainees in the North Western Region. *Br Med J* **298**, 1432–4

Smith, L.F.P. (1991) GP trainees' views on hospital obstetrics training. *Br Med J* **303**, 1447–50

Smith, L.F.P. (1992) Roles, risks and responsibility in maternity care: trainees' beliefs and the effects of practice obstetric training. *Br Med J* **304**, 1613–15

Tait, I. (1987) Agreed educational objectives for the hospital period of vocational training. *J Assoc Course Organisers* **2**, 179–82

Appendix: Blackburn vocational training scheme: obstetrics core curriculum

	Comment	Date

Antenatal care

Basic knowledge of the principles of human reproduction and family planning

Prepregnancy counselling, including high- and low-risk factors etc.

Clinical assessment of the changes which occur in the mother and fetus during a normal pregnancy and all routine procedures used in antenatal care

Awareness of the interrelationships between general disease and pregnancy

Range and interpretation of screening procedures, including ultrasound, carried out during this period. Methods of detection of fetal abnormalities

Recognition and management of problems treatable by a GP:
    vaginal discharge
    urinary infection
    anaemia etc.

Recognition of possible abnormalities requiring specialist or hospital attention

Importance of social and emotional factors in pregnancy and childbirth

Relationships with other members of the obstetric care team. Shared care or full care?

Assessment and appropriate management of bleeding in early pregnancy, including the initial management of common emergencies

Counselling after miscarriage, still birth etc.

Labour

Indications for the induction of labour

continued

Appendix: *continued*

	Comment	Date
Insertion of prostaglandin pessaries and their mode of action		
Amniotomy		
Recognition of the signs and symptoms of the onset of labour		
Assessment, understanding and significance of the normal progress of labour including vaginal examination and assessment, and all other routine procedures used in normal labour		
Normal delivery, including detailed record keeping		
Use of intrapartum fetal monitoring		
Recognition of possible deviations from the norm during labour		
Low cavity forceps delivery, including local anaesthetic techniques		
Assisted breech delivery, multiple pregnancy		
Ability to suture episiotomies and lacerations		
Postpartum haemorrhage and its management. Manual removal of placenta		
Resuscitation of shocked mother		
Home deliveries and the risks involved		
Alternative positions for childbirth, birthing stools etc. 'Natural Childbirth'. Awareness of the emotional aspects of childbirth, including management of maternal (and paternal) anxiety		
Resuscitation of the newborn		
Principles of counselling parents faced with fetal abnormalities		

Postnatal care

Care, examination and assessment of the newborn

continued

Appendix: *continued*

	Comment	Date

Recognition of common diseases of the
newborn also congenital

Care, examination and assessment of the
mother, including advice about the pros and
cons of the various methods of feeding,
contraception etc. Also postpartum exercises

Awareness of the psychological and psychiatric
complications following confinement

Understanding of the normal involutional
processes in the postpartum period

Gynaecology

Taking a history of, assessing, advising and
managing where appropriate common
gynaecological conditions including:
    Vaginal discharge
    Abnormal uterine bleeding

Ability to manage:
    Abortion
    Emergency
    Counselling
    Aftercare

Premenstrual syndrome

Management of common problems relating to
menstruation

Physiology and management of the
menopause, HRT

Infertility, both male and female

Investigation and treatment of pelvic pain and
discomfort, including pelvic inflammatory
disease

Abnormalities found on vaginal examination,
including erosions, masses, prolapse and its
complications etc. Early diagnosis of neoplasia
of the genital tract

continued

Appendix: *continued*

	Comment	Date
Ability to recognise common gynaecological emergencies requiring urgent intervention and ability to provide first aid measures		
Prevention of gynaecological disease, e.g. carcinoma of cervix, sexually transmitted diseases etc.		
Sexual counselling		
Family planning in all its aspects		
Vaginal and pelvic examination		
Taking a vaginal smear, collecting of samples for various investigations etc.		

Other requirements

Knowledge of ethical and legal aspects of gynaecological problems:
    Age of consent
    Rape
    STD, etc.

Knowledge of the epidemiology of maternal and paternal morbidity and mortality

All trainees should have experience of being a member of a cardiac arrest team

Maintaining one's level of knowledge, skills and attitudes, by personal reading, informal discussions with colleagues, attendance at formal teaching courses

Chapter 29

The education and training of midwives

Christine Henderson

'Would you tell me please, which way I ought to go from here?'
'That depends a good deal on where you want to get to,' said the cat.
'I don't much care where . . .' said Alice.
'Then it doesn't matter which way you go,' said the cat.
(*Alice's Adventures in Wonderland*, 'The Pig and the Pepper', Lewis Carroll)

If we are concerned about the care of women in childbirth, the outcome of birth and its effect on the welfare of the mother, baby and family then we need to examine critically the way in which we train those involved to ensure the provision of a maternity service which is responsive to the needs of women. We need to be clear about the way we should proceed in the training of midwives and doctors. Evidence received by the government, during its review of the maternity services in 1992 (House of Commons Health Select Committee 1992) and the findings of the Expert Maternity group (Department of Health 1993) was explicit about the kind of service that users want. The government has endorsed the recommendations and wants health authorities and trusts to make known their purchasing plans for 1994/5 (National Health Service Management Executive 1994). The report acknowledges the importance of education and training and calls for a review of the roles, responsibilities and training of midwives, senior house officers in obstetrics, general practitioners and obstetricians.

This chapter will seek to put midwifery education into context by identifying briefly the main stages in its development. It will then examine in more detail the present system of educating midwives before reflecting on those issues likely to influence its future.

The training of midwives has undergone a number of changes since the 1902 Midwives Act first established a formal training programme. Midwifery education has evolved and developed considerably over the years and there are a number of sources where these are documented (Towler and Bramall 1986; Donnison 1988; Upritchard 1987; Bennett and Brown 1993). Curriculum changes have occurred as a result of government initiatives, consumer pressures and professional demand. These include an increase in length and content, the introduction of a variety of teaching and learning strategies coupled with various assessment methods to evaluate achievement.

Figure 29.1. Length of training for certification or registration as a midwife. RGN: Registered General Nurse; RSCN: Registered Sick Children's Nurse

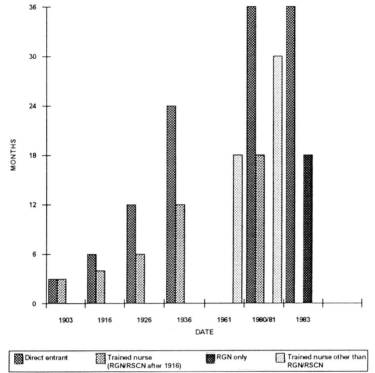

Reproduced from Bennett, V.R. and Brown, L.K. (1993) by kind permission of Churchill Livingstoi

Conjoint validation of midwifery education programmes, between higher education institutions and the English National Board, to degree and diploma level has inevitably brought significant curriculum changes notably in the theoretical component.

Prior to 1902 many women practising midwifery were apprenticed to older women and had no nurse qualification. With the introduction of a statutory framework regulating the training and practice of midwives those without a nurse background had, from 1916, to undertake a longer programme of training. To become a midwife in 1902 the requirements included three months' instruction by attending a series of lectures and attending those in childbirth under the supervision of a midwife. The emphasis was on practice and the prospective midwife could not take the examination without the certificate from the supervising midwife. With the changing place of birth from home to hospital, the introduction of the health service, an increase in technology and medical advances, the length of the training period increased to accommodate an ever expanding body of knowledge and practice. Figure 29.1 illustrates the changing length of the training period from, three months to six months in 1916 and then to 12 months in 1938

Figure 29.2. Routes to registration

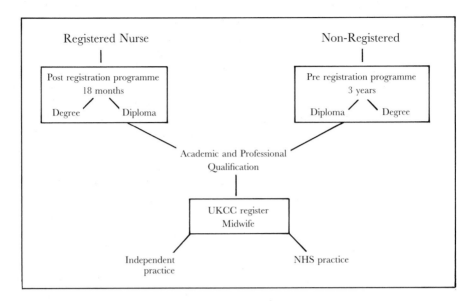

Note: Diploma and Degree levels were introduced in the late 1980s.

to be taken in two parts. This was changed to a single period of one year in 1971.

By 1981 the training period was increased to take into account the EEC Midwifery Directives (European Economic Community 1980a, b); for Registered Nurses this was 18 months, and for those without a nurse qualification it was three years (Figure 29.2).

Lack of opportunity for career progression for the 'direct entrant' contributed to reduced numbers in training and by 1980 only two training institutions provided this training (later referred to as Pre-registration Midwifery Education). The passing of the Nurses Midwives and Health Visitors Act in 1979 meant that the education of midwives became part of the debate related to the education of the nurse. The whole issue of the education and training needs of the future nurse and midwife has been the focus of reports for some time (Committee on Nursing 1972; Royal College of Nursing 1985; Royal College of Midwives 1987; English National Board 1985). In 1986 the publication of the United Kingdom Central Council's (UKCC) report (1987) on the Future Preparation of Nurses, Midwives and Health Visitors (Project 2000) stimulated the profession to argue that midwives should be viewed as different from nurses and that their preparation for practice should remain separate and that the 18-month and three-year programmes of training should continue unchanged.

Professional pressure, predicted manpower shortages, the need to recruit and retain midwives and the cost of training led the Department of Health to fund a research study focusing on the 'Direct-entrant' midwife (Radford and Thompson 1988).

Based on its findings the government in 1989 provided funds to assist in the development of seven three-year pre-registration programmes, one in each region. The number of pre-registration programmes approved by March 1993 totalled 31, 25 at diploma and six at degree level with 51 postregistration (18-month) diploma programmes for Registered Nurses. The demand for pre-registration midwifery programmes continues to rise and the figures given by the Nurses and Midwives Clearing House in March 1993 were 6532 applicants for 452 places (English National Board 1994). Advocates for the three year programme of education for 'non-nurses' argue that the students are highly motivated, they want to become midwives, not nurses, are not socialised into the NHS system and are therefore more likely to be critical of practice. Radford and Thompson (1988) in their study reported that these students would be more open to women's needs with the potential to become a more independent practitioner. It is considered by some to be the better route and many argue that it is the most cost-effective way to educate midwives. The importance of these developments could have far reaching effects on health resources and the delivery of care so the government in 1990 commissioned research to evaluate the effectiveness of these programmes (Kent and Maggs 1992).

However, many regions are already reducing the numbers of students in training especially those holding a registered nurse qualification and are targeting funds for pre-registration midwifery programmes only (Henderson 1993). In discussions with colleagues and from my own observations, drawn from experience of both programmes it does appear that the three-year programme is producing a more questioning and assertive midwife. However, whichever route is chosen, in order to practise as a midwife, the institution providing the educational programme must ensure that by the end of training the student achieves the outcomes contained in the Midwives Rules (UKCC 1993 pp.12–14) and that she is therefore able to fulfil the definition of a midwife as it appears in 'A Midwife's Code of Practice' (UKCC 1991). This is the definition adopted by the International Confederation of Midwives and the International Federation of Gynaecologists and Obstetricians following amendments to the World Health Organisation's original definition. The midwife:

> ... must be able to ... give the necessary supervision, care, advice to women during pregnancy, labour and the postpartum period ... conduct deliveries on her own responsibility ... care for the newborn infant ... she has an important task in health counselling and education which extends to areas of gynaecology, family planning, child care ... she may practise in hospitals, clinics, health units, domiciliary conditions or in any other service.

Practice is an important element of the educational programmes and a substantial period of time is allocated to experience in the clinical setting. Table 29.1 illustrates the allocation of hours to each programme and shows the proportion of time spent between theory and practice. This is an example from one training institution but guidance from the statutory body requires that a minimum of 33 per cent of the programme must be theory and 50 per cent practice.

Table 29.1.   Number of hours theory/practice in Midwifery Diploma Programmes e.g. of one institution

Educational programme	Total theory hours	Practice hours
Preregistration 3 years	1998 (1152)	2052 (1402)
Postregistration 18 months (RN)	862 (345)	1668

Other factors have necessitated changes to the curriculum, for example the changing pattern of provision of maternity services influenced by changes in government policy towards the National Health Service and the creation of Trusts and market forces. Altered working practices and a contracting workforce has meant reductions in the numbers of students being trained which will lead to a smaller but more educated workforce. With the amalgamation of colleges of nursing and midwifery and the move into higher education there are issues concerned with where and how midwifery education should be delivered. Currently there is an interest in shared learning and teaching. This is seen as a way forward in the hope that interprofessional learning will assist in the development, at an early stage, of relationships that create a foundation for working within a multidisciplinary team. However, interprofessional initiatives in education, elsewhere has caused organisational and attitudinal difficulties (Runciman 1989) and they need to be carefully planned to prevent detracting from the prime purpose of the required outcomes of a particular programme. An area where shared learning could work well is with those already qualified. Wherever interprofessional discussion takes place there are opportunities for learning but the value of these learning experiences depends heavily on the personalities involved. There are courses being developed for interprofessional groups (Horder 1992; Storrie 1992) and perhaps it is in this area that we should concentrate. There are concerns that programmes may become more academically orientated to the detriment of practice (Jackson 1993). Midwife teachers must continue to work alongside students and, in liaison with clinical staff, be involved in practice developments. In so doing they will remain in touch with users and carers and thus assist the integration of practice and theory.

The move into higher education is both stimulating and challenging and I believe that it will greatly enhance midwifery education by encouraging a spirit of enquiry that will inevitably lead to a more empowered workforce. Practice needs to be based on theory and that, in turn, should be based on a sound evaluation of practice. The opportunity to share with academics in a higher education environment will be beneficial to all groups particularly if there is teaching and research across disciplines.

On completion of training, midwives have acquired a broad knowledge base, have highly developed skills and may practise independently or within the NHS. The investment in training is considerable and yet many midwives within the

NHS fail to carry out the total role of the midwife, a situation that has caused concern for many years. The Ministry of Health in 1949 stated that, 'the midwife should be the practitioner of normal, she is the expert in normal childbearing in all its various aspects. The doctor is her partner in the detection and treatment of abnormalities'. Since that time concern has continued to be expressed regarding the underuse of the midwife's skills (Ministry of Health 1959; Royal College of Midwives 1977; Department of Health and Social Services 1980) and the duplication of roles in caring for women during childbearing (Robinson 1985).

The interrelationships between midwife, obstetrician and general practitioner are complex and varied. However, I believe that unless we recognise the contributions made by each and formally recognise the midwife as an expert in normal childbirth we will not achieve a 'woman'-centred service that is accessible and responsive to client need. Where midwives have the authority they are providing such a service in collaboration and in co-operation with medical colleagues.

Some new skills will be required to fulfil the total role and these need further discussion. Other aspects of training may need greater emphasis, for example, evaluative techniques, reflective practice, multicultural studies, interpersonal skills, problem solving and the ability to interrogate information systems.

There will be a need to review the practice element of the programme to ensure that appropriate preparation has been given to mentors and that the environment is suitable for education and is appropriately resourced, including access to the Cochrane database. Teachers will need to rethink their roles in terms of clinical input and research.

The value of education beyond registration was recognised in 1917 (Campbell 1917) but it was not until the 1950s that periodic refresher courses of one week's duration were introduced and became a statutory requirement. The nature of these has changed to allow midwives to explore ways of updating and developing their practice and there will be further changes as a result of the UKCC (1990) proposals. There are many continuing education opportunities in existence and still more are being developed to take into account the many organisational changes and altered patterns of care. These are accredited by institutions of higher education and many utilise a building blocks approach enabling midwives to work progressively towards diplomas, undergraduate and Masters degrees. Flexible approaches to learning using reflective practice techniques and contracted learning are helping practitioners to become confident and make innovations and change established practices. Educational programmes should be dynamic and sensitive to the changes brought about by practice developments, research or government policy. Existing programmes of education have a lot to commend them but we constantly need to ask, 'Are we preparing practitioners appropriately and adequately?'

The question can be answered by looking at the contribution practitioners make to care and the response of women receiving care. The care that we give should be based, as far as possible on reliable research and should be 'seamless' with each professional contributing in the most appropriate way for each woman and her baby. This has become a reality in some authorities where change is happening in an evolutionary way and consumer views are known and acted upon.

Elsewhere a revolution is necessary. The government appears to strongly want to promote and ensure a 'woman centred service'. It has accepted that the majority of births are normal and that the skills of the midwife should be utilised to the full. We must liaise, co-operate, collaborate and be committed to taking the challenge of this forward and decide upon how best we prepare ourselves, both midwives and doctors, so that we are 'fit for the purpose' i.e. to serve women in their childbearing experiences in the safest and best possible way.

References

Bennett, V.R. and Brown, L. (Eds) (1993) *Myles Textbook for Midwives* 12th edn. Edinburgh: Churchill Livingstone

Campbell, J.M. (1917) Report on the physical welfare of mothers and children in England and Wales Vol 2: Midwives and Midwifery. Carnegie Trust: Tingling and Co.

Committee on Nursing (1972) Report of the Committee on Nursing (Briggs Report) CMND 5115. London: HMSO

Department of Health (1993) *Changing Childbirth*. London: HMSO

Department of Health and Social Security (1980) *Second Report: Perinatal and Neonatal Mortality*. London: HMSO

Donnison, J. (1988) *Midwives and Medical Men: the History of the Struggle for the Control of Childbirth*. London: Historical Publishers

English National Board (1985) Professional Education/Training Courses Consultation Paper. London: ENB

English National Board (1994) *Midwifery Factfile*. London: ENB

European Economic Community (1980a) Recognition of diplomas, certificates and formal qualifications of midwives and right to provide services 80/154/EEC 21st January. *Off J Eur Commun* 23(L33) Feb 11, 1–7

European Economic Community (1980b) Pursuit of activities by midwives 80/155/EEC 21st January. *Off J Eur Commun* 23(L23) Feb 11. 8110

Henderson, C. (1993) Seminar paper: Pre-registration midwifery programmes, recruitment and selection. Doctoral studies. Birmingham: University of Birmingham

Horder, J. (1992) A national survey that needs to be repeated. *J Interprofessional Care* **6**, 65–71

House of Commons Health Select Committee (1992) *Second Report on the Maternity Services*. London: HMSO

Jackson, K. (1993) Midwifery degree programmes: who benefits? *Br J Midwifery* **1** 274–5

Kent, J. and Maggs, C. (1992) An evaluation of the effectiveness of pre registration midwifery education in England. Working paper 1 Research design. Bath: Maggs Research Associates

Ministry of Health (1959) Report of the Maternity Services Committee (Chairman Lord Cranbrook). London: HMSO

National Health Service Management Executive (1994) Woman-centred maternity services. EL(94)9. Leeds: Department of Health

Radford, N. and Thompson, A. (1988) Direct Entry: a preparation for midwifery practice. University of Surrey. Crown

Robinson, S. (1985) Midwives, obstetricians and general practitioners: the need for role clarification. *Midwifery* **1**, 102–3

Royal College of Midwives (1977) *Evidence to the Royal Commission on the NHS*. London: RCM

Royal College of Midwives (1987) *The Role and Education of the future Midwife in the United Kingdom*. London: RCM

Royal College of Nursing (1985) Commission on Nursing Education. The Education of Nurses: A New Dispensation (Judge Report). London: RCN

Runciman, P. (1989) Health assessment of the elderly at home: the case for shared learning. *J Adv Nurs* **14**, 111–19

Storrie, J. (1992) Mastering interprofessionalism. An enquiry into the development of Master's programmes with an interprofessional focus. *J Interprofessional Care* **6**, 253–9

Towler, J. and Bramall, J. (1986) *Midwives in History and Society.* London: Croom Helm

United Kingdom Central Council for Nursing, Midwifery and Health Visiting (1987) The future preparation of nurses, midwives and health visitors. *Project 2000.* London: UKCC

United Kingdom Central Council for Nursing, Midwifery and Health Visiting (1990) Report of the Post Registration Education and Practice Project. London: UKCC

United Kingdom Central Council for Nursing, Midwifery and Health Visiting (1991) *A Midwife's Code of Practice.* London: UKCC

United Kingdom Central Council for Nursing, Midwifery and Health Visiting (1993) *Midwives Rules.* London: UKCC

Upritchard, M. (1987) The evoluation of midwifery education. *Midwives Chronicle* January, 3–9

Chapter 30

Training of obstetricians

William Dunlop

Introduction

Almost all specialists in obstetrics and gynaecology in the United Kingdom are members of the Royal College of Obstetricians and Gynaecologists. They have obtained a basic specialist qualification (MRCOG) and have subsequently completed a period of higher training. The entire training programme currently occupies a minimum of seven and a half years (Figure 30.1).

In order to obtain the basic qualification of Membership of the Royal College of Obstetricians and Gynaecologists it is necessary to possess a recognised medical qualification, to complete and log a prescribed programme of training, to submit a book of case records and commentaries, to be recommended by two referees and to pass (or obtain exemption from) two examinations: Part 1 MRCOG, a multiple choice questionnaire in relevant basic science topics, and Part 2 MRCOG, a written, clinical and oral examination related to clinical practice.

Once MRCOG has been obtained, it is necessary to spend at least three years in higher training, a minimum of two at the grade of senior registrar. Training for one of the subspecialties in obstetrics and gynaecology (fetal medicine, gynaecological oncology, reproductive medicine and urogynaecology) requires additional specialised training and a period undertaking research. All training posts are inspected regularly by teams of visitors, in order to ensure that comparable standards are maintained.

Specialist medical training has come under considerable scrutiny in the past year, as the result of the report of the working group convened by the Chief Medical Officer (Department of Health 1993). Although final details have yet to be announced, it is certain that there will in future be a single training grade replacing those of registrar and senior registrar and that training will be more structured, so as to streamline the acquisition of knowledge and clinical skills leading to the award of a certificate of completion of specialist training (CCST). This process will be enhanced by the fact that postgraduate deans now have substantial responsibility for the payment of the salaries of trainees and are thus in a position to ensure that adequate training is provided independently of service needs (Department of Health 1991).

Figure 30.1.   Training in obstetrics and gynaecology in the UK

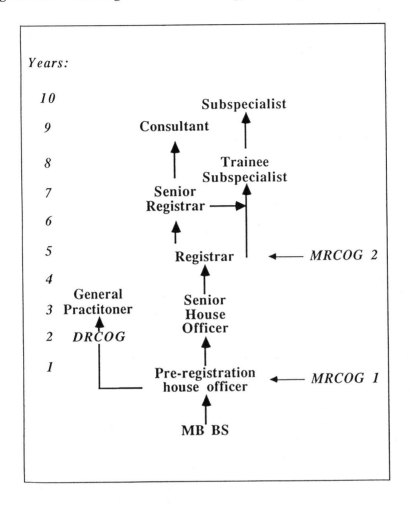

The Royal College of Obstetricians and Gynaecologists has been in the vanguard of planning for structured training (RCOG 1993b) and, as part of this process, educational aims and objectives of training in obstetrics and gynaecology have been defined (RCOG 1991) (Table 30.1). How will these objectives be met?

Structured training

A comprehensive syllabus of knowledge, skills and attitudes has been constructed. This has provided the framework for the development of a structured training

Table 30.1. MRCOG working party: educational objectives of training in obstetrics and gynaecology

Aim 1. To ensure that at the time of accreditation specialists have attained standards of knowledge and clinical skills adequate to permit them to undertake fully independent clinical practice.

Objectives
1. To establish a system of formative assessment continuing throughout the training period.
2. To provide at a suitable point during the training period a summative assessment. This will require:
   (a) the provision of a syllabus, the content of which should be reviewed regularly.
   (b) the definition of the clinical abilities which should have been acquired.
   (c) the definition of those personal and professional attributes which are desirable in a specialist.
3. To incorporate into both formative and summative assessments objective criteria for the evaluation of achievement.

Aim 2. To encourage the recruitment into and progress within the specialty of junior doctors of high calibre.

Objectives
1. To encourage the design and use of promotional material.
2. To publicise new developments in the specialty.
3. To encourage involvement in elective periods of clinical practice in obstetrics and gynaecology during undergraduate training.
4. To encourage undergraduates to undertake intercalated degrees involving aspects of obstetrics and gynaecology.
5. To devise structured training programmes which will permit postgraduates to fulfil their training needs throughout the range of specialist practice.
6. To ensure that individual postgraduate training programmes are supervised by a designated consultant in each training unit.

Aim 3. To encourage the philosophy of acquiring, assessing and applying new information and techniques in order to improve standards of practice.

Objectives
1. To ensure that clinical practice is based upon sound scientific principles.
2. To ensure that access to facilities for postgraduate training is provided for all trainees.
3. To ensure that assessments of training reflect new developments in the specialty.
4. To arrange regular meetings for the critical review of new clinical and scientific developments.
5. To arrange for formal appraisal of standards of practice.
6. To encourage research and ensure that recognition is given for research training.

Table 30.2.   DRCOG working party: educational objectives of training

Aim 1.   To ensure that doctors completing a defined programme of training have acquired knowledge, clinical skills and attitudes to enable them to undertake the practice of obstetrics and gynaecology within the setting of primary health care.

Objectives
1. To provide a syllabus for training, listing the knowledge, skills and attitudes to be acquired by trainees.
2. To ensure that the educational needs of trainees are met in the most effective way.
3. To devise systems of assessment, both formative and summative.

Aim 2.   To encourage the philosophy of updating knowledge and skills by means of further training or study.

Objectives
1. To devise training programmes for those trainees who wish to obtain special skills in addition to those required for DRCOG.
2. To ensure that relevant new information can be rapidly and widely disseminated to diplomates.

Aim 3.   To facilitate the integration of primary and secondary health care in relation to obstetrics and gynaecology.

Objectives
1. To involve general practitioners and midwives in training programmes.
2. To involve trainees in the evaluation of management beyond the hospital setting.

programme, ready to be implemented as soon as final decisions are made by the General Medical Council about the exact timing of specialist training in relation to general professional training.

The first six months of this programme coincides precisely with the requirements of the DRCOG, for which corresponding educational objectives have recently been set (RCOG 1993a) (Table 30.2). During this six months, it is considered essential that trainees, whether intending a career in general practice or in specialist obstetric practice, obtain instruction in and experience of normal pregnancy and childbirth. We consider that the health professionals most appropriate to provide that instruction include midwives and general practitioners and have been very pleased at the positive responses which the Royal College of Midwives and the Royal College of General Practitioners have made to our proposals to become more formally involved in the training of these doctors.

It is likely that structured specialist training can be completed within five years (Figure 30.2), a considerably shorter time than the average duration of training at present. Discussions about additional components of training, whether within the

Figure 30.2. Structured training in obstetrics and gynaecology

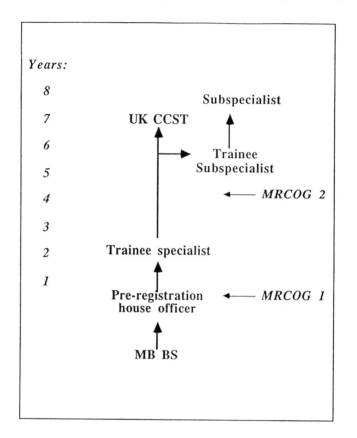

specialty (for example, towards subspecialist practice), in research or in other disciplines (as in our current MRCOG regulations) are still in progress.

Assessment

There will continue to be summative assessments at appropriate times during the training programme. Specialist trainees will continue to undertake a multiple choice examination in basic sciences and to prepare a book of case records and commentaries before being accepted for summative clinical assessment. A new feature of the MRCOG clinical assessment will be observation at the place of work by a visiting examiner, trained to assess a range of clinical skills and attitudes. Only when this component of the assessment exercise has been completed, will it be possible for a trainee to progress to the centrally organised examination.

Table 30.3. Scale for assessing competence in clincial skills

0 = insufficient opportunity to observe
1 = observer status
2 = assistant status
3 = requires close supervision
4 = competent with indirect supervision
5 = competent to be left unsupervised

The DRCOG and MRCOG examinations are currently undergoing substantial restructuring, however, in order to improve their validity and reliability. Both will contain an objective structured clinical examination (OSCE) and it is likely that there will also be some modification of the written components of both examinations. A strict timetable for these changes has been agreed: the first of the new DRCOG examinations will be held in November 1994, while the new MRCOG assessment arrangements will be in place by 1996.

Potentially of more importance than any of these developments, however, is the introduction of a clearly defined system of formative assessment, to be undertaken throughout the duration of training. The competence of each trainee will be assessed by those responsible for training at that time, thus providing immediate feedback for the trainee and identifying areas of strength and weakness. Assessors will include not only district tutors in obstetrics and gynaecology (one of whom has been identified in every training unit) but also other members of staff with direct responsibility for supervising the task under consideration. Thus midwives, general practitioners, registrars, senior registrars and other consultants will be involved in this exercise. A simple but realistic scale for assessing competence has been devised (Table 30.3) and appropriate targets at various points duing training have been assigned for every clinical skill in the syllabus. Work is already well advanced for the implementation of formative assessment during the first six months of training and pilot schemes are being devised for the assessment of the remainder of the syllabus in time to coincide with the implementation of the changes in summative assessment.

Conclusion

Within the last three years, the Royal College of Obstetricians and Gynaecologists has made considerable efforts to define clearly the educational objectives of training, to formulate structured programmes intended to meet these objectives within an appropriate timescale and to improve the efficacy of its assessment processes. Implementation is now being actively pursued.

References

Department of Health (1991) Postgraduate Medical and Dental Education. Unnumbered working paper. London: Department of Health

Department of Health (1993) Report of the Working Group on Specialist Medical Training. London: Department of Health

Royal College of Obstetricians and Gynaecologists (1991) Report of the MRCOG Working Party. London: RCOG

Royal College of Obstetricians and Gynaecologists (1993a) Report of the DRCOG Working Party. London: RCOG

Royal College of Obstetricians and Gynaecologists (1993b) Report of the RCOG Working Party on Structured Training. London: RCOG

Chapter 31

The role of the anaesthetist

Anthony P. Rubin

Many women require advice and care from anaesthetists before, during or after childbirth. This is frequently urgent, and may occur by day or night.

The antenatal period

The anaesthetist may be involved in discussion about methods of pain relief in labour, their advantages and disadvantages and their availability. This may be done at parentcraft classes, by individual consultation or by prepared material ideally in relevant languages.

Where problems have arisen in a previous confinement, women may have anxieties that can often be allayed by an appropriate consultation.

The anaesthetist should also be involved in the assessment of those women with medical or obstetric conditions that might influence choice or method of analgesia or anaesthesia or increase the likelihood of it being required.

Anaesthetic staffing

Anaesthetic deaths, both in total numbers and as a contributor to maternal mortality, have continued to fall, from 10.5 per million in 1973–75 to 1.7 per million in 1988–90 (Department of Health 1994).

Recent figures show a fall in deaths directly due to anaesthesia from six in 1985–87 to only four in 1988–90. There was also one late death in which anaesthesia was the most important factor, aspiration of gastric contents having occurred during induction of anaesthesia.

However, there is no room for complacency as most of the deaths have avoidable factors, and we do not have accurate figures for the morbidity resulting from 'near misses'. There must be provision of a 24 h anaesthetic service with adequately trained anaesthetists.

It is accepted that obstetric analgesia and anaesthesia requires particular skills and has particular dangers that make it unsuitable for unsupervised first-year trainees or occasional anaesthetists. There must be a named consultant with responsibility for the organisation and management of obstetric analgesia and anaesthesia. There should be at least one consultant session per 500 deliveries up to 3000 and full time cover above that number (Association of Anaesthetists of Great Britain and Ireland and the Obstetric Anaesthetists Association 1987).

There will need to be additional consultant input of particular skills, e.g. intensive care management.

> Great strides have been made in the provision of dedicated consultant sessions for obstetric anaesthesia during the past decade, but the direct supervision and training of junior staff by consultants is still inadequate in a number of hospitals. (Department of Health 1994)

> The provision of adequate consultant supervision is particularly difficult in the smaller hospitals and in those with separate maternity units and every effort should be made to bring maternity services onto the main hospital site. (Department of Health 1994)

Adequate arrangements for study leave for consultants to maintain their skills and knowledge by continuing medical education must be provided. Locum cover is unlikely to be satisfactory in the obstetric unit where teamwork is essential.

There should be adequate numbers of trainees to avoid onerous hours and to permit proper training with direct consultant supervision. There should be regular assessment of their skills, knowledge and performance. There should be adequate time for regular teaching episodes, and a number of multidisciplinary sessions are essential.

Techniques

Epidural as well as other methods of analgesia should be widely available and the epidural should include the possibility of bolus and infusion methods. Recent figures show variation in different regions of the country, but overall only 71 per cent of units provide Entonox, pethidine and epidurals (Chamberlain *et al.* 1990).

About 25 per cent of women chose epidural analgesia as a method of pain relief in labour in units where it was available on a 24 h basis, but the figure is much higher if Caesarean sections are included (Chamberlain *et al.* 1990).

> Epidural anaesthesia can allow a woman, if she wishes, to remain fully conscious and aware during birth, even when delivered by Caesarean section. Moreover it can be a safer option than general anaesthesia. (Department of Health 1993)

Anaesthesia for operative obstetrics should include both regional and general anaesthesia. The anaesthetic response time should enable a Caesarean section to start within 20 min of the clinical decision to proceed. This will be facilitated if the anaesthetist has prior knowledge of the particular problem and has been able to assess the woman in advance. It also presupposes that there is a dedicated anaesthetic assistant available who must be an Operating Department Practitioner, midwife or registered nurse who has completed the ENB 182 course in anaesthesia (Assistance for the Anaesthetist 1988): A postoperative pain relief service if it exists for surgical patients should be extended to include the obstetric unit (HMSO 1994).

Complicated obstetrics

The anaesthetist should be involved as early as possible where complications are likely or have occurred. This has been stressed repeatedly but still only too rarely happens:

> Anaesthetists have a crucial role to play in the care of some women who become acutely ill in pregnancy, labour and following the birth. To minimise mortality and ill-health it is essential that anaesthetists are involved as early as possible when these complications occur or are anticipated. (Department of Health 1993)

It is difficult to understand the occasional failure to recognise the often insidious deviations from normal labour, and the reluctance to invite relevant specialists to advise. 'Above all it is vital that all professionals involved in the provision of maternity services hold paramount the safety of the women and babies entrusted to their care' (HMSO 1994).

Neonatal resuscitation will usually be managed by the paediatric service but all staff including midwives, obstetricians and anaesthetists should be familiar with the full skills of neonatal resuscitation.

Back-up facilities

There must be adequate back-up facilities including pathology, blood transfusion and pharmacy. Adequate operating theatre, recovery room, resuscitation, high dependency unit and intensive therapy unit facilities must be available.

Recovery room facilities

Deaths to which anaesthesia contributed included six deaths which were associated with substandard postoperative care. 'Midwifery staff deputed to look after post-operative patients should be specifically trained in monitoring, the care of the airway and resuscitative procedures and should be supervised by a defined anaesthetist at all times' (HMSO 1994).

Resuscitation

Facilities and skills in maternal resuscitation must be available and all staff should be trained in the methods, aware of the particular problems, and undergo regular refresher courses and re-assessment. Often this will be supervised by a resuscitation trainer but in their absence the anaesthetic department should take responsibility.

High dependency (HDU) and intensive care (ICU) facilities

Many complications of childbirth require HDU or ITU facilities. It has been estimated that about 10 HDU cases will arise per 1000 deliveries (Weaver personal communication). It is likely that at least one ITU case per 1000 deliveries is also the minimum to be expected (Graham and Luxton 1989).

There should be adequate premises, equipment, and medical and specialist support staff. Skill in the insertion of central venous and arterial lines must be provided to aid in the management of severe haemorrhage. The group with these skills are likely to be anaesthetists as they regularly insert these lines and manage massive haemorrhage in the operating theatre. Many 'routine' surgical operations result in blood loss that in the obstetric unit would certainly be defined as massive haemorrhage:

> It should be standard practice to insert large bore IV cannulae and a CVP line, and to call for more senior obstetric and anaesthetic assistance as soon as severe blood loss is observed or suspected. Summon all extra staff required, including obstetricians, midwives and nurses. In particular the duty anaesthetic registrar should be contacted immediately as in most obstetric units the anaesthetist will take over the management of the fluid replacement. (HMSO 1994)

In the latest report, 44 out of 238 direct and indirect deaths were due to adult respiratory distress syndrome (ARDS) or associated complications, of whom 18 had hypertensive disorder of pregnancy (HMSO 1994).

The vast majority of ITUs in this country are run by anaesthetists who have acquired the requisite skills and knowledge to be able to care for the sick patient with ARDS or multi-organ failure. The obstetric patient who requires HDU or ITU care should be given the benefit of advice from a suitable anaesthetist while the midwife and obstetrician remain closely involved in their care.

There must be recognised routes of access to HDU and ITU facilities together with equipment and personnel for safe transfer when required.

Education

Anaesthetists have an important role to play in the teaching of midwives and subjects in which they might be involved include pain relief in labour, the assessment and identification of anaesthetic problems, the preparation and problems of regional and general anaesthesia, resuscitation and high dependency and intensive care.

They should play their part in the setting up of protocols for the management of the aspects and complications of childbirth in which they have expertise and are likely to be involved. In view of their wide involvement in many aspects of the care of the woman in childbirth, they also have a clear role in the teaching of undergraduates attached to the obstetric unit.

Audit

Data are required on work-load, safety, patient satisfaction and clinical practice aspects. These data should be analysed to identify deficiencies and to facilitate modification of practice where appropriate.

Research

Research is essential to ensure progress and introduction of new ideas after adequate trial and proof of their benefit. It should be seen to be an asset rather than a disadvantage and to enhance the quality of care and not just the prestige of the individuals.

Conclusions

Every mother is entitled to full information about childbirth. This must include the role of the anaesthetist in the provision of pain relief, anaesthesia for operative obstetrics, post-partum pain relief and the management of associated problems. They should see the anaesthetist as a friend and advisor and not as a threat.

We feel that we are the group who offer the most choice to the women, and that it is wrong that midwives as the primary carer should have the sole right to influence women in their choices. We, as professionals, know our role in childbirth as well as other professional groups, and expect to be able to ensure that the woman receives the most complete and best information and advice.

For the safety of the mother we have to try to see as many as possible, if not during the antenatal period, then during their hospital admission. This is the anaesthetist's duty and the mother's right. We take the responsibility for any anaesthetic involvement including epidurals and we cannot perform this duty unless we are in possession of all the material facts about the woman. If we are not, unacceptable delay may arise while history taking, examination and explanation takes place, and the outcome may be jeopardised, e.g. the increased and unnecessary use of general anaesthesia.

We have to be allowed to do our job properly. We cannot accept lower standards than it is possible to provide and stand by while unacceptable morbidity and mortality happens.

References

Association of Anaesthetists of Great Britain and Ireland and the Obstetric Anaesthetists Association (1987) *Anaesthetic Services for Obstetrics – A Plan for the Future*. London: Association of Anaesthetists

Association of Anaesthetists of Great Britain and Ireland (1988) *Assistance for the Anaesthetist*. London: Association of Anaesthetists

Chamberlain, G., Wraight, A. and Steer, P. (Eds) (1990) *Pain and its Relief in Childbirth: The Results of a National Survey Conducted by the National Birthday Trust*. Edinburgh: Churchill Livingstone, pp. 47, 51

Department of Health (1993) *Changing Childbirth*. Part 1: Report of the Expert Maternity Group. London: HMSO

Department of Health (1994) *Report on Confidential Enquiries into Maternal Deaths in the United Kingdom 1988–1990*. London: HMSO

Graham, S.C. and Luxton, M.C. (1989) The requirement for intensive care support for the pregnant population. *Anaesthesia* **44**, 581–4

Chapter 32

The role of the paediatrician

B. Garth McClure

The training of obstetricians, general practitioners and midwives by paediatricians is fundamental in their professional careers since all will be concerned with the successful outcome of pregnancy. The core of knowledge to be conveyed is the same for all three groups but will vary considerably in emphasis and degree. For example, the general practitioner would be more interested in the long-term outcome of children, the midwife would be concerned about the effects of pregnancy problems on the fetus and the obstetrician must have a very profound knowledge of the prenatal environment and of the effects of disease of pregnancy on the outcome of babies and children.

Who should do the training?

The training should be given by a *neonatologist*, not by a paediatrician. The neonatologist has the knowledge of the events in life that occur prenatally or in the labour ward and their primary role is to understand the pathophysiology of neonatal disease in order that it may be prevented in future cases.

Where should training take place?

The most appropriate place where training of all three groups can take place is in the neonatal unit of a busy maternity hospital. In such units, the treatment of sick newborn babies is a daily occurrence and this is the only place where any person can gather sufficient experience in a relatively short period of time to gain any level of expertise. It is the view of many that obstetricians in training should spend at least six months in a neonatal intensive care unit with responsibility for care of the new born in the labour ward and also for doing follow-up clinics with the neonatal consultants. This would allow the obstetrician to gain deeper insights into the prevention of problems and the management and treatment of sick babies and be better able to plan their obstetric practice. For the general practitioner trainee, the experience related to neonatal resuscitation techniques learned is applicable to all ages and they will also learn a great deal about child development, together with deviations from the norm. The midwife would gain insight into the effects of pregnancy on newborn babies and develop skills in resuscitation, and in many cases, may choose a career in neonatal medicine.

The role of the neonatologist

The first role of the neonatologist is to describe the potential and limitations of neonatology. It is surprising how often other health professionals have preconceived ideas of neonatal paediatrics – they either view neonatologists as some form of 'wunderkind' or, on the other hand, as people who keep alive children who would be better off dead. This requires the neonatologist to explore with the three groups what is done in principle for sick babies, describe the limitations of his knowledge and to indicate where research may be carried out in future.

Occasionally one gains the impression that the neonatologist's function is purely to criticise obstetricians and midwives and their management of particular patients. This is and should remain far from the case. Both the Royal College of Obstetricians and Gynaecologists and the British Association of Perinatal Medicine have addressed the issue of perinatal medicine and what it means. Quite clearly, what we are seeking is a marriage of different disciplines to achieve the best possible outcome for the mother and the baby. This can only be achieved with a profound knowledge of what perinatal medicine is. Caring for pregnancies can only take place at the highest possible level if there is very close cooperation between all health professionals concerned. This means constant analysis of outcomes and it must mean from time to time that there is conflict. However, it must be said that such controversial issues are inevitable and it is only by full discussion of all the events that we can all take part in the learning process. There is no room for foolish pride in the field of perinatal medicine; this can only lead to harm being done to our patients.

One major function of the neonatologist is to reinforce in other health professionals the knowledge that obstetrics is unpredictable and that the diagnosis of normal pregnancy and outcome can only be made retrospectively. There is a rather dangerous idea currently in vogue that low risk pregnancy and labour can be identified before the event. This is most certainly not the case for all patients. Every obstetrician and neonatologist in practice can think of occasions when an apparently normal pregnancy has developed rapid, serious complications which required the cooperation of a whole team of people in order to ensure a successful outcome. Every one of us has experienced a sudden cord prolapse or abruption or a baby who has been born in need of resuscitation when no indication of such a condition was apparent. Most neonatologists are firmly of the belief that delivery in hospital is preferable if one is to consider the baby as the end product of pregnancy and not the by-product. All the three health professionals should be made totally familiar with the examination of the normal newborn baby. All babies should be examined properly to detect any obvious malformation but deviations from the norm, especially those that are subtle, can only be detected if expert attention is given. It is fairly straightforward to diagnose a condition such as Down's syndrome or spina bifida but there are many more subtle signs of latent disease in babies that can be detected only by expert observation. For example, anybody who looks after newborn babies relies very heavily on the nursing staff to detect and describe signs which are not obvious on only one examination. For example, cardiac disease is very often not detectable in the newborn period but careful observation by a trained nurse may alert the attending paediatrician to potential cardiac problems, e.g. if the nurses discover unusual respirations, difficulty with feeding, or perhaps the most important sign of all, that the baby 'does not feel right'. A great deal of experience is needed if one is to become well versed in the nature of latent disease in babies but I feel that if we have inculcated into our staff the ability to always ask the question 'Does the baby look well?' then we will have gone some way towards achieving this goal.

The neonatologist must instruct all three groups on resuscitation of the newborn. Even in the best run hospitals babies are born who unexpectedly require help immediately and the person present at the delivery must be able to apply simple resuscitation measures. The techniques of resuscitation are simple and most neonatologists do them reflexly but such people are doing these tasks regularly and in well-equipped units with assistance and the staff are properly qualified. The Cumberlege Report has recently suggested that home confinement should be allowed provided *two* professionals trained and practised in neonatal resuscitation are present at the delivery so that one is free to provide resuscitation if necessary. However, the need would not be often and such professionals would have difficulty in retaining skills at resuscitation if they were only using them infrequently.

The care of the low birthweight baby is in the remit of the neonatologist and it is not necessary that the neonatologist trains all three groups in all that he does in the intensive care unit. However, what is of fundamental importance is first that he can convey to the three groups how their actions affect the outcome of the baby. Most of us feel the condition of the baby at the time of birth is of major significance in terms of the long-term outcome. Anyone then who is responsible for delivering mothers should be in a position to ensure the condition of the baby at birth is optimal. It is known for example that diseases of pregnancy affect the fetus and that drugs used in the therapy for such conditions or analgesics in labour also have major affects on the newborn. There are many obvious examples, such as the administration of steroids and the use of anticonvulsant agents in pre-eclampsia. The second important point is that the delivery of a low birthweight infant requires an expert attendant. Gentle, controlled delivery of the low birth-weight baby has an advantageous effect on the outcome as, probably, has the timing of cord clamping etc., but in practice there seems to be an unseemly haste to get the baby into the hands of the neonatologist. I would advocate control, coupled with gentleness and I would suggest that the beneficial effects of these one or two minutes may be of major significance with regard to the outcome for the newborn infant.

It is of vital importance that all those concerned with pregnancy are aware of the long-term outcome studies that have been carried out extensively in babies with a variety of conditions. This is particularly true of the low birthweight baby and each hospital should have its own data. In my own hospital we know that the handicap rate for babies born less than 1500 g is 5 per cent, that the mean IQ of the non-handicapped children is 100 and that 20 per cent have learning difficulties. These data only apply to the Royal Maternity Hospital, Belfast in 1990 and to no other hospital at any other time. Of particular interest is the child with a congenital malformation. The development of ultrasound and various other genetic tests have led to an increased awareness of prenatal malformation. However, the effects of such malformations require to be explained to all three groups by the neonatologist or the genetist. The reason for stating this is that there may be an unreal perception of the effects of such conditions on the babies and the long-term outcome. For example, it is distressing to see people advocating termination of pregnancy for malformations which are in fact correctable by surgeons.

There is also some evidence to suggest, for example, that the method of delivery may influence the outcome for certain congenital malformations and this evidence should be known by the obstetricians. In addition, it is quite clearly necessary from time to time to consult with the paediatric or cardiac surgeons prior to the delivery of the baby, and at that stage, it is reasonable that the timing of the delivery be discussed. Optimal care can only be given when those who are having to look after the baby after birth are immediately available at the time of the birth. This clearly means an organisational problem in that obstetricians, neonatologists and paediatric surgeons must agree on a time that suits all three teams. It is really not good enough in the 1990s to deliver a baby semi-electively with no provision being made for intensive care or paediatric surgery.

In conclusion, the neonatologist's role is to stress the team approach to perinatal care, to provide training related to neonatal resuscitation and stress the importance of assessing outcome.

Chapter 33

How can we promote learning together?
Discussion

Patel: A number of reports, from Winterton (House of Commons Health Select Committee 1992), Cumberlege (Department of Health 1993), the RCOG (1991; 1993), the joint RCOG, RCM and RCGP report (1992) relating to change, all stressed the need for interprofessional involvement in training. To bring it up to date, the Implementation Group of the RCOG is currently looking at ways to involve midwives and general practitioners. We hope to produce educational targets in terms of training of vocational trainees and obstetricians in the first six months of training where the midwives and the GPs will be involved.

Dunlop: We hope that learning together will be an important part of future training of obstetricians, of general practitioners, and of midwives. But I do find myself confused about a number of things and one of them is about the precise role of the general practitioner in providing maternity services in the future. If we are not clear about that it is difficult to define aims and objectives of training general practitioners.

Do Dr McKinlay and Dr Styles have a clear view about the aim of training of general practitioners in obstetrics?

Styles: The role is perhaps becoming clearer as a result of these discussions. The general practitioner's role is changing not just in relation to obstetrics, but in the whole provision of primary care services. In the past as general practioners we prided ourselves on the one-to-one relationship we had with our patients and the consulting skills that we had been able to develop and deploy in the consulting room. It is clear since 1990 and the Health Service reforms that now we shall have to develop skills outside the consulting room, to meet the health care needs not just of the patient on a one-to-one basis but the whole population of patients that is registered with us. That is a fundamental change in role and responsibilities for us and we shall have to adapt our training programmes so that we can deal with populations of patients. We will have to be able to make assessments of the health care needs of these populations and then be able to go and either meet these needs directly or else purchase (if we are fundholders) or commission other services.

If we apply that pattern of responsibility to obstetric services, then our role begins to emerge a little more clearly and it is different from the responsibilities that we have had hitherto. Some general practitioners will want to be able to provide the whole range of obstetrics services including intrapartum care; they are likely to be a minority. Others will be purchasing intrapartum care either directly or through commissioning arrangements. Some general practitioners will want to continue to be involved in antenatal care and postnatal care only; the proportion of general practitioners who will want to be involved in this way is unknown.

But I would see the general practitioners' prime role in the future in relation to maternity services, is ensuring that mothers have available to them maternity care of high quality, whether provided from within the practice or from services, midwifery and obstetrics services, outside the practice. In effect we are becoming much more the monitors of the provision of care rather than the direct care providers.

Patel: In that scenario does Dr Lindsay Smith have any comments about how each profession's involvement in the vocational training of obstetricians might develop?

Smith: It is worth emphasising that we really must decide what services we intend to provide in obstetrics, gynaecology and family care as GPs; that future service provision should determine the training which we undergo. I can see a looming conflict between possible service requirements in junior hospital posts against the educational needs that future vocational GPs would have, and I think it will become increasingly difficult to balance one against the other.

At the present time most partners required to be eligible for the obstetric list need to do six months obstetrics and gynaecology. I understand there are moves to abolish the obstetric list and if that occurs it will be interesting to see how many trainees continue to do obstetrics and gynaecology, particularly if only a minority of GPs will provide intrapartum care. Perhaps the majority will start purchasing or commissioning care and not providing it within the practice. But it is rather difficult to say how the training should go at the moment because we are very much in a situation of flux and not knowing quite how the GPs' role in women's health care will develop over the next five to ten years.

Dunlop: Service needs are considerably less important than they were at one time now that postgraduate deans in England and Wales hold 50 per cent of the salaries for trainees and in Scotland 100 per cent. As we move forward in training we will see that SHOs have much less service involvement than they have had in the past.

The other feature that we might address is whether in fact every hospital in the country needs to be a training hospital; that would not be the case in most European countries, nor in North America, or in Australia. Service needs perhaps can be overemphasised in this context and whereas they may be important at the moment, in five or ten years time they could be much less important than now.

Young: I think there will be a gradual change brought about by how women choose what they want from maternity services. If midwifery can provide as good continuity now as most general practitioners do, general practice involvement antenatally will gradually diminish because women will prefer to go to see midwives. Any kind of blanket shift at the moment would be precipitate; we have no evidence that shifting general practitioners out of antenatal care would be of benefit to women in this country. There needs to be a gradual change with women being offered a real choice. My guess is that most will head towards midwives as midwives can be seen to provide continuity.

What I would hate to see is the removal of general practitioners from obstetric care because someone deems it to be a good thing. We do not know it will be a good thing. There would be a rather looser and hard-to-define loss to the whole practice of family medicine in the UK if family doctors had no experience at all of what pregnancy and childbirth meant. I cannot see that we can be good doctors to our female patients, to their children and to their partners if we lose the complete experience of what pregnancy and birth is about.

Jenkins: I should like to raise a structural problem over the joint learning experiences between midwives and doctors learning obstetrics. The midwife in training is still undergoing her pre-diploma or undergraduate training, whereas the doctor learning obstetrics is already a qualified doctor and is beginning his specialty training in some way, whether it is obstetrics or it is general practice. That raises an issue of whether we should be looking back into undergraduate medical and midwifery training programmes to make some initial links as well as the link that happens later.

I believe there are certain communication modules that we should be encouraging at that very basic level so that there could be an initial understanding of the different roles of the two groups.

Patel: I shall come back to that comment about midwives being involved at the stage of vocational training or initial training of obstetricians. We must remember that undergraduate training varies a lot from university to university.

Downe: How do the others involved in delivering maternity care, including anaesthetists and the paediatricians, feel about refresher courses and how they perceive that the skills of the various professionals are kept up to date over time? Perhaps it is particularly a question for the GPs. Clearly midwives cannot continue to practise if we do not maintain our skills under statutory requirements. I am not necessarily saying that the refresher courses we attend are proven in terms of their outcomes, but certainly the intent is there that maintenance of skills must be formally kept up. I am wondering how the other professional groups view this.

Patel: General practitioners, midwives and obstetricians have mandatory Continuous Medical Education (CME). The RCOG started this on 1 January 1994 and we may all be obliged to produce evidence of our Continuing Medical Education.

Styles: GPs' continuing education is not mandatory but each gains a postgraduate education allowance when participating in approved courses. More than 90 per cent are successful in achieving the minimum requirement of five days' study a year.

Patel: So money makes it mandatory. We need to discuss how in the future we can learn together as a specialist, a midwife, or a general practioner to ensure that we understand what services we provide and how we relate.

Hall: I acknowledge that the training of general practioners in hospitals has been execrable. They should have some of their training in general practice, their obstetric training, but there is a problem of volume of work. They have only a small chance of seeing some of the important obstetrical complications that they would have to detect, such as pre-eclampsia. The incidence of that condition is such that if they only have experience of 100 women over a year, they may not even see one case of severe pre-eclampsia.

We fully acknowledge the need for us to pay attention to the trainees' educational objectives but we should not throw the baby away with the bathwater.

Rubin: Clearly people need basic training and then they need refresher courses. The problem is that the numbers of sick women involved are very small. Our paediatrician made this very clear about neonatal resuscitation. Similarly it is impossible, even with refresher or CME courses, for people to maintain their skills in maternal resuscitation if they are doing it infrequently and the same applies to HDU and ITU for the numbers are just too small. Data from Birmingham suggest that 1/100 maternities need HDU care and 1/1000 need ITU care. No amount of refresher courses could enable people to maintain the necessary skills when numbers are so small. The only people who can maintain the necessary skills are the people who are doing it all the time.

McKinlay: We have some experience of trainee GPs and health visitors in training meeting together and that experience was depressing. The prejudices were already ingrained and the learning that went on was cathartic. I do not think however that means we would shy away from it. My suggestion is that training in the future would be community based and released to hospital rather than hospital based and released to community. For a low-tech training, a release to the hospital for certain experiences might be useful.

Coming back to the original question of the role of the GP, the woman will still come to the GP for the diagnosis of her pregnancy and for a discussion of what facilities are available to her. What do midwives feel about their role in the pregnancy that does not go on to childbirth such as the counselling of the woman who is contemplating termination of pregnancy? As a GP I have recently had a difficult time with a woman who has had this terrible decision to make.

The loss of bonding with the mother by the doctor not being present at her children's births affects the continuing care of the mother throughout her life and the whole family. Since my facilities for GP-maternity were taken away from me it is one of the things that I miss more than anything. For the reasons that Professor McClure mentioned, if women are to deliver in the community, the midwife, an essential part of the primary health care team, and the GP, should both be there.

Walkinshaw: The study group is about the maternity services and we can now begin to see some of the threads coming together about the impact of the changes in education on how we are capable of delivering the service. If I put on my clinical director hat, then I think that if the GPs are marginalised within maternity care there will be fewer SHOs.

The three Cs, as I call them, Cumberlege, Calman and CME, buffet consultant obstetricians in trying to free time to train and teach. It is highly likely that soon the number of bodies that we actually have within a consultant unit will be many fewer than we have at the moment. My fear is that I am not sure that midwifery training and consultant Continuing Medical Education is moving quickly enough to fill a gap that will probably be there within the next five years. We will not have as many SHOs or registrars. There may be more consultants although it is not clear who will give me the money to employ them. These developments will influence how the service is put together and probably much more quickly than most of us appreciate.

Zander: It is too early to say what the role of the general practitioner is likely to be. If we go into the functions of an educational programme, it is to teach knowledge and skills, but also to teach attitudes, a theme which has come through this meeting. Returning to the earlier discussion whether there are fundamental differences between the attitudes of doctors and midwives, I believe that there would be a great deal to be gained for the trainee general practitioners if they had a greater input in their learning from midwifery, from a greater integration in the teaching and learning together. If the emphasis for the trainee general practitioners was much more focused on normality and many of the things which govern the training of midwifery, it would make the working of the primary care team much more productive.

One of the difficulties we have as doctors and midwives in general practice is that the doctor is to a very large extent seen somehow in the obstetric model whereas it does not fit in the primary care scenario. If we can really get together as teachers, midwives, obstetricians and GPs, and organise the educational programme to achieve certain attitudes, that would be productive. Whether that happens in hospital or in the community, will vary in different localities.

Dunlop: There is a substantial need to integrate undergraduate teaching with midwifery teaching. We are fortunate in Newcastle in having a BSc course in midwifery. Those midwives participate in some of our undergraduate sessions and some of our undergraduate teaching is conducted by midwives, and both work very well. There is a need, however, for integration at postgraduate level as well.

Some of the targets can only be assessed by people who are supervising the actual skill being tested; if that is normal delivery or repairing episiotomy it is very likely to be a midwife. There may be other aspects which would be better supervised by general practitioners and we would very much hope to see an integration at that sort of level. One thing that it might be important to set down, that we found difficult when establishing our BSc course in midwifery, was the entrance requirements for university matriculation which are really quite different from the entrance requirements to nursing. I would be interested to hear what the entrance requirements are for midwifery training in the Netherlands where they have a rather more elaborate training programme than we have here.

Eskes: Last year we started a four-year course. Students must have completed secondary schooling and have an A-grade in biology and chemistry. They get a full-time four-year course and in that time they do between 40 and 50 deliveries. They also get theoretical courses in physiology, chemistry, the normal birth, the pathology of obstetrics and some gynaecological training.

Smith: The service requirement of SHOs is diminishing and is likely to reduce further in the future. SHOs are now meant to be supernumerary on the labour ward and perhaps soon in the antenatal clinic as well; they are there to learn rather than to make decisions about care. It is my belief that one can make a good case for most obstetrics, gynaecological and family planning training to be practice based with sessional release during the day to special hospital clinics such as those in gynaecology or fertility. The trainee could provide a one in four on-call service provision in the hospital for night care. Thus it would be perfectly feasible instead of having the six-months job based in hospital with the occasional half-day release into practice, to have a six-months post based in the community with release for specific learning experieces in hospital out patients, and also to be on call in the hospital to learn the emergency experience that we all need for things we may have to deal with rarely as GPs.

On the matter of CME, re-certification of GPs is coming, probably every five years, to show that they are competent at various procedures. As with the other add-on extras which GPs do, such as child health surveillance and minor surgery, the maternity services will require a five-year re-certification if they are to continue to provide maternity care.

Patel: If the SHOs are based in the community and come in to learn obstetrics, what would they do outside? Now when they do their SHO post for vocational training in the hospital, they are concentrating on getting obstetrical and gy-naecological experience. If they are outside how will they get the concentrated experience that they get now?

Smith: A large percentage of my consultations every day concern gynaecology and family planning. We could take a larger view and say that the majority of obstetric vocational training for general practice should be practice based, as it is in other specialties. Most training in obstetrics for obstetricians is in their specialty and it seems crazy that most of the training for GPs is not in their chosen specialty but is in hospital jobs of various types. There is a strong case that most of the training that GPs have, should be practice based and that over that period of two or three years, they would gain probably as much experience as the hospital six months but it would be less concentrated. They could also have sessional release for paediatric on call over a period of time, or psychiatric on call, and they could build experience not dissimilar to what they get at the moment but over a longer period of time.

Page: The proposals made through *Changing Childbirth* will inevitably mean that the majority of maternity care takes place in the community. The schemes that have been successful have put into practice the principle of the midwife following the woman and her family through the system and we have to conceive of an integrated maternity service where the hospital is a part of that service. Inevitably that will mean that the majority of midwives are working very closely with the primary healthcare team although there will always be specialist midwives who work in high-risk areas and work in hospital for various reasons.

The English National Board is moving very quickly to help ensure that midwives are trained to put into practice the requirements that are described in *Changing Childbirth*; there is a strategy already in place and we are moving very quickly with that. The majority of midwives would welcome shared learning with other health professionals because there are so many skills and ideals that we share. As far as entry requirements are concerned, there are minimum standards but they tend to vary according to the validating institution; because we are now moving into higher education some of the entry requirements are higher in some areas than in others. For instance, for the honours degree programme in Oxford the requirement was three A levels but that could be challenged. In general, the academic standing was very high and we had 115 applicants for 11 places in the first year. I think we will inevitably see a higher academic standing and we are already seeing a different quality of midwife graduating from our diploma and degree programmes.

Direct entry is for the midwife who is not qualified as a nurse. A few years ago those midwives were regarded as rather lower status and they were often regarded as the midwives who did not have high academic standing. I think that we are reversing that situation now. The degree programme in Oxford is direct entry and we particularly emphasise the academic requirements of that programme, so that understanding of midwives who went into direct entry programmes who had lower academic standing is being changed.

Rodeck: The trainees of all healthcare professions learn while they are working and work while they are learning. If they are to be encouraged to work together the dfferent groups should do both together. There are several potentially innovative things one could do on a day-to-day basis cheaply and effectively such as having joint case conferences, joint audit sessions, ward rounds or meetings after clinics.

Lewison: Users are available to help with education, perhaps in situations where there is shared learning, and particularly at the early stages of their education.

The student midwives I talked to recently who are a few months off qualifying said they wished they had had their session with me right at the beginning before they got the ingrained attitudes about user involvement from some of the midwives they had worked with. We have two specific contributions. One is to give midwives and doctors the chance to share the sort of skills that we have in working with women, woman-centered, participative learning skills. Also the chance to have feedback on how our clients talk to us about the service they receive. The other thing is learning to understand the concept of consumerism and how user representation can be used for the good in service planning and provision.

Chamberlain: At the beginning of training we have the apprentice system of waiting till someone turns up in the surgery or into the hospital and teaching on that. But we are moving away from that and are moving towards structured training. It is the better way of learning for people are grouped into seeing conditions and seeing problems in a structured way.

I also am concerned that the GMC-proposed changes will take away so much obstetrics and gynaecology from undergraduate teaching that the specialty will become a postgraduate subject. Doctors of the future will arrive at SHO level with very little understanding of obstetrics or gynaecology. Although we have talked mostly about obstetrics, gynaecology is such an important subject in general practice that some intensive training will be required.

For these reasons I would not wish to see the removal of the practitioner from the hospital for training. The hospital is the concentration point where problems are brought together and trainees can see a lot of material when working on it and discussing it in a short period of time.

Styles: I want to try to reverse a trend that seems to have crept in – the general practitioner as the consumer of education. We can also be the providers of education. We have a lot that we can offer midwives and obstetricians in terms of education and I should like to see obstetricians and trainee midwives spending time with us in our practices. We can offer education in terms of how to deal with undifferentiated problems and how to reach early diagnoses. We have developed skills in doctor-patient communication. We can demonstrate the effects of psychological and social factors on people's health. In the RCGP at the moment we are preparing a series of objectives that we think would be appropriate for future hospital specialists spending some time in general practice as part of their general professional training. We shall be publishing these in the next few months and I hope that they will be useful.

If we want to promote multi-professional education, then the place to begin is with the teachers in our various disciplines. Until they get together in a multi-professional way we shall be slow in making headway. There might be some merit in a few experimental, pilot occasions, when the teachers from the various disciplines represented in this study group get together to address the whole issue and the problems surrounding multi-professional learning.

Coats: We have talked considerably, and very properly, about the academic updating and training, but also the aspect of skills being maintained and being seen to be maintained. We have talked about attitudes, which is somewhat more difficult to address. But what has been left out is aptitude. In disciplines outside of medicine aptitude is one of the things that is looked at the beginning of their training process. Within the profession I suppose this reflects on carer advice, when people have reached a certain point in training, and perhaps we do need to give and receive more frank career advice. There are some midwives who will never be able to get under the skin of the the mother, and know all that needs to be known to help her, and there are others who will never be very good in the delivery suite. Likewise there are obstetricians and general practitioners who have their forte. Maybe that needs to be addressed in the course of monitoring all that we are doing.

Allison: I have been involved in interdisciplinary education with GPs and that was excellent. As a head of a faculty of midwifery I find the concept of joining in training laudable, but that faculty is many miles away from any medical school and I am not sure how it would work. There must be other teaching centres of midwifery that are so far away from any medical school that it would be impossible. We would have to decide if it was desirable or mandatory that it happened, but if it became mandatory it could put certain midwifery schools in jeopardy.

References

Department of Health (1993) *Changing Childbirth.* London: HMSO

House of Commons Health Select Committee (1992) *Second Report on the Maternity Services.* Volume 1: Report. London: HMSO

RCGP, RCOG (1992) Recommendations for arrangements for general practitioner vocational training in obstetrics and gynaecology. London: Royal College of General Practitioners

RCOG (1991) Report of the MRCOG Working Party. London: Royal College of Obstetricians and Gynaecologists

RCOG (1993) Report of the DRCOG Working Party. London: Royal College of Obstetricians and Gynaecologists

RCOG, RCM, RCGP (1992) Maternity Care in the New NHS: A Joint Approach. London: Royal College of Obstetricians and Gynaecologists

SECTION V
FUTURE

Chapter 34

Development of service: models of care

Mary McGinley and Deborah Turnbull

Midwifery development unit

In 1991 the Scottish Office Home and Health Department invited interested Health Boards to submit bids for funding of up to £300 000 over three years to establish a Midwifery Development Unit in Scotland. The aim of the Midwifery Development Unit was to achieve and promote excellence in midwifery care. Glasgow Royal Maternity Hospital was delighted to have been successful in attracting the United Kingdom's first Midwifery Development Unit to Rottenrow, Glasgow. A Midwifery Development Unit is a setting which aims to achieve and promote excellence in midwifery care. It is geared towards improving midwifery care and practice in a climate where each person's contribution is valued and an open, questioning and supportive approach is fostered. Midwifery Development Units provide a focus for developing practice. It is appreciated that the development of education, research and management may also occur but the development of practice is seen as being of primary importance.

Statement of purpose

The purpose of the Unit is to improve the quality of care provided to women during pregnancy and childbirth. At the outset we set ourselves clear objectives and these were:

1 to introduce a total midwifery care programme for pregnant women considered to be at low risk;
2 to encourage participating midwives to utilise their skills to the full;
3 to develop audit and educational tools for use by the midwifery profession;
4 to monitor and evaluate the Unit.

It was recognised that if we were to be successful in establishing such a Unit then it was important that we cooperated with others who were involved in maternity care provision. We established contacts with obstetricians, general practitioners, public health, colleagues in the University Departments of Social Sciences, Nursing

Studies and Medical Education as well as representatives from our consumers. The links forged with these various groups were to prove valuable, both in development of the service specification and the programmes of care as well as providing representatives for the multidisciplinary steering group which was to oversee the new programme.

Development of the new model of care

In developing our new model of care we considered it essential that the maternity care provided should reflect the philosophy statement of our integrated midwifery team. This philosophy states that maternity care should be provided in a way which ensures that the dignity, privacy and individual choice of each woman is respected at all times. That it must recognise the diversity of cultures, education, social and economic circumstances of the population being served and ensure that programmes of care which are sensitive to individual needs are developed. It states that women should be cared for in a holistic manner and that partners or significant others should have the opportunity to participate in care and health promotion programmes. This philosophy provided the backdrop to the development of the new programme.

It was also considered essential that the programme should take account of good research-based practice. We found Chalmers *et al.*'s (1989) *Effective Care in Pregnancy and Childbirth* an invaluable resource during our workshops with the midwives and incorporated the findings from these studies in our new programme of care.

We appreciated that it would be essential to incorporate women's views when planning the new programme of care and for this reason decided to apply the QAMID Quality Assurance Model for Midwifery (World Health Organisation 1991) in developing the new programme. The QAMID Model was developed at a World Health Organisation Conference on quality held in Belgium in June 1991, but had yet to be applied in practice.

Consumers' views

The QAMID Quality Assurance Model followed the usual quality assurance cycle of defining the requirements, setting the standard, implementation and evaluation followed by taking action to improve the standard following the evaluation. Where QAMID differs from other health-care quality assurance models is that it is the users of the service that identify the need rather than the providers of the service.

The starting point for the model is the generation of information on clients needs. We invited the Glasgow Health Council, East End Initiative Group and the National Childbirth Trust to nominate a representative to participate in the QAMID Group. We also invited these representatives to provide market research or survey data which they considered would assist the group to determine the maternity care needs of the consumers. A survey on local women's views was carried out (Mason 1989) and in addition the Midwifery Development Unit research team carried out open-ended interviews with women attending for care. The findings from this local market research as well as consideration of national research reports and surveys were discussed by the QAMID Group which had both consumer and midwife representation.

Service specifications

From the review it was clear that women in Glasgow were identifying similar needs to those views reflected in the evidence submitted to the Select Committee's enquiry on maternity care. Women wanted continuity of care and carer. They wanted individual informed care planning and they wanted more information and choice. Three service specifications were developed from these needs statements:

1 *Service specification – continuity of care and carer.* Healthy women being cared for by the MDU Midwives can expect to be cared for by a named midwife and three associate midwives, from booking through to transfer to the health visitor postnatally.
2 *Service specification – individual informed care planning.* The MDU will facilitate individual informed care planning: each woman will hold her own midwifery care plan which will contain clinical progress notes as well as her personal choices for care, antenatally, postnatally and her birthplan. During the final episode of care, the midwife will evaluate the care plan with the woman prior to it being returned to the case record.
3 *Service specification – information and choice.* Every woman being cared for in the MDU will receive a basic information pack. In addition, there will be an ongoing assessment of specific information requirements which will be tailored to the individual woman's circumstances. The midwife will allow time to discuss information and choices with each woman.

In this chapter I will concentrate on the implementation of one of the service specifications, that of continuity of care and carer.

In order to achieve greater continuity of care and carer it was appreciated that we would have to change radically the way in which midwives were deployed. Review of the current deployment model for midwives shows that midwives normally work in one of the following functional units, either community antenatal and postnatal care, hospital-based antenatal outpatient and day care, inpatient antenatal, labour ward or inpatient postnatal. This style of working encourages what Kotler and Clark (1987) refers to as a production-orientated type of care. Midwives provide all of the care within their own section and then transfer the women to the next functional unit where care is provided by a different team of midwives. If we were to achieve a customer/service orientation then we agreed that we would have to change this production process orientation style of working. The implementation plan had to look at developing more flexible rosters which would allow midwives to work in all areas in order to provide greater continuity of care for their own caseload. The 20 midwives who were to be involved in

Figure 34.1.   MDU midwife deployment model

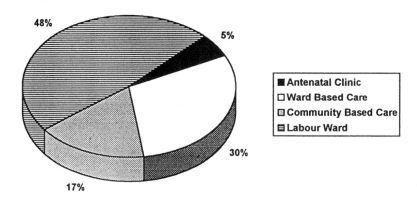

75 hours per fortnight

providing the new programme of care were given the opportunity to help to develop the new deployment model (Figure 34.1) and had the opportunity to pilot it prior to recruitment of women to the programme. This deployment model represents a compromise in that while the midwives were keen to provide greater continuity of care and wished to provide all of the planned inputs for their own caseload, they considered that an on-call roster would not allow them to balance both their family and social commitments with their work commitments. They also considered that if they were on-call and had to attend a woman out of hours they might not be fit to provide care the next day for the women attending their antenatal session. It was this reality of trying to balance women's needs while at the same time providng an efficient service that proved challenging. It is accepted that women would prefer to see one or two care providers as opposed to the current situation where they may be seeing more than eight care givers during pregnancy and more than three midwives during labour (Flint and Poulengeris 1989).

   The implementation plan also had to consider the resource implications of providing such continuity of care and carer. This resource review takes on board Vuori's (1982) assertion that health care providers should seek to provide optimum quality as opposed to maximum quality as the cost of this would be too great. Maxwell's (1984) efficiency criteria for quality in health care also insist that the client's needs/demands are balanced against efficiency and effectiveness. It was for these reasons that it was decided that a named midwife would provide the majority of the planned care, both antenatal and postnatal, for her caseload but that she would be supported by three associate midwives who would provide care in labour and additional support postnatally. The midwives were satisfied that the agreed service specification was such that it did not compromise safety or breach the Midwives Code of Professional Conduct or Practice rules. I think this example illustrates that it is possible to set service standards which are led by the consumer but which also give an opportunity for negotiation around resource use and maintaining professional standards.

Another way of achieving greater continuity of care is by avoiding duplication or over-provision of care. Most women are currently seen by general practitioners, midwives and obstetricians who may repeat certain aspects of care. They are also seen more often than current research evidence suggests to be necessary. There is widespread agreement with the findings of Hall and Chong (1982) whose research suggested that no more than eight to ten antenatal attendances should be necessary for a healthy woman. Howie *et al.* (1991) also highlighted the fact that most women have at least 14 antental visits irrespective of whether they are considered high or low risk. This suggested that there was scope to reduce the frequency of care and perhaps avoid duplication of care. This would not only represent a better use of resources but would also help achieve the objective of greater continuity of care and carer. The model of care developed is shown in Figure 34.2.

In addition to reviewing the frequency of care it was also appreciated that it was important to review the content of care and to look at the research evidence supporting the various investigations which are at times routinely carried out. The new programme of care does not advocate routine weighing at every visit. Frequency of screening has been reduced to reflect current good practice. Women are given the opportunity to discuss the various screening tests and examinations available to them prior to these being carried out. Scanning is not carried out routinely at booking but offered to the woman after discussion. Women are not routinely monitored using electronic fetal heart monitoring while in labour. Women are encouraged to be ambulant in early labour and to adopt whichever position they find comfortable for delivery. Should they wish fluids or a light diet in labour, this is available.

Evaluation

The Midwifery Development Unit setting has encouraged us to develop a model of care which is women-led and in which midwives are encouraged to question current practice and to implement a programme of care which reflects current research thinking. The final step in the QAMID cycle is evaluation; the service specifications are being audited individually and the whole programme is being subjected to a randomised control trial.

The Midwifery Development Unit programme has now been running for 12 months and in that time we have recruited 575 women to each arm of the trial. About one-third of our women have delivered. Each midwife has a caseload of around 29 women and we look forward to receiving results from both the audit and the randomised control trial. Our final report will be available in 1995 and if outcomes are favourable then we would hope to be able to offer women the

Figure 34.2.   Midwifery Development Unit Glasgow Royal Maternity
Hospital: Care Programme

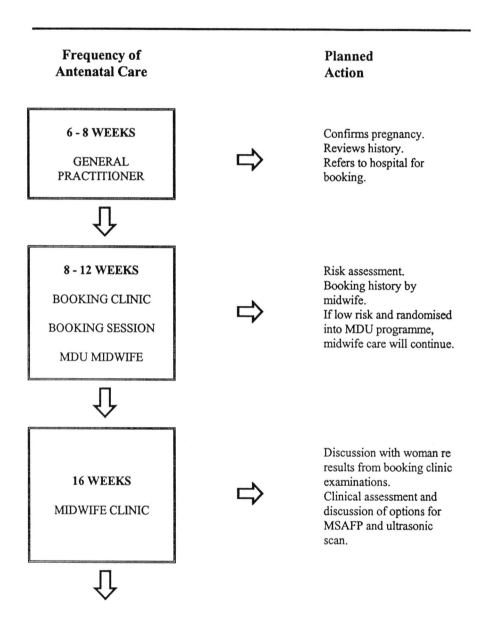

Frequency of
Antenatal Care

Planned
Action

6 - 8 WEEKS

GENERAL
PRACTITIONER

Confirms pregnancy.
Reviews history.
Refers to hospital for
booking.

8 - 12 WEEKS

BOOKING CLINIC

BOOKING SESSION

MDU MIDWIFE

Risk assessment.
Booking history by
midwife.
If low risk and randomised
into MDU programme,
midwife care will continue.

16 WEEKS

MIDWIFE CLINIC

Discussion with woman re
results from booking clinic
examinations.
Clinical assessment and
discussion of options for
MSAFP and ultrasonic
scan.

Figure 34.2.   *continued*

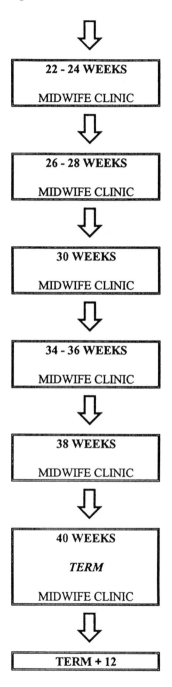

16 - 40 WEEKS

AT EACH VISIT:

Full clinical examination, action and update of maternity care plan.

Venepuncture and investigations will be planned or carried out by midwife as required.

Health education and place of care will be tailored to women's needs.

* AT ALL VISITS:

In the event of deviation from normal, referral to a senior medical staff member will be made.

If undelivered, discuss plan for delivery with consultant.

option of midwife-led care should they wish this. We also hope that the Midwifery Development Unit care programme will serve as an example for others who are attempting to implement change within the maternity services.

References

Chalmers, I., Enkin, M. and Keirse, M. (1989) *Effective Care in Pregnancy and Childbirth.* Oxford: Oxford University Press

Flint, C. and Poulengeris, P. (1989) The 'Know Your Midwife', a randomised trial of continuity of care by a team of midwives: *Midwifery Int J* **5**, 11–16

Hall, M. and Chong, P.K. (1982) Antenatal care in practice in M. Enkin and I. Chalmers (Eds) *Effectiveness and Satisfaction in Antenatal Care.* Oxford: Spastic International Medical Publication, Heinemann Medical Books

House of Commons Health Select Committee (1992) *Second Report on the Maternity Services,* Vol. 1. London: HMSO

Howie, P.W., McIlwaine, G.M., D.U. and Florey, C. (1991) What is antenatal care in Scotland? Health Services Research Committee Final Report

Kotler, P. and Clark, R.N (1987) *Marketing for Health Care Organisations.* New Jersey: Prentice Hill Publication

Mason, V. (1989) *Women's Experience of Maternity Care: A Survey Manual.* Social Survey Division of Office of Population Censuses and Surveys. London: HMSO

Maxwell, R. (1984) Quality assessment in health. *Br Med J* **288**, 1470–2

United Kingdom Central Council for Nursing, Midwifery and Health Visiting (1992) *Code of Professional Conduct* 3rd Edn. London: UKCC

Vuori, H. (1982) Quality Assurance in Health Services, World Health Organisation, Regional Office for Europe. Public Health in Europe No. 16

World Health Organisation (1991) *Midwifery Quality Assurance.* Report of a World Health Organisation Workshop

Chapter 35

Development of service: advances in clinical practice

Stephen A. Walkinshaw

Any of the developing models of care evolving in response to the proposals within *Changing Childbirth* (Department of Health 1993) must incorporate advances in clinical practice taking place within the specialty of obstetrics. The models must acknowledge the unpredictability of risk assessment, both antenatally and intrapartum, and that highly technical and labour intensive back-up will be required for many women. The models must acknowledge that some of what is performed within maternity services may be useful to the health of the community but may not be absolutely necessary for effective maternity care.

Advances in clinical care are difficult to define but a group of recent and potential advances in care which any new system of delivering maternity care must attempt to address are considered below.

Cochrane Collaboration: pregnancy and childbirth module

Perhaps the greatest advance in clinical practice over the last 10 years has been the appreciation by medical and midwifery staff that much of the care offered to both low- and high-risk pregnant women is poorly supported by rigorous research. The more scientific approach to maternity care has been pioneered by the National Perinatal Epidemiology Unit at Oxford, aided by the Oxford Database of Perinatal Trials, culminating in the publication of *Effective Care in Pregnancy and Childbirth* (Chalmers *et al.* 1989). This has evolved into the Cochrane Collaboration, now encompassing many specialties, but with its core Pregnancy and Childbirth Module. This bi-annual user-friendly computer disc contains up-to-date information from randomised trials in obstetric and midwifery practice.

The speed of electronic publishing, allied to the recent popularity of large trials with sufficient potential power to answer a clinical question in a single trial (e.g. CLASP or term PROM trials), means that basic practices can, and should, be capable of rapid change. Any evolving model of care must be flexible enough to meet this challenge. The recommendation to both purchasers and providers to utilise up-to-date overviews of practice, such as is made by Mersey Region in its

Consensus Statement on Maternity Care (Mersey Regional Health Authority 1994), is long overdue.

Antenatal screening for fetal malformation

No single area of care exemplifies the effect advances in clinical care can have on the organisation of services better than the field of prenatal diagnosis. Although the morality of deliberate screening for malformation, the psychological sequelae of false positive screening, and the lack of precise information on the value of routine ultrasound screening (Ewigman *et al.* 1993) are important brakes on the use of prenatal screening, there is little doubt that in clinical practice most couples wish the reassurance of the normality of their baby. Assessment for abnormality includes, as core functions, the availability of first trimester diagnosis of genetic and chromosomal disease, serum screening for autosomal trisomy and neural tube defects, and ultrasound diagnosis of major malformation. Additional complexity is provided by targeting of particularly high risk groups such as diabetic women and those with multiple pregnancy, and by the increasing recognition of both minor markers of trisomy and minor malformations (Nicolaides *et al.* 1992). Current systems therefore require the ability of very rapid referral for early prenatal diagnosis, accurate gestational ageing prior to serum screening, close collaboration and communication between clinical and laboratory services, meticulous and consistent counselling, easy access to a range of karyotyping procedures, and well-organised, well-staffed and well-trained sonography services with speedy access for detected malformations to practitioners versed in the counselling and management of antenatally detected malformations.

Potential developments within the field include the possibility of carrier screening for cystic fibrosis, the development of first trimester serum markers for trisomy, the possibility of screening for genetic and chromosomal disease from maternal blood, and the use of earlier ultrasound examination to detect structural malformation. The common theme of these advances is to push prenatal diagnosis into the first trimester. If these techniques prove effective the current infrastructure will need to be reorganised and the organisational complexities which will allow most women access to these facilities at these gestations are formidable. It could require an almost 'walk in' approach to prenatal diagnosis.

Identification of the 'at risk' fetus

Care within the maternity services would be simplified if it were possible to identify clearly pregnancies at risk of major problems. Unfortunately, few real advances have been made in the identification of fetuses at risk of premature delivery, hypertension or growth failure. Recent work in preterm labour has focused on the role of microorganisms (Lamont and Fisk 1993) but it remains to be demonstrated that large-scale screening and treatment of genital tract colonisation will reduce the incidence of spontaneous preterm delivery. Similarly screening for hypertensive disorders of pregnancy has been disappointing, although the use of uterine Doppler (Steel *et al.* 1990) and family history (Morris 1993) show promise. Although clinical screening may identify some fetuses destined to be growth retarded, current methods, both clinical and sonological, falsely identify too many women as at risk to be useful. Novel approaches, looking at growth velocity (Deter *et al.* 1986) or relating size to other confounding variables of birthweight using computer assistance (Wilcox *et al.* 1993), may fare better.

All of these potential advances will require the availability of sophisticated facilities for all women, if they are to be effective.

Antepartum fetal monitoring

Over the last decade the number of antenatal beds required for a given population has fallen dramatically. In part this has resulted from more appropriate use of outpatient facilities, in particular, the movement of antepartum fetal assessment into ultrasound departments and 'day assessment units'. It is rarely necessary on medical grounds nowadays to admit a pregnant woman for fetal monitoring. Already many areas have arrangements with GPs and community-based midwives to ensure easy access to such facilities and this will need to be encouraged. Clear protocols of care, including the setting of indicators for referral, will be needed to avoid overuse of facilities. Many envisage day assessment areas as the hub of hospital-based antenatal care rather than the conventional antenatal clinic.

Units will need to examine critically the choice of fetal monitoring techniques given the lack of data on many of the testing strategies currently employed. There is increasing evidence that umbilical Doppler velocimetry should be part of these strategies (Neilson 1993).

Specialist clinics

Increasingly obstetricians have attempted to concentrate resources on women at particular risk. The most obvious example is women with co-existent medical disease. However there are many examples of other groups, often arising out of local audits of outcome and satisfaction, where such focused attention may have been of benefit. These include clinics for multiple pregnancy, drug users, previous preterm labour, and teenagers. Such clinics allow a concentration of all services – medical, midwifery, professionals allied to medicine, social services and external bodies. Although there is at present little hard evidence of their benefit, feedback suggests that such 'special care' and continuity of care is found to be helpful.

Novel models of care must allow for the benefits of such facilities, often midwife led, even if this means that the care is not in the community.

The community health

Pregnancy provides an opportunity to examine a number of public health issues. It may be one of the few times that women of this age attend health care professionals. It provides a chance to promote healthy lifestyles with advice on diet, smoking, alcohol and exercise. It provides an opportunity to screen for cervical cancer, for immunity to rubella, and to identify blood group. In some areas it allows access to screening for important public health issues such as hepatitis and HIV. The issues around trisomy screening and screening for genetic disease such as cystic fibrosis fall as much within the domain of public health as within the maternity service. For all of these, there may be some impact on maternal and perinatal outcome, but the main impact is in other spheres, not confined to medicine. More contentious are the issues around screening for gestational diabetes. There is at present no evidence that such screening or the treatment of biochemical glucose abnormalities so revealed have any impact on perinatal outcome (Walkinshaw 1993). Its role within a maternity system must therefore be questioned. However, women with impaired glucose tolerance in pregnancy are at substantial risk of developing non-insulin dependent diabetes in later life, a condition with appreciable morbidity and mortality. The identification of such a predisposition might allow intervention to prevent or modify later disease, an important public health issue. Therefore more universal screening may be justified despite the lack of benefit at the time. Systems of care and their funding must allow for the use of the maternity system as a public health tool.

Intrapartum care

Within the delivery suite setting, advances in clinical practice have been closely linked to critical evaluation of much of the routine processes and procedures which have evolved. This has led to a gradual demedicalisation of procedures on the labour ward, whilst recognising the effectiveness of some interventions. It has also led to the confirmation that the most effective routine 'intervention' on the labour ward is to provide the pregnant woman with continuous skilled support throughout her labour (Walkinshaw 1994). Considerable advances have been made in providing a better environment for childbirth within the hospital setting, with developments such as the Leicester 'Home from Home' model. Better guidance is now provided for both midwifery and junior medical staff by the development of labour ward protocols and guidelines, and by their rigorous updating. The importance of senior support on the labour ward and its effect on the quality of intrapartum care are increasingly recognised by doctors and managers. The reduction in antenatal work for consultant staff which will result from re-organisation will free skills and experience for utilisation on the delivery suite.

With the broadening of the midwifery base involved in intrapartum care to provide better overall continuity, vigilance will be required to ensure that carefully crafted, research-based delivery suite guidelines continue to be the cornerstone of intrapartum care. Awareness among doctors and midwives of the principles of such care will need to be increased.

Whichever models of care are adopted, all must recognise the need to provide easily accessible specialist services, whether for particular high risk groups or for screening for risk. As advances in clinical practice arrive, a community-based service will be challenged to find innovative ways of ensuring that all women have a choice of all options, including access to highly specialist facilities. It is to be hoped that these choices will be real as unproven practices in both midwifery and obsterics are phased out, and effective practices and advances in practice of proven benefit are introduced across a wider spectrum of care.

References

Chalmers, I., Enkin, M. and Keirse, M.J.N.C. (1989) *Effective Care in Pregnancy and Childbirth.* Vols 1 and 2. Oxford: Oxford University Press

Department of Health (1993) *Changing Childbirth.* London: HMSO

Deter, R.L., Rossavik, I.K., Harrist, R.B. and Hadlock, F.P. (1986) Mathematical modelling of fetal growth: development of individual growth curve standards. *Obstet Gynecol* **68**, 156–61

Ewigman, B.G., Crane, J.P., Frigoletto, F.D. *et al.* (1993) The RADIUS study group. Effect of prenatal ultrasound screening on perinatal outcome. *N Engl J Med* **329**, 821–7

Lamont, R.F. and Fisk, N. (1993) 'The role of infection in the pathogenesis of preterm labour' in J. Studd (Ed.) *Progress in Obstetrics and Gynaecology* Vol 10, pp. 135–58. Edinburgh: Churchill Livingstone

Mersey Regional Health Authority (1994) *Changing Childbirth in Mersey – a Consensus Statement.* Liverpool: Mersey Region Health Authority

Morris, P. (1993) Screening for gestational hypertension. M Obstet Gynaecol Thesis. University of Liverpool

Neilson, J.P. (1993) 'Doppler ultrasound in high risk pregnancies'. Review No. 03889 in M.K. Enkin, M.J.N.C. Keirse, M.J. Renfrew and J.P. Neilson (Eds) *Cochrane Database of Systematic Reviews: Pregnancy and Chilbirth Module.* Cochrane Updates on Disk. Issue 2. Oxford: Update Software

Nicolaides, K., Snijders, R.J.M., Gosden, C.M., Berry, C. and Campbell, S. (1992) Ultrasonographically detectable markers of fetal chromosomal abnormality. *Lancet* **340**, 704–7

Steel, S.A., Pearce, J.M., McParland, P.M. and Chamberlain, G.V.P. (1990) Early Doppler ultrasound screening and prediction of hypertensive disorders of pregnancy. *Lancet* **335**, 1548–51

Walkinshaw, S.A. (1993) Dietary regulation for 'gestional diabetes' Review No. 06649 and Diet plus insulin versus diet alone for 'gestional diabetes' Review No. 06650 in M.K. Enkin, M.J.N.C. Keirse, M.J. Renfrew, and J.P. Neilson (Eds) *Cochrane Database of Systematic Reviews: Pregnancy and Childbirth Module.* Cochrane Updates on Disk. Issue 2. Oxford: Update Software

Walkinshaw, S.A. (1994) 'Is routine active medical intervention in spontaneous labour beneficial?' in G.V.P. Chamberlain and J.O. Drife (Eds) *Contemp Rev Obstet Gynaecol* (In press)

Wilcox, M.A., Johnson, I.R., Maynard, P.V., Smith, S.J. and Chilvers, C.E.D. (1993) The individualised birthweight ratio: a more logical approach to birthweight. *Br J Obstet Gynaecol* **100**, 342–7

Chapter 36

Areas of future research

Charles H. Rodeck

The only predictable thing about future research is its unpredictability. Three important aspects will be discussed here:

1 the nature of research
2 the areas of research likely to be of interest in the future
3 pragmatically, the most important question in the short term: who will do the research?

The nature of research

A number of questions need to be considered:

1 What is the aim of research? To obtain new information that is true, i.e. verifiable and predictive.
2 What is the relationship between research and audit? Much of scientific work progresses by formulating hypotheses and then designing experiments to refute them. Randomised clinical trials are a variant of this type of enquiry. Much clinical science is observational and overlaps with audit. Here the questions may be about the efficacy or safety of a procedure. The information obtained in audit is not necessarily novel or original, but is intended to modify clinical practice.
3 Where is research done? This depends on the source of funding which includes the universities, the Medical Research Council, the National Health Service, charities and drug companies. The important role that the National Perinatal Epidemiology Unit and the Perinatal Trials Database have played deserves emphasis. In the past, the traditional esteem in which 'pure' research has been held in relation to 'applied', or theoretical versus practical research, has been profoundly damaging. This division is being overcome in many quarters (although not all) by the multidisciplinary nature of much of modern research and by target-orientated research. The latter may be illusory, but so is the other extreme view that 'basic' science is inherently superior to 'clinical' science.

4 The role of research and development (R and D) in the NHS. The stated aim is to base NHS practice on research and to initiate a research culture in the NHS. This has involved a redistribution of research funds, establishing new methods of dispensing them, identifying priority areas and defining targets. The efficacy of this policy has yet to be assessed.

What areas of research?

These may be divided into (1) basic science, (2) clinical science, (3) behavioural science, (4) health services research. The following is a list of topics where a great deal of research is required. Criteria for inclusion on this list are that it is a subject either of outstanding importance or ignorance, or both. The list is of course by no means exhaustive.

1. Basic science
  (a) The Human Genome Project
  (b) Developmental biology
  (c) Implantation and placentation
  (d) Growth, differentiation, maturation

2. Clinical science
  (a) Causes and management of early pregnancy loss
  (b) Causes and management of congenital malformation
  (c) Genetic screening
  (d) Gene therapy
  (e) Disturbed fetal growth and oxygenation
  (f) Pre-eclampsia
  (g) Labour and pre-term labour
  (h) Fetal monitoring
  (i) Pain relief in labour
  (j) Effects of fetal life on later health

3 Behavioural science
  (a) Emotional effects of screening
  (b) Adaptation to pregnancy
  (c) Effects of pregnancy loss and its management
  (d) Psychological adaptation to parenthood ('bonding')
  (e) Prediction and management of postnatal depression

4. Health Services research
  (a) Maternal mortality
  (b) Infant nutrition
  (c) Health education
  (d) Population control
  (e) Evaluation of new technologies
  (f) Evaluation of innovative clinical practices

Many of these examples will have more cross-category relevance and influence than within, e.g., findings from the Human Genome Project are likely to affect genetic screening policies, as may behavioural science research. Developmental biology, until recently an area of huge ignorance, is now succumbing to molecular analysis, and in the future will increase our understanding of the congenital malformations. The maintenance of a healthy scientific environment therefore depends on a creative pluralism based on free dialogue between the various categories and disciplines outlined above.

Who will do the research?

It follows that effective and appropriate research involves the skills of many, such as scientists, doctors, midwives, epidemiologists, psychologists and others. It is to be hoped that the R & D Directorate will initiate and foster such collaborations and create a research culture in the NHS. Unfortunately a number of recent trends are in danger of promoting an anti-research culture.

1 The need to do a higher degree such as Doctor of Medicine (MD). In most clinical specialties, trainees aiming for a good consultant post have been under pressure to work for a higher research degree. This has been both good and bad. Good in that it has been an excellent training for many and has led to much first class work; bad in that some have done it unwillingly and merely to dress-up their curriculum vitae. Research performed and supervised by amateurs is unlikely to be of good quality. If the need to do an MD is removed, both types of research, good and bad, are likely to diminish. The clinical scientific community must be concerned to preserve the former and not the latter.
2 The effects of the purchaser/provider arrangements in the NHS on the facility to perform clinical research are not yet known. The worry of many clinical academics is that the changes may be detrimental. The future deployment of Service Increment for Teaching and Research (SIFTR) is another unknown which is of potential concern.
3 The advent of structured training programmes will produce specialists more efficiently and after a shorter training, and hopefully as well trained as in the past. There will be less time for research and it is likely that fewer trainees will do any.

A possible solution is to improve the organisation of research training and to make it more professional. All specialists should have some understanding of statistics and research methodology and can be capable of critical evaluations of the literature. The majority need not do independent research themselves, however. Structured training programmes should therefore all have an appropriate component of research training. A second, more advanced level of training should be available for those that wish to do research. This would be appropriate for subspecialty or academic trainees. These individuals are likely to spend two or three years in research, ideally in research training fellowships or they may have done an MB–PhD programme. It is vital that some clinicians also have a training in basic science because the gap between the languages of scientists and clinicians is widening. There is also a need for more obstetric researchers to be skilled in epidemiology and an MSc course in Perinatal Epidemiology would be an influential innovation.

Scientific research has for long been subjected to peer review of grant applications and submitted papers, but in the future, audit of research will feature more prominently. The Higher Education Funding Council (HEFC), formerly the Universities Funding Council, conducts extremely detailed three- or four-yearly research assessments of all institutions and their departments. Achievement of a higher grade results in a larger grant and vice versa. NHS R and D funded research will also be monitored closely to see whether set targets have been reached and 'value for money' is being obtained.

As more research information becomes available, the need for its wide dissemination and efficient utilisation will become increasingly important.

Chapter 37

Areas of future research in the maternity services

Jennifer Sleep

Historically, the issue of determining priorities for health care research has been influenced or dictated by a number of factors. For example, by the personal choice or preference of the individual researcher, by the needs/interests of a specific organisation, by the requirement to gain a higher degree or to achieve promotion or by the dictate of a funding agency. Clearly such factors exert a constraining and extremely limiting effect on the scope and appropriate direction of research to address the needs of the policy makers, service providers and the recipients of care.

For the first time in England there is now a concerted effort to undertake a national agenda setting exercise to determine a cohesive strategy for future research in the maternity services. Scotland and Wales are also currently conducting a similar exercise. This impetus has been fuelled by a number of important recent initiatives.

First, the publication of *Effective Care in Pregnancy and Childbirth* (Chalmers *et al.* 1989) and *A Guide to Effective Care in Pregnancy and Childbirth* (Enkin *et al.* 1989). These companion volumes use systematic literature reviews to identify areas where research relevant to the care of women, their babies and their families has been thorough and convincing and areas where more research is needed. Appendices 2 and 3 provide a 'shopping list' of interventions for which further research is needed in order to determine their outcome on care. These volumes provide an unique resource for clinicians, educators and managers working within the field of maternity care. However, by their very nature, these publications are already out of date but we do have access to the Cochrane Collaboration Pregnancy and Childbirth Database (CCPC) which provides an updated synthesis of controlled trials of relevance to maternity care.

Second, the first Research and Development Strategy for the NHS (DoH 1991) which was designed to strengthen the commitment to systematic enquiry, evaluation and knowledge-led practice throughout the NHS. In a follow-up to this report, Professor Peckham (DoH 1993a) called 'for a more robust and productive relationship between health problems and scientific investigation' so that the 'imbalance between investigator-led research and problem-led research' can be addressed. Furthermore, the report identifies six overlapping dimensions which provide a necessary framework for debating the issues under the following themes:

1 Disease-led or practice related issues
2 The organisation and management of services
3 The needs of specific client groups
4 Consumer issues
5 Evaluating health technologies
6 The use of a range of methodologies

For the first time, these reports emphasise the importance of a multidisciplinary approach to research. This initiative is to be warmly welcomed. As a relatively recent development the Central Research and Development Committee (CRDC) has undertaken the first in a series of priority-setting exercises. The list has just been published. It does not contain much of a focus on the maternity services but, hopefully, future rounds will be more comprehensive.

Third, *Health of the Nation* (DoH 1992) identifies maternal and child health not as a priority but as an area where developments in practice must be sustained and developed. However, priority areas, for example, mental health do incorporate aspects of maternal and child health such as postnatal depression.

Fourth, *The Report of the Taskforce on the Strategy for Research in Nursing*, Midwifery and Health Visiting (DoH 1993b) considered the role and contribution of research by these professions and, in particular, the mechanisms for identifying research and development priorities. The report emphasises that these professions have much to gain from being proactive in this process highlighting that this will:

... stimulate collaboration within the professions, and enable them to play their rightful part in health services research.

... coordinate the financial and staff investment in research and development (R&D), to ensure that limited funding is concentrated in areas of greatest need and that the expertise of skilled researchers is employed to greatest benefit.

... consolidate effort in expanding research-based information for the professions by building up a cumulative information base on which to make informed decisions.

The report acknowledges that research in these professions is still relatively new and that there are challenges to be faced in developing research within a multidisciplinary setting.

Fifth, the *Changing Childbirth* Report (Department of Health 1993c), the recommendations of which have now been fully accepted by the government, stresses the need for sound evidence to inform practice highlighting the importance of basing priorities for evaluation upon the needs of women for example, perineal care and breast feeding.

These combined resources provide a powerful impetus to the agenda setting exercise. However, establishing priorities is a multifaceted process. For example, literature reviewing and consulting with researchers are essential parts of the process but on their own this is not enough. There is also a need to identify questions arising from clinical practice, perhaps not yet addressed in the literature.

Table 37.1

Areas identified from systematic reviews

The provision of antenatal classes

Sodium chloride for leg cramps

Amniotomy to augment spontaneous labour

Syntometrine vs oxytocin for third stage of labour

Routine administration of Vitamin K to neonates

Oral proteolytic enzymes for breast engorgement

Routine iron or folate supplements

Routine witholding of fluids or food in labour

Fetal weight estimation as a guide to care for preterm labour

Non-pharmacological methods of pain relief

Areas of importance to clinicians

Evaluating the pattern and effectiveness of postnatal care

The effect of part-time employed staff on the continuity of care

Evaluating strategies for the effective dissemination of research relevant to
practice

What pattern of care do women really want?

Routines in care

Areas of importance to women

Perineal care both during and after delivery

Methods of alleviating the unpleasant common symptoms in pregancy

Interventions aimed at babies, for example, giving Vitamin K and testing blood
glucose levels

Methods of alleviating sore breasts

Areas of importance to purchasers

Resource implications of using antibiotics prior to elective Caesarean section

Resource implications of providing additional support to enable mothers to keep
breast feeding

Resource implications of providing a 24 h epidural service

The skill mix necessary to provide an optimum level of care

Questions asked both by caregivers and by women and their families who use the services.

I would suggest that there are three important criteria to be addressed in identifying issues and in determining priorities for future research in the maternity services. The proposed research must:

1 meet the expressed needs of women, their babies and their families;
2 offer the potential to improve the provision and standards of care;
3 be cost-effective in ensuring the most efficient use of service resources, research funding and research expertise.

These criteria have been used to formulate the aims of an important midwifery study which is currently in progress. In the wake of these recent initiatives, its conduct is timely. It comprises a three-part national survey designed to identify and prioritise research issues of relevance to users, purchasers and providers of the maternity services. It is an unique study in concurrently exploring not only the views of professional groups but also the views of maternity organisations and of purchasers and providers of the service. The study has been funded by the Department of Health but accesses a sample representative of all the countries in the UK. It forms part of the Midwifery Research Programme at the National Perinatal Epidemiology Unit. It is planned that the results will be reported by the early Autumn of 1994.

A tentative list is given here (Table 37.1) which perhaps serves to demonstrate the diversity of the issues seen from differing perspectives.

Clearly, priority setting is a dynamic process, to be revisited regularly to ensure that it is responsive to new developments and ideas. The process must ensure that there is a balance between identified needs and the stimulus of new ideas, technologies, clinical advances and changes in the service provision and pattern of care.

References

Chalmers, I., Enkin, M. and Keirse, M.J.N.C. (Eds) (1989) *Effective Care in Pregnancy and Childbirth*. Oxford: Oxford University Press

Department of Health (1991) *Research for Health. A Research and Development Strategy for the NHS*. London: HMSO

Department of Health (1992) *Health of the Nation*. London: HMSO

Department of Health (1993a) *Research for Health*. London: HMSO

Department of Health (1993b) *Report of the Taskforce on the Strategy for Research in Nursing, Midwifery and Health Visiting*. London: HMSO

Department of Health (1993c) *Changing Childbirth*. London: HMSO

Enkin, M., Chalmers, I. and Keirse, M.J.N.C. (Eds) (1989) *A Guide to Effective Care in Pregnancy and Childbirth*. Oxford: Oxford University Press

NHSME (1993) *A Vision for the Future: The Nursing, Midwifery and Health Visiting Contribution to Health and Health Care*. London: NHS Management Executive

Chapter 38

How to ensure research-based practice

Julia Allison and Suzanne Tyler

Introduction

It is now almost universally accepted that practice – midwifery, obstetric and general medical – should be research-based. The message of Enkin *et al.* (1989) is beyond dispute: differences in practice which exist between countries, communities, institutions and even between care-givers can only be resolved by research. Cormack (1984), too, gives us a number of good reasons why we should understand research:

1 to establish scientifically defensible reasons for activities
2 to find ways of increasing cost-effectiveness
3 to satisfy academic curiosity
4 to provide evidence of the weaknesses and strengths of existing practice
5 to provide evidence to support demands for resources
6 to earn and defend professional status.

To this we would add 'improving client/patient satisfaction'.

The leaders of each of the professions must achieve a happy marriage between published research and clinical wisdom.

In discussing how this might be achieved for midwifery we want to highlight four needs:

1 we *need* midwives doing research
2 we *need* research which is accessible to midwives
3 we *need* a truly multidisciplinary approach to research
4 we *need* research which is clinically relevant.

Research by midwives for midwives

Research which is defined and undertaken by midwives remains a fledgling discipline. It was only in 1962 that the government health departments first began to build a framework to support the nursing professions in developing their research potential.

It was only in 1979 that the first national 'Research and the Midwife' conference was organised to provide midwives and others with a platform to present their research findings.

However, as Alexander *et al.* (1990) demonstrate, these conferences have been enormously successful year after year in fostering midwives who have the confidence and competence to undertake research. The research which has been undertaken during this short period has already had a profound impact on practice.

The proceedings of the first two conferences (Robinson and Thomson 1979–80 unpublished) included papers on:

1 feeding and sleeping in the early weeks and the mother and child relationship
2 interaction in antenatal clinics
3 the effectiveness of predelivery shaving.

In 1980 it was still largely held to be true that routine predelivery shaving of pubic hair was necessary to prevent infection. The fact that this is no longer the case shows how long-held beliefs can be challenged effectively and existing practice turned on its head.

The research evidence presented at the Research and Midwife Conference in 1980 by Mona Romney demonstrated that there was no benefit to the procedure but that it created a great deal of discomfort for women. This, together with doubts about the effectiveness of shaving in general surgery, has led to an almost total abandonment of the procedure.

By the 1992 conference, midwives had become increasingly sophisticated and rigorous in their research. The proceedings included (Robinson and Thomson, 1992 unpublished):

1 long-term health problems after childbirth (an investigation into 11th 701 women delivered in Birmingham)
2 psychological and social aspects of screening for fetal abnormality during routine antenatal care.

The most important aspect of midwifery research undertaken by midwives is that it moves beyond a purely medical paradigm. Like the care midwives give, their research embraces the physical, psychological and social aspects of pregnancy and childbirth, such as:

1 communication during antenatal booking interviews
2 the psychology of pregnancy
3 emotional problems associated with childbearing
4 teenage mothers
5 the retaliation of marginalised fathers (Alexander *et al.* 1993).

Midwifery research brings together women's needs, midwives' activities and outcomes. The small but growing cadre of midwifery researchers need support and development from their professional organisation, their employers, government and statutory bodies and other professions. Midwife researchers need to publish widely and to engage in public speaking to disseminate their work. They particularly need financial support, be it paid time-off from work or an increase in the scholarships and awards available from charities and trusts. A financial commitment from the Department of Health to supporting midwifery research would bolster the confidence of all involved in undertaking research and send a strong signal to the rest of the profession about the importance of research-based practice.

Midwives using research

Although not every midwife can or indeed should be undertaking research, all should be confident and competent in handling/assessing research material. Every midwife should be expected to be reflective about her practice and able to challenge traditional assumptions. By being able to use research, midwives should have the technical and scientific data upon which to make rationale, sensible and informed decisions.

Being a research-based practitioner requires an acceptance that the way things have always been done, is not necessarily the way they should always be done.

According to Robinson and Thomson (1988) translating research into practice requires a commitment to:

1 base activity in available research findings
2 develop skills to evaluate literature
3 keep up-to-date
4 support colleagues undertaking research
5 identify areas worthy of research.

However, ensuring research-based practice is not merely a matter of individual responsibility.

Midwives' education from pre-registration onwards needs to prepare them to handle and analyse research data. This includes being able to read research intelligently, being able to understand methodologies and findings and being able to see the relevance to practice. Midwife teachers must ensure that their teaching is based on research, midwife managers must give staff the time to learn about research. Midwives' careers must reward and encourage a research-based approach.

Perhaps more importantly midwifery research needs to be accessible, both physically, in libraries associated with hospitals and teaching institutions, and written in a manner which makes it usable. Guides such as *Effective Care in Pregnancy and Childbirth* and *Midwifery Practice: A Research Based Approach* have been enormously helpful in presenting research in clear straightforward terms. This type of work needs to be widely disseminated and widely available.

Collaboration between the professions

Just as collaboration and a genuine respect for the skills of others is the basis of providing good maternity care, so it should be the basis of good maternity research.

Traditionally it has been medical research that has dominated policy-making and practice in maternity care. Over the last ten years, as midwives have begun to reassert control over normal pregnancy, they have become more confident in articulating their own research.

Now, however, is the time to begin moving forward together. Researchers in any discipline need to keep an open mind. Few profit from isolated research undertaken within a single discipline. Research must have a specific purpose, such as, for example, Julia Allison's own research into the work of district nurses. Often there is no clear distinction between obstetric research and midwifery research, so collaboration based on mutual recognition of abilities and respect must be the most effective way to proceed.

The National Perinatal and Epidemiology Unit has been the most marvellous inspiration for all practitioners in showing how joint working can be profitable and productive.

There are plenty of other examples of midwives working with obstetricians and GPs in a productive research relationship such as:

1 Obstetrician Peter Howie's work on breastfeeding. Much of this research has been undertaken in collaboration with midwives.
2 Midwife Phillipa Gunn and Obstetrician Geoffrey Chamberlain's work on place of birth
3 Midwife Anne Wraight and Obstetrician Geoffrey Chamberlain's work on pain
4 Midwife Patricia Rouse and GP Kevan Thorley's work in Newcastle-under-Lyne on antenatal care which builds on the earlier work of Marion Hall.

The three Royal Colleges should be taking the lead in promoting collaboration; by working together at a national level they would set a positive example to all of their members. Perhaps the time has come to hold a joint three-Colleges research conference or perhaps the research advisory groups of the three Colleges should meet together to explore the potential for joint activity?

Clinically relevant research

The final 'need' serves as something of a warning to eager researchers everywhere who may be tempted to start down obscure alleys in the hope of being original. Research must be clinically relevant if it is ever to be translated into practice. Each profession must ensure that valuable research resources are not wasted in the pursuit of the esoteric. We must avoid the pitfalls of much academic research where career progression is based on the number of papers published regardless of their worth.

In midwifery there remains much that still requires proper examination and analysis such as:

1 the place and type of care given to women who experience problems during pregnancy
2 antenatal care that is geared to women's needs

3 evaluating pain relief
4 strategies to promote successful breastfeeding
5 prevention of incontinence
6 communication between midwives and women which allows women to determine the care that suits them (Robinson and Thomson 1988).

The gaps in our knowledge base are constantly being uncovered by those already engaged in research. Achieving good practice must be a marriage of clinical wisdom based in traditional practices and thorough research and scientific evaluation.

Conclusion

The final chapter of the *Guide to Effective Care in Pregnancy and Childbirth* (Enkin *et al.* 1989) discusses some of the ways in which research may or may not be applicable to practice. They highlight:

1 evidence that should guide the development of broad policies relating to the provision of care
2 increased diagnostic accuracy to assist care-givers in identifying women who respond in a typical way to care
3 knowledge of the effects of care as a prerequisite to making choices, for both providers and users of services.

It is perhaps also worth looking at the common factors involved where research has changed practice. The first issue here is where the research is undertaken and where it is published. Research done outside the UK never seems to attract the attention it deserves, there is often the feeling that 'it doesn't apply to us'. This is a dangerous belief for anyone to hold. In many cases we must rely on research undertaken abroad. For example, in the UK now, perinatal and maternal mortality is so low that researching the causes and procedures to adopt when things go badly wrong is likely to be problematic. It may be that from a research point of view it is countries with higher rates of mortality that could teach us the most. Finding the appropriate place to publish is also crucial to actually influencing opinion to change practice. Journals such as the *British Medical Journal* appear far more effective in influencing all types of professionals and policy-makers.

The second point about change is also a warning. Do we change our practice because the research has convinced us, or because we did not like performing the procedure anyway and the research satisfies our objection? I believe it is likely that the speed with which routine enemas and shaves were abandoned owes as much to professional dislikes as sound understanding. Being committed to research-based practice is, however, more than looking for justification of our own prejudices. It is also of no use to the women we serve if we abandon procedures virtually overnight without explanation, support and counselling. I do not believe that women's interests were served by forcing them all to have enemas one week and refusing them the next.

Finally, much recent work, particularly by Lomas in Canada, demonstrates clearly that research is not translated into practice unless there are 'change agents' prepared to put personal energy into convincing colleagues of the worth of any given change. The study of vaginal birth after Caesarean has now been picked up widely in this country (Lomas *et al.* 1991). His studies show that merely circulating data does not change practice, opinion leaders within the workplace are needed if guidelines are to be translated into action.

Perhaps above all else ensuring research-based practice requires us all, policy makers, managers, educationalists and clinicians to have the humility to accept that we might not always get it right and the commitment to making the changes to remedy this.

References

Alexander, J., Levy, V. and Roch, S. (1990) *Midwifery Practice: A Research Based Approach.* (Three volumes (i) Antenatal Care (ii) Intrapartum Care (iii) Postnatal Care) London: MacMillan

Alexander, J., Levy, V. and Roch, S. (1993) *Midwifery Practice: A Research Based Approach.* London: MacMillan

Cormack, D.F.S. (1984) *The Research Process in Nursing.* London: Blackwell

Enkin, M., Keirse, M.J.N.C. and Chalmers, I. (1989) *A Guide to Effective Care in Pregnancy and Childbirth.* Oxford: Oxford University Press

Lomas, J., Enkin, M., Anderson, G.M. *et al.* (1991) Opinion leaders vs audit and feedback to implement practice guidelines. *JAMA* **265**, 2202–7

Robinson, S. and Thomson, A. (1979–80) Research and the Midwife: Conference Proceedings. Unpublished paper

Robinson, S. and Thomson, A. (1988) *Midwives Research and Childbirth*, vols 1 and 2 . London: Chapman and Hall

Robinson, S. and Thomson, A. (1992) Research and the Midwife: Conference Proceedings. Unpublished paper

Chapter 39

How to ensure research-based practice

Alastair G. Donald

In this section we are looking into the future and in particular at the problem of ensuring a comprehensive research base in relation to maternity care in the community.

In general practice research is taking place at a number of levels, the first of which is that initiated by individual doctors in their own practices. I am happy to be able to say that the number of research papers coming from these individuals in practice has never been higher nor of better quality than at the present time and the academic journals of general practice are finding increasing difficulty in accommodating the number of papers presented to them that they would wish to publish.

The majority of these published papers from practice have been concerned recently with the safety of maternity units run by general practitioners and the satisfaction levels of the mothers who have their confinements in these units (Garrett *et al.* 1987; Lowe *et al.* 1987; MacAlister-Smith 1989) This type of research will be ensured so long as we are producing doctors with enquiring minds who are given the opportunity of time to undertake research projects.

Audit in general practice is now well established and we are following the lead of our obstetric colleagues who have demonstrated to us the importance of a careful analysis of our work in practice identifying ways in which the clinical care we offer can be improved. Provided that Government support to the medical audit programme continues, audit activity can be ensured into the future.

General practice also enables data to be collected from the observations of a very large number of doctors and their patients which can then be collated and analysed centrally. General practitioners have a defined population from which to identify subjects of interest and a suitable comparison group. They also maintain comprehensive, life-long records of illnesses occurring in their patients, including those reported by their hospital colleagues. Two studies conducted by the Manchester Research Unit of the RCGP have exploited this opportunity.

The Oral Contraception Study began in 1968 when 1400 general practitioners throughout the United Kingdom recruited 23 000 women who were using the pill and a similar number who had never used these preparations (RCGP 1974). The family doctors have supplied at regular intervals information about all hormonal prescriptions, any illnesses and, when appropriate, causes of death. Twenty-five years since its start, the study is still following up approximately 14 000 of the original cohort. It has now accumulated more than half a million woman-years of observations making it one of the largest investigations in the world able to provide a comprehensive assessment of the risks and benefits of oral contraception. Its results have often been replicated by other investigations.

The study was the first to show a direct relationship between the progestogenic content of the pill and the risk of hypertension and arterial disease (RCGP 1977; Kay 1982). This observation led to the introduction of preparations with lower doses of both hormonal components, and more recently, stimulated the pharmaceutical industry to introduce a new generation of progestogens. The study also demonstrated much higher risks of arterial disease among pill users who are older and who smoke (RCGP 1981). Consequently, most clinicians would now probably be reluctant to prescribe the pill to smokers aged more than 35 years. Results from the study also remind us that oral contraception is associated with major health benefits, such as a reduced risk of ovarian and endometrial cancer (Beral *et al.* 1988), effects which may well redress any adverse effects of the pill.

The Attitudes to Pregnancy Study was a joint observational study between the RCGP and the Royal College of Obstetricians and Gynaecologists (Kay and Frank 1981). Between 1976 and 1979, more than 1500 general practitioners recruited about 7000 women who had an unplanned pregnancy which was terminated and 7000 women who had an unplanned pregnancy which ended naturally. Nearly 800 gynaecologists, working in both the private and NHS sector, supplied details of the operation, including any immediate complications. The women were observed for up to ten years in order to evaluate the long term complications of this unfortunately all too common operation. The study has found that there are no major effects on the woman's fertility or her next pregnancy (Frank *et al.* 1987, 1991, 1993). Unpublished data also show that there are no major psychiatric complications from the operation.

General practice is capable of being organised to provide numerical power to research activity in the community and we can only ensure the continuation of that research activity through central funding by the Department of Health and from the pharmaceutical industry. Fortunately that funding has been forthcoming to support the unit in Manchester since 1968 but there is no guarantee that it will continue into the future. We can only ensure the continuation of that aspect of research study by the quality of the applications we make to funding bodies and demonstrate the importance of the studies we wish to undertake.

We are, however, placing great store on the ability of the new National Centre for Research and Development in Primary Health Care to develop adequate research programmes in the community that will address many of these problems. It is a matter of great concern to the RCGP that research appointments within the National Health Service are so dominated by appointments in the hospital sector without adequate opportunities to train doctors in general practice for high quality research activity.

In general practice there is one research fellow for approximately 160 general practitioners and there is an urgent need to redress that balance through adequate funding for research posts in practice and in academic departments of general practice. The implementation of such a programme of training of young doctors in research method who will work in the community and the provision of research appointments is the principal way in which we can ensure rsearch-based practice in the future.

Since 1989 my College has been calling through its academic plan for general practice for the funding of 12 research fellowships in each Health Service Region and with the new Health Service structure that means approximately 22 research fellowships for each of the new Regions of England and Wales. In addition the College has been calling for the same number of general practices to be selected on the basis of their research record and recognised as research practices and funded like training general practice. We see these appointments as fundamental to ensure the continuing of research-based practice.

In the Report on Maternity Services from the House of Commons Health Select Committee (1992), the importance of an adequate research programme to be conducted by midwives and general practitioners, as well as by our colleagues in hospital, was strongly stressed. The report expressed astonishment at how little is known by the Department of Health, for example, about the relative costs of different aspects of the maternity services, with particular reference to team midwifery, domino deliveries and peripheral maternity units. Antenatal care was widely acknowledged as being inefficient, over-provided and inappropriate, and there was strong criticism of interventions in interpartum care which had not been evaluated in terms of cost–benefit or indeed of the reactions of women who undergo them. Criticism too was directed to the area of postnatal care where the Committee concluded that there was little or no effort made to assess the social or medical costs of neglecting women and leaving them unsupported at a crucial time. The report suggested that maternity services should be a priority area for research and that research should clarify its goals and objectives which will lie, and I quote, 'Not so much in the glamorous areas of high level, high tech research' but in the area of 'soft outcomes such as consumer satisfaction and the widely defined area of morbidity rather than mortality'. The report went on to welcome the recognition by Professor Peckham that, 'The science of evaluation is an area of neglect between bio-medical research and clinical practice'.

It may be fitting at the conclusion of this volume in a section devoted to the future, to make reference to developments in the field of reproductive medicine that are beginning to cause concern within our profession and, more importantly, in society itself, with the recent decision by Government to seek the views of the public into the ethics of research with respect to *in vitro* fertilisation and the use, for example, of ova from fetuses. Scientific advance is accelerating in these areas at an alarming pace and a heavy responsibility will lie on our profession, and not least in general practice, as the advocate of our patients' interests, to contribute sensibly to perhaps one of the most important social debates to confront society in relation to fundamental aspects of the human condition. The inexorable progression of objective scientific advance is leading us into confrontation with instinctive inherited, subjective beliefs in relation to human values. As doctors we will have a particular responsibility to contribute to this quite fundamental debate and we must do so, as far as we can, by providing evidence in relation, for example, to the role of love in the reproductive process, the implications for parents and children of *in vitro* fertilisation by donor, the long-term psychological and emotional effects of the use of a surrogate uterus, and, most alarming of all, the possibility of the full replacement of a human uterus by one artificially provided in the laboratory. The combination of genetic engineering, chromosomal screening, and *in vitro* human development, provides a scenario which many will not wish to contemplate but which others may welcome. Crucial to the outcome of these developments will be much stronger evidence than we have at present of the physical, psychological and emotional importance of procreation as an act of love and the development of children in a warm, secure, loving environment throughout pregnancy and childhood. Forty years ago, as a medical student, I remember being ridiculed for daring to ask if it would ever be possible to transplant a heart from one human being to another and we have to face the real possibility that someone somewhere will in the foreseeable future succeed in developing a human being designed to meet the specifications laid down by parents, or should I say purchasers.

To refer to the spectre for the future is, I believe, to be realistic rather than alarmist and adds emphasis to the importance of the work which all of you do, to ensure that our children are created and nurtured to their best possible advantage. The time may not be far off when all of you will be required to contribute to that debate and it is not premature to be directing your thoughts to some of the implications as they affect maternity care. The joint Report of the RCGP/RCM Working Party on Maternity Care in the Community stated that it, 'Involves an interest reaching back before conception and well into the post-natal period'. I would extend that interest to adulthood which is increasingly being shown to be determined by influences on pregnancy.

References

Beral V., Hannaford, P. and Kay, C. (1988) Oral contraceptive use and malignancies of the genital tract. *Lancet* **ii**, 1331–5

Frank, P., Kay, C.R., Scott, L.M., Hannaford, P.C. and Haran, D. (1987) Pregnancy following induced abortion: maternal morbidity, congenital abnormalities and neonatal death. *Br J Obstet Gynaecol* **94**, 836–42

Frank, P., McNamee, R., Hannaford, P.C., Lay, C.R. and Hirsch, S. (1991) The effect of induced abortion on subsequent pregnancy outcome. *Br J Obstet Gynaecol* **98**, 1015–24

Frank, P., McNamee, R., Hannaford, P.C., Kay, C.R. and Hirsch, S. (1993) The effect of induced abortion on subsequent fertility. *Br J Obstet Gynaecol* **100**, 575–80

Garrett, T., House, W. and Lowe, S.W. (1987) Outcome of women booked into an isolated general practice maternity unit over eight years. *J R Coll Gen Pract* **37**, 488–90

House of Commons Health Select Committee (1992) *Second Report on the Maternity Services.* London: HMSO

Kay, C.R. (1982) Progestogens and arterial disease – evidence from the Royal College of General Practitioners' study. *Am J Obstet Gynecol* **142**, 762–5

Kay, C.R. and Frank, P. (1981) Characteristics of women recruited to a long-term study of the sequelae of induced abortion. *J R Coll Gen Pract* **31**, 473–7

Lowe, S.W., House, W. and Garrett, T. (1987) Comparison of outcome of low-risk labour in an isolated practice maternity unit and a specialist maternity hospital. *J R Coll Gen Pract* **37,** 484–7

MacAlister-Smith, E. (1989) Support for GP units. *Health Service* **99,** 1037

Royal College of General Practitioners, (1974) *Oral Contraceptives and Health.* London: Pitman Medical

Royal College of General Practitioners (1977) Oral Contraception Study. Effect on hypertension and benign breast disease of progestogen component in combined oral contraceptives. *Lancet* **i,** 64

Royal College of General Practitioners (1981) Oral Contraception Study. Further analyses of mortality in oral contraceptive users. *Lancet* **i,** 541–6

Chapter 40

How to ensure research-based practice

Geoffrey Chamberlain

Research results from a series of observations, often made in the laboratory or in the clinical area. It consists of the collection and the appropriate analysis of data. It should also include the proper promulgation of any results. Research however is too often not concerned with what is done with that information. Reasearchers produce it in journals, and lectures, and often do not go any further than that.

Compare this with audit. Audit is the collection of data, usually of an observational nature. It is then analysed and the results are promulgated. Suggestions are then made about change. In a good audit one comes back and re-audits to see what difference the changes have made. Audit is a cyclical process which is very helpful if looking at research-based practice. Research is important to raise the questions and audit is a parallel handmaiden which tries to find solutions to them.

We have been reminded, by Professor Lilford, of the adage that we know what we believe and only believe what we know. Research that is to dominate and rule practice must be believed, it must be credible and it must be promulgated in a way that people can understand.

What are the styles of research at the moment in the maternity services? There is at the lowest level the straightforward, simple hospital study. This is published, often in a comparative way, comparing two groups of patients treated by similar but different regions. Most units are too small to do very big studies and so we move to multicentre studies. These need tight definitions and great enthusiasm to organise. If they are not big enough, we turn to the isolated meta-analysis of several independent studies that contain sufficient similarities of data collection to enter the analysis. These add power to the numbers.

In addition we have population surveys; for these the Region is probably the smallest survey unit in this country that will provide enough material in most conditions. We then have the national cohort studies of the total population of the United Kingdom. These have been performed by the National Birthday Trust for many years. Finally we have statutory collected information which various governmental agencies collect from total UK populations continuously and publish intermittently, usually annually. We had a great reputation in this field and we should be making sure that our government realises that we are gravely disappointed in the Government Statistical Service's monitoring of the healthcare of the country.

It has deteriorated enormously in the last six years and whatever the reasons given by learned ministers, this is still a problem.

Those are the types of studies. I will take two examples. First, a special study of what should be virtually statutory collected data, the Confidential Enquiries into Maternal Deaths. This has been done for a long time; the data are well founded, the reports are something most people read, but not much action has been taken on it. Those who read reports carefully will note that this year, the scientific advisers and their teams have actually gone out to find information that results from the surveys. They looked at haemorrhage and at hypertension and in the report we find some information about how many units have blood banks, how many units have places to refer mothers with hypertension. They have actually started the beginning of audit.

At the RCOG, we have gone further and issued to all Fellows and Members a series of questions based on the Report of the Confidential Enquiries into Maternal Deaths so that they can audit their own units, looking at the points, we have learned about maternal mortality. For example, on hypertensive diseases of pregnancy:

- Are there guidelines for the management of hypertension?
- Is there a regular centre for transfer of difficult cases?
- Have the guidelines been agreed by the junior staff, the midwives and the anaesthetists?
- What are the arrangements for instructing medical and midwifery staff in the immediate management?
- Are new medical and midwifery staff provided with personal copies?

These are simple questions one can ask and one can get replies to them fairly swiftly. They will tell how efficient a unit is. Changes can then be made according to answers and then a re-audit can be done. There are three pages of such simple audit projects and we hope our fellows and members will pick this up.

We are using audit based data that can be used to look back now to see what is being done and then advance ideas.

The next area of report in research is a rather sadder one. The Oxford Database on Perinatal Trials (the Cochrane database) is well known to everyone; most are converted and are happy with it. However, a recent publication (Paterson-Brown et al. 1993) referred to a study when the workers, in March 1993, got in touch with the teaching hospitals of England and a randomised half of the district hospitals in England – 24 teaching hospitals and 74 district hospitals. They then asked the nominated consultant in each department whether the Oxford database was available to them. In 15/24 (62 per cent) of the teaching hospitals it was, but in only 12 (16 per cent) of the district hospitals was it available. Thus it was not available in 38 per cent of teaching hospitals and 84 per cent of non-teaching hospitals. Many will find that amazing because of the fuss the Department of Health made in 1992 about this. Adequate databases against which to set new decisions are not available.

This research group then went further and looked at the use of the Oxford Database in the places which had a copy, in the 15 teaching hospitals and 12 district hospitals. In education it was used in 13/15 teaching hospitals and 7/12 district hospitals; one might have expected that. Finding references for further reading naturally was more frequently used in teaching hospitals than the district hospitals. For designing protocols, though, its use was respectively 10/15 and 8/12, a cheering point that a large number of the district hospitals were using it to design their protocols. They were using research-based data to run their service.

How do we ensure that teaching and practice are research based?

1 Make it known: research that is done and not reported may as well not be done. We must ensure that editors of journals are prepared to publish trials with negative results as well as those with positive ones. There is a bias for all editors of journals to publish positive data, something one can grip and get professional publicity. It is important however that they publish some negative results as well because they contain important information. We must ensure that if someone has performed a piece of work that they can talk about it and have it published. They must not just sit on it.

2 People have to like it. It is no good having research they are not going to like, for they will not believe it; if they do not believe it, they will not act on it. It has got to be acceptable research to people written up in a way that makes it interesting and that they understand.

3 One should audit it; research must be audited to make sure that what is happening is getting through, that we are learning from it. Then it is the area that must be audited again. This is what the RCOG has recommended with aspects of maternal mortality. They are asking people to look at their own practice.

4 We have to ensure that the audit loop is closed. Audit is a cyclical business and therefore we have to re-audit to see what has happened as a result of any action taken from the findings of the research.

We have considered how we can best use research in our practices and how to ensure that research-based practice is seen, understood and used.

The Executive of the NHS will be convening a group to ask for our help in the implementation of the published recommendations. Those who read the Executive Letter will see that they will be sending out their ideas to the health authorities in the next few months. When we are asked to help in the implementation I hope we go as a group of people who believe in what we have talked about over the past two days. If we do then we will have a much better service for the women we all try to serve.

Reference

Paterson-Brown, S., Wyatt, J.C. and Fisk, N.M. (1993) Are clinicians interested in up-to-date reviews of effective care? *Br Med J* **307**, 1467

Summary of the main areas of agreement

Introduction

In January 1994 the recommendations made in the report *Changing Childbirth* were adopted as government policy. On 7th and 8th February 1994, representatives from the Royal College of Obstetricians and Gynaecologists, the Royal College of Midwives and the Royal College of General Practitioners met in London with neonatal paediatricians, anaesthetists, perinatal epidemiologists, the Department of Health and women who use the service.

The following summary of the main areas of agreement was distilled from notes made during the discussion periods and a recording of the final session. It was sent to all members of the group and edited by:

Miss Debra Kroll, RCM
Mrs Helen Lewison, NCT
Dr Naren Patel, RCOG
Dr Lindsay Smith RCGP
Mr John Spencer, RCOG
Dr Gavin Young, RCGP

Creating a framework for informed change

Achieving change

Purchasers and providers should take account of the needs and preferences of local users of maternity services when implementing changes in services and patterns of care. Areas of further research regarding the provision of maternity care need to be identified and resources allocated.

Resources will be required to bring about changes in maternity services. There is a lack of data about the cost of maternity services as currently provided and it cannot be assumed that new services will necessarily cost less. New services should be subject to further evaluation and costing once they are in place. Purchasers and providers should be aware that the contract price for services may not yet necessarily reflect the true cost of providing those services.

291

A purpose-designed national maternity record is required. This needs to link relevant parents' circumstances with all maternity care received, including that from general practice, social services and hospital and community provider units. This would enhance data collection to give a fuller picture of the care provided which, in turn, would assist the estimation of the true cost of maternity services.

In the absence of additional funding, monies saved within the maternity services by improved efficiency should be reinvested to implement changes which may result in better outcomes.

Information and data collection

Data need to be readily available from primary sources. The items collected should describe the population receiving care, reflect service provision, and measure short- and long-term outcomes for mother and baby both for the population and for individual users. Local data collection systems must be capable of readily providing relevant information for collection at national level.

National Health Service data collection systems need to be revised and improved to make them more accurate, relevant and up to date in order that women and professionals can see what is happening in all places where maternity care is provided.

Contracts

Representatives from lay groups as well as professional groups from the provider units should join with purchasers when discussing contract setting. The local Maternity Services Liaison Committee (MSCL) is the ideal forum for this activity. It is the responsibility of each District Health Authority to establish an MSLC and it is the duty of purchasers, providers and user groups to ensure that it is both representative and effective.

Ensuring quality woman-centred care

Emotional support

Emotional support and antenatal education, to help each woman take care of her own health during pregnancy and childbirth and in preparing for parenting, are important parts of the programme of maternity care.

Information

Each woman needs as much information as possible during pregnancy in order to make informed choices. The new *Pregnancy Book* (published by the Health Education Authority) should be given to each woman early in pregnancy.

Choice

More attention needs to be paid to the concept and complexities of maternal choice. The role of partners in influencing choice also needs recognition. In particular, the following should always be considered:

- providing full information to help each woman make appropriate choices
- facilitating the making of choices
- how choices are to be offered
- the cost of having choices available.

Options should be available so each woman can make real and relevant choices. An integrated maternity service, that offers a choice of carer and a choice of place and style of care, should be available to each woman. All caregivers should empower each woman to achieve autonomy.

Continuity

Lack of continuity of carer can result in poor care. Each woman should have the opportunity to establish a good relationship with a lead professional based on kind, polite, sensitive and truthful communication. The resulting care will allow her to maintain control and to make choices. Each woman should know that she has the opportunity to change her lead professional if she feels that the relationship is unsatisfactory, though this may be difficult in isolated rural areas.

Pre-pregnancy care

Primary health-care teams should have an agreed policy on pre-pregnancy care. A good, extended medical and family history can sometimes help to identify potential genetic risks before pregnancy. Should genetic counselling be appropriate, copies of a written summary of the discussions should be retained in the hospital notes and made available to the couple, their general practitioner, and the referring practitioner.

Pre-pregnancy consultations provide the opportunity to give information and offer general health advice related to pregnancy. In addition, checking of rubella status, and specific advice regarding medical conditions, can be offered. Many pre-pregnancy therapies are of unproven value but folate supplements can reduce the risk of recurrence of neural tube defect.

Place of birth

Each woman needs to be given full information about the facilities available at her chosen place of birth. The choice of home birth may be partly a reflection of the unwelcoming care and environment in some hospitals. Improving the quality of care should include attention to the attitudes of caregivers and to the environment. It may be appropriate to reconsider the role of peripheral or isolated units as part of a general improvement in service provision and choice in some rural areas.

Risk

Assessment of risk should be person and not population specific, and should be undertaken at each contact with a caregiver since the degree of risk may increase or decrease during the pregnancy. There is a need to develop effective systems for identifying, at all stages of pregnancy, features which may be associated with adverse outcomes. These may lead to the development of nationally accepted guidelines.

The effects of risk attribution on clinical care and outcome need further research, particularly focusing on whether such assessment can usefully form the basis of professional advice and the choices of each woman.

Technology

There should be more information and advice on the appropriate use of technology. Given the complexity of technologies employed, each woman and her caregivers must distinguish between the use of technology to improve outcome and the use of technology for the convenience and comfort of either party.

The lead professional should be able to refer directly for appropriate diagnostic tests. However, such access must remain within local and nationally agreed guidelines which ensure appropriate use of resources and optimal interpretation of results.

Standards of care

Clinical standards, which reflect collective beliefs, should be based on research evidence where it exists. Active promotion of good clinical standards is required if they are to be effective. National guidelines are required for informed clinical practice and should be reviewed regularly; there is room for innovation and for a large improvement in the proper evaluation of many antenatal investigations.

Clear protocols for referral to and from specialist care during pregnancy and labour, agreed by all the professional groups involved, are required at local level.

Optimal, rather than maximal, quality standards should be set taking account of existing resources. The process of standard setting requires user involvement. It should begin at local district health authority level (even if informed by national guidelines) and should be monitored in a structured manner by the MSLC.

Standard setting and audit are the responsibility both of purchasers and providers and should be major functions of the MSLC. Audit of maternity services is a responsibility that should be shared by the professional groups involved with providing care and undertaken jointly with service users.

Audit should be used to ensure that care is both effective and efficient. For example, it should ensure that the service purchased adheres to clinical standards that are research based where this is possible. Results from audit can be used to refine standard setting as well as to identify areas for further research. National guidelines for reporting and auditing critical incidents are required.

A formal, rigorous, evaluation of pilot studies of GP fundholders purchasing maternity care is required. Full consultation, with the involvement of the 'Changing Childbirth' Advisory Group, is recommended before general developments occur along this line. If fundholding general practices are to purchase maternity services they should be represented on their local MSLC.

The role of professionals

Provision of care

More research is needed into alternative models for delivery of care.

The lead professional

Each woman may choose a midwife, a general practitioner, or an obstetrician as her lead professional who should be identified at the booking consultation. Each lead professional should work within the framework of multidisciplinary collaboration which facilitates, as necessary, the involvement of a midwife, a general practitioner, and an obstetrician. In addition to contributing substantially to the provision of care, the lead professional should be accountable for planning care in consultation with each woman concerned and for managing the programme of care agreed with her. This includes the co-ordination and facilitation of appropriate referrals to other professionals.

The role of the lead professional should be pivotal in linking primary and secondary care provision. The lead professional needs to ensure that each woman is aware of the role of all health-care personnel who might be directly involved with her care. When continuity of care and carer are discussed, their precise monitoring should be defined.

Professionals working together

Power and control over maternity service provision should not be exclusively the province of any one professional group. Professional rivalries need to be overcome so that optimal care can be provided. Caregivers from each professional group need to acknowledge that a woman may not wish to see them during pregnancy. Nevertheless, each woman should be offered the opportunity to consult a member of any professional group during pregnancy.

The primary role of all caregivers is to assist each woman to make decisions about her care. Sufficient time needs to be available for effective communication between a woman and her caregiver. Where a woman has more than one caregiver, they need to communicate effectively with each other to minimise duplication of care and contradictory advice. This may mean more than just a note in the hand-held records. Each caregiver remains responsible for ensuring that their own contribution to the programme of care is in accord with the overall wishes of the woman.

In addition to continuing care from a midwife, each pregnant woman should be offered a medical assessment by a doctor (general practitioner or obstetrician) early in her care. Community midwives should be able to work with the primary health-care team. Midwives should not refer to junior medical staff with insufficient experience of the problem to be discussed. Direct access to appropriately trained and experienced medical staff should be available to the lead professional at all times.

When not the lead professional, the general practitioner should continue to contribute to pregnancy care if the woman wishes. Local lists of general practitioners should distinguish between those who offer the whole package of antenatal, intrapartum and postnatal care and those who offer only antenatal and postnatal care. General practitioners providing intrapartum care should receive appropriate remuneration which should relate to continuing education and experience.

Responsibility for care

Giving each woman choice, and encouraging her to take responsibility for her choice, does not mean that professionals abdicate responsibility for care. Professionals have a duty to indicate the known benefits and risks of alternative treatment patterns. An honest approach is required when knowledge in a particular area is insufficient. Uncertainties, where they exist, should be acknowledged.

Professionals should understand the potential influence of their advice and care on the self-esteem of each woman. Sometimes a woman will want advice. However, it should be normal practice to give information encouraging each woman to take the lead in decision-making. This approach is new to many caregivers.

Role of the anaesthetist

Anaesthetists should contribute to the information that is given to each pregnant woman. If she wishes, each woman should have the opportunity to discuss specific needs or identified potential problems regarding analgesia with an anaesthetist at any time before or during labour. There is a need for better post-operative pain relief.

The essential contribution of anaesthetists to the management of severe maternal complications on the labour ward should begin as soon as a problem is identified.

Role of the paediatrician

Each woman should be given the opportunity to meet a paediatrician should she wish. Early involvement of paediatric staff is essential whenever a neonatal problem is anticipated.

A greater understanding of the implications and limitations of perinatal care needs to be developed. Continuing education about neonatal resuscitation for all professionals involved with childbirth needs to be frequent and up to date.

Training

Joint education and training

There could be more joint education and training of doctors and midwives, involving the input not only of obstetricians and midwives but of primary health-care and other appropriate professionals as well as users of the maternity services.

A larger proportion of general practitioner obstetric and gynaecology training should occur in a primary care setting. The content (service and training) of SHO training posts should relate to their future needs (knowledge, skills and attitudes) as potential caregivers of maternity services, whether as obstetricians or general practitioners in the community.

Multi-professional training courses for teachers of maternity care are recommended to help promote joint learning and better teamwork in the provision of maternity services. Training should encourage a philosophy of acquiring and updating knowledge, and methods of assessment need to be reliable and valid.

Recommendations

Framework for change

1 All proposals to change maternity services should take account of user views.
2 Standard setting and audit should be major functions of Maternity Services Liaison Committees.
3 User representatives should be involved with contract setting between purchasers and providers.
4 Effective mechanisms of data collection are badly needed to get comparable national, regional and local data which are relevant to maternity care.

Quality of care

5 The importance of social and psychological support needs to be recognised by caregivers and should be incorporated with the plans of their care.
6 Continuity of care is an essential component of quality care and should be achieved through locally agreed protocols.
7 Women should be empowered to make informed choices throughout pregnancy.
8 Caregivers have a duty to provide accurate and unbiased information and should give advice only when appropriate and requested.
9 The poor value of risk assessment in predicting the outcome of an individual pregnancy should be made clear to each woman.
10 Clinical practice should be based on the best research evidence available.
11 Home birth is an acceptable option and appropriate information should be provided.

Role of professionals

12 A lead professional should be agreed with each pregnant woman at booking to ensure continuity of carer.
13 The lead professional should be responsible for identifying the needs of each pregnant woman throughout her pregnancy to ensure appropriate care, including referral if necessary.

14   The lead professional should be able to refer directly for appropriate diagnostic tests.

15   Each pregnant woman should be offered the opportunity to consult a member of any relevant professional group.

Training

16   There should be joint education, training and updating of midwives, general practitioners and obstetricians with input from users as well as from each professional group.

Index